DC 121 ETH

ETHICS and POLITICS

in

Seventeeth-Century France

Top portrait, Louis XIV, bottom left Richelieu,
and bottom right, Retz.

ETHICS

and

POLITICS

in

Seventeenth-Century France

Essays in Honour of Derek A. Watts

Edited

by

Keith Cameron and Elizabeth Woodrough

UNIVERSITY
of
EXETER
PRESS

First published in 1996 by
University of Exeter Press
Reed Hall, Streatham Drive
Exeter EX4 4QR
UK

British Library Cataloguing in Publication Data
A catalogue record of this book is available
from the British Library

ISBN 0 85989 466 5

Printed and bound in Great Britain by
Antony Rowe Ltd, Chippenham

CONTENTS

PART I: THE ETHICS OF ACTION

Contents

Derek Watts

Lecturer, Senior Lecturer, then Reader in Classical French Literature at the University of Exeter, Derek Arthur Watts has had an academic career which many of us would envy. Its bare facts, even with their prestigious connotations, do not do justice to the man, whose warmth and personal charm have been appreciated by all who have known him.

A veritable child of the twentieth century, he has known its vicissitudes and tribulations. A pupil of Battersea Grammar School, he was to experience the doubtful pleasures of being evacuated to Hertfordshire, then after the second World War reached its end, he joined the ranks of the young and the demobbed at Cambridge, to devote himself, as Exhibitioner and subsequently Scholar at Jesus College, to the study of French and German. Thence across the channel to spend four fruitful years at the Ecole Normale Supérieure in the rue d'Ulm, a sojourn which enabled him to form a network of relationships which still remains. Derek's friends are not only to be found in the upper *échelons* of Academe but are also in government and the administration.

It was in Paris that he was able, thanks to patient hours of toil in the Bibliothèque nationale, to bring to fruition his research on *Le Cardinal de Retz moraliste*, research that was to reveal unknown aspects of the Cardinal, to receive the congratulations of his examiners, to make him a *Docteur de l'Université de Paris* and to establish the young Watts as a scholar of repute. Like many aspirants of his day, he was eventually obliged to serve the nation and was fortunate enough to be placed in the Education branch of Her Majesty's Royal Air Force. A testing ground for his teaching abilities, and his patience, but which was a useful preparation for his first lecturing post, in 1955, at the University College of Wales in Bangor. There he was to make the acquaintance of, amongst others, Ron Grimsley and William Barber, under the philosophical eye of Ian Alexander. It was in Bangor that he met Gwen, his late wife; together they formed a union which saw the birth of six children and has left Derek with many happy memories.

In 1964, Robert Niklaus was inspired to appoint Derek to the staff of the University of Exeter, where he has brought his patience, his affability and his expertise. His publications have earned him a place amongst the leading seventeenth-century scholars of this century; whether it be his seminal book on the *Cardinal de Retz: The*

Ambiguities of a Seventeenth-Century Mind, his edition of *Cinna*, or *La Conjuration de Fiesque* or his recent monographs on *La Rochefoucauld* and *Rodogune and Nicomède*, his critical editions for the Exeter *Textes littéraires*, his articles, or his papers at conferences both national and international, all have in common an outstanding erudition and, collectively, constitute a remarkable contribution to our knowledge of the theatre, ethics and politics in seventeenth-century France. Derek is a man for whom quality of production has been more important than quantity.

His standing was recognized by the editors of the *Revue d'Histoire littéraire de la France* who invited him to be their British correspondent from 1975 until 1990, and by the Society for XVIIth Century Studies which he chaired from 1984 until 1987.

For five years (1982-1987) he led the Department of French and sustained an atmosphere of goodwill, learning and high standards in spite of the ever worsening economic climate. He showed himself to be an approachable and democratic Head of Department; one who was dedicated to the welfare of both staff and undergraduates. With characteristic modesty and efficiency, he was able to introduce into the life of the department his love of the French cinema and his lifelong passion for music.

His students and colleagues will miss his critical acumen, his humanity and his dry humour, but they are consoled by the knowledge that he will be at hand to help and answer their queries as he has so often done in the past. His retirement is one which is well deserved yet one during which, characteristically, he intends to pursue his fervent interest in French life and culture.

This present collection of essays, so readily contributed to by colleagues and friends, bears witness to the affection and the esteem in which he is held.

Keith Cameron

DEREK WATTS

BIBLIOGRAPHY

1958
'The Enigma of Retz', *French Studies*, XII, pp. 203-21.

1964
(ed.) Pierre Corneille, *Cinna*, Critical edition with introduction and notes. London, University of London Press ('Textes français classiques et modernes'), 182 pp.

1966
'Corneille's Defence of his Art', *Forum for Modern Language Studies*, II, 1, pp. 42-7.

1967
(ed.) Cardinal de Retz, *La Conjuration de Fiesque, édition critique publiée d'après le texte de 1665, avec des variantes provenant de manuscrits inédits.* Oxford, Clarendon Press, xxxiv 121 pp.

'Quelques réflexions sur *La Conjuration de Fiesque*', *Revue des Sciences humaines*, 126, pp. 289-302.

1971
(ed.) Jean Rotrou, *Hercule mourant, édition critique avec introduction et notes.* Exeter ('Textes Littéraires', II), xxx + 94 pp.

1975
'Le sens des métaphores théâtrales chez le cardinal de Retz et quelques écrivains contemporains', *Mélanges offerts à Monsieur René Pintard*. Strasbourg et Paris, Klincksieck, pp. 385-99.

'Testimonies of Persecution: Four Huguenot Refugees and their Memoirs', *Studies in Eighteenth-Century Literature presented to Professor Robert Niklaus*, eds J.H. Fox, M.H. Waddicor and D.A. Watts. University of Exeter, pp. 319-33.

'Self-portrayal in Seventeenth-Century French memoirs', *Australian Journal of French Studies*, XII, pp. 263-85.

1977
Thomas Corneille, *Camma, tragédie, édition critique avec introduction et notes.* Exeter ('Textes Littéraires', XXV), xxxiii + 102 pp.

'Retz and Tacitus', *The Classical Tradition in French Literature. Essays presented to R.C. Knight.* London, Grant and Cutler, pp. 135-44.

1979
'La Notion de patrie chez les mémorialistes d'avant la Fronde. Le problème de la trahison'. *Les valeurs chez les mémorialistes français du XVIIe siècle avant la Fronde.* Paris, Klincksieck, pp. 195-209.

1980
Cardinal de Retz. The Ambiguities of a Seventeenth-Century Mind. Oxford, Clarendon Press, 300 pp.

'The Fronde as seen in the Memoirs of Retz and La Rochefoucauld'. *Newsletter of the Society for Seventeenth-Century French Studies,* II, pp. 21-8.

'Seventeenth-century French memoirs: new perspectives'. *Journal of European Studies,* X, pp. 126-41.

1982
'Rotrou's problematical tragedies', *Form and meaning. Aesthetic Coherence in Seventeenth-Century French Drama. Studies presented to Harry Barnwell.* Amersham, Avebury, pp. 75-91.

1983
Jean Rotrou, *Cosroès, tragédie, édition critique avec introduction et notes.* Exeter ('Textes Littéraires', LI), xxxviii + 102 pp.

'*Cosroès* - a Providential Tragedy?' *Papers on Seventeenth-Century French Literature,* X, 19, pp. 589-615.

1988
'La présentation et l'évolution du *moi* dans les *Mémoires* de Retz'. *Cahiers de l'Association Internationale des Etudes Françaises',* XL, pp. 51-68.

'A further look at *Rodogune*', *Ouverture et Dialogue. Mélanges offerts à Wolfgang Leiner.* Tübingen, Narr, pp. 447-63.

1989

'Les Journées des Barricades racontées par les mémorialistes', *La Fronde en questions. Actes du dix-huitième Colloque du Centre Méridional de Rencontres sur le XVIIe siècle*, Marseille, pp. 51-62.

1990

(ed.) Jean Rotrou, *Venceslas, tragi-comédie, édition critique avec introduction et notes*, Exeter ('Textes Littéraires', LXXIX), xxxii + 104 pp.

1991

'Jugements sur la cour chez le Cardinal de Retz et quelques écrivains contemporains'. *La Cour au Miroir des mémorialistes.* Paris, Klincksieck, pp. 123-33.

1992

Corneille: 'Rodogune' and 'Nicomède'. (Critical Guides to French Texts, no. 94). London, Grant and Cutler, 93 pp.

'Une correspondance peu ecclésiastique: les lettres du cardinal de Retz à l'abbé Charrier (1651-1652)'. *Correspondances: mélanges offerts à Roger Duchêne.* Tübingen, Narr and Aix-en-Provence, Publications de l'Université de Provence, pp. 315-24.

1993

La Rochefoucauld: Maximes. (Glasgow Introductory Guides to French Literature, no. 24). Glasgow, University of Glasgow, 92 pp.

1994

'La Rochefoucauld between Baroque and Classicism', *Seventeenth-Century French Studies,* XVI, pp. 65-81.

[In addition, some fifty reviews, published mainly in *French Studies, Modern Language Review* and *Papers on Seventeenth-Century French Literature.*]

CONTRIBUTORS

MARK BANNISTER
Head of School of Languages, Oxford Brookes University

MADELEINE BERTAUD
Professeur, Université des Sciences Humaines, Strasbourg

SIMONE BERTIÈRE
Professeur émérite,Université de Bordeaux-III

RICHARD BONNEY
Professor of History, University of Leicester

WILLIAM BROOKS
Reader in French, University of Bath

KEITH CAMERON
Professor of French and Renaissance Studies, University of Exeter

JOHN CAMPBELL
Senior Lecturer in French, University of Glasgow

DAVID CLARKE
Senior Lecturer in French, King's College, London

YVES COIRAULT
Professeur émérite, Université de Paris-Sorbonne (Paris IV)

JOHN CRUICKSHANK
late Professor of French, University of Sussex

EDWARD FORMAN
Senior Lecturer in French, University of Bristol

C. J. GOSSIP
Professor of French, University of New England, Armidale,
N.S.W., Australia

NOÉMI HEPP
Professeur émérite, Université de Strasbourg-II

WILLIAM D. HOWARTH
formerly Professor of French, University of Bristol

COLIN JONES
Professor of History, University of Warwick

MARGARET MCGOWAN
Professor of French, University of Sussex

WENDY PERKINS
Senior Lecturer in French, University of Birmingham

HENRY PHILLIPS
Professor of French, University of Manchester

JEAN ROHOU,
Professeur, Université de Rennes II-Haute Bretagne

GUY SNAITH
Lecturer in French, University of Liverpool

ELIZABETH WOODROUGH
Lecturer in French, University of Exeter

PART I

THE ETHICS OF ACTION

INTRODUCTION

Ethics and Politics in Seventeenth-Century France

ELIZABETH WOODROUGH

Ne piu ne pari—none greater nor equal—the young Louis XIV's distinctive *devise* for the Carrousel of 1662 may be taken as the measure of a generation and more of image-conscious men of action and letters in seventeenth-century France, and also of the women of the period to the lesser degree that circumstance permitted. The remarkable concurrence of noble heroes and writers of supreme distinction who dared to compare their singular *belles actions* and multiple *chefs-d'œuvre* to the best in the ancient world, and also to break the mould, eclipsing all their predecessors, presents posterity with a unique challenge. Such eloquent claims to excellence require constant critical evaluation, as well as the praise, admiration and adulation which have made cult figures of the Sun King and of so many of those in his service.

This collection of twenty essays, written by leading English and French literary and historical scholars, deconstructs the ethical and political framework supporting and circumscribing the actions of a powerful elite in France between the early 1600s and the final years of Louis XIV's reign. Reflecting a diversity of individual concerns, the essays represent a radical rethinking of the absolute values on which was founded the authority of the established Church and the king. Discussion of the twin themes of the book has been divided into two parts, in acknowledgement of the importance accorded in this study to the fact of history and to the virtual reality of dramatic representation.

Part One, 'The Ethics of Action', evaluates, against the background of the climate of belief and the new civility in social relations, the evolution of the deontological debate about the nature of heroism which marked the century. The argument focuses on some of the most notable conflicts opposing the prince-generals, cardinal ministers and others who used and abused the privilege of birthright or the accident of authority in the name of the king. The initial essays reassessing the importance attached to independence of thought in a period of apparent conformism are followed by a series of individual or comparative studies of the most independent-minded ministers and nobles of the age: Richelieu, La Rochefoucauld, Henri de Montmorency, Mazarin, Condé, Retz, Fouquet and Colbert. This sequence of political profiles, superimposed one on another and refracted through the prism of first-person and third-person memoirs, rich in textual images of the violent clashes between the new and old servants of the crown which threatened royal authority, is a study in loyalty and resistance, failure and reconciliation, exclusion and submission.

The volume opens with an overview by Bill Howarth of alternative ethical systems which deflects the reader's gaze from the certainties of the classical age towards the ideological challenge presented to the prevailing morality and theology of seventeenth-century France by a number of non-conformist individuals, and invites comparison with the enlightenment. Three key stages in the development of manners and mentalities are highlighted, foregrounding many of the themes addressed in later essays. *Libertinage* is explored through the work of the marginal *poètes maudits* who dared, often at the risk of their own lives, to celebrate free-thought in obscene verses, anti-novels, memoirs, and treatises in the face of hypocritical condemnation, before being driven underground by a determined policy of conformism. *Gloire* on the grand scale, the driving force behind Retz, Condé, La Rochefoucauld and the generation of the Fronde, is shown ultimately to have been absorbed within the code of *honnêteté* according to Méré and Mitton, which became the standard for courtly behaviour, but was all too frequently devoid of the transcendental dimension on which Pascal insisted.

The second essay by John Cruickshank, which may itself be classified as a layman's *Introduction à la vie dévote* in early seventeenth-century France in the tradition of Saint François de Sales, meets the challenge of spreading belief beyond the cloisters, by focusing on an important form of religious non-conformism as popular among women as men: lay piety. Four reasons are given for the remarkable renewal of faith outside the Church at the dawn of the new century: the conclusion of the long Wars of Religion that had increased the climate of fear; the growth of printing and literacy; the increased influence of high-minded women, like Mme Acarie, however stereotypical this view might seem; and the Catholic Reformation supported by acts of charity.

'L'illustre solitaire, le trois fois grand Balzac, ce démon du savoir', whose name is associated with many of the major religious and political upheavals of the first half of the century might have appeared in this volume in various guises. In her essay, Margaret McGowan shows how the letters he wrote from Rome in the 1620s served to extend the theme of independence of thought as a civilising force to the act of imitation of the greater by the lesser. Only a shadow of his real self when he returned to France, but contemptuous of too literal an admiration for the physical remains of antiquity, Balzac's appreciation of Corneille's successful removal, in *Cinna,* of Rome to Paris, without breakages, is indicative of the originality of his own response to the eternal city, where invention has as great a part to play as mimesis. McGowan shows how Balzac transmitted his imaginative vision of an assimilation of all the refining influence of *urbanitas* to Madame de Rambouillet, helping to turn the glorious heroes of the battlefield into the urbane *habitués* of the salon, well versed in the art of polite conversation.

The historical perspective of other essays by Richard Bonney and Mark Bannister in this first part confirms the shift in the balance of power back towards the centre in mid-century, following the series of unsuccessful revolts and rebellions, which culminated in the complex alliances and realliances of the Fronde. As the *Fronde parlementaire* gave way to the *Fronde des princes,* the noble warriors and aspirants to high office of the first half of the century—Condé, La Rochefoucauld and Retz—became the *grands frustrés* of the new reign and tempers boiled over. In just one of many colourful episodes recounted in the memoirs of prominent Frondeurs, the duplicitous Retz, so keen to win the cardinal's hat that he simultaneously supported and undermined the opposing sides and even suggested the formation of a third faction to defeat both the Princes and Mazarin, had his head jammed in a set of doors in the Palais Royal by the duc de La Rochefoucauld. Divided amongst themselves, the anti-Mazarin factions could not capitalize on the minister's two periods of exile and fell to the wayside. Like the duc de Montmorency who had been beheaded after the 1632 coup in the Languedoc, and all the others who had tried to oppose the Bourbon kings since the days of the Catholic League at the end of the sixteenth century, they failed, hastening the displacement of the high aristocracy as the ruling class in Louis XIV's reign.

In the memoirs discussed here in successive essays by Simone Bertière, Noémi Hepp, Colin Jones and myself, the opponents of the regime may judge themselves, like La Rochefoucauld, as victims of fate, or like Retz, as responsible rebels, fulfilling their duty in the tradition of the great noble alliances of earlier generations, who provided the necessary heroic models whatever their individual shortcomings. Those that pronounced judgement upon them as traitors and ungrateful hypocrites did little more than create a new set of tragic martyrs to the cause. Similarly, the ministers who were the main focus of discontent may portray themselves as selfless defenders of the crown, or be portrayed by their enemies, whether by accident or design, as clever villains or farcical charlatans, more likely to damage the health of the body politic than to cure its ills, or else as greedy self-seekers who must be removed. However persuasive the rearguard defence offered to posterity by both sides in their memoirs, such testimonies merely confirm that those who had always sought to serve the king the better to preserve their own *gloire* found themselves increasingly isolated by an inflexible political philosophy at the centre of government which would not tolerate acts of courage at the expense of the state, any more than excessive self-confidence in those who held the highest offices, but did not have the machiavellian cunning to match their position.

With the reaffirmation of the royal prestige in the 1650s, it had become clear that, though even Condé might be rehabilitated for ceremonial purposes, there was no room for the morally autonomous aristocrat within the new political order. Mark Bannister suggests that fear of the uncontrollable in power and passion had made the diplomatic skills of the *honnête homme*, or even on rare occasions of the *honnête femme*, more appropriate, as a later essay by Wendy Perkins on the conscious and unconcious political significance of the Marquise de Villars, wife of an ambassador to the Spanish court, would also suggest. While John Campbell muses on the moral ambiguity of a good mother's advice on marriage and the use of an imperfect subjunctive in *La Princesse de Clèves*, Yves Coirault brings Part One to a close with a meditation on the mythogenesis of the heroic caste. In this essay, Coirault takes us far back upstream to the socio-political structures of the privileged race of the Franks, in an examination of Boulainvilliers's systematic bid at the beginning of the 18th century, as Louis XIV's reign came to an end, to prove that the institutions of the French nobility and monarchy were synchronic in origin and should therefore remain on an equal footing.

Part Two, 'The Politics of Theatre', transposes the action and the debate to the contemporary stage where, for their particular pleasure and instruction, the makers of myth and history were confronted with the past-in-the-making of other nations, rewritten in their own image but with any personal likenesses cleverly disguised. Essays on Corneille, Tristan, La Calprenède, Quinault, Racine and others situate tragedy on parallel axes of power, politics and passion, occasionally traversed by more idealistic tragi-comedies on political subjects. These dramatists of unequal reputation demonstrate varying degrees of commitment to serious and sentimental issues, but are all shown to have greater political consciousness than has been generally allowed. A substantial number of the plays concerned examine the conflicting imperatives of the king and the nobility through the enactment of the excesses of heroism, the debilitating burden of monarchy, and the clash of tyranny and sedition. In almost all, it is the apolitical force of love which energizes or incapacitates the hero; concerns of state are dramatized only in so far as they control the destiny of lovers of noble or royal birth. The effect of such a *parti pris* is to place the emphasis on the individual moral dilemmas of those who act to fulfil their public function. Not surprisingly, *raison d'état*, which advocated the division of public and private morality and was closely associated with Richelieu's ministry, is one of the most important theoretical undercurrents in plays of the period. In a reversal of the logic of this deeply unpopular philosophy of government, the fate of the heroes made to suffer its consequences, or of the monarchs who agonize over the cruel judgements it forces them to make, overshadows all interests of state in tragic drama.

What distinguishes Corneille, who is inevitably in the first rank of dramatists in the study of the politicization of French seventeenth-century theatre, is his attempt to subsume passion within a shared ethical system which accepts the necessity of heroic action, but must in turn be subsumed within the new political order, as the hero is increasingly isolated from the heroic group. In Henry Phillips's essay on ethics and politics in Corneille's theatre, the major plays are shown to mark the passage of the tragic hero from the reverse dependency of noble king-maker to hero-king, capable of an act of great generosity which makes him the supreme value within the state by virtue of his own heroic performance, allows him to become once again the guardian of history, but still requires Christian legitimation through the reinforcement of the mystical theory of divine monarchy, fusing political, religious and ethical issues and unifying the state.

In the essays that follow, it is openly acknowledged that the lesser-known dramatists under consideration—all of whom were influenced by Corneille to a greater or lesser degree—have a tendency to repeat simple formulae from play to play and rarely take a clear political line. As Madeleine Bertaud shows in her essay on the failure of the conspiracy in *La Mort de Sénèque*, only Tristan, who had served on both sides in the sieges and revolts of the 1630s, and felt troubled by the Christian implications of tyrannicide, could be said to portray the opposing interests of an all-powerful monarch and of the heroes who must accept his authority, with anything like the same depth of conviction as Corneille. Guy Snaith argues that the theatre of La

Calprenède may, nevertheless, be valued for its special study, in the context of *raison d'état*, of the pressures to which kings are subject. Set in remarkably undifferentiated times of crisis, these plays cannot be said to constitute a philosophy of government, though regicide, rebellion and usurpation give rise to a whole panoply of often fascinating personal dilemmas, as private passions and fatherly duties conflict with national interests and the duties of state. The tender Quinault is similarly concerned with the difficulty of balancing personal concerns and public duty in extreme situations. It is Bill Brooks' contention that the repetition from play to play of commonplaces about the status and psychology of kings to complicate and sustain the love interest should not, however, be allowed to mask the increasing variety and prominence of political material in Quinault's later plays.

French dramatists of a more romantic disposition, anxious to renew the theatre after the departure of Corneille and Racine, may not have been much better placed in the late 1670s and 1680s, than was La Calprenède in 1637, to appreciate the complex motives and alliances of the court of Elizabeth of England. Nevertheless, Chris Gossip suggests, their enduring fascination for the trial of the Earl of Essex and the dilemma of a foreign queen who has to sacrifice her rebellious lover to achieve peace within her kingdom, and then finds herself overcome with remorse, is an important reminder that passion and guilt are accorded a better part than valour in the lesser, as well as in the great tragedies of the later period. A further reflection by Edward Forman on the nature of the tragic hero in *Phèdre* and in Euripides's play on the same subject reviews the concept of *hamartia* which prevents Racine's Hippolyte from fulfilling his political destiny by virtue of a passion which is decisive in the making of a suitably sympathetic character. Racine's preface presents Theseus' son's love for Aricie as a fault for which he feels more than a little guilt towards his father, but his desire for her, like Phèdre's desire for him, it is argued, may in fact be both politically and morally justifiable in terms of the play. The problem is that it leads both characters to make a fatal miscalculation, or error of judgement, preventing them from appreciating the dangers which others, and the gods to whom they are related, represent.

When tragic drama makes passion both the pretext of history and the message of myth, women may more easily enter stage politics, however opposed to the empowerment of their sex the regimes directly and indirectly represented in the plays. As David Clarke demonstrates, most of the male playwrights of this period portray controversial female characters who have either inherited power or who actively seek to challenge royal authority, partly in response to a growing demand for star actresses on the Paris stage. The increasing feminization of the acting profession in the 1630s and 1640s authorized the exploitation of a narrow range of subjects drawn from Roman sources which might satisfy the exigencies of Richelieu's political programme for the arts and offer a series of pro-active roles for Mlles Lenoir, Bellerose, Beauchâteau and their contemporaries. Exotic queens and tragic victims like Dido, Sophonisbe, and Cleopatra, or the lovely Lucretia, and their attendants and confidants, were given a new lease of life by Mairet, Benserade, Chevreau and Scudéry, though such dramatists tended to emphasize mainly the decorative aspects of the roles.

As his contemporaries acknowledged, it was again Corneille who provided the definitive examples of hero(in)es who, whether temptresses or matrons, were prepared ardently to defend the principle of subsidiarity in love with the same, if not greater, ardour than their menfolk, according to the stringent code which placed public image and duty above private sentiment. In the reordering of patriarchal roles in *Le Cid* and *Cinna*, Chimène and Emilie, though still dependent on decisions taken by the opposite sex, may be said to represent major obstructive forces, helping to bring the king to accept the code of the heroic group as part of his own political vision. The more politically conscious Emilie has her counterpart in Epicaris, the only hero(ine) of Tristan's '*Contre-Cinna*', prepared to sacrifice her life for her fellow conspirators. In a way such 'feminism' represents little more than a degenerate form of heroism, but the enforced acknowledgement in such plays of the legitimacy of an all-powerful emperor, whether benevolent or tyrannical, allowed women to borrow enough charisma from their defeated heroic allies to overshadow them in the political debate.

Acknowledging the devaluation of the *grands hommes* view of history, Jean Rohou, in the final essay in this series, drafts a balance sheet of the influence on the development of literature, and of theatre in particular, of Louis XIV's personal greatness as individual and king, distinguishing the man from the character, and highlighting the themes of many of the plays of the period. A great king, as much by virtue of historical and political circumstance as personality and acumen, the limitations of Louis XIV's intelligence of anything other than the theatrical role of hero-king suggest that other factors may have determined the patronage of writers during his reign. Most of the great writers, apart from Racine, were already established in Paris before the death of Mazarin. Much of the direction of the prestigious cultural and media programme, so influential in the promotion of the king's glorious reputation as patron of the arts, and the manner of government was left to Colbert. Well-rewarded women like Mme de Montespan and her sister may be said to have been more influential in patronage of the arts in the early decades when, in singling himself out from the heroic group, the king took the first steps towards tyranny. We are reminded that budget allocations to writers, although far more important than in the previous reign, represented only an insignificant proportion of total expenditure even in the 1660s and 1670s, and disappeared altogether towards the end of the century when the king ceased to take an active interest in literature as he turned to religion which might provide an ethical basis for a politics of domination.

Thus brought to account in a collection of essays which amounts to a twenty-point audit of seventeenth-century moral values and the literary and political landscape of the *ancien régime*, Louis XIV, the cardinal ministers, and Frondeurs seem less than equal to the image they would project of themselves, but ever more fascinating in the conflicts and contradictions which characterise their relations with each other, to which the memoirs and plays of the period add a further dimension. It is to be hoped that this binary study offers a true and fair statement of the nature of belief and the exercise of power in monarchical society, which will give renewed impetus to French seventeenth-century studies in the twenty-first century and beyond.

CHAPTER ONE

'Alternative' Ethical Systems in France during the *Grand Siècle*

WILLIAM D. HOWARTH

A prominent feature of the intellectual history of the *Grand Siècle* in France is the close alliance of Church and State in the interests of uniformity: this was a period during which the suppression of doubt and debate was designed to ensure political and social cohesion as well as religious orthodoxy. As a result, between the intellectual curiosity of the Renaissance (and such practical implementation of religious tolerance as marked Henri IV's reign) on the one hand, and the challenge to received ideas that we associate with the Enlightenment on the other, there was a long period of reaction, characterized by the repression, and even the persecution, of intellectual independence. It will be the purpose of this essay to take stock of the survival of independent thought beneath the conformist surface; and more specifically, to consider the extent to which examples of such survival may have provided the basis for anything that might be called an 'alternative' life-style.

The officially approved life-style of the period is of course one which was prepared to sacrifice worldly pleasure in this life for a reward in the life to come. Though many of today's readers—not excluding those with sincere Christian convictions, I suspect—may feel uncomfortable with the calculating casuistry with which Pascal seeks to bring persuasion to bear on readers of his own day, there can be no doubt of the genuine intellectual and moral commitment which inspired the *pari*. Nor can we doubt the genuineness of the intellectual conviction and religious zeal which produced such outstanding examples of piety and *dévotion* as the lives of Saint François de Sales, Saint Vincent de Paul, Bossuet or Fénelon—even if in the case of Bossuet, for example, a characteristic mark of his zealous fervour was a determination to coerce others into sharing his own uncompromising orthodoxy. Less conformist, but equally genuine, is the witness of those groups—the Jansenists, the Huguenots—who built a way of life on the sacrifices and suffering they were forced to endure for their beliefs.

But as we know, this was also a century marked by the opportunist conformism of the self-seekers: on the one hand, the 'fausse dévotion' of Molière's 'grand seigneur méchant homme' which had its real-life models, the playwright would have us believe, in the hypocrisy of Conti and other powerful aristocrats; and alongside this the much more numerous, if socially less objectionable, courtiers who adopted an outward show of religious practice to cover their more mundane ambitions: the real-life originals of La Bruyère's *dévot* who would have been 'athée sous un roi athée'.

On a more private level, there is ample evidence of the role played by the confessor, or by the lay *directeur de conscience*, in the domestic interior of the comfortably-off bourgeois. This was sometimes, no doubt, little more than a status symbol; but not all *directeurs de conscience* were Tartuffes, and we may assume that most *bons bourgeois* were motivated by a genuine concern for the moral welfare, as for the religious orthodoxy, of those dependants for whom they were responsible. As for the humblest levels of French society, it is hardly surprising that such testimony as has survived confirms the role of the parish priest in determining the social and moral conservatism of the urban artisan class, as well as of the rural peasantry; while the limited educational opportunities, and the dependent social status, of women of all ranks of society, meant that they naturally tended to be even less likely than their menfolk to challenge the established order of things.

So much for the conventional picture: a very summary sketch, but one that is supported in general terms by the documentary evidence of the time, and accepted as such by three hundred years of historical tradition. It shows us a society which, from the King to the lowliest of his subjects, subscribed—officially at any rate—to the received doctrine as expounded in the pulpit and the confessional, and to a set of moral values and a code of social behaviour deriving directly from the Church's teaching. When we come to look more closely at the reality underlying this picture of moral and social conformism, it is easy enough to find evidence for a sometimes glaring gap between precept and practice—again, from the King himself downwards. Nor is it difficult to find examples of individuals who quite clearly rejected the moral teaching, and flouted the doctrinal sanctions, of the Church, in order to exploit the orthodox belief, or manipulate the credulity, of their fellows. I am not concerned here, however, with individual cases of anti-social behaviour such as are recorded by Tallemant in his *Historiettes*, or catalogued by Félix Gaiffe in *L'Envers du Grand*

Siècle; but rather with groups or communities whose 'alternative' life-style was based on a more systematic rejection of the Church's teaching in favour of a social structure independent of transcendental sanctions.

The clearest example of anything like an organized fellowship dedicated to the liberation of the social life of the individual, and of the community to which he belonged, from the centuries-old domination of the Church, can be identified in the group of young free-thinkers who, round about 1615 to 1620, made up the entourage of Théophile de Viau. Théophile's own formative years had given him an enquiring mind, very ready to reject conventional morality and religious authority in all its forms; and when he arrived in Paris in about 1615 he was able to satisfy his desire for an independent life-style as a member of a group of like-minded young noblemen and men of letters. Some professed atheism, some were deists, but what distinguishes them from the *libertins érudits* of the following generation is that they proclaimed their godlessness quite openly, making it the basis of a life-style. To quote Antoine Adam: 'L'athéisme à cette date ressortit bien plus à la sociologie qu'à l'histoire abstraite des idées philosophiques'.[1] This 'libertinage de mœurs' acknowledges the influence of sixteenth-century Italian free thought; and the brief period during which moral libertinage was able to flourish unchecked represents a sustained attempt to practise an Epicurean way of life based on the gratification of the senses, a sometimes provocative hostility to repressive dogma, freedom from prejudice and hypocrisy. The best-known surviving reflection of this life-style can be seen in the notorious collections of scurrilous verse such as *Le Cabinet satirique* (1618), *Les Délices satiriques* (1620), or *Le Parnasse satirique* (1622), which Adam characterizes in this way:

> Ces poésies sont avant tout des œuvres de clan. C'est pour les agapes du groupe, c'est pour les joyeuses réunions autour d'une table chargée de bouteilles que ces vers ont été composés. Sorte de liturgies à rebours, opposées au culte de la religion officielle.[2]

However, blasphemous and obscene poems are not the only testimony. E. Roy, editor of Sorel's *Francion*, calls the first (1623) edition of this work 'le manuel du parfait libertin'; and there are certainly to be found, alongside the more Rabelaisian type of anecdotes, passages that would bear this out:

> Depuis que je m'estois veu bien en couche, j'avois acquis une infinité de cognoissances, de jeunes hommes de toutes sortes de qualitez, comme de nobles, de fils de Justiciers, de fils de Financiers

et de Marchands; tous les jours nous estions ensemble à la desbauche, où je faisois tant que j'emboursois plutost que de despendre. Je proposay à cinq ou six des plus grands, de faire une compagnie la plus grande que nous pourrions, et de personnes toutes braves et ennemies de la sottise, et de l'ignorance, pour converser ensemblement, et faire une infinité de gentillesses.

Mon advis leur plût tant, qu'ils mirent la main à l'œuvre, et ramasserent chacun bonne quantité de drosles qui en amenerent encore d'autres, de leur cognoissance particuliere. Nous fismes des loix qui se devoient garder inviolablement, comme de porter tous de l'honneur à un que l'on esliroit pour Chef de toute la bande, de quinze jours, de s'entresecourir aux querelles, aux amours, et aux autres affaires, de mespriser les ames viles de tant de faquins qui sont dans Paris, et qui croyent estre quelque chose à cause de leurs richesses ou de leurs ridicules Offices. Tous ceux qui voulurent garder ces ordonnances là, et quelques autres de pareille estoffe, furent receus au nombre des braves et genereux, (nous nous appellions ainsi), et n'importoit pas d'estre fils de Marchand, ny de Financier, pourveu que l'on blasmast le trafic et les Finances. Nous ne regardions point à la race, nous ne regardions qu'au merite.[3]

Adam goes so far as to suggest that an embodiment of Théophile himself is to be seen in Sorel's hero, who makes what Roy calls 'cette déclaration libertine':

Je semois parmy eux le plus qu'il m'estoit possible, les enseignements de la nouvelle philosophie, dont je vous ay desja parlé. Quelques esprits y prenoient du goust, et ne s'en falloit guere qu'ils ne desirassent la pouvoir suivre, mais d'autres barbares et stupides, luy faisoient un si mauvais acceuil, que j'eusse voulu ne leur en avoir jamais parlé. Mesme, comme c'est l'ordinaire de la bestise des hommes, ils vindrent à m'accuser de folie, ce qui me fascha tant que je me resolus de tenir comme un thresor caché ce que je sçavois, puisqu'il n'y avoit personne qui eust la volonté de s'en servir. Il ne m'importe, ce dis je en moy mesme; les hommes refusent leur bien que je leur presente, ils en porteront la peine; il est vray que j'en patiray quelque peu, mais quoy il faut s'accomoder au temps; la mort viendra bientost me delivrer de ces angoisses.[4]

And there is always the distinctive character of Théophile's own writing: in general terms his sensuous delight in the natural world as a manifestation of a universal principle—a 'pantheistic naturalism', according to J.S. Spink[5]—as a coherent basis for a life-style independent of Christian doctrine:

Les planettes s'arresteront,
Les eslements se mesleront
En ceste admirable Structure

Dont le Ciel nous laisse jouyr.
Ce qu'on voit, ce qu'on peut ouyr
Passera comme une peinture:
L'impuissance de la Nature
Laissera tout évanouyr.
Celuy qui formant le Soleil,
Arracha d'un profond sommeil
L'air et le feu, la terre et l'onde,
Renversera d'un coup de main
La demeure du genre humain
Et la base où le Ciel se fonde:
Et ce grand desordre du Monde
Peut-estre arrivera demain.[6]

There is enough evidence to support Adam's view that we are here on the verge of a break-through of tremendous importance: 'La génération de 1620 a failli orienter la pensée française dans un sens hardi et nouveau. La révolution qui s'est faite dans les esprits vers 1750 aurait pu se produire 130 ans plus tôt'.[7] And not only might Théophile and his band of young free-thinkers have achieved an *intellectual* 'revolution': they came near to establishing—for a self-selecting elite, it goes without saying—the viability of a liberal, cultured life-style freed from the repressive constraints of a backward-looking theology. But the forces of reaction were too strong, and the warnings were too fearsome to ignore: Vanini burnt at the stake at Toulouse, Théophile himself sentenced to exile, then driven to an early death by his sufferings in prison. Sorel, Balzac, Boisrobert and others who had shown sympathy lost little time in distancing themselves from the expression of dangerous views; and orthodox and conformist behaviour became the order of the day.

In Richelieu's France, and the France of Louis XIV, there was to be no further room for attempts to found an alternative society on a basis of openly acknowledged free thought. The typical *libertins* of the middle of the century are either private scholars who pose no threat to the social order; or powerful, self-indulgent noblemen whose rejection of religious sanctions assumed a much more violently anti-social character than the harmless orgies of Théophile and his brother *généreux* had done. What has survived of the writings of the *poètes maudits* of the mid-century does, it is true, suggest a paler imitation of these earlier gatherings, but there is a repetitive, second-hand flavour to both their blasphemy and their obscenity. At all events, any chance of a revival of a flourishing *libertin* community must have been killed off by the exemplary warnings conveyed through the executions of Chausson and Fabry for sodomy in 1661, and of Claude Le Petit, burnt at the stake in 1662 'pour avoir fait un livre intitulé: *Le Bordel des Muses,* escrit *l'Apologie de Chausson, le Moyne renié* et autres compositions de vers et de prose pleines d'impiétés et de blasphèmes, contre l'honneur de Dieu, de la Vierge et de l'Estat'.8

The most exciting pieces of writing to come out of the *libertin* tradition in the middle of the century are without a doubt Cyrano de Bergerac's two companion works forming his *L'Autre Monde.* But it is cosmological concepts on a grand scale which give the creative stimulus to Cyrano's imagination; he is inspired by the Copernican challenge to the Ptolemaic system, not by the moral and social possibilities of an Epicurean alternative to the Christian way of life. His critique of social practices and moral prejudices hardly goes beyond the satirist's standard device of constructing a 'monde à rebours'. He illustrates his belief in the arbitrary and relativist nature of all customs by imagining an ideal lunar society in which virginity is a crime; in which it is the young to whom their elders pay respect; in which the carrying of a sword as an emblem of noble birth is replaced by the wearing of a large phallic symbol:

> quoi! les grands de votre monde sont enragés de faire parade d'un instrument qui désigne un bourreau et qui n'est forgé que pour nous détruire, enfin l'ennemi juré de tout ce qui vit; et de cacher, au contraire, un membre sans qui nous serions au rang de ce qui n'est pas, le Prométhée de chaque animal, et le réparateur infatigable des faiblesses de la nature!9

and in which the honourable burial of the dead is replaced by a celebratory feasting on the flesh of the departed. Entertaining and stimulating as such *jeux d'esprit* may be, they cannot be seen, any more than can Rabelais's *Abbaye de Thélème,* as the blueprint for a new way of life.

Though later generations were to give him an honourable place in the development of seventeenth-century free thought, Cyrano's impact on his contemporaries seems to have been minimal. *Les Etats et empires de la lune* was published in an abridged version for reasons of prudence, and *Les Etats et empires du soleil* in incomplete form after the author's death. Cyrano himself, despite his affiliation to thinkers such as Gassendi, was very much an individual writer, and neither his life nor his creative imagination suggests a challenge to the dominant life-style of his contemporaries, any more than did the reclusive scholarship of *libertins érudits* such as Naudé or La Mothe le Vayer.

Long before Octave Nadal gave currency to the term 'l'éthique de la gloire', the psychological and moral motivation of Corneille's characters had been the subject of critical scrutiny. However, it was left to Paul Bénichou (*Morales du Grand Siècle*, Paris, 1948) and to Nadal (*Le Sentiment de l'amour dans l'œuvre de Pierre Corneille*, Paris, 1948) to complete the discrediting of the precise parallel drawn by Gustave Lanson between the Cornelian hero and the 'généreux selon Descartes'.[10] Bénichou insists that the psychology of Corneille's characters has been seriously misunderstood through 'un emploi erroné des concepts de volonté et de raison';[11] while in his 'Etude conjointe: De quelques mots de la langue cornélienne, ou D'une éthique de la gloire'—by far the most valuable part of his *Sentiment de l'amour...*—Nadal reaches a similar conclusion in respect of the terms *mérite, devoir, vertu, générosité, gloire*. For Bénichou, 'l'horreur profonde de toute humiliation infligée au moi est bien la source de toute la vertu cornélienne';[12] and for Nadal the concept of *la gloire* is the key to an equally self-centred ethical system: one that the reader must be careful never to confuse with 'la morale commune' or the morality taught by religion:

> Dieu, ni la conscience morale, n'orientent le cornélien. Seule la gloire est le principe et la fin, la loi et la foi de cette morale particulière.[13]

That Corneille's 'éthique de la gloire' had its real-life counterpart, in what Alban Krailsheimer felicitously calls 'le moi soleil',[14] is abundantly documented; and that this phenomenon was regarded by churchmen as an insidious challenge to Christian precept is equally clear:

> La gloire: qu'y a-t-il pour le chrétien de plus mortel? Quel appas plus dangereux? Quelle fumée plus capable de faire tourner les meilleures têtes?[15]

However, by the time Bossuet wrote these lines in 1670, it was a second generation of the faithful whose piety was at risk from the contagion of *la gloire*. This worldly ethic had made its most heady appeal to the generation of the Frondes; it was around 1650 that it came nearest to constituting a coherent life-style, and its most notable exponent was the Cardinal de Retz, whose *Mémoires* offer such a frank portrait of a man driven by an all-consuming ambition.

A basic attribute for those seeking to live according to the 'éthique de la gloire' is an obsessive sense of caste. Krailsheimer quotes the following passage in which Retz asserts his aristocratic pride as a reason for not relying on the support of members of his household in a certain crisis:

Il n'y eût rien eu de si odieux que de mettre les gens, ou du peuple ou du bas étage, dans ces sortes de lieux où l'on ne laisse entrer, dans l'ordre, que des personnes de condition.

And comments that 'the habit of treating people as things, which in his own class applied to individuals, in the classes below applied to the mass collectively'.[16] Tallemant records, among the characteristic components of Retz's *gloire*, as well as his fierce pride, the propensity to a spontaneous liberality that brings to mind the sort of *acte gratuit* that will be associated with Molière's Dom Juan:

Dez le college, l'Abbé fit voir son humeur altiere: il ne pouvoit guères souffrir d'egaux, et avoit souvent querelle; il monstra aussy dez ce temps son humeur liberale; car ayant appris qu'un gentilhomme qu'il ne connoissoit point estoit arresté au Chastelet pour cinquante pistolles, il trouva moyen de les avoir et les luy envoya.[17]

Part of the fascination of the *Mémoires* lies in the blatant contrast between Retz as an unabashed practitioner of the most worldly of ethical systems, and the same man as a prince of the Catholic Church who, while admitting to his worldly goals, nevertheless pretends to a respect for traditional Christian virtues—a contradiction underlined by the author himself when he writes:

Je pris une ferme résolution de remplir exactement tous les devoirs de ma profession, et d'être aussi homme de bien pour le salut des autres, que je pourrais être méchant pour moi-même.[18]

But the constant proclamation of his preoccupation with the self—Pascal's 'moi haïssable'—betrays the incompatibility of Retz's concern for 'le salut des autres' with any genuinely Christian motivation.

Pascal's 'la plus grande bassesse de l'homme est la recherche de la gloire'[19] inspires the following commentary by Bénichou:

Cependant toute la gloire du moi, ainsi démentie par la faiblesse de l'homme au sein de l'univers, pourrait trouver refuge dans le désir même que la gloire inspire, s'il était prouvé que ce désir fût noble. C'est à quoi s'emploie la morale aristocratique quand elle représente l'amour de la gloire comme un mouvement vers un bien immatériel, par lequel l'âme échappe à l'injurieuse dépendance des choses, comme une démarche spontanément idéale de la nature humaine.[20]

In his article 'L'Ethique de la gloire au dix-septième siècle', Nadal characterizes the aspiration of this 'morale aristocratique' as 'l'ultime relèvement en France d'un esprit chevaleresque mais non chrétien'.[21]

'Chivalric', 'romanesque', 'theatrical': all these epithets have rightly been applied to the heroic exertions of the leading players on the public stage of the *Fronde des Princes*. The affinity between the real-life exponents of *la gloire* and Corneille's characters like Nicomède, Sertorius or Cléopâtre is no mere superficial coincidence of themes and vocabulary; we can see on both sides a continuation of the chivalric, aristocratic values inherited from a feudal society, while on both sides too there is a compulsion to play to the gallery: self-advertisement and self-justification, a constant need for the approval and the admiration of others, are of the essence of the 'éthique de la gloire'.

Such a perspective is decisively rejected by Pascal, most notably in the important fragment on 'l'amour propre' which so eloquently defines the 'misère de l'homme':

> La nature de l'amour propre et de ce moi humain est de n'aimer que soi et de ne considérer que soi. Mais que fera-t-il? Il ne saurait empêcher que cet objet qu'il aime ne soit plein de défauts et de misère ... C'est sans doute un mal que d'être plein de défauts; mais c'est encore un plus grand mal que d'en être plein et de ne les vouloir pas reconnaître, puisque c'est y ajouter encore celui d'une illusion volontaire.[22]

Not only was this 'illusion volontaire' condemned by Christian thinkers, it was soon also to be found wanting as the basis of a worldly ethos, once the volatile, exhibitionist activity of the Frondes had given way to the more stable social structures of 'la Cour et la Ville'.

An illustration of this change in life-style after the turbulent years of the Frondes, from the self-assertive 'éthique de la gloire' to the self-effacing values of *honnêteté*, has frequently been recognized in the career of La Rochefoucauld. Wounded in battle, unsuccessful in politics and disappointed in love, the future author of the *Maximes* made the transition from public to private life with some difficulty—and with less than total success, if we are to believe the portrait by Retz:

> Il n'a jamais été guerrier, quoiqu'il fût très soldat. Il n'a jamais été par lui-même bon courtisan, quoiqu'il ait eu toujours bonne intention de l'être. Il n'a jamais été bon homme de parti, quoique toute sa vie il y ait été engagé. Cet air de honte et de timidité que vous lui voyez dans la vie civile s'était tourné dans les affaires en air d'apologie. Il croyait toujours en avoir besoin; ce qui, joint à ses *Maximes*, qui ne marquent pas assez de foi en la vertu, et à sa pratique, qui a toujours été de chercher à sortir des affaires avec autant de plaisir qu'il y était

entré, me fait conclure qu'il eût beaucoup mieux fait de se connaître
et de se réduire à passer, comme il l'eût pu, pour le courtisan le plus
poli, et le plus honnête homme, à l'égard de la vie commune, qui eût
paru dans son siècle.[23]

La Rochefoucauld's own self-portrait, published in 1659—which
Emile Magne calls 'une sorte de manifeste'[24]—while it claims a
single-minded pursuit of the new goal of *honnêteté*, surely also
suggests a residue of aristocratic pride which he did not always find it
possible to subdue:

> J'ai les sentiments vertueux, les inclinations belles, et une si forte
> envie d'être tout à fait honnête homme que mes amis ne me sauraient
> faire un plus grand plaisir que de m'avertir sincèrement de mes
> défauts ... L'ambition ne me travaille point. Je ne crains guère de
> choses, et ne crains aucunement la mort. Je suis peu sensible à la
> pitié, et voudrais ne l'y être point du tout. Cependant, il n'y a rien
> que je ne fisse pour le soulagement d'une personne affligée; et je
> crois effectivement que l'on doit tout faire, jusqu'à lui témoigner
> même beaucoup de compassion de son mal; car les misérables sont
> si sots que cela leur fait le plus grand bien du monde. Mais je tiens
> aussi qu'il faut se contenter d'en témoigner et se garder
> soigneusement d'en avoir. C'est une passion qui n'est bonne à rien au
> dedans d'une âme bien faite, qui ne sert qu'à affaiblir le cœur et
> qu'on doit laisser au peuple, qui, n'exécutant jamais rien par raison, a
> besoin de passions pour le porter à faire les choses ...[25]

In the *Maximes*, it is the ethical values of *honnêteté* that provide the
positive reference-point against which the overall catalogue of man's
egoism can be measured:

> Les faux honnêtes gens sont ceux qui déguisent leurs défauts aux
> autres et à eux-mêmes; les vrais honnêtes gens sont ceux qui les
> connaissent parfaitement et les confessent.
> Le vrai honnête homme est celui qui ne se pique de rien.[26]

And whatever influence of Jansenist doctrines it would be proper to
acknowledge in shaping La Rochefoucauld's characteristically cynical
view of human nature, it must be clear that the moral concerns
expressed in the passage quoted from his self-portrait owe little to
Christian teaching, and that in his case the ideal of *honnêteté* retains a
good deal of the elitist self-regard of the 'éthique de la gloire'.[27]

What one might call 'main-line' *honnêteté* is sufficiently well
defined to qualify without difficulty as the third of our secular life-
styles. However, despite the dominant contribution of Méré to its
definition, it is not Méré, but Mitton, who is taken to task in the

Pensées as the exponent of a worldly way of life lacking the extra dimension provided by Christian belief. Mitton's succinct summary of the characteristic features of this way of life is as follows:

> L'honnête homme ... n'est point intéressé ... Sa conduite est toujours réglée, et jamais il ne vit dans le désordre ... L'honnête homme fait grand cas de l'esprit, mais il fait encore plus de cas de la raison ... Il veut tout savoir et ne se pique de rien savoir; il prend garde à tout; il n'estime les choses que selon leur véritable valeur ...
>
> L'honnête homme enfin ne dit et ne fait jamais rien qui ne soit agréable et raisonnable, et qui ne tende à faire que tous les hommes soient heureux.[28]

Pascal brings a threefold charge against Mitton's *honnête homme*:

> Reprocher à Miton de ne point se remuer.
> Le moi est haïssable. Vous, Miton, le couvrez, vous ne l'ôtez point pour cela: vous êtes donc toujours haïssable.
> Miton voit bien que la nature est corrompue et que les hommes sont contraires à l'honnêteté. Mais il ne sait pas pourquoi ils ne peuvent voler plus haut'.[29]

The first reproach is the same as that made against Montaigne: that he aspires to a virtue 'couchée mollement dans le sein de l'oisiveté tranquille', and shows 'une nonchalance du salut, sans crainte et sans repentir';[30] in other words, Pascal recognizes, and denounces, a Stoic ataraxia as one of the characteristic objectives of *honnêteté*. As regards the celebrated 'moi haïssable', Mitton would very reasonably have countered this reproach with the safeguard that the *honnête homme*'s activity in society is limited by regard for others: such a defence is indeed put into his mouth by Pascal, and expanded in Mitton's own words as follows:

> Pour se rendre heureux avec moins de peine, pour l'être avec sûreté, sans craindre d'être troublé dans son bonheur, il faut faire en sorte que les autres le soient avec nous: car si l'on prétend songer seulement à soi, on trouve des oppositions continuelles, et quand nous ne voulons être heureux qu'à condition que les autres le soient en même temps, tous obstacles sont levés, et tout le monde nous prête la main. C'est ce ménagement de bonheur pour nous et pour les autres que l'on doit appeler honnêteté, qui n'est, à le bien prendre, que l'amour propre bien réglé.[31]

This last sentence expresses, more effectively than any text by Méré or Saint-Evremond, the moral acceptability of the 'éthique de la gloire' for something much nearer to an Epicurean ideal, in which the pursuit of worldly pleasure readily acknowledges the constraints imposed by consideration for one's fellow-men. It quite fails, of course, to address itself to the metaphysical dimension of Pascal's reproach: that human nature is essentially corrupt, and cannot be redeemed without divine aid.

Round about 1660, Sorbière wrote a valuable paragraph on the distinction between the terms *homme de bien, homme dévot, honnête homme* and *galant homme*; the *honnête homme* is defined as follows:

> bien plus éclairé que l'homme de bien, ... il ne suit pas les seules lumières qui conduisent l'homme dévot. Il se laisse guider aussi aux clartés naturelles du bon sens et de l'équité vers lesquelles il fait autant de réflexion que sur celles que la piété lui donne. C'est pourquoi sa vie est plus en dehors; sa science est plus étendue et ses actions, de même que ses paroles, sont plus accommodées à quelque bienséance et à quelques civilités, par lesquelles il tâche de se rendre utile et agréable à tout le monde. Ses pensées sont plus vastes que celles de l'homme de bien et elles lui font entreprendre plus de choses qu'il ne ferait, s'il renfermait son activité dans une moindre sphère. Sa vertu est plus détachée de la matière: et ses maximes d'honneur lui font trouver de quoi enchérir sur la pratique ordinaire de ses concitoyens. Il veut faire plus que les Loix ne commandent, et il ne s'estimerait pas digne du titre qu'on lui donne, s'il ne faisait que ce que doivent faire les autres hommes. Il est soigneux de tenir ce qu'il a promis, et jamais il ne cherche de prétexte pour s'empêcher de faire du bien à ceux qui ont besoin de lui.[32]

This generous appreciation suggests that the secular ideal of *honnêteté* is able to find, for the practice of charity towards one's fellows, an alternative source to the traditional Christian injunction to love one's neighbour; and this is a useful reminder when we come to Méré, the supreme theoretician of *honnêteté*, who sometimes gives the impression that the *honnête homme* is to be judged by aesthetic rather than by moral criteria, and that he can be adequately identified by externals. In fact, Méré has had a bad press among some modern critics; Magendie for instance writes of him:

> L'outrecuidance de Méré est insupportable; son rôle de professeur écouté l'a comme grisé; il cherche toutes les occasions de donner de lui une idée avantageuse.[33]

However, there is no denying Méré's importance; even if Borgerhoff is right to stress the anomaly of his position as 'that lonely being, the professional amateur', the range of attitudes and activities that he documents is unequalled elsewhere in the writings on *honnêteté*; and the force of his personal convictions is persuasive precisely because 'this teacher of the art of pleasing and of being pleased wanted to be his own best example'.[34]

The *honnête homme* as defined by Faret had been a bourgeois outsider seeking a key to social success; and the way of life advertised in *L'Honnête Homme, ou l'Art de plaire à la cour* (1630) contains more than a little of what Krailsheimer, borrowing the term from Stephen Potter, calls 'lifemanship'. Méré's *honnête homme*, on the other hand, does not have to worry about his social standing; and to the extent that his various writings can be regarded as forming a composite gentleman's vade mecum, this is less for the use of the social climber than of the man of breeding and taste with an established position in society, who needs some guidance as to how to protect his position of privilege and distinction from the possibility of contamination.

However, breeding is more important for Méré than noble birth: though he acknowledges the advantage 'une heureuse naissance' can bring, he is certain that 'il faudrait choisir les plus honnêtes-gens, plûtôt que les grands Seigneurs, pour instruire les jeunes Princes'. And he disapproves of a society in which deference is shown to rank for its own sake:

> un de mes amis me déplut extrêmement de s'être avancé pour aider un jeune homme à monter à cheval, parce qu'il étoit Duc et Pair: Que s'il se fût empressé de la sorte pour un homme indisposé, j'eusse loüé son action ... [35]

Méré's *honnête homme* is distinguished by his modesty:

> Il n'y a rien qui s'accommode plus mal avec un honnête-homme que la vanité, ni qui convienne mieux, que les sentiments du vrai honneur;[36]

and by his refusal to impose himself on others in society:

> je me souviens qu'un des meilleurs Esprits de la Cour m'assuroit, qu'il n'avoit jamais rien tant souhaité que d'être honnête-homme, et que tout ce qui l'en avoit le plus reculé, c'étoit une passion violente et dereglée de divertir toute sorte de gens.[37]

He must aim to be an all-rounder, and must distance himself from anything that might suggest the specialist:

> Parmi tous les airs qu'on remarque, je n'en vois d'agréable que celui des Cours et du grand monde: de sorte que dans la vie ordinaire tout ce qui tient du métier, déplaît. Ce n'est pas qu'un galant homme ne

> doive rien dire de la pluspart des Arts, pourvû qu'il en parle en
> homme du monde, plutôt qu'en artisan: mais c'est un malheur aux
> honnêtes gens, que d'être pris à leur mine, ou à leur procédé, pour
> des gens de métier, et quand on a cette disgrace il s'en faut défaire, à
> quelque prix que ce soit ...38

Conventional ambition is to be deplored; and even the ambition to
make one's mark as an *honnête homme* must not be overdone:

> même le talent d'honnête homme, le plus beau qu'on se puisse
> imaginer, n'a pas tous les agrémens, à moins que de paroître plus
> negligé, que ajusté, parce qu'en l'affectant, ce seroit en faire une
> espece de métier, comme si l'on étoit Gouverneur d'un jeune Prince,
> et toûjours prés à lui donner des Leçons. Cette manière, à mon sens,
> auroit si peu de grace, que je voudrois qu'on fût honnête homme,
> sans témoigner d'en avoir jamais eu la pensée.39

Once inculcated by birth and breeding, this social ideal must be
pursued in the company of other *honnêtes gens*—and particularly
through the 'commerce des dames':

> Il me semble donc, que le commerce des honnêtes gens est à
> rechercher; mais les entretiens des Dames, dont les graces font
> penser aux bienséances, sont encore plus nécessaires pour s'achever
> dans l'honnêteté.40

An arduous pursuit, but one that will bring great rewards; for
honnêteté is 'la quintessence de toutes les vertus ... Cette science est
proprement celle de l'homme, parce qu'elle consiste à vivre et à se
communiquer d'une manière humaine et raisonnable'.41 If we ask: was
Méré deliberately putting his 'science de l'homme' forward as an
'alternative' ethical system? I think the answer must be that he
prudently maintained—and possibly did genuinely believe—that
honnêteté was not only not incompatible with Christian doctrine, but
was capable of making its own contribution to a life of piety:

> Je prens garde aussi, que la dévotion et l'honnêteté vont presque les
> mêmes voïes, et qu'elles s'aident l'une à l'autre. La dévotion rend
> l'honnêteté plus solide et plus digne de confiance; et l'honnêteté
> comble la dévotion de bon air et d'agrément: Elles s'unissent donc
> fort bien, car comme Dieu ne commande que des choses justes, et ne
> défend rien, qui ne soit mauvais; quand un homme ne sauroit pas
> tous les Préceptes divins, il y en a bien peu, qu'il n'observât de lui-
> même; encore suis-je persuadé qu'un honnête homme ne tombe dans
> le désordre, que bien rarement; et que si ce malheur lui arrive, il
> n'est pas longtemps à s'en repentir: De sorte que l'honnêteté n'est pas
> inutile au salut, et qu'elle y contribuë extrêmement, mais la dévotion

en est la principale cause. Je ne voudrois pas que dans la vie ordinaire on fît le dévot de profession: le Sauveur nous ordonne de cacher nos bonnes œuvres; surtout je n'approuve pas que les personnes du monde se mêlent de catéchiser: cela leur sied mal, et sent l'hipocrite.[42]

However, one does not need to be a Pascal in order to read into everything that Méré writes a virtually complete disregard of any transcendental dimension, amounting—in Pascal's terms—to nothing less than a 'nonchalance du salut'. And if we are looking for supporting evidence of Méré's independence of the Christian tradition, J.G. Benay sees in his known love for nature, so unusual for someone of his generation, a definite link with Théophile's naturalistic philosophy; for Méré, he argues:

[la nature] est bonne, elle est belle, elle agit sur les sens. Méré qui fait profession d'épicurisme et qui certainement continue la tradition de Théophile revient sans cesse sur ce thème.[43]

Méré's interest in the world about him is not the interest shown by a baroque poet like Saint-Amant; it shows a more genuinely philosophical preoccupation with the place of man in the cosmos, and he chides his contemporaries for lacking such an interest:

Mais si nous regardons les divers ouvrages de la nature, le coucher du Soleil, une nuit tranquille, et ces astres qui roulent si majestueusement sur nos testes, nous en sommes toujours étonnez. Ceux qui ne pensent qu'à leur fortune, sont occupez d'un petit monde artificiel qu'ils sçavent fort bien; mais ce grand monde naturel leur est inconnu.[44]

Evidence of *libertin* ideas underlying Méré's profession of *honnêteté* is also to be seen in a letter of La Rochefoucauld's which is of capital importance. The letter reports a conversation with Méré on the subject of Epicurus:

Vous me faites souvenir, lui dis-je, de cet admirable génie qui laissa tant de beaux ouvrages, tant de chefs-d'œuvre d'esprit et d'invention, comme une vive lumière dont les uns furent éclairés et la plupart éblouis. Mais parce qu'il était persuadé qu'on n'est heureux que par le plaisir, ni malheureux que par la douleur, ce qui me semble, à le bien examiner, plus clair que le jour, on l'a regardé comme l'auteur de la plus infâme et de la plus honteuse débauche; si bien que la pureté de ses mœurs ne le put exempter de cette horrible calomnie. Je serais assez de son avis, me dit-il, et je crois qu'on pourrait faire une maxime que la vertu mal entendue n'est guère moins incommode que le vice bien ménagé. Ah, monsieur! m'écriai-je, il s'en faut bien garder; ces termes sont si scandaleux qu'ils feraient condamner la chose du monde la plus honnête et la plus sainte. Aussi n'usai-je de ces mots, me dit-il, que pour m'accommoder au langage de certaines gens qui donnent souvent le nom de vice à la vertu et celui de vertu au vice. Et parce que tout le monde veut être heureux et que c'est le but où tendent toutes les actions de la vie, j'admire que ce qu'ils appellent vice soit ordinairement doux et commode, et que la vertu mal entendue soit âpre et pesante. Je ne m'étonne pas que ce grand homme ait eu tant d'ennemis; la véritable vertu se confie en elle-même, elle se montre sans artifice et d'un air simple et naturel, comme celle de Socrate. Mais les faux honnêtes gens, aussi bien que les faux dévots, ne cherchent que l'apparence, et je crois que, dans la morale, Sénèque était un hypocrite et qu'Epicure était un saint.[45]

Mention of Epicurus in connection with *honnêteté* brings us finally to Saint-Evremond, who although he left no blueprint for an alternative life-style, and was placed by force of circumstances in a situation in which it was difficult for him to influence the thinking of his fellow-Frenchmen, does nevertheless usefully round out the picture of the *honnête homme* drawn by Méré. H.T. Barnwell writes of him:

Ne suivant aucun système orthodoxe en religion, en philosophie, en morale ou en littérature, Saint-Evremond n'en construisit pas de nouveau à son usage, et n'en légua pas à ses successeurs. Mais s'il se méfia des systèmes et de l'orthodoxie, il ne s'y attaqua pourtant pas directement: il s'en servit plutôt pour former sa propre pensée et sa morale personnelle.[46]

If he was content to adhere formally to the religion of his fathers, his ideal was a Catholicism purged of the intolerance and fanaticism which led to the persecution of so-called heretics, forced conversions and the revocation of the Edict of Nantes; as he writes with uncharacteristically savage irony:

Toutes ces belles controverses
Sur les religions diverses
N'ont jamais produit aucun bien:
Chacun s'anime pour la sienne;
Et que fait-on pour la chrétienne?
On dispute, et l'on ne fait rien.

Comment! on ne fait rien pour elle?
On condamne les *juifs* au feu!
On extermine l'*infidèle*!
Si vous jugez que c'est trop peu,
On fera pendre l'*hérétique*;
Et quelquefois le *catholique*

Aura même peine à son tour.
Où pourrait-on trouver plus de zèle et d'amour?[47]

Like Méré, Saint-Evremond seems less concerned about his 'salut' than about his happiness in this life, and to look to Epicureanism for the definition of that happiness. His 'Jugement sur les sciences où peut s'appliquer un honnête homme' reviews the various intellectual disciplines on offer, and on mathematics he makes this comment, which seems to encapsulate a pure Epicureanism:

Il n'y a point de louanges que je ne donne aux grands mathématiciens, pourvu que je ne le sois pas. J'admire leurs inventions, et les ouvrages qu'ils produisent; mais je pense que c'est assez aux personnes de bon sens de les savoir bien employer; car, à parler sagement, nous avons plus d'intérêt à jouir du monde qu'à le connaître.[48]

His self-portrait, written when he was in his eighties, shows his moral goal to be the Epicurean one of moderation in all things:

C'est un philosophe également éloigné du superstitieux et de l'impie; un voluptueux qui n'a pas moins d'aversion pour la débauche que d'inclination pour les plaisirs ...

– and its concluding lines show us a man at peace with the world he lives in, and free of worry about the possibility of a world to come:

De justice et de charité,
Beaucoup plus que de pénitence,
Il compose sa piété;
Mettant en Dieu sa confiance,
Espérant tout de sa bonté,
Dans le sein de la Providence
Il trouve son repos et sa félicité.[49]

The first of the three secular ethical systems under review, *libertinage de mœurs*, once driven underground by a determined policy of political and social conformism, was to stay underground. To the extent that the *ideas* of the free-thinkers proved resistant to such repression, and resurfaced to play an important part in the shaping of Enlightenment thought, this was through the writings of *vulgarisateurs* such as Bayle and Fontenelle, rather than the practical example of a viable life-style. Unprincipled libertines there would always be, but free thought as the proclaimed principle of a society organized on enlightened humane grounds was to disappear without trace.

The *éthique de la gloire* was too much a response to those particular political and social challenges of the years of the Frondes to have a long-term viability as a way of life, even for a princely elite: the example of le Grand Condé, *assagi* in his later years and settled into a life of pious conformism, is a case in point. More generally, ambition on the grand scale was replaced by petty vanity; the *gloire* of Corneille's heroes gave way in practice to the banal self-seeking of the placemen at Versailles.

The fate of *honnêteté* was rather different. It became assimilated, losing much of the ideological underpinning of its Epicurean origins, to the point at which it could be taken for granted as the outward manner of any courtier; and as La Bruyère warns us, *honnêteté* in this debased form did not have much to recommend it:

> L'honnête homme tient le milieu entre l'habile homme et l'homme de bien, quoique dans une distance inégale de ces deux extrêmes. ... L'honnête homme est celui qui ne vole pas sur les grands chemins et qui ne tue personne, dont les vices enfin ne sont pas scandaleux ...[50]

If we look further ahead, and attempt to assess the legacy of these alternative life-styles to the century of Voltaire, it is surely not too imaginative to interpret the cynical egoism of a Valmont as a travesty of the generous spirit of seventeenth-century *libertinage*. The noble impulses of the 'éthique de la gloire' at its best are replaced by the vain posturings epitomized in the phrase 'un homme de ma qualité ...' and pilloried in Destouches's *Le Glorieux*. And should we perhaps be justified in seeing an appropriate memorial to the fall from grace of the *honnête homme* in Voltaire's Pococuranté, in whom 'la science de la vie' has degenerated into an all-encompassing *taedium vitae*?

Notes:

1   *Théophile de Viau et la libre pensée française en 1620*, Paris, 1935, p. 127.
2   Ibid., p. 128.
3   *Francion*, ed. E. Roy, Paris, 1924, II, pp. 116–7.
4   Ibid., II, p. 173.
5   *French Free Thought from Gassendi to Voltaire*, London, 1960, p. 44.
6   'A Monsieur de L. sur la mort de son père', *Œuvres poétiques, seconde et troisième parties*, ed. J. Streicher, Geneva, 1958, p. 217.
7   Op. cit., p. 431.
8   *Le Cabinet secret du Parnasse*, ed. L. Perceau, Paris, 1935, p. 153. See also *Les Libertins au xviie siècle: textes choisis et présentés par A. Adam*, Paris, 1964.
9   *L'Autre Monde*, ed. H. Weber, Paris, 1959, p. 148.
10   'Le Héros cornélien et le généreux selon Descartes', first published in *Hommes et livres*, Paris, 1895.
11   Op. cit., p. 25.
12   Ibid., p. 53.

13   Op. cit., p. 305.
14   *Studies in Self-interest*, Oxford, 1962, p. 7.
15   Bossuet, 'Oraison funèbre de la Duchesse d'Orléans' (1670), in *Oraisons funèbres*, ed. J. Truchet, Paris, 1961.
16   Op. cit., p. 76.
17   *Historiettes*, ed. A. Adam, Paris, 1960–1, II, pp. 304–5.
18   Quoted by Krailsheimer, op. cit., p. 63.
19   *Pensées*, ed. P. Sellier, Paris, 1976, fragment 707.
20   Op. cit., pp. 100–1.
21   *Mercure de France*, CCCVIII, Jan.–April 1950, pp. 21–34 (p. 24).
22   Ed. cit., fragment 743.
23   Quoted in La Rochefoucauld, *Œuvres complètes*, ed. L. Martin-Chauffier, Paris, 1950, pp. 588–9.
24   *Le Vrai Visage de La Rochefoucauld*, Paris, 1923, p. 127.
25   *Œuvres complètes*, ed. cit., pp. 29–30.
26   *Maximes*, nos. 202, 203.
27   See Krailsheimer, op. cit., p. 96.
28   Quoted in D. Wetsel, 'Pascal and Mitton: Theological Objections to 'l'honnêteté' in the *Pensées*', *French Studies*, XLVII, 1993, pp. 404–11 (p. 405).
29   Ed. cit., fragments 433, 494, 529.
30   Quoted by Wetsel, art. cit., p. 405.
31   Ibid., p. 406.
32   Quoted in A.M. Boase, *The Fortunes of Montaigne*, London, 1935, p. 319.
33   M. Magendie, *La Politesse mondaine et les théories de l'honnêteté en France*, Paris, 2 vols, 1925, p. 743.
34   E.B.O. Borgerhoff, *The Freedom of French Classicism*, Princeton, 1950, p. 83.
35   *Œuvres complètes du Chevalier de Méré*, ed. C.-H. Boudhors, Paris, 1930, III, pp. 70, 76, 144.
36   Ibid., III, p. 146.
37   Ibid., III, p. 77.
38   Ibid., III, pp. 142–3. Cf. Pascal: 'C'est donc une fausse louange qu'on donne à un homme quand on dit de lui, lorsqu'il entre, qu'il est fort habile en poésie et c'est une mauvaise marque, quand on n'a pas recours à un homme quand il s'agit de juger de quelques vers', ed. cit., fragment 486.
39   Ibid., III, p. 143.
40   Ibid., III, p. 75. In saying this, Méré is anticipating La Bruyère's 'Une belle femme qui a les qualités d'un honnête homme est ce qu'il y a au monde d'un commerce plus délicieux: l'on trouve en elle tout le mérite des deux sexes' (*Caractères*, ch. IX, para. 13).
41   Ibid., III, pp. 71–2.
42   Ibid., III, pp. 101–2.
43   'L'honnête Homme devant la nature, ou la philosophie du Chevalier de Méré', *P.M.L.A.*, LXXIX, 1964, pp. 22–3 (p. 24).
44   Quoted by Benay, art. cit., p. 31.
45   Quoted by Spink, op. cit., p. 142.
46   *Les Idées morales et critiques de Saint-Evremond*, Paris, 1957, p. 216.
47   *Œuvres mêlées*, Amsterdam, 1706, III, pp. 105–6.
48   *Œuvres*, ed. R. de Planhol, Paris, 1927, I, p. 86.
49   Ibid., I, pp. 5–6.
50   *Caractères*, ch. XII, para. 55.

CHAPTER TWO

A Note on Lay Piety in the Early Seventeenth Century

JOHN CRUICKSHANK†

One of the most notable features of religious life in France during the 1590s and early 1600s is the degree of its intensity. Within a short number of years a complete 'psychological revolution'[1] had occurred, taking the form of deep, personal piety and mystical fervour. This change is all the more striking since it occurred so soon after the Wars of Religion. The wars, waged intermittently between 1562 and 1594, pitted Catholic against Protestant. They gave Christianity a bad name in many quarters because of its apparent inseparability from sectarian killing and widespread brutality. Thus the Huguenot François de la Noue, writing while the wars were still being fought, saw them as a major source of contemporary atheism:

> Si on demande qui a produit telle génération (d'incroyants et de libertins), on ne répondra pas mal que ce sont nos guerres pour la religion qui nous ont fait oublier la religion. Et ne faut point que ni les uns ni les autres disent: c'est le parti contraire qui engendre les athéistes, car de toutes parts ils se rencontrent.[2]

And in 1601 Charron took it upon himself to warn against religious zeal and zealots: 'Quelles exécrables méchancetés n'a produit le zèle de religion?' Later he added: 'cette guerre intestine ... est un venin qui consomme toute l'humanité'.[3]

Nevertheless, although the years of civil and religious war did much to blunt sensibilities, render human life cheap, and generally loosen most forms of moral restraint, they also appeared to issue in a wave of individual piety in many areas of society—the Catholic Reformation. In particular, a new sense of the desirability and possibility of a direct relationship with God was widespread among both clergy and laity. As one scholar writes: 'In a host of souls the Catholic Reformation fostered not merely obedience to the Church but also that spontaneous love of God which joyfully expresses itself in affection and service towards man'.[4] It is striking that this religion of love should follow so quickly the religious wars of a few years earlier.

In what follows I shall first look at some proposed reasons for this dramatic transition from fanaticism and cruelty to faith and love, and then attempt to describe some of the distinctive forms taken by the piety of lay people in particular.

In examining the sudden change of attitude just mentioned, Lucien Febvre emphasizes the brutalizing effect of religious war on the men fighting on both sides, and the general immorality of their conduct. He underlines equally the remarkably large number of individuals, in the final years of the sixteenth century, who were beginning to practise private prayer and meditation. This type of silent, meditative prayer, largely confined in earlier times to the world of the cloister, now extended well beyond the cloister walls. Having accepted the sharpness of this contrast, Febvre goes on to consider evidence of the attitude of the majority of women in the provincial nobility, the *bonne bourgeoisie*, and the artisanal classes. Unlike many of their menfolk they reacted vigorously against cruelty and licentiousness, and in many cases they responded positively to a variety of ideals including the concept of love taught by Neoplatonism. M.-C. Gueudre[5] appears to support Febvre's thesis by pointing out that the better-educated 'femmes du monde', partly through the intellectual salons which a number of them had established, encouraged high-minded and reflective attitudes, refined manners, and generally contributed to the growth of *civilité*.[6] This idealism, refinement and thoughtfulness helped to provide a soil in which religious devotion could grow and flourish. This is Febvre's view and it accounts, incidentally, for the fact that women at large, and laywomen in particular, played such a prominent part in the Catholic Reformation. It has been widely accepted although it depends, of course, on a stereotype of women (at least of women during the transition from the sixteenth to the seventeenth centuries) as being in general more sensitive, more gentle, and more high-minded than men.[7]

There is a sense in which the growth of printing and the spread of literacy contributed significantly to the development of spirituality. Printing, for example, gradually led to what has been called the 'privatization' of the Bible.[8] For an elite at least, the Bible was no longer simply a book to be listened to as it was read aloud in church, but a book which individuals could own, read and re-read, and meditate upon. Increased literacy and the availability of biblical and other devotional texts led to silent reading which was more naturally accompanied by reflection and self-scrutiny. This was an experience which in earlier times had been available only to the clergy, whether regular or secular. Individual piety developed and grew stronger, among clergy and laity alike, as increasing emphasis was laid on *examen de conscience*, confession, and the prayerful study of certain devotional works. Furthermore, this happened against a background of growing moral austerity, and with the help of a widespread campaign against many fashionable social evils from duelling to swearing. In addition, among those who adopted high standards of personal piety, a significant number appear to have been convinced that Christianity, with its emphasis on love of God and love of one's neighbour, could transform civil society and lead it in a direction which many people desired, shocked and disillusioned as they were by the moral and material dislocation of wars ostensibly fought in the name of religion.

René Bady's explanation of the sudden transition from sectarian fighting to Christian love is somewhat different. It has to do with the ability of profound, religious conviction to comfort and console those living through times of particular fear and danger. This can be seen as a fairly complex instance of a familiar psychological phenomenon: physical fear or moral desperation can give rise to what is often an unexpected or uncharacteristic invocation of divine help and wisdom.

There is much to be said for the view that a sense of fear was one of the most common constituents of the average mind of the early modern period. Many features of the age justified such apprehension, from the dangers of childbirth to the prevalence of homicide. Travel could be extremely dangerous, marauding gangs often terrorized rural areas, starvation and plague were a frequent menace. To these were added the horrors of war—killing, wounding, rape and pillage. Delumeau properly writes of 'le climat de 'mal aise' dans lequel l'Occident a vécu de la Peste Noire aux guerres de Religion'.[9] It is not surprising, then, that late sixteenth and early seventeenth-century moralists wrote a good deal on the subject of fear. As an example, Bady turns to the thought of Loys Le Caron (Charondas) whose *De la Tranquillité de l'esprit* appeared in 1588. It is significant that the full title of this work includes the phrase: *Traité grandement nécessaire pour le temps présent*. Similarly, the *Excellents Discours ...* of Jean de Lespine, published in 1587, includes in its full title the phrase: *contenant infinies doctrines et fermes consolations à toutes sortes de personnes affligées en ces derniers temps*. These writers, like others of the period, distinguish between what threatens the body and what menaces the soul, and exhort their readers to see in the teaching of Christ that perfect love which casts out fear.[10] In this sense Christian piety was interpreted as the one true source of consolation in a world of danger and death created by human sinfulness.

For many thoughtful observers the spectacle of violence, death, and general moral breakdown encouraged a return to the view that human nature can only be redeemed by God's grace. Du Vair, for example, in *De la sainte philosophie* (*c*.1580), affirms that 'si autre chose ne nous peut faire haïr à nous-mêmes et détester notre vie pécheresse, considérons autour de nous cette hideuse et effroyable image de la mort, à laquelle notre péché nous a livré'.[11] He adds later that only through a return to Christian values will human life resume its proper nature: 'Notre lumière, notre guide, notre appui, c'est la révélation que Dieu nous a donnée de sa volonté ... '[12] Finally, Du Vair appears to confirm the general line adopted by Bády that fear and desperation can sometimes trigger a return to religious values. He writes: 'Rebelles et malins serviteurs que nous sommes, nous ne révérons notre maître que quand il a le bâton levé sur nous; nous ne lui crions Merci que quand il nous tient le couteau sur la gorge'.[13]

To sum up, then, the rapid reappearance of piety after the Wars of Religion has been mainly explained in one of two ways. In largely secular terms it can be seen as the outcome of female sensitivity and high-mindedness. In a more religious context, it has been explained as the result of a new sense of human sin and of the need to return to dependence on God's grace. It seems likely that these two factors are not totally separate, that they carried different weight with different individuals or groups, and that they were assisted by other more indirect influences such as the popularization of works of devotion through the spread of printing.

Lay piety in particular has to be seen first of all within the wider context of the Catholic Reformation. Although the influence of the Council of Trent was relatively slow in reaching France because of strong Gallican influences within the Church, various French clerics, including Cardinal de Bérulle and Adrien Bourdoise, were soon to act upon their conviction that proper spiritual training of the clergy, and of the parish clergy in particular, was a prerequisite of effective christianization of the laity. Bérulle's Oratorian priests (founded in 1611) played a particularly prominent part in providing support and training for parish priests and encouraging an 'inner sanctity' among priests and parishioners alike. At the same time, some outstanding lay figures had already exerted influence in the opposite direction, acting as spiritual counsellors not only to fellow-laypeople, but even to members of both the regular and secular clergy. From the 1590s, for example, Madame Acarie, a housewife and mother of six, began to counsel various ecclesiastics including Bérulle, and eventually she trained young girls to become Carmelite, and later Ursuline, nuns. Her influence among the devout of Paris and further afield was immense. Again, for thirteen years, Jean de Bernières de Louvigny, *trésorier de France* in Caen, was sole spiritual director of Mère Mechtilde de Bar who founded the Bénédictines du Saint-Sacrement. His friend Gaston de Renty also displayed particular gifts as a spiritual director and was referred to as 'le premier homme de son siècle en matière de spiritualité'.[14]

Inevitably, the campaign to christianize clergy and laity alike was accompanied by efforts to eradicate the general grossness of behaviour and language specially characteristic of the late sixteenth and early seventeenth centuries. The most concerted attack against prostitution, duelling, blasphemy, pornography, and street violence was made by members (both lay and clerical) of the Compagnie du Saint-Sacrement, first conceived by the Duc de Ventadour in 1627. Groups varying from twenty to fifty members met weekly throughout France, headed by a lay *supérieur* and a clerical *directeur*. Prayer and Christian teaching, as well as plans for moral reform and charitable work, occupied an important part of these meetings. Later, with the death of Gaston de Renty in 1649 and the withdrawal of Oratorian support, the Compagnie became increasingly oppressive and meddlesome. In its prime, however, it was what has been called 'le centre d'attraction et d'action des laïcs les plus pénétrés par l'esprit chrétien.'[15]

The year 1608–1609 saw the appearance of three devotional works which made an immediate impact on many laypeople. The Jesuit Pierre Coton published his *Intérieure occupation d'une âme dévote* and the Capuchin Benoît de Canfield his *Règle de perfection* (which had been circulating in manuscript form since 1592 or 1593). But undoubtedly the most influential person to define and encourage lay piety was François de Sales, bishop of Geneva from 1602 to 1622. Whereas the influence of Coton and Canfield, though considerable, had waned before the end of the seventeenth century, François de Sales's popular devotional work, his *Introduction à la vie dévote*, is still highly regarded today.

At this time the term *dévot* was applied to a political grouping which was anti-Protestant in home affairs and opposed Richelieu's anti-Hapsburg foreign policy which involved several alliances with Protestant countries. More commonly, the term was used of individuals whose religious ideals corresponded closely to those set out by François de Sales.[16] In this latter sense the word could carry a pejorative meaning, but could equally be a term of high praise. For some a *dévot* was a killjoy, a bigot, and almost certainly a hypocrite. For others the word implied single-minded love of God and a determination to bring one's will into close conformity with divine purpose. It had to do with living what Anglicanism terms a 'godly, righteous and sober' life. Inevitably, the concept of *dévotion* began to deteriorate as it spread further. It gained the apparent approval of the court of Louis XIII and, as it grew more fashionable, it proved for some a useful means of social or political advancement. Claims of hypocrisy became increasingly justified,[17] though the most fair-minded described a religious hypocrite not as a *dévot* but a *faux dévot.*

François de Sales was one of those who gave *dévotion* a good name. He defined its essence clearly in a letter which he wrote to Madame Brûlart in October 1604:

> La vertu de dévotion n'est autre chose qu'une générale inclination et promptitude de l'esprit à faire ce qu'il connaît être agréable à Dieu; c'est cette dilatation de cœur de laquelle David disait: 'J'ai couru dans la voie de vos commandements quand vous avez étendu mon cœur'. Ceux qui sont simplement gens de bien cheminent en la voie de Dieu; mais les dévots courent, et quand ils sont bien dévots, ils volent.[18]

The original aspect of the *Introduction* lies above all in the fact that it was addressed, not to monks and nuns but to a spiritual elite among the laity committed to living a Christian life while remaining in the world. This went against the well-established tradition that high spiritual attainment was only possible in a life of monastic withdrawal. Indeed, there were those who argued strongly that to continue living in the secular world would be to render salvation a near impossibility. However, François writes firmly in his preface:

> Mon intention est d'instruire ceux qui vivent ès villes, ès ménages, à la cour, et qui par leur condition sont obligés de faire une vie commune, quant à l'extérieur; lesquels bien souvent sous le prétexte d'une prétendue impossibilité, ne veulent seulement pas penser à l'entreprise de la vie dévote, leur étant avis que ... nul homme ne doit prétendre à la palme de la piété chrétienne, tandis qu'il vit emmi la presse des affaires temporelles. Et je leur montre que comme les mères-perles vivent emmi la mer sans prendre aucune goutte d'eau marine ... ainsi peut une âme rigoureuse et constante vivre au monde sans recevoir aucune humeur mondaine, trouver des sources d'une douce piété au milieu des ondes amères de ce siècle ...[19]

This is why François insists that it is 'une erreur, ains une hérésie, de vouloir bannir la vie dévote de la compagnie des soldats, de la boutique des artisans, de la Cour des Princes, du ménage des gens mariés'.[20] So piety or *dévotion* does not necessarily demand monastic isolation. Part III of the *Introduction* is particularly concerned with the practice of devotion in society and deals with such topics as society and solitude, friendship, wealth and poverty, dress, flirtation, advice to married couples, etc. It is made clear that love of God, contemplative prayer, devotional reading, *examen de conscience*, chastity, humility, simplicity, patience, temperance and love of one's neighbour are all virtues that can be exercised under secular conditions and must be the permanent concerns of all Christians.

The ideals of Christian belief and behaviour set out by François de Sales and others do not, of course, constitute actual evidence of pious practice. Evidence can be found, however, in many sources ranging from contemporary biography or correspondence to the growth of devout *cénacles* and of Christian charity among the sick and the poor. The outward forms of Christian worship were increasingly reinforced by 'interior religion' which sought 'personal sanctification and flight from the corruption of the world'.[21]

What was known as 'oraison mentale' was one of the most distinguishing features of these 'chrétiens intérieurs'. It was essentially silent devotion which involved not only requests or thanksgiving, but lengthy meditation on Christian truths by an individual who had emptied his or her mind of all worldly preoccupations and become wholly responsive to the promptings of the Holy Spirit. Etienne Bernard, an important legal figure in the provinces, is known to have spent two hours daily in such prayer. Other high officials, including Michel de Marillac who was *garde des sceaux* between 1626 and 1630, were known as 'men of prayer'.[22] Similarly, a number of the great ladies of Paris, including some like Louise de Bourbon who were much involved in court life, spent anything up to three or four hours a day in prayer.[23] Increasingly, too, devotional exercises were practised by a whole family assembled together morning and evening as recommended by various catechisms of the time. Inevitably, the demands of devotion and spirituality required an unwavering personal commitment beyond the capacity of many. Some reacted by indulging in excessively ostentatious outward observance. Others simply experienced inadequacy and guilt.[24] It was in part for such individuals that manuals of model prayers for private use were published. They ranged from Jean de Ferrières's *Trésor des prières, oraisons et instructions pour invoquer Dieu en tout temps* (1585) to Antoine Godeau's *Instructions et Prières chrétiennes pour toutes sortes de personnes* (1646). Ferrières included prayers to be said by a young woman contemplating marriage, by a child about to begin its lessons, or by anyone in time of plague. Godeau's *Instructions* contained prayers appropriate for a minister of the crown, a financial official, a husband on the death of his wife, etc. This makes clear the extent to which such collections of prayers were specifically directed towards laypeople.

Many members of the laity who practised contemplative prayer also nourished and fortified their faith by reading the Bible, more particularly the Gospels and the Psalms. Those among them who were legal or financial officials had no difficulty in reading the Vulgate. For those who depended on the vernacular the so-called Louvain Bible, first published in 1550, was available and enjoyed 'a sort of tacit approval' by the Church authorities.[25] There also existed pious compilations containing a large number of biblical quotations. These included *Le Palais de l'amour divin* (1602 and 1614) by Laurent de Paris, and Benoît de Canfield's *Le Chevalier chrétien* (1608). Antoine Godeau, writing of Denis de Gordes who was a *conseiller* at the Châtelet, recalls: 'Encore que la lecture de l'Écriture sainte à table ne soit pas ordonnée aux laïques, il la faisait faire néanmoins le soir et le matin ...'[26]

At the same time, Catholic attitudes to laymen reading the Bible were somewhat ambivalent. François de Sales does not appear to have encouraged it, and his disciple and biographer, Jean-Pierre Camus, bishop of Belley, expressed the view in his *Acheminement à la dévotion civile* (1624) that the proper interpretation of Holy Writ could only be entrusted to the clergy. Some laymen, however, including Marillac, published translations of the Psalms. A few even wrote commentaries on the Scriptures.

Some pious women, both lay and religious, regularly adopted so-called *horloges spirituelles*. Their aim was to live in continuous consciousness of God's presence always remembering, in the words of the Capuchin Cyprien de Gamache 'qu'il est devant vous, à vos côtés, en vous-même, qu'il vous voit et vous considerè'.[27] The *horloges spirituelles* indicated short prayers to accompany regular actions of the day—getting up, washing, dressing, etc., and they also proposed topics for contemplation at other times—God's act of creation, Christ's Incarnation, the Passion, etc., thus uniting the individual with the deity at regular intervals. Furthermore, all the activities of the day were consecrated to God, recalling George Herbert's resolution: 'And what I do in anything, / To do it as for thee'.[28]

It is also in the early seventeenth century that the laity achieved a new awareness of a major duty to the poor and the sick. Although lay piety put so much emphasis on the inner life of the individual, it was conscious too of the need to combine loving God with loving one's neighbour. Social action, based on traditional Christian teaching concerning 'l'éminente dignité du pauvre' and the conception of the poor man as *alter Christus*, was a preoccupation of many pious laypeople. Indeed, 'in the seventeenth-century mind, charitable works were not the responsibility of the priest, still less of the religious.

They fell to the layman and laywoman as their appointed lot, the means of their salvation'.[29] François de Sales had made this clear in the *Introduction*:

> Aimez les pauvres et la pauvreté ... Rendez-vous donc servante des pauvres;
> allez les servir dans leur lit quand ils sont malades, je dis de vos propres mains;
> soyez leur cuisinière, et à vos propres dépens; soyez leur lingère et blanchisseuse.[30]

By around 1660 the state had begun to step in to deal with the poor who were increasingly regarded as anti-social malcontents rather than images of Christ. But in the first half of the century pious men and women—and particularly women—did much to fulfil one or more of the traditional 'corporal works of mercy' (i.e. feeding the hungry, giving water to the thirsty, offering hospitality to strangers, visiting prisoners, caring for the sick, clothing the naked, burying the dead). Some laypeople contributed through their membership of groups such as confraternities, or the parish *charités* established by Vincent de Paul; others made private and individual contributions. In both cases there were those whose effort was mainly financial, whereas others dressed wounds in hospitals or cooked food and took it to the houses of the poor. As early as the 1590s Madame Acarie was tending the war-wounded in the Saint-Gervais hospital, as well as working frequently, and for long hours, among the sick poor of the Hôtel-Dieu in Paris. In general, *dévot* charity put considerable emphasis on the salvation of souls, as well as on the care of bodies, so that both God and neighbour might be served.

As the years passed, an increasing number of strong and devout country girls accustomed to hard work volunteered to carry out tasks among the poor which many gently nurtured ladies could not bear to perform—and would not have been expected to perform in their own households. This fact reminds us that secular piety was not confined to the nobility and bourgeoisie.

It is from such lay charitable efforts that Vincent de Paul's specifically trained Dames de la Charité and Filles de la Charité developed from the 1630s onwards. Around 1660 the *Dames* were about 150 in number, while the *Filles* were 800 strong, spread throughout France but under firm central direction. Although secular in the strictest sense, the *Filles* obeyed a Rule and took simple vows. In this way they represent the beginning of a very significant revolution which was taking place within the Catholic Church. The later relaxation of enclosure among certain orders of nuns who combined contemplative religion with direct service to the community outside their convent walls, is the outcome of that remarkable lay piety which generally transformed religious life in the early years of the seventeenth century.

Notes:

1   This is the term used by Lucien Febvre in 'Aspects méconnus d'un renouveau religieux en France entre 1590 et 1620', *AESC*, 13, 1958, pp. 639–50.
2   François de la Noue, *Discours politiques et militaires*, 1587. Quoted in R. Bady, *L'Homme et son 'Institution' de Montaigne à Bérulle, 1580–1625* , Paris, 1964, p. 15.
3   Pierre Charron, *De la sagesse*, 1601. Livre II, ch. 5 and Livre III, ch. 4.
4   A.G. Dickens, *The Counter Reformation*, London, 1968, p. 200.
5   M.-C. Gueudre, 'La femme et la vie spirituelle', *XVIIe Siècle*, 62–3, 1964, 47–77 (p. 47).
6   For a short list of sixteenth-century works on *civilité* published in France or translated into French between 1547 and 1613, see Ruth Murphy, *Saint François de Sales et la civilité chrétienne*, Paris, 1964, p. 219.
7   Febvre, pp. 644–5: 'La femme, pendant que le mari, au loin, menait dans les camps et les villes conquises, sans retenue, la vie libre du soudard et du chef, la femme restée au foyer entretenait un idéal vivace. Et sur nos listes d'adeptes de la Réforme il y a beaucoup de femmes ...'
8   Gabriel Josipovici, *The Book of God: a Response to the Bible*, New Haven and London, 1988, p. 32.
9   J. Delumeau, *La Peur en Occident (XIVe –XVIIIe siècles). Une Cité assiégée*, Paris, 1978, p. 19.
10   See 1 John IV. 18.
11   Guillaume Du Vair, *De la sainte philosophie*, edited by G. Michaut, Paris, 1945, p. 27.
12   Du Vair, p. 49.
13   Du Vair, p. 31.
14   C. Berthelot du Chesnay, 'La spiritualité des laïcs', *XVIIe Siècle*, 62–3, 1964, pp. 30–46 (p. 40).
15   Berthelot du Chesnay, p. 38.
16   Some *dévots*, of course, belonged to both groups, and both groups provided members of the Compagnie du Saint-Sacrement.
17   See, for example, various references in the chapter entitled 'De la mode' in La Bruyère's *Caractères*.
18   François de Sales, *Œuvres*, 26 vol, Annecy, 1892–1932, XII, pp. 346–7. The quotation is from Psalm CXIX. 32.
19   François de Sales, *Introduction à la vie dévote*, edited by C. Forot, Paris, 1934, pp. 3–4.
20   François de Sales, *Introduction*, I, iii, p. 16.
21   P. Janelle, *The Catholic Reformation*, Milwaukee, 1949, p. 186.
22   See Berthelot du Chesnay, pp. 41–4.
23   See Gueudre, pp. 55–6.
24   This is a phenomenon well described and analysed by Robin Briggs in '*Idées* and *mentalités*: the case of the Catholic Reform movement in France', *History of European Ideas*, 7, 1968, 9–19 (pp.14–15).
25   R.A. Sayce on French translations of the Bible in *The Cambridge History of the Bible*, edited by S.L. Greenslade, 3 vols, Cambridge, 1963, III, p. 114.
26   Berthelot du Chesnay, p. 36.
27   Gueudre, p. 51.
28   From 'The Elixir' in Herbert's collection of poems, *The Temple* (1633).
29   E. Rapley, *The 'Dévotes': Women and Church in Seventeenth-Century France*, Montreal and Kingston, 1990, p. 76.
30   François de Sales, *Introduction*, III, XV, pp. 161–2.

CHAPTER THREE

Guez de Balzac: The Enduring Influence of Rome

MARGARET McGOWAN

Balzac's visit to Rome in 1620, which lasted eighteen months, had an abiding influence upon him, guiding his moral and aesthetic judgements and offering examples (to which he frequently returned) of ethical and political behaviour which, he argued, could find their counterparts in contemporary France. In a letter to his cousin, Monsieur de Brye, (10 May 1635), he confessed:

> Il y a longtemps que j'ay donné mon cœur à l'Italie ... Si j'eusse gouverné ma vie à ma volonté je serois Citoyen Romain dez l'an 1620, et je joüirois presentement du bien que vous me faites voir en peinture.[1]

The emotion and the nostalgia recorded here are not isolated sentiments in Balzac's work; he undoubtedly longed for direct sights of the monuments of the imperial city and for contact with those minds and the texts which had formed his own style and thinking. In a late, undated letter, sent to Monsieur de Morin, thanking him for a gift of grapes, Balzac reveals how meditation upon ancient Rome was the most effective, and his most frequent, source of consolation:

> Il vaut mieux, à mon ordinaire, avoir recours à ma vieille Rome, qui ne me manque jamais au besoin.[2]

Indeed, as he had written to Boisrobert in 1623,[3] it was only his shadow that had returned to France, his real being resided in Rome which was a constant point of reference. For instance, when he sought to praise Jean de Silhon's Latin prose, he declared it worthy of the heroic times of Roman eloquence.[4]

Nonetheless, Balzac's projections of Rome in the letters he sent back to France differed greatly from the views expressed by contemporary French travellers; and it is instructive to recall their impressions[5] which highlight the difference. All those who made the journey to Rome agreed on the benefits of travel which the Sieur de Villamont summarized in his introductory remarks to his *Voyages*:

> ceux qui avoyent beaucoup voyagé ... estoient beaucoup plus propres au maniement des affaires que ceux qui s'estoient contentez de vivre en leurs maisons et fueilleter leurs livres.[6]

Straightaway it is the practical effects for the conduct of business and public matters which are stressed. Yet, Villamont also emphasized the need for accuracy in observation, for setting down very precisely the actual size of buildings and monuments. So, for example, he gave the dimensions of the amphitheatre he encountered on 15 January 1590 on the way out of Rome.[7] This mathematical approach to recording was adopted by many: Jean Rigaud,[8] for instance, or Peiresc whose letters testify to an addiction for systematic counting, careful drawing, and accurate records.[9] Figures seemed somehow to compensate for the inability to describe adequately the powerful impressions which were received in Rome; while arguing the necessity of leaving a record, Jean Rigaud often refused to describe,[10] or concentrated on the wild and desert-like character of some of the hills of Rome. Similarly, Florisel de Claveson, who went to Rome in 1608 and found difficulty in conceptualizing and articulating the detail of ruins and the richness of the many buildings, wrote:

> Il est comme impossible de particulariser les ruines des anciens bastiments, lesquels manquent encor quelle estoit la grandeur de l'Empire Romain; plus difficile encor de descrire la quantité des Palais magnifiques ...[11]

Counting, measuring, naming and listing were characteristic responses in guidebooks and in the accounts of travels to Rome. More rare, in the seventeenth century, were the penetrating comments of Pierre Bergeron who saw the civilizing effects of the city, the capacity to 'adoucir et polir tant de nations Barbares';[12] or the highly personalized response of Jean-Jacques Bouchard who was overcome with emotion at the sight of Rome—face to face with

> Cette grande et belle Rome, je me sentis saisir premierement d'une certaine horreur religieuse et devote, pensant à toutes les grandes et belles choses qui se sont faites autrefois là dedans.[13]

It is against this varied context of reaction that Balzac's own experience must be judged. He did not, of course, ignore the weight of history that Bouchard evoked, but he did abandon the scholarly authentication of presence, and this was a conscious withdrawal that was to inform both his style and judgement.

Guez de Balzac went to Rome in the autumn of 1620 as the agent of Monsieur de la Valette and in the company of Sébastien Bouthillier, abbé de la Cochère, who journeyed there at the behest of the queen mother and of Richelieu, still Bishop of Luçon, and in search of his cardinal's hat. Naturally, Balzac did not go unprepared, for Nicolas de Bourbon (1574–1644), whom he had met about 1615, had inculcated in him a knowledge of and an admiration for Rome's greatness. Through this future Oratorian, Balzac sharpened his judgement of writers, learnt to distinguish styles, and to separate the good from its mere outward and deceptive appearance; and, through him, he fired his imagination and creativity. This inspiration is readily acknowledged in the *Œuvres*:

> Ce fut luy [Bourbon] qui me refit et me reforma l'esprit. Il m'annonça le premier la grandeur et la majesté de Rome, que je ne connoissois point, et m'en remplit l'imagination. J'appris de luy, à juger du merite des Autheurs; à distinguer les Stiles et les Characteres; à faire difference entre le bien et l'apparence du bien.[14]

This generous statement gives some indication of the depth and range of Balzac's concerns, and these are also apparent from the eighteen letters which survive and which he sent home from Rome.

It has to be remembered that letters sent under such circumstances were rarely intended for the private consumption of the addressee. They were, at this time, often carefully wrought pieces designed to impress through their style and content. Thus they must be interpreted with some caution. When Balzac writes to Monsieur de la Valette (28 April, 1620) that he is off to 'resver à mon ayse dans les ruines de la vieille Rome',[15] he appears to take for granted his recipient's knowledge of the nature and status of those ruins. To Nicolas de Bourbon, he asserts:

> il est certain que je ne monte jamais au mont Palatin, ni au Capitole que je ne change d'esprit et qu'il ne m'y vienne d'autres pensées que les miennes ordinaires. Cet air m'inspire quelque chose de grand et de genereux que je n'avois point auparavant. Si je resve deux heures au bord du Tybre, je suis aussi sçavant que si j'avois estudié huit jours.[16]

Here he is setting forth a process of transformation and of recollection, modes of assimilation and a vision of the dignity (physical and mental) of ancient Rome—a vision that Freud has explained so cogently.[17] It is noticeable that Balzac's emphasis is on the effect on his mind and imagination of simply being in Rome amidst the recollected greatness through books and through the signs in the ruins, recalled but not spelt out, assimilated but left unmeasured and even unnamed. Only general evocations of the places he visited are given—the Tiber, the Palatine hill, the Capitol. Such generality is in marked contrast to the scrupulous descriptions of earlier travellers and of some contemporary writers. Balzac's letter attempts to give no record but rather to suggest his own personal sense of uplift and the promise of the great work that is to flow from the experience. There is something in the air of Rome that prepares for and reminds one of achievement;[18] and, in a letter to Richelieu, Balzac promises never to forget what Rome stands for and how he personally is committed to respond: 'je n'oublieray pas le lieu où je suis, afin de ne concevoir rien qui ne soit digne de la vieille Rome'.[19]

It is not, however, the visible remains of Rome that retain his attention, nor the artefacts that could be found there in such quantity, as he wrote to Bouthillier who was temporarily in Naples at the end of December 1622, and after Balzac himself had returned to France. While requesting him not to forget to remit the details of his travels and of what he saw, Balzac adds:

> ce n'est pas toutefois que j'aye beaucoup de curiosité pour ces choses-là, ni que j'admire du marbre qui ne parle point; et des peintures qui ne sont pas si belles que la verité.[20]

Here, very deliberately, Balzac adopts an antagonistic stance, asserting his own difference against the enthusiasm which travellers to Rome had poured on the pictures and statues which crowded the palaces there and which French princes had sought to emulate.[21] To ensure that there is no doubt about his views, Balzac goes on to spell out the intensity of his antagonism, adopting a rather superior attitude:

> il faut laisser cela au peuple, dont les mesmes objects bornent l'imagination et la veüe, et qui de tous les temps ne regarde que le present, ny de toutes les choses que l'apparence. Mais pour moy je suis d'une autre opinion. Il n'y a point au monde de Palais si beaux, ni si eslevez, qui ne soient au dessous de mes pensées.

Here, Balzac advances ideas that are quite novel, for his attack on the visible remains of antiquity and on the adulation accorded to them is not the well-rehearsed attack which Protestants had mounted against images, but a much more thoughtful opposition which saw these objects as blocks to creativity, as hindrances to the development of his own originality.

Out of this difference, Balzac sought to create values and a style which matched the ambitions which he began to reveal as he wrote in more nuanced ways about his response to Rome. He does dream among the ruins and he walks in the steps of those who triumphed over kings in search, not of medals for which most men crave, but of something of the mind of Sylla or the glory of Pompey. The presence of history is undeniable but it is significant only in so far as it can affect Balzac himself. To Monsieur d'Amberville who plans to visit Rome, he writes:

> Je vous diray le reste sur le bord du Tybre, et dans les ruines precieuses, où je vais resver une fois le jour, et marcher sur le pas de ceux qui ont mené un peu de la bonne fortune de Sylla; et de la grandeur de Pompée, au lieu des médailles qu'on y cherche, j'aurois meilleure raison de vous convier d'y venir.[22]

And yet, Balzac is all too conscious of the fragility of such things and even of language itself as a persuasive instrument when faced with the brutality of war.[23] This vein of realism does not, however, deter him. On his return to France he will publish the letters from Rome in which he implicitly sets out a programme which privileged (as he was later to declare) 'la force, la vigueur et la lumière de Rome', as represented by the thoughts and style of Livy, Cicero and Salluste.[24] He reassured Richelieu (letter of 16 September, 1622) that his pursuit of an eloquence endowed with the power of those who had argued on behalf of the Republic or of the oppressed, and worthy of the distinction that Richelieu embodied, was undiminished. He saw this task as eventuating in a persuasive force that would worthily and justifiably dominate souls—an eloquence, as he put it, 'qui commande partout où elle est, et qui particulièrement est si propre au gouvernement des ames, que c'est la seule puissance à qui elles veulent se sousbmettre'. Such was his aim—to influence the mind through the penetration of his style which he had only begun to refine.

In Rome, his indifferent health threatened his resolve to write things worthy of the place, and led Balzac to make somewhat contradictory statements about his experience of the city. Sometimes, while acknowledging the impact of beautiful objects, Balzac undermined their power by contrasting expressions of yearning for his family and friends whom he had left behind.[25] The vision of opulence nonetheless lingered on and, in the *Entretiens*, he evoked modern Rome splendidly rebuilt, shining in its marble and gold, and with its many churches and palaces, gloriously resurrected from the dead:

> Mais luy souffrirez-vous de parler, comme il [Maynard] [26] fait de
> Rome, qui est encore aujourd'huy si pompeuse et si superbe, qui est
> toute de marbre et toute d'or, soit en ses Palais, soit en ses Eglises. Il
> me semble qu'il ne faudroit point parler de cercueil, après une si
> glorieuse Resurrection.[27]

Then, back in Rome, his ill health so absorbed him that he cared for
himself as though he were made of glass and he warns his patron that
he may fail in his aims to produce great works destined to improve the
public. What plans can a man have, he writes in despair, when he
hovers perpetually 'entre le sentiment du mal et l'appréhension de la
mort'?[28] He is aware too of his own shifting attitudes that change from
day to day and of the ambiguous nature of the city itself. To his
friend, Monsieur d'Amberville, he wrote on Christmas day 1621,
'Vous devez sçavoir qu'il n'y a lieu au monde, où la vertu soit plus
proche du vice, ni où le bien soit plus meslé avec le mal'. To his
patron—now Cardinal de la Valette preparing to go to the conclave in
Rome, 1623—he maintained the same see-saw movement of thought.
In February 1621, Balzac had advocated a visit to Rome as the most
appropriate form of enlightenment for his gifted supporter: 'si vostre
grand esprit cherche de grandes choses pour s'occuper, il les trouvera
infailliblement à Rome'.[29] Two years later, such confidence has been
modified. On the one hand, he admits the importance of history, the
power of stones which call forth Caesar and Pompey and their gods,
of ruins whose age and impressiveness still command admiration; but
is this enough to keep a fine mind busy and alert, he asks, and to meet
the moral and political demands that daily assail it? This time, the
doubts thrown upon the value of the physical sights of Rome and the
memories they recall are no longer attributed to Balzac himself but are
opened out in this way:

> A Rome, vous marcherez sur des pierres qui ont esté les Dieux de
> César et de Pompée: vous considererez les ruines de ces grands
> ouvrages dont la vieillesse est encore belle, et vous vous promenerez
> tous les jours parmi les histoires . . . Mais ce sont des amusemens
> d'un esprit qui se contente de peu . . . Je ne doute point que . . .
> vous ne vous lassiez à la fin du repos et de la tranquillité de Rome,
> qui sont deux choses beaucoup plus propres à la nuict et aux
> cimetières, qu'à la Cour et à la lumière du monde.[30]

It is interesting to see how the standard references to history, to ruins
and to heroes such as Caesar and Pompey, are set aside as occupations
suitable for leisure perhaps but not designed to fill the mind of an
active churchman/politician.

This impression of acknowledged greatness with limited effect, despite its careful articulation (with Balzac building on the expected response to Rome before undermining that process completely with powerful images of light and dark, death and the living), is not maintained consistently. On the contrary. When, in 1631, Balzac writes to Madame de Villesavin on the return of her son from Italy, he is at pains to paint the visit there as a source of stimulation both with respect to the acquisition of knowledge and for the encounters with rare minds which he has made: 'Il a puizé [en Italie], je m'asseure, tres-abondamment, à la source de la prudence humaine, et s'est rempli l'esprit de hautes et rares connoissances'.[31] The tone is insistent and unquestioning. What then of the letter of 1623 to Cardinal de la Valette? The advice may have been couched simply to impress by its unusual character; it may have been a simple piece of flattery for an ambitious patron; or it may be a record of what Balzac himself experienced.

Undoubtedly his own response to Rome was complex, and that response is made the more difficult to assess in that it is recorded in forms whose conventions are not easy to read, and whose success depended on lightness of touch, wit, hiding the work involved and an ability to combine tones and styles which are not often linked—the letter form, and pieces written for discussion in highly specific social situations.

Letters were a way of living in society and influencing its discussions even when ill health or travelling kept Balzac far from the Court and from Paris. Letters passed from hand to hand, introduced topics of conversation, influenced the outcome and helped shape styles of discussion, values and even social behaviour.[32] It was in a letter to his old tutor that Balzac articulated most fully his profound attachment to Rome and the influence that radiated out from that source of civility and fountainhead of all civilizing activities: morals, arts and sciences.

> Il n'y a qu'à Rome où la vie soit agreable, où le corps trouve ses plaisirs et l'esprit les siens, et où l'on est à la source des belles choses. Rome est cause que vous n'estes plus ni Barbares ni Payens, Car elle vous a appris la civilité et la Religion; Elle vous a donné les loix qui vous empeschent de faillir, et les exemples à qui vous devez les bonnes actions que vous faites. C'est d'icy que vous sont venuës les inventions et les arts, et que vous avez receû la science de la paix et de la guerre.[33]

There is no reason to doubt that Balzac believed these positive sentiments expressed in such rousing and well-balanced cadences; he was to repeat them fifteen years later in another letter, this time to his cousin Monsieur de Brye who had just returned from Rome. You have, Balzac argued, 'acquis de nouvelles grâces au pays de Cicéron, et l'air de Rome a purgé vostre esprit de toutes les pensées du vulgaire'.[34] This purifying, civilizing effect was expressed in a matching style which was inspired, in content and form, from Cicero and Livy but which was not inhibited by that borrowing from the creation of an individual style. Balzac was categorical about his own originality in this context. 'Je prens l'art des anciens', he admitted to Boisrobert, 'mais je ne despends pas servilement de leur esprit'; on the contrary, I am myself: 'j'invente plus heureusement que je n'imite'.[35] In trying to define what this manner he had invented was, Balzac had recourse to the non-pedantic approach spelt out by Quintilian in his *Institutio*, and one can find practical exemplification in the *Epîtres latines* where, to Silhon, he praises the manner and life style of Maffei as having achieved the very difficult combination of seriousness and politeness (humanitas); 'Huius, Silhoni, ut vita, ita oratio consecuta mihi videtur difficilimam illam societatem gravitatis cum humanitate'.[36] This amalgam of seriousness and levity which aimed to please and to instruct, and ultimately to seduce, Balzac sought to produce in his own writing where one finds an ease of delivery, the cultivation of a certain negligence which was fitting in the social contexts for which he composed his letters and *entretiens*. The style seems eminently accessible, the thoughts—however grave— composed with a deft touch so that their impact steals upon the reader without effort. As Bernard Beugnot has argued,[37] Balzac thought he had found this art of negligence in Rome—an art which he called *Urbanitas*, defining this term as 'la science de la Conversation et le don de plaire dans les bonnes compagnies'.[38] His own mode of pleasing was threaded through with allusions and examples from Rome. The enduring nature of the influence which permeates the letters is perhaps best captured by the works he wrote at the instigation of Madame de Rambouillet and in his views on Corneille's *Cinna*. Before examining these works, however, it is appropriate to consider how Balzac envisaged the transfer of style and ideas from Rome to France. Many contemporaries had understood this process as the literal transfer of artefacts or as the translating of key texts into French.[39] Balzac had a more subtle approach.

In reflecting on the impossibility of having trivial ideas in a place like Rome, Balzac immediately juxtaposes 'tous les triomphes des anciens, et toute la gloire de nostre siècle'.[40] This conformity and continual *va-et-vient* between Rome and Paris is the foundation on which Balzac built his analysis of the contemporary scene and advocated appropriate moral and political values. To Chapelain, he advised the reading of an epigram from Martial 'qui parle de Paris en parlant de Rome';[41] and to Nicolas Bourbon he had asked the question: these virtues that you so admire at the French Court, are they not Roman and Madame la marquise [de Rambouillet] 'n'est-elle pas Romaine'?[42] It was natural that she, the 'Romaine', and the one who had taught the social values of politeness and civil exchange[43] (which paralleled Balzac's own views both of what was to be commended and what was his own practice), should be the recipient of his specifically Roman works. He had announced in early February 1639 that he was working on a *Discours sur les Romains* at the behest of Madame de Rambouillet; and, just over one year later, he wrote to the Comte de la Vauguion, sending him a copy of what had become *De la Conversation des Romains*, telling him: 'vous y trouverez ce que vous cherchez en la mienne'.[44] In other words, there was no discrepancy in manner and content between his own performance and that which he praised in the Romans.

In the *Œuvres*, *Le Romain* heads the series of *Dissertations politiques*, and in the opening speech, addressed directly to Madame de Rambouillet, we find again assertions about Rome as the source of divine inspiration and influence for future generations: 'Rome estoit la boutique où les dons du Ciel estoient mis en œuvre, et où s'achevoient les biens naturels' (I, p. 420). The city was that great artisan of works of power—'des actions militaires, aussi bien que des affaires civiles'. These statements are exemplified through Caesar whose innate authority (military genius and patriotism) is displayed. Balzac here demonstrates his ability to call up these spectres from the past and to give them dramatic presence and persuasive weight. There is, for example, the ghastly appearance of Appius Claudius in the Senate where, in his decrepitude, he upbraided his colleagues for daring to consider giving way to Pyrrhus. In this dissertation, Balzac argues, more forcibly than in his correspondence, how the richness of Rome and its values have been preserved even in its ruins:

> lorsque Rome n'est plus que le sepulchre de Rome, la Nature voulant à mon advis, conserver ses droits, et faire voir que les cendres, les matières souverainement excellentes, sont encore riches et precieuses (II, p. 424).

It was not at all unusual to link Rome with the idea of sepulchre (see Montaigne's *tombeau*), yet by giving emphasis to the personalized nature of the opinion Balzac reinforces the paradoxical effect of the juxtaposition.

The second dissertation begins with a verse quotation from an author who urged his reader to admire the achievements of the heroic souls of Rome, while recognizing that they belong to an age that has gone and will not return. Balzac agrees that it is no longer appropriate to think of the rugged virtue of a Cato reborn, 'nous ne sommes pas de la force de ces gens là' (II, p. 428). But we can still touch them beneath the ruins and through their books: 'Il les faut aller chercher sous des ruïnes et dans les tombeaux. Il faut adorer leurs reliques ...'(II, p. 429).

Madame de Rambouillet had, however, demanded more than this; she had ordered Balzac to discover and reveal Romans in their privacy, 'quand ils se cachoient, et que je vous ouvrisse la porte de leur cabinet' (II, p. 429). It is this more intimate, social dimension which allows Balzac to effect the transformation of the heroic into that civilized being that could inhabit the salon without losing a sense of the values which had originally characterized the hero. From the primitive austerity of his distant ancestors, Augustus had developed that social virtue, *la Politesse*, which extended across all social spheres, and had banished Greek Atticism to install the most polished value of all—*l'Urbanité* (II, p. 434). Balzac expands at some length on the nature of this social virtue,[45] placing it at the centre of good behaviour, 'un certain air du grand Monde, et une couleur, et peinture de la Cour—un génie secret, que l'on perd en le cherchant'. While no other country in Europe (except Rome) had contrived to acquire this polish, it is clear from the way Balzac defines it that he believes that Paris has mastered its secrets. The skilled response which he reports Fabritius to have made to Pyrrhus gains its full effect from the panache with which Balzac tells the tale, and the praise and admiration are equally shared between the original speaker and the modern re-teller of the story.[46] In expressing his regret at the number of works that have not survived, Balzac reveals how his reading of those that do is coloured by his search for their conformity with contemporary French ideas and manners 'à qui a tant de rapport et de conformité avec les Temps que nous avons veûs' (II, p. 441). It is perhaps not surprising that when he looks at the history of Rome to find adequate parallels, it is to Augustus that he turns: 'le siecle d'Auguste a jugé des choses bien subtilement'; and, as he develops his opinions on this reign, it is evident that he is offering judgements that also belong to other contemporary evaluations: 'Tout s'est poli et s'est raffiné sous ce Regne: Tout estoit sçavant et ingenieux en cette Cour' (II, p. 442).

It is but a small step to *Cinna* (1643) which Balzac regarded as a wonderful elaboration of the very qualities he had explored in his

Conversation des Romains. In his letter of congratulation to Corneille, he begins by affirming, 'Vous nous faites voir Rome tout ce qu'elle put être à Paris, et ne l'avez point brisée en la remüant'.[47] The transfer of Rome to Paris is now complete. Through his genius, Corneille has been able not only to dramatize with truth and fidelity the Rome of Livy and Augustus, he has also penetrated the depths of Rome's ruins to find the ancient pride and the nobility and magnanimity which belonged (according to Balzac) to the time of Augustus along with the refined exchanges of the inhabitants of the Court and their urbane behaviour which finally triumphed over conspiracy and civil uproar. Balzac's final peroration sees Rome rebuilt in France, a 'glorious Resurrection' in Paris itself:

> Aux endroits où Rome est de brique, vous la rebastissez de marbre. Quand vous trouvez du vuide, vous le remplissez d'un chef d'œuvre; et je prens garde que ce que vous prestez à l'Histoire, est toujours meilleur que ce que vous empruntez d'elle.

Here, Balzac has borrowed the words of Augustus himself (if we are to believe Alberti) to underline the significance of the transplantation.

Lest it should be thought that the marriage of Rome and Paris, of Roman and French, was restricted to Balzac's own perceptions, consider the letter he wrote in 1636 to the king's councillor, Monsieur l'Huillier. There, he describes the celebrated gallery of Monsieur de Thou which was full of 'des plus nobles despoüilles de l'Antiquité, et des richesses Grecques et Romaines', and was also inhabited by 'toutes les Graces du siecle present, et par toutes les vertus sociables et civiles'.[48]

For Balzac himself, Rome had entered so deep into his being that when, for example, he wished to congratulate a patron (like the Comte de Schomberg) on his recall to power by Louis XIII, he likened him to Phidias 'ou quelque autre de ces anciens ouvriers, à qui on eust lié les mains, et osté d'autour de luy le marbre, l'or et l'yvoire'.[49] It was natural, too, that when joking about his illness, he should appropriate Rome to his person and transform his bed into an amphitheatre and his body into the spectacle to be viewed.[50] For the wider public, it was Balzac's transposition of *urbanitas* from Rome to Paris which had the most enduring impact. Mademoiselle de Scudéry, for instance, opens her remarks on *De la politesse* with the strong statement: 'je suis persuadé que la vraye politesse est cette urbanité des anciens Romains dont Balzac a si noblement parlé',[51] a sentiment taken up by Andry de Boisregard, some years later, and consistently argued for in his *Réflexions*.[52]

Letters were an integral part of social discourse; in a sense, they constitute modes of dialogue and social exchange that we can still hear as living conversation. As François Ogier remarked, 'La pluspart des lettres sont des conversations par escrit'.[53] Rome was a dynamic force in this exchange and the qualities of its citizens became players on the seventeenth-century scene. Between Balzac and Chapelain, for example, there was—as Youssef has observed [54]—a tacit understanding with regard to Roman virtues: a mere reference to a name or a quality evoked a density of resonance which did not need spelling out. The extent of Balzac's assimilation of Rome was appreciated by his contemporaries who also recognized the individuality of his response. The most pertinent assessment was probably that of François Ogier who recalled the great number of volumes written on the city, the vast legions of people who had visited Rome and yet none of these had given the quality of presence of its remains nor responded with the singularity of Balzac. Ogier's apology, with its rising tones and rhetorical questions which echo Balzac's own words, provides a fitting end to this study of Balzac's response to Rome and of the civilizing effects he drew from the experience.

> Il s'est fait des livres entiers des antiquitez de Rome; et ceux qui les ont esté voir sur les lieux, ont veû par terre les idoles des Payens, encor toutes noires de la fumée de leurs sacrifices: mais de tous ceux-là, qui a esté si hardy de s'imaginer qu'il marchoit sur des pierres qui ont esté les Dieux de César et de Pompée? Qui a considéré si hautement que Monsieur de Balzac les ruines de ces grands ouvrages, dont la vieillesse est encore belle?[55]

Notes:

1   I have used the 1665 *Œuvres complètes* (O.C.), 2 vols checked against the H. Bibas & K.T. Butler edition of the early letters, Droz, 1933, 2 vols (referred to henceforth as B & B), and supplemented by Bernard Beugnot's edition of the *Entretiens*, Paris, 1972, 2 vols.

2   O.C., I, p. 661.

3   O.C., I, p. 77, le 1er août, 1623.

4   *Epîtres latines*, eds Jean Jehasse et Bernard You, Saint-Etienne, 1982, p. 102; in similar vein, the defence of Plutarch in Letter XIII, pp. 109–113.

5   These impressions will be discussed in more detail in the context of my forthcoming work on the vision of Rome in the late French Renaissance.

6   Sieur de Villamont, *Voyages*, Paris, 1600, sig. â iij.

7   Ibid., f. 111 verso.

8   Jean Antoine Rigaud, *Bref recueil des choses rares*, Aix, 1601, or an anonymous account recently edited by Michel Bideaux, *Voyage d'Italie* [1606], Slatkine, 1981, p. 232.

9   Peiresc, *Lettres*, ed. Tamizey de Larroque, Paris, 1894, 7 vols, where there are many examples showing Peiresc's concern to have the details of medals carefully drawn while he maintained nonetheless that 'une veüe oculaire a un merveilleux advantage sur toute sorte de relations ou portraictures', I, 1628, p. 547.

10 Rigaud, op. cit., f. 59 verso, and f. 51.

11 The journey is described in a manuscript, BN Clairambault, 1006, and the passage cited can be found on f. 49.

12 Pierre Bergeron, *Le voyage d'Italie*, BN Ms.fr. 5560, f. 4. Bergeron spent two years in Italy between 1601 and 1603.

13 *Œuvres de Jean-Jacques Bouchard*, [in Rome in 1632], ed. E. Kanceff, Turin, 1977, 2 vols, II, p. 474.

14 O.C., II, p. 368.

15 B & B, II, pp. 121–123.

16 B & B, II, pp. 106–108, le 25 mars, 1621.

17 Sigmund Freud, *Civilisation & its Discontents*, ed. London, 1982, pp. 6ff.

18 He had written to de la Valette, for instance, le 1er août, 1621 (B & B, I, pp. 22–24) :'Vous n'avez garde de trouver mauvais l'air qu'a respiré toute l'ancienne République, ni le Soleil qui a aidé à faire tant de conquérans et esclairé de si beaux triomphes'.

19 Le 12 avril, 1622 (B & B, I, pp. 31–33).

20 Le 28 décembre, 1622 (B & B, I, pp. 122–127).

21 Cardinal de Richelieu, we learn from Peiresc's correspondence and from work on *L'Album Canini*, acquired a huge collection of statues in the 1630s, see Marie Montembault and John Schloder, *L'Album Canini du Louvre et la collection d'antiques de Richelieu*, Paris, 1988.

22 Le 25 décembre, 1621 (B & B, I, pp. 193–196).

23 On his arrival in Rome, Balzac lamented the superior force of arms over the pen; in an early letter to de la Valette, he wrote: 'Deux livres de poudre bien mesnagée feront plus d'effet que toute la rhétorique de Cicéron, assistée de tous les arguments d'Aristote ... Il faut quelque chose de plus fort que le discours, pour agir sur des ames si dures que sont les nostres', le 11 septembre, 1620 (B & B, II, pp. 48–52).

24 See letter to the Jesuit father Dalmé, le 3 avril, 1643, O.C. I, p. 527.

25 Letter to M. de la Magdeleine, le 1er août, 1622 (B & B, I, pp. 215–217).

26 Balzac much admired François Maynard's *Ode à Alcippe* where Rome is depicted as a coffin; see pp. 161–163 of Ferdinand Gohin's edition of the *Poésies*, Paris, 1927.

27 *Entretiens*, ed. cit., II, p. 401.

28 Letter to de la Valette, le 27 février, 1621 (B & B, I, pp. 218–220). See also the letter to Richelieu, le 10 avril, 1622 (B & B, I, pp. 31–33): 'je me conserve aussi soigneusement que si j'estois de crystal'; and again, back to de la Valette, le 27 février, 1621 (B & B, I pp. 218–220), 'Comment pensez-vous que je conçoive des choses éternelles, moi qui dois finir à tous les momens?'

29 B & B, I, pp. 218–220.

30 Letter, le 3 juin, 1623 (B & B, I, pp. 18–21).

31 O.C., I, p. 270.

32 For a discussion of the social implications of letter writing, see Frank Sutcliffe, *Guez de Balzac et son temps*, Paris, 1953, p. 107.

33 Letter to Nicolas Bourbon, le 25 mars, 1621 (B & B, II, pp. 106–108).

34 Cited by G. Guillaumie, *J.L. Guez de Balzac et la prose française*, Paris, 1927, p. 67.

35 Letter, le 11 février, 1624 (B & B, I, pp. 143–148).

36 *Epîtres latines*, ed. cit., p. 103. The combination of gravitas and frivolity in the way of seeking to seduce his reader has received attention from Marc Fumaroli, *L'Age de l'éloquence*, Droz, 1980, pp. 543ff.

37 *Entretiens*, ed. cit., p. xxx. See also the discussion of the early letters by Jean Jehasse, *Guez de Balzac et le génie romain*, Saint-Etienne, s. d., p. 202.

38 O.C., II, p. 434; Zobeidah Youssef has studied the formative nature of Balzac's early contacts in Rome in *Polémique et Littérature chez Guez de Balzac*, Paris, 1972, especially pp. 109–110, 113–114, and p. 309. *Urbanitas* had, by 1640, become an accepted way of describing the polite style which conferred wit, grace and elegance on what was said: 'qui plaist et chatouïlle agreablement l'imagination'; see my article, 'Autour d'Amphitryon', in *L'Image du Souverain dans les lettres françaises*, Actes du Colloque de Strasbourg no. 24, Paris, 1985, pp. 281–291.

39 See Roger Zuber, *Les 'Belles Infidèles' et la formation du goût classique*, Paris, 1968, especially pp. 400–411.

40 Letter to Richelieu, le 10 avril, 1620 (B & B, I, pp. 31–33).

41 Letter, le 20 décembre, 1636, O.C. I, p. 737.

42   Letter, le 25 mars, 1621 (B & B, II, pp. 106–108).

43   Segrais maintained that Madame de Rambouillet 'a enseigné la politesse à tous ceux de son temps qui l'ont fréquentée'; Mademoiselle de Scudéry made a similar point, describing her as 'la femme du monde qui savait le mieux la politesse', *Nouvelles conversations*, Paris, 1684, I, p.121. These observations are discussed by Magendie in *La Politesse mondaine*, Paris, s. d., 2 vols, I, p. 125.

44   O.C., I, p. 610, letter, le 28 mars, 1640.

45   Balzac goes on to comment thus on *Urbanité*: 'C'est ainsi, Madame, qu'ils l'appelèrent après l'avoir pratiquée plusieurs années, sans luy avoir donné de nom asseuré', O.C., II, p. 434.

46   Balzac remained firmly convinced of Fabritius' quality; in the *Entretien* XXI, Réponse à trois questions à Monsieur Conrart : 'C'est pourtant un homme et qui a esté, et que j'ay pris plaisir de faire revivre. Ce n'est pas un fantosme formé par l'imagination et par le désir. Rome ne fut jamais animée d'une âme plus belle, plus grande, ni plus forte que celle-là', ed. cit., II, p. 322.

47   Letter, A M. de Corneille, le 17 janvier, 1643, O.C., I, p. 675.

48   Letter, le 23 novembre, 1636, O.C., I, p. 402.

49   Letter to Schomberg, le 20 août, 1624 (B & B, II, pp. 22–23).

50   'Mon lit a esté mon Amphitheatre, et le premier spectacle n'a point eu de spectateurs', this ironic comment appears in *Mémoires pour l'Histoire de Balzac à Monsieur* [Costar], *Entretiens*, ed. cit., II, p. 69.

51   *Conversations nouvelles*, Paris, 1685; cited in Beugnot, *Guez de Balzac. Bibliographie générale*, Montréal, 1967, p. 120.

52   Ibid, p. 121.

53   Ogier, *Apologie pour Monsieur de Balzac* [1627], in O.C., I, p. 181.

54   Youssef, op. cit., p. 381.

55   O.C., I, p. 136.

CHAPTER FOUR

L'Image de la Ligue
dans les *Mémoires* du Cardinal de Retz [1]

SIMONE BERTIERE

Dans la nuit du 26 au 27 août 1648, après l'arrestation du conseiller Broussel, Paris se couvre de barricades. Difficile de ne pas penser à l'épisode qui marqua un tournant dans l'affrontement entre Henri III et le duc de Guise: les barricades du mois de mai 1588. Dans les deux cas, l'émeute eut pour résultat une rupture entre le roi et sa capitale. Henri III s'enfuit dans l'après-midi du 13 mai. Il temporisa jusqu'en décembre, puis fit mettre à mort les chefs adverses, suscitant contre lui dans Paris une flambée de haine. Il voulait n'y revenir qu'en vainqueur et s'apprêtait à l'attaque lorsque, le 1er août 1589, il fut assassiné par le moine Jacques Clément. Son successeur Henri IV assiégera la ville à plusieurs reprises, en vain. Il n'y sera accueilli, le 22 mars 1594, qu'après avoir pacifié le reste du royaume et abjuré la religion réformée. Les choses furent plus rapides et moins dramatiques lors de la Fronde. Mazarin attendit d'avoir calmé les esprits par quelques concessions, puis il fit partir la reine et le petit Louis XIV pendant la nuit du 6 janvier 1649. Le siège de la capitale ne dura que deux mois, jusqu'à la paix de Rueil, signée le 11 mars. Pendant ce siège les meneurs, et notamment le coadjuteur de Paris, futur cardinal de Retz, bien conscients des analogies entre les deux situations, s'efforcèrent de tirer de l'exemple antérieur des enseignements pour leur propre action.

On ne s'étonnera donc pas de rencontrer dans les *Mémoires* un nombre assez important d'allusions à la Ligue, surtout situées au début du récit, dans l'évocation de la Fronde parlementaire. On en retrouve aussi vers la fin, lors de la guerre condéenne, quand Gaston d'Orléans et Retz s'interrogent sur les moyens de se tirer d'affaire.[2] Attention! Beaucoup d'entre elles sont placées dans des dialogues ou des discours et il convient de leur apporter deux correctifs. On doit d'abord se demander qui parle et à qui: le coadjuteur modulait en effet ses arguments selon qu'il s'adressait au duc de Bouillon, très lié à l'Espagne, au prince de Condé, premier prince du sang et descendant d'un des chefs réformés, ou à Gaston d'Orléans en quête d'une voie moyenne entre les partis. On ne doit pas oublier d'autre part que ces discours et ces dialogues, bien qu'ils paraissent relever du passé, sont récrits de mémoire vingt-cinq ans après l'événement, et qu'ils sont donc influencés par l'expérience ultérieure du mémorialiste et probablement gauchis pour donner de son action d'autrefois une image compatible avec les idées et les valeurs qui prédominent vers 1675.

En dépit de ces réserves, il n'est pas impossible de dégager des diverses allusions à la Ligue éparses dans les *Mémoires* une image de ce qu'elle représentait pour Retz. Image ambiguë, jugement contrasté. À propos de la Ligue se posent deux questions. Avait-elle raison ou tort dans son principe? Pourquoi a-t-elle échoué? Le mémorialiste est aussi explicite sur la seconde qu'il est discret sur la première. Je tenterai de montrer ici qu'il porte à ses dirigeants une admiration certaine, qu'il gomme les ombres qui pourraient nuire à leur image et qu'il tente de les décharger, au moins en partie, de la responsabilité de l'échec.

Indulgence aisément explicable. Entre la Ligue et la Fronde, il n'y a que deux générations d'écart. Les Frondeurs sont les petits-fils de ceux qui ont vécu les guerres du siècle précédent et ils doivent souvent à la transmission familiale, orale, l'idée qu'ils s'en font. Or, si la Ligue a perdu la partie, on ne peut en dire autant de la noblesse ligueuse. Ceux de ses membres qui ont survécu ont brillamment tiré leur épingle du jeu. Henri IV a acheté—très cher—leur ralliement, à coup de faveurs, de places, de pensions, de prébendes. Le troisième des frères de Guise, le duc de Mayenne, chef du parti après la mort des deux autres, s'est vu offrir un pont d'or bien qu'il eût été battu à plates coutures sur le terrain. Seul le duc d'Aumale, réfugié à Bruxelles et refusant tout accommodement, a payé le prix de son intransigeance: il est 'tombé à rien dès qu'il n'[a] eu que la protection d'Espagne'.[3] Les autres, tous les autres, les Guise, les Brissac, et aussi des membres de la noblesse de robe comme Villeroy ou Jeannin, avaient retrouvé dans le royaume la place qui était la leur et transmis à leurs descendants charges et fonctions. Ces derniers ont vu Louis XIII reprendre à son compte un des objectifs de la Ligue, l'élimination de l'état dans l'Etat que constituaient les protestants autour de leurs places de sûreté. Pourquoi rougiraient-ils de l'action de leurs aînés qui, dans leur volonté de rétablir l'unité religieuse du royaume, n'ont eu que le tort d'être en avance sur l'histoire? Ils sont nombreux à trouver que Richelieu s'est arrêté trop tôt en chemin. Aussi les voit-on se regrouper dans le parti dévot et les diverses associations qui travaillent à la reconquête pacifique des âmes. Et ils réprouvent l'alliance avec les pays protestants sur lesquels s'appuie le ministre dans la lutte qu'il mène contre la très catholique maison de Habsbourg.

Or les appartenances familiales du jeune Paul de Gondi le situent dans cette mouvance. Non que ses ancêtres paternels aient été ligueurs. Albert de Gondi et son frère Pierre, évêque de Paris, savaient leur fortune trop fraîche et ils étaient trop sages pour s'engager dans une aventure dont ils mesureraient pleinement les risques. Le premier se tint à l'écart et le second, après avoir tenté de jouer les médiateurs, finit par déserter son siège épiscopal pour se rallier à Henri IV, dont il négocia la réconciliation à Rome.[4] Mais la génération suivante, alliée aux plus grandes familles françaises, résista moins bien à la contagion. L'aîné des fils d'Albert se fit tuer dans les rangs des ligueurs. Le troisième, Philippe-Emmanuel—le père du futur meneur de la Fronde—dut à son jeune âge d'échapper à la tentation d'un engagement irréfléchi, mais, par l'entremise de sa femme, familière de la célèbre Mme Acarie,[5] il rencontra le cardinal de Bérulle, devint un membre actif du parti dévot, patronna les activités de Vincent de Paul et se fit prêtre à l'Oratoire après son veuvage. Quant aux ascendants maternels de Paul de Gondi, les Silly, issus de vieille noblesse, ils avaient leurs terres patrimoniales en Champagne et en Lorraine, provinces guisardes, et, sans avoir milité expressément dans la Ligue, ils avaient des sympathies pour la cause catholique. Et le couple Du Fargis, oncle et tante du jeune Paul, travaillait pour le parti dévot. Le jeune coadjuteur est dans la droite ligne des options familiales lorsqu'il s'illustre dans des 'disputes' théologiques avec l'espoir de convertir des réformés ou lorsqu'il se fait le porte-parole des déçus du traité de Westphalie, qui réclament à grands cris la 'paix générale', c'est-à-dire la paix avec l'Espagne.

Aucune prévention n'anime donc Retz contre l'esprit de la Ligue, ni contre les grands seigneurs qui en prirent la tête. Au contraire. Dans sa mythologie personnelle François et Henri de Guise font figure de héros. Des héros comparables à Condé, lequel est comparé à César et à Alexandre! Monsieur le Prince, est-il dit dans la fameuse galerie de portraits, a manqué d' 'esprit de suite':

> Ce défaut a fait ... qu'ayant toutes les qualités de François de Guise, il n'a pas servi l'Etat, en de certaines occasions, aussi bien qu'il le devait; et qu'ayant toutes celles de Henri du même nom, il n'a pas poussé la faction où il le pouvait. Il n'a pu remplir son mérite, c'est un défaut ; mais il est rare, mais il est beau.[6]

Guerriers prestigieux, chefs d'un parti puissant, les Guise sont de grands hommes habités de 'vastes desseins',[7] promis à une 'belle et vaste carrière'8 et capables d'entreprendre de ces actions hardies, aux frontières de l'impossible, à quoi l'on reconnaît les êtres d'exception:

> Toutes les grandes choses qui ne sont pas exécutées paraissent toujours impraticables à ceux qui ne sont pas capables des grandes choses; et je suis assuré que tel ne s'est point étonné des barricades de M. de Guise, qui s'en fût moqué comme d'une chimère, si l'on les lui eût proposées un quart d'heure auparavant qu'elles fussent élevées.9

La mise à mort tragique du duc et du cardinal à Blois les a transformés en martyrs et a permis à leur frère et successeur à la tête du parti de recueillir le prestige qui s'attachait à eux:

> M. du Maine, l'un des plus grands hommes de son siècle, fut obligé de faire un traité qui a fait dire à toute la postérité qu'il n'avait su faire ni la paix, ni la guerre. Voilà le sort de M. du Maine, chef d'un parti formé pour la défense de la religion, cimenté par le sang de MM. de Guise, tenus universellement pour les Maccabées de leurs temps : d'un parti qui s'était déjà répandu dans toutes les provinces, et qui avait déjà embrassé tout le royaume.10

La propagande ligueuse ne disait pas autre chose. Certes le coadjuteur parle ici au duc de Bouillon. Mais le mémorialiste n'a pas cru bon d'atténuer cette louange. Les propos tenus à Condé rendent un autre son de cloche: la cause de la Fronde y est donnée pour très 'au-dessus de celle de la Ligue'11 et le duc de Mayenne comme très inférieur à l'orgueilleux et irascible prince, qu'il faut convaincre de soutenir le Parlement rebelle. Mais la comparaison, même défavorable au dernier des Guise, confirme que la Ligue et ses chefs sont aux yeux de Retz, pour juger du présent, une référence incontournable.

Mayenne, un grand homme? L'éloge est paradoxal, s'agissant d'un personnage sur la médiocrité duquel les contemporains s'accordaient déjà: pour l'intelligence, la hardiesse, le 'charisme', comme nous dirions aujourd'hui, il était loin de valoir le Balafré. Quant à ce dernier, il faut pour le transformer en héros, ignorer délibérément quelques aspects de son action.

Ainsi voit-on le mémorialiste, dans le rapide survol des siècles antérieurs, passer négligemment sur les affrontements civils très graves qui affectèrent le règne des derniers Valois:

> Sous Charles IX et sous Henri III, la cour fut si fatiguée des troubles, que l'on y prit pour révolte tout ce qui n'était pas soumission.12

C'est tout. C'est peu, s'agissant d'une crise au cours de laquelle faillit sombrer la monarchie! Silence complet, ou presque,[13] sur les menées du duc de Guise pour évincer Henri III, l'enfermer dans un couvent et prendre sa place sur le trône. C'est qu'un tel objectif discréditerait irrémédiablement le héros. Au XVIIe siècle, dès le temps de la Fronde, toute mise en question de la légitimité monarchique est impensable. L'assassinat d'Henri III, mais surtout celui d'Henri IV, fondateur de la dynastie régnante et bientôt surnommé Henri le Grand, ont fait du régicide un crime inexpiable. La présence sur le trône d'un enfant permet de détourner vers les 'mauvais conseillers' la colère des opposants, qui épargne ainsi l'institution royale. La personne du roi est plus que jamais sacrée.

On conçoit donc que Retz, héritier de la tradition ligueuse dans son admiration pour les Guise, se refuse à la suivre quand elle prétend canoniser Jacques Clément. Écoutons le mémorialiste. Le 27 août 1648, le coadjuteur parcourt les rues de Paris hérissées de barricades:

> J'y vis encore quelque chose de plus curieux: M. de Brissac me fit remarquer un hausse-cou, de vermeil doré, sur lequel la figure du jacobin qui tua Henri III était gravée, avec cette inscription: «Saint Jacques Clément». Je fis une réprimande à l'officier qui le portait, et je fis rompre le hausse-cou à coups de marteau, publiquement, sur l'enclume d'un maréchal. Tout le monde cria: «Vive le Roi!», mais l'écho répondait: «Point de Mazarin !».[14]

Retz sait-il qu'au plus fort des violences ligueuses, ce sont les images d'Henri III que les Parisiens, fanatisés par les sermons de leurs prêtres, martelaient pour les réduire en miettes? Sans doute. Mais on touche ici à un autre aspect de la Ligue—et, à un moindre degré, de la Fronde—que le mémorialiste réprouve a posteriori: l'engagement direct des gens d'Eglise dans la rébellion armée. Il se montre d'autant plus critique, après coup, que lui-même s'est vu reprocher d'avoir prononcé, le 25 janvier 1649, un sermon séditieux, puis solennellement béni le régiment dit des Corinthiens avant de l'envoyer se faire battre par les troupes royales. Episodes peu glorieux, qu'il s'est efforcé d'oublier. La *Satire Ménippée* a attaché un ridicule indélébile aux déambulations de moines affublés de casques, traînant mousquets et rapières. La 'procession de la Ligue' sert à deux reprises, dans les *Mémoires*, de contre-exemple grotesque.[15] Reconnaissons au moins au cardinal disgracié le mérite d'avoir choisi, pour défendre son archevêché, la voie légale d'un recours à Rome, au lieu d'écouter ceux qui le poussaient à se réfugier dans une place forte de l'Est et à se lancer comme Condé dans la lutte armée, aux côtés des Espagnols.

Cette remarque nous conduit à la question de l'appui espagnol: autre point délicat sur lequel les mentalités ont évolué. Au XVIᵉ siècle la France servait de champ clos aux rivalités internationales. Les ligueurs n'avaient pas hésité à s'allier à l'Espagne, contre un parti huguenot soutenu par l'Angleterre et par les princes réformés d'Allemagne. L'or venu du Nouveau Monde permettait aux envoyés madrilènes d'inonder Paris de ce que la *Ménippée* appelle le *Catholicon*: de beaux doublons sonnants et trébuchants qui venaient renforcer le prétendu zèle religieux des catholiques. L'expression, passée dans la langue courante, vient tout naturellement sous la plume de Retz pour désigner l'aide espagnole.¹⁶ Nous connaissons aujourd'hui, par des documents d'archives, le montant considérable des sommes perçues par le duc de Guise comme agent et agitateur au service de Philippe II. Retz, sans doute moins bien informé, savait cependant que la Ligue était inféodée aux Espagnols, tout comme les conspirateurs successifs—Montmorency, Cinq-Mars—qui tentèrent d'éliminer Richelieu. La chose paraissait admissible encore, au moment de la Fronde, bien que la guerre fût alors déclarée entre les deux pays. Mais plus le temps passe et plus il paraît déshonorant d'avoir négocié avec l'ennemi. Hors du royaume, point de salut. Les alliances de jadis prennent rétrospectivement un fâcheux parfum de trahison. Au moment où écrit le mémorialiste, mieux vaut en parler le moins possible.¹⁷

Retz souligne donc, comme il se doit, sa répugnance à faire appel au soutien espagnol. Non sans quelques flottements, lorsqu'il s'abandonne à ses souvenirs. Il est difficile de savoir si le recours à l'Espagne est à ses yeux une faute morale ou seulement une erreur tactique. Il explique, par exemple, qu'il refusa longtemps, en dépit de ses amis, de solliciter du secours à Bruxelles. Il n'y consentit, dit-il, qu'à regret et faute d'une autre solution:

> Quoique je sentisse dans moi-même beaucoup de peine à être le premier qui eût mis dans nos affaires le grain de catholicon d'Espagne, je m'y résolus par la nécessité.¹⁸

Et il y renonça dès que se présenta 'un moyen plus agréable et plus innocent', l'adhésion au parti de la duchesse de Longueville et du prince de Conti. De même il insiste plus loin sur l'importance qu'il y avait à faire prendre au Parlement, et non aux seuls grands seigneurs frondeurs, la responsabilité d'un traité avec l'Espagne—perçu comme moralement répréhensible.

On rapprochera ces réticences d'une condamnation explicite du traité de Joinville, signé par les Guise avec Philippe II à la fin de 1584, et du manifeste commun publié à Péronne le 31 mars 1585:

La Ligue fit une guerre où le chef du parti commença sa déclaration par une jonction ouverte et publique avec Espagne, contre la couronne et la personne d'un des plus braves et des meilleurs rois que la France ait jamais eu; et ce chef de parti, sorti d'une maison étrangère et suspecte, ne laissa pas de maintenir dans ses intérêts [le] Parlement ... .[19]

Mais ce passage se situe dans un discours adressé à Condé, au temps où celui-ci avait choisi de soutenir la cour face à la Fronde parlementaire: le coadjuteur, qui tente de l'y entraîner, serait mal venu à lui chanter les louanges de la Ligue.

Nul blâme, en revanche, ne semble peser sur les engagements politiques du duc de Bouillon:

Je considérais M. de Bouillon, soutenu par l'Espagne, avec laquelle il avait, par la considération de Sedan, les intérêts du monde les plus naturels, comme un nouveau duc du Maine, qui en aurait mille autres, au premier jour, tout à fait séparés de ceux de Paris, et qui pourrait bien avec le temps, assisté de l'intrigue et de l'argent de Castille, chasser le coadjuteur de Paris, comme le vieux M. du Maine en avait chassé à la Ligue le cardinal de Gondi, son grand-oncle.[20]

La décision de pactiser ou non avec l'étranger relèverait, en somme, de considérations purement personnelles. Si Retz hésite à s'y aventurer lui-même, c'est pour des raisons très terre-à-terre: il craint de ne pas faire le poids aux yeux des Espagnols et de leurs alliés français. Et en cas de défaite, une fois privé de l'archevêché, fondement de son pouvoir, il ne lui resterait plus qu'à se réfugier à Bruxelles pour y devenir 'l'aumônier du comte de Fuensaldagne'.[21] Le sens de son intérêt, bien plus que le sentiment national, lui conseillait de rester sur la défensive face aux offres espagnoles.

Il est cependant un domaine dans lequel morale et politique consentent à converger. C'est celui du recours au peuple. A l'idée d'un soulèvement massif qui déclencherait dans Paris des émeutes incontrôlables, Retz et son allié Beaufort reculent:

Pour ce qui est du crédit que M. de Beaufort et moi avons dans les peuples, il est plus propre à faire du mal au Parlement qu'à l'empêcher de nous en faire. Si nous étions de la lie du peuple, nous pourrions peut-être avoir la pensée de faire ce que Bussy Le Clerc fit au temps de la Ligue, c'est-à-dire d'emprisonner, de saccager le Parlement. Nous pourrions avoir en vue de faire ce que firent les Seize quand ils pendirent le président Brisson, si nous voulions être aussi dépendants d'Espagne que les Seize l'étaient. M. de Beaufort est petit-fils d'Henri le Grand, et je suis coadjuteur de Paris. Ce n'est ni notre honneur ni notre compte ...[22]

Réflexe de grand seigneur qui méprise les classes populaires et qui s'en défie. L'éthique aristocratique autorise la guerre civile, pourvu qu'on reste entre gens de qualité. On peut à la rigueur susciter dans la rue une 'émotion' ponctuelle, d'extension limitée. Mais il serait déshonorant pour un Condé, un Beaufort, un Gondi même de se faire le tribun d'un authentique mouvement populaire.

Ce serait également dangereux:

> Nous soulèverions demain le peuple si nous voulions ; le devons-nous vouloir? Et si nous le soulevons, et si nous ôtons l'autorité au Parlement, en quel abîme jetons-nous Paris dans les suites? Tournons le feuillet.[23]

L'histoire de la Ligue vient confirmer ces craintes. Mayenne se servit du peuple pour écraser le Parlement, faute de réussir à le rendre docile et à se faire accorder par lui une espèce de légitimité. Mais il faillit ensuite être débordé:

> M. du Maine, trouvant dans le Parlement cet esprit que vous lui voyez, qui va toujours à unir les contradictoires et à faire la guerre civile selon les conclusions des gens du Roi, se lassa bientôt de ce pédantisme. Il se servit, quoique couvertement, des Seize, qui étaient les quarteniers de la Ville, pour abattre cette compagnie. Il fut obligé, dans la suite, de faire pendre quatre de ces Seize, qui étaient trop attachés à l'Espagne. Ce qu'il fit en cette occasion pour se rendre moins dépendant de cette couronne, fit qu'il en eut plus de besoin pour se soutenir contre le Parlement, dont les restes commençaient à se relever.[24]

Ainsi s'explique, selon Retz, l'échec de la Ligue. Il ne précise pas, mais tout le monde savait au XVIIe siècle, que la Ligue avait eu deux visages et que le mouvement urbain échappait en partie à l'autorité des Guise. Après le drame de Blois notamment, Paris s'était doté d'une organisation autonome de forme plus ou moins démocratique, avec responsables élus, qui régnaient par la terreur. Ce n'est pas seulement parce qu'ils étaient 'trop attachés à l'Espagne', mais parce qu'ils avaient instauré un contre-pouvoir menaçant d'ébranler l'ordre social tout entier, que Mayenne se décida à les abattre. Entre temps, la terrifiante dérive populaire de la Ligue parisienne avait déclenché l'union sacrée chez les grands, qu'ils fussent catholiques ou protestants: elle accéléra les ralliements à Henri IV.

Et le souvenir des embarras inextricables qu'elle valut à ses chefs[25] hantera durablement les Frondeurs. Beaucoup en concluront qu'un bon accommodement avec la cour est préférable à un saut dans l'inconnu.

Les réflexions qui précèdent permettent de mieux comprendre le jugement porté par Retz sur la Ligue et les Ligueurs et d'en lever en partie les ambiguïtés. Le mémorialiste impute les fautes de la Ligue et l'échec qui en découla aux initiatives populaires, qui vinrent fausser le jeu des princes: c'est pour avoir dû mater les violences parisiennes que Mayenne se retrouva face à l'Espagne dans une position d'étroite dépendance, au lieu d'être pour elle un allié parlant d'égal à égal. Un tel raisonnement fait bon marché des liens qui asservissaient depuis longtemps les Lorrains à Philippe II. Mais il permet à Retz de laver François et Henri de Guise des deux reproches qui, au XVIIe siècle, risqueraient de ternir leur image—avoir été à la solde de l'Espagne, et avoir mis en danger l'institution monarchique—et de les dissocier du moine régicide issu du peuple parisien fanatisé. Retz partage les préjugés de ses pairs: la rébellion sied aux grands seigneurs, à condition qu'elle ne sorte pas du cadre traditionnel des guerres nobiliaires. On conçoit aisément qu'il s'efforce de faire entrer dans ce cadre l'histoire dérangeante de la maison de Guise et de la Ligue. Mais c'est un lit de Procuste où elle se trouve si violentée que nous avons parfois peine à la reconnaître ...

Notes:

1   Je me propose de développer ici des thèmes que j'ai déjà effleurés dans l'*Introduction* de mon édition des *Mémoires*, Classiques Garnier jaunes, 2 vol., 1987. C'est à cette édition que je renverrai pour les citations.

2   En voici les références: t. I, pp. 284, 318, 345, 347, 348, 359–360, 372, 391, 404–405, 408–409, 418, 432, 478, 521; t. II, pp. 51, 169, 217, 294, 338, 353, 391–392, 409, 423–424, 447.

3   I, p. 418.

4   Pendant la Fronde, Paul de Gondi prend à l'occasion celui-ci pour modèle et s'inspire de telle ou telle de ses démarches avec un bonheur inégal. Par exemple, le cardinal de Gondi avait consenti, pour acheter de quoi nourrir les Parisiens affamés, à faire fondre les vases sacrés des églises. Mais une initiative analogue de son petit neveu souleva un tollé, dont le mémorialiste préfère ne pas se souvenir. En revanche, lorsque Retz se rend à Compiègne, en septembre 1652, pour paraître jouer un rôle dans les retrouvailles du roi et de sa capitale, il évoque explicitement l'ambassade menée par son grand-oncle auprès d'Henri IV au mois d'août 1590 (II, p. 392).

5   Barbe Avrillot était la femme du maître des comptes Pierre Acarie, l'un des fondateurs de la Ligue parisienne. Tous deux s'étaient dépensés sans compter, pendant le siège de Paris, pour secourir les malades. Leur adhésion au mouvement insurrectionnel relevait d'une foi ardente et désintéressée.

6   I, p. 372. On se souviendra que le terme de *faction* n'est pas nécessairement péjoratif au XVIIe siècle. Cf. aussi I, p. 347, où il est dit que les circonstances offraient à Condé l'occasion de courir 'une carrière plus belle et plus vaste que celle que MM. de Guise avaient courue'.

7   I, p. 284.

8   I, p. 347.

9   II, p. 423–424.

10   I, p. 409.

11   I, p. 345.

12   I, p. 284.

13   Cf. le passage du t. I, p. 345, que nous citons plus loin.

14   I, p. 318.

15 I, p. 348, et II, p. 409.

16 I, p. 348 et 478.

17 En témoignent les remarques manuscrites faites par Caumartin en marge d'une copie des *Mémoires* que le cardinal lui avait soumise, et notamment celle qui porte le n°11 (*Œuvres*, éd. des G.E.F., t. II, p. 236, n. 4). Caumartin conseille à Retz de se démarquer plus fermement des partisans de l'alliance espagnole. Sur ces remarques, cf. Simone Bertière, 'Une lecture critique des *Mémoires* de Retz: les annotations de Caumartin à la copie Caffarelli', dans *Revue d'Histoire littéraire de la France,* 89e année, n°1, janv.–févr.1989, p. 39–48.

18 I, p. 348. Il veut parler ici d'une demande de secours pour le parti frondeur. Rien ne permet d'en conclure qu'il avait touché personnellement de l'argent espagnol. Ses adversaires l'en accusèrent, mais la chose n'est pas prouvée. Après son évasion en tout cas, il traverse l'Espagne sans s'y arrêter. Tandis que le traité des Pyrénées rouvre aux Condéens les portes de la France, il reste banni et clame que c'est son refus de servir l'Espagne qui lui vaut cette épreuve: 'C'est ma fidélité que l'on punit. On ne me tient exilé que parce que je n'ai pas mérité de l'être.' (*Lettre à tous les évêques, prêtres et enfants de l'Église* ... ,du 24 avril 1660, dans *Œuvres*, coll. des Grands Ecrivains de la France, t. VI, p. 408–409).

19 I, p. 345.

20 I, p. 391.

21 I, p. 419.

22 I, p. 404.

23 I, p. 405. Cf., dans ma *Vie du cardinal de Retz,* le développement intitulé: «Devenir populaire» ou Du bon usage de l'émeute, p. 191–195.

24 I, p. 408–409.

25 Cf. II, p. 294.

CHAPTER FIVE

The Political Testaments of Richelieu and La Rochefoucauld

ELIZABETH WOODROUGH

> Qui meurt a ses droits de tout dire
> (Villon)

The closing moments of the lives of Richelieu and La Rochefoucauld might not have been entirely out of place in one or other of Molière's medical comedies. Richelieu's death on 4 December 1642 aged fifty-seven, following years of ill health, was precipitated by the burden of office and the Cinq-Mars conspiracy. Louis XIII publicly accused the terrible doctor Bouvard of having killed his patient.[1] Rumours of the king's private reaction to the event, however, suggest that, much like Argan's second wife, Béline, in the scene of the *fausse mort* engineered by the good Doctor Toinette in *Le Malade imaginaire*, he was in fact delighted to be rid of his chief minister.[2] Anxiously attentive at Richelieu's bedside on the night of 2 December, when he fed the moribund two egg yolks, Louis XIII was heard to release a strange nervous laughter as he left the Palais Cardinal for the Louvre, though on his final visit the next day he seemed more disturbed than the members of his retinue.[3]

The exchange of correspondence between La Rochefoucauld's doctor, the abbé Bourdelot, and Fagon, the first doctor to the king and queen, concerning La Rochefoucauld's death in March 1680, following an acute attack of gout, might in turn almost have been inspired by the farcical diagnosis given to that specimen of porcine good health who is the eponymous hero of Molière's earlier medical comedy-ballet, *Monsieur de Pourceaugnac*. Messieurs Bourdelot and Fagon are no less insistent than the pair of pompous practitioners in Molière's play that their reluctant patient should be 'phlébotomisé libéralement, c'est à dire que les saignées soient fréquentes et plantureuses'.[4] Whilst not subscribing to the comic doctors' theory that such bleedings are best conducted in even numbers, rather than odd, their conclusions as to the correct course of treatment in La Rochefoucauld's case are not so very different.

Bourdelot opens the discussion of the results of the autopsy with a description of the concentrations of blood in the upper part of the body:

> A l'ouverture du thorax, je vis la plèvre au même endroit toute livide, visante à gangrène, mais les poumons qui étaient noirâtres, étaient si gonflées et si gorgés de sang, qu'ils bousèrent hors de la capacité quand l'ouverture en fut faite. Nous y donnâmes quelques coups de bistouri, le sang en ruissela, fondu, brun et rabide, et ensuite le pus. Il ne faut pas chercher ailleurs la cause de sa mort, qu'à la suffocation de cette partie.[5]

Final responsibility for the patient's death is made to rest with the family:

> La mort est survenue faute d'avoir vidé les vaisseaux; les Médecins n'ont point consulté pour le Malade, qu'ils n'aient proposé la saignée; mais les parents assistants, par tendresse ou mal persuadés sur les remèdes, n'y ont point voulu consentir.[6]

Very sick men, as Molière's Béline is so anxious lest her hypochondriac husband forget, need to consult their lawyers about the disposal of their estate, as well as learned doctors about their state of health. Unable to hold a pen, Richelieu dictated the long and detailed *testament civil* he made at Narbonne shortly before he died. An abscess on his right arm troubled him throughout his final years, increasing his dependency on his team of secretaries. 1.5 million *livre*s were left to the crown, though the state in fact took much more. The cardinal left most of the rest of his fabulous wealth, possessions, public and private papers, and debts, to his young grand nephew, the duc de Richelieu, and his niece, the duchesse d'Aiguillon, who also inherited all the attendant problems of administering this complex and much challenged document.[7]

No less than three separate holograph wills in the name of François, duc de La Rochefoucauld, prince de Marcillac, baron de Verteuil, Montignac et Cahuzac, have been discovered in the family archives at the Château de Combreux, all signed with the famous closed S or 8, which La Rochefoucauld also occasionally used in correspondence to underline his *fermesse*.[8] Two are dated the same day, 20 September 1653, following his terrible injury during Condé's last stand in the *Fronde des princes*, when he received the full blast of a musket shot in the face. A third *testament et ordonnance de dernière volonté*, again substantially unaltered, was made five years later. In all three, La Rochefoucauld's wealth and possessions, much depleted by his insurrectionary activities,[9] are bequeathed without an inventory to his wife and family, and though Andrée de Vivonne predeceased her husband by ten years, no later will has been found.

It has been suggested that if only marginal political significance can be attached to Richelieu's last will and testament, it is probably because his political philosophy is to be found in a text first published with considerable success in Amsterdam in 1688 by a French Protestant under the illustrious title, *Le Testament politique ou les maximes d'Etat d'Armand du Plessis, cardinal duc de Richelieu, pair et grand amiral de France, premier ministre du Conseil d'Etat sous le règne de Louis XIII, roi de France et de Navarre, commandeur des ordres de Sa Majesté, évêque de Luçon, confondateur et bienfaiteur de la maison de Sorbonne.*[10] There is some anecdotal evidence to suggest that this adjunct to the cardinal's will, which remains a model for modern French statesmen, was located among the papers bequeathed to the duchesse d'Aiguillon on his death.[11]

The nearest we have to a political treatise in the name of Richelieu, the *Testament politique* formally bequeaths to a master known to dislike long speeches, the sum of his first servant's knowledge, experience and advice on the government of the state, and has been organised with the Cartesian rigour we associate with the cardinal.[12] The text, which has been rather arbitrarily divided into two parts and abounds in maxims that have given Richelieu the reputation of a 'moraliste consommé', appears unfinished at times.[13] It may nevertheless be regarded as the final statement to be issued in his name on one of the central problems of government in seventeenth-century France, namely the exercise of the king's authority through a first minister to the exclusion of other members of the royal family and the great aristocracy. The *Testament* is based on a summary of Louis XIII's reign to 1638,[14] suggesting that it was in fact written some time before Richelieu's final illness.

The dedication to the king explains that the *Testament* was originally intended as a full history of the reign, but was constantly interrupted by illness. The 'brefs mémoires' which are all that remain of this vast project are formally presented as a last will and testament, to be revealed only after death, though there is some suggestion that a wider circle of beneficiaries may also be envisaged:

> Cette pièce verra le jour sous le titre de mon testament politique, parce qu'elle est faite pour servir, après ma mort, à la police et à la conduite de votre royaume, si V.M. l'en juge digne, parce qu'elle contiendra mes derniers désirs à cet esgard, et qu'en vous la laissant, je consigne à V.M. tout ce que je lui puis léguer de meilleur quand il

plaira à Dieu m'appeler de cette vie [...] Si mon ombre qui paroîtra
dans ces mémoires peut, après ma mort, contribuer quelque chose au
règlement de ce grand Estat, au maniement duquel il vous a plu me
donner plus de part que je n'en mérite, je m'estimeray extremement
heureux.

There are three further instances of the word 'testament' in the final
chapters of Part One, justifying a critical section on the state of the
king's household. Before outlining a detailed complaint, the author
explains that he is here writing with 'la sincérité que doit avoir un
homme qui fait son testament',[15] and confesses that '[ce présent
testament révèle] beaucoup d'intentions que le testateur n'avait osé
divulgé pendant sa vie'.[16] A further reference to the status of the
document as an expression of Richelieu's last will and testament is
included in a subsequent defence of the position of chief minister,
where the writer calls upon God as his witness: 'Diverses
expériences m'ont rendu si sçavant en cette matière que je penserois
estre responsable devant Dieu si ce présent testament ne portoit pas
en termes exprez qu'il n'y a rien de plus dangereux en un Estat que
diverses authoritez esgales à l'administration des affaires'.[17]

The Christian dimension of the *Testament* has been shown by
Madeleine Bertaud to be one of the factors distinguishing this book
of advice to the prince from the machiavellian model which it in part
resembles.[18] As he reviews his life in politics in preparation to meet
the Supreme Judge, the cardinal is determined to look fixedly upon
the fact of his own mortality, and to encourage the king to do the
same. Having preached the cause of peace at court and in
Christendom in the name of God, and having written at times as
though it had been achieved during his ministry,[19] Richelieu
promises the king in his final sentence: 'il ne sera jour de ma vie que
je ne tâche de me mettre en l'esprit ce que j'y devrois avoir à l'heure
de ma mort sur le sujet des affaires publiques, dont il lui plaît se
décharger sur moi'.[20]

Although we know how much Louis XIII valued Richelieu's
advice and memoranda during his lifetime,[21] and that he respected
many of the cardinal's wishes after his death, including the choice of
Mazarin as a successor, it is not recorded what use, if any, the king
made of such a document in the five months of life that remained to
him, or whether he actually ever saw it. The debate about the
authenticity of the *Testament*, which was fuelled by Voltaire who
regarded the work as 'un monument d'absurdité, que les ignorants
admirèrent, séduits par un grand nom',[22] is unresolved. This highly
personalised dialogue with the king, where Richelieu refers to
himself either directly in the first person or infers his presence as

one of Louis XIII's Council and his most faithful servant and creature, remains in search of an author or authors. Of the seventeen known manuscript versions, none are signed. The manuscript used for the original edition was apparently written hurriedly in two different hands, without correction.[23] Louis André, who produced the first scholarly edition of the *Testament* in 1947, favoured the theory that Richelieu was indeed the principal author, assisted by père Joseph. The idea that the cardinal's *éminence grise* might have been his main collaborator in this instance is discredited by Françoise Hildesheimer, the most recent editor of the text, who also rejects André's choice of the Sorbonne manuscript of the *Testament* in favour of a more complete manuscript, located in the archives of the French Foreign Office, which comes directly from Richelieu's papers.

Closely related to a number of other documents issued from the cardinal's office which raise similar questions of authorship, some parts of the *Testament* have been identified as modifications of other texts written in what appears to be the cardinal's distinctive hand where the letter 'i' is not dotted.[24] However, the fragility of this method of authentification has been exposed by Christian Jouhaud in his study of the hidden hand or hands of Richelieu's amanuensis: 'Pendant quinze ans une main inconnue a écrit pour Richelieu. Ce n'est ni la sienne ni celle d'un secrétaire. ... Cette main sans nom se dessine donc comme une grande ombre menaçant tout système de preuves graphiques.'[25] Other scholars have argued that parts of the text offer further evidence of the 'private, collaborative enterprise of king and minister, designed to justify, glorify, and encourage royal acts'.[26] Calling for a still broader concept of authorship, Hildesheimer is content to conclude with Roland Mousnier and other historians that the *Testament* may well have been the result of a team effort, which nonetheless 'exprime bien [la pensée de Richelieu] ou du moins celle de son entourage penétré de sa doctrine'.[27]

La Rochefoucauld who was only sixteen when Richelieu's ministry began and whose political influence was restricted by what he refers to as 'une longue suite de disgrâces'[28] is not among the nobles who figure in the *Testament*. The celebrated author of the *Maximes*, this duke and peer whose family claimed recognition as *princes étrangers* and who would in another age have sat in the highest Council of State, remains the *grand seigneur* of French seventeenth-century literature. He is further distinguished by the fact that versions of the *Mémoires,* a genre which was usually published posthumously appeared in his name during his lifetime.[29] However, although his personal papers were burnt before his death, a number of other manuscripts in his hand, including additions to the *Mémoires*, came to light in the nineteenth century. The first edition to include Part I, bounded by the dates of the cardinal's ministry, did not appear until 1817. The opening paragraph explains the writer's recall of events in reverse order, mirroring the eventual order of publication, which at last brings him back to his youthful experiences, as the prince de Marcillac, of Richelieu's rise to power:

> J'ai passé les dernières années du ministère du cardinal Mazarin dans l'oisiveté que laisse d'ordinaire la disgrâce: pendant ce temps j'ai écrit ce que j'ai vu des troubles de la Régence. Bien que ma fortune soit changée, je ne jouis pas d'un moindre loisir: j'ai voulu l'employer à écrire des événements plus éloignés où le hasard m'a souvent donné quelque part.
>
> J'entrai dans le monde quelque temps devant la disgrâce de la Reine mère, Marie de Médicis ...
>
> Le cardinal de Richelieu gouvernait l'Etat, et il devait toute son élévation à la Reine mère.[30]

Long obscured by the importance attached to the *Maximes*, it is only in recent years that the quixotic *Mémoires* have become valued as a challenging analysis of the political situation of the day with paradoxes and ambiguities of their own.[31] Begun as an account of La Rochefoucauld's disastrous escapades in the *Fronde des princes*, and narrated in the third person in Parts III to VI, this catalogue of his misfortunes in love and war is successively dominated by the political personalities of the three cardinals, Richelieu, Mazarin and Retz, and the rebellious Prince de Condé, with the queen and La Rochefoucauld's mistresses, who were all enemies of one cardinal or another, as supporting cast.

It is not altogether surprising that these *Mémoires*, which underline the role of chance and the passions in the affairs of man, have not been more frequently compared to the *Testament politique*, which stands for reason (referred to on 70 occasions),[32] and the supremacy of the national interest over the interests of the individual. However, despite their formal differences, these two texts may both be seen as examples of the memoirs genre which each offer their own testament to the age of Richelieu. Just as the metaphor of a last will and testament is in some ways only an extension of the tendency among seventeenth-century memoirs-writers not to seek to publish their work during their lifetime, so Part I of La Rochefoucauld's *Mémoires,* which escaped publication for so long, may be regarded as one of his *ultimes oeuvres*. Both La Rochefoucauld and Richelieu were members of the *noblesse poitevine*, although Richelieu never enjoyed quite the same social distinction. La Rochefoucauld remained fascinated by the figure of the minister who had replaced his caste in the king's confidence.[33] Having in his youth witnessed at first hand the impact of the policy of *raison d'état* on the great aristocracy, La Rochefoucauld proceeds in his personal account of the ministry to draw a silhouette of the cardinal in red blood around the various court intrigues which he himself observed or in which he played some small part.

Presented as a tale of relationships with people with whom La Rochefoucauld tells us, 'j'ai été lié[s] d'intérêt et d'amitié',[34] his own role in the events of Richelieu's ministry is limited to a few juvenile adventures, undertaken 'à un âge où on aime à faire des choses extraordinaires et éclatantes',[35] but which in fact amount to nothing very much. Chosen to reflect his unfailing loyalty to the queen, who at one stage asks him to prepare her flight to Brussels, the events recounted are complicated by a half-hearted attempt to protect the scheming Mme de Chevreuse, which eventually lands him in the Bastille for a week. Central to the plot of every episode, however, is the tyrannical and vengeful cardinal. Whether recruiting English spies in the case of the duke of Buckingham and the missing royal diamonds, or facing, more bravely than might have been expected, an assassination attempt where La Rochefoucauld is but an innocent bystander, it is Richelieu whom we see manipulating the king, undermining the queen, and punishing the aristocracy from Chalais to Cinq-Mars. If the cardinal shows an exceptional degree of leniency towards La Rochefoucauld, the affair of Mme de Chevreuse and the Book of Hours with the wrong colour-coding, where La Rochefoucauld's celebrated irresolution is amply enough demonstrated to warrant a public warning, serves no less as an illustration of Richelieu's autocratic style of government than the account of the major historical episodes of the ministry which follows.

Although as a young hero La Rochefoucauld shows himself to have been ever at the mercy of events, his critical study of a deeply unpopular cardinal, for which his self-portrait is the pretext, has been constructed with classical rigour. The work of one of the finest portraitists of the age, this analysis of the events of the ministry illustrates the effects of the cardinal's three main policies, and is framed at either end by mirror images of the cardinal's profile.[36] The first glimpse we have of him is as an evil genius, who totally eclipses a king who seeks to be governed rather than to govern:

> Il avait l'esprit vaste et pénétrant, l'humeur âpre et difficile; il était libéral, hardi dans ses projets, timide pour sa personne. Il voulut établir l'autorité du Roi et la sienne propre par la ruine des

huguenots et des grandes maisons du Royaume, pour attaquer ensuite la maison d'Autriche et abaisser une puissance si redoubtable à la France. Tout ce qui n'était pas dévoué à ses volontés était exposé à sa haine, et il ne gardait point de bornes pour élever ses créatures ni pour perdre ses ennemis.[37]

It is this determination to get his own way by whatever means which characterises the cardinal's behaviour in the narrative that follows, as Noémi Hepp observes: 'Excellent dans l'art de s'informer, Richelieu ne l'est pas moins dans l'art d'agir, qui seul rend le premier utile. ... La troisième caractéristique de la politique de Richelieu est l'art de s'imposer aux esprits.'[38] In his final retrospective portrait La Rochefoucauld, having witnessed the terrible civil strife of the Fronde which followed Richelieu's ministry, suddenly reverses his judgement of the cardinal with the benefit of hindsight, recognising him as having been the right man at that time:

> Quelque joie que dussent recevoir ses ennemis de se voir à couvert de tant de persécutions, la suite a fait connaître que cette perte fut tres préjudiciable à l'Etat, et que, puisqu'il en avait osé changer la forme en tant de manières, lui seul la pouvait maintenir utilement, si son administration et sa vie eussent été de plus longue durée. Nul que lui n'avait bien connu jusqu'alors toute la puissance du Royaume, et ne l'avait su remettre entière entre les mains du Souverain. La sévérité de son ministère avait répandu beaucoup de sang, les grands du Royaume avaient été abaissés, les peuples avaient été chargés d'impositions mais la prise de La Rochelle, la ruine du parti huguenot, l'abaissement de la maison d'Autriche, tant de grandeur dans ses desseins, tant d'habileté à les exécuter, doivent étouffer les ressentiments particuliers, et donner à sa mémoire les louanges qu'elle a meritées. [39]

The dual portrait of Richelieu in La Rochefoucauld's *Mémoires* may be viewed with the self-portrait in the *Testament Politique* as a kind of triptych. Such a montage by different hands, where the central panel still requires some finishing touches and may be a complete forgery,[40] clearly lacks the symmetry of Philippe de Champaigne's celebrated triple portrait of the cardinal. Interfacing these three opposing judgements drawn from contemporary sources may nevertheless allow us to focus more clearly on the political legacy of what has been called 'l'énorme abstraction nommée Richelieu, le pouvoir de Richelieu ou le pouvoir-Richelieu'.[41]

Dedicated to the glory of the divine ruler, the *Testament* gives a full-length portrait of the cardinal in his ecclesiastical robes, in the image of the perfect counsellor, at the right hand of Louis the Just, a shining example of the benefits of 'la vertu masle' in political life. Women, who are judged never to have had the vigour to govern well, are all but excluded from the scene.[42] The cardinal himself virtually disappears from view in the introductory chapter, entitled *Succincte narration des grandes actions du roy jusqu'à la paix faite en l'an...*,[43] which is the best known part of the *Testament*. He does not deny responsiblity for the main policies of the reign. In the most celebrated line in the work which is also repeated in the penultimate chapter, Richelieu explains, in terms remarkably similar to those reiterated at the beginning and end of Part I of La Rochefoucauld's *Mémoires* cited above, how his main aims and objectives have been to 'ruiner le parti huguenot, rabaisser l'orgueil des grands, réduire tous ses sujets en leurs devoirs et relever [le nom du roi] dans les nations estrangères au point où il devoit estre'.[44]

Yet it is the king who is presented as the principal agent of the successful implementation of these plans, with God's assistance. He it is who is praised for having defeated the Protestants at La Rochelle and for taking on the Spaniards on all fronts, even when incapacitated by illness. Louis XIII is also credited with having calmed the frequent storms at court, caused by the machinations of other members of the royal family. He is given full responsibility for the exemplary punishment exacted on Montmorency-Bouteville and Dechapelles and numerous other unruly nobles, insufficiently grateful for the honours already bestowed on them. Whilst it is admitted that the king may not be absolutely infallible and that it may have been a hasardous enterprise to engage in so many wars at once, His Majesty is shown often to have succeeded against all the odds; his very appearance on the scene is sufficient to change the course of a battle. Even the costs of continual warfare in terms of men, money and equipment are presented as a tribute to the king's greater glory.

Richelieu is altogether more discreet about his own role in the running of the country. As he explained at the outset, however, that it was his entry into the king's council which was the decisive moment of the reign, marking a transformation of king and country from weakness and failure to almost constant good fortune, it is difficult not to see the cardinal behind every action accredited to his master.[45] Richelieu seems confident, however, that he has already assured his own reputation for integrity and determination, without needing to exceed the bounds of modesty that should restrain the good adviser. At the most delicate moments in the narrative, he merely reminds us that he was present, strengthening the king's resolve. At Montmorency-Bouteville's execution, for instance,

Richelieu confesses to an almost overwhelming feeling of compassion. He explains to the king that, though much moved by the floods of tears shed by the condemned man's wife, he was only able to overcome his natural inclination because 'les ruisseaux de sang de votre noblesse qui ne pouvoient estre arrêtés que par l'effusion du leur me donnèrent la force de résister à moy-mesme et d'affermir V.M. à faire exécuter pour l'utilité de son Estat ce qui estoit quasi contre le sens de tout le monde et contre mes sentimens particuliers'.[46]

When it comes to the matter of his own part in the exclusion of the rest of the royal family from the king's council, the cardinal is particularly careful to present himself in a favourable light, as one who sought only reconciliation with 'la Mère et le Fils', and to humour the queen. Richelieu praises the king for his continued generosity towards his family, no matter what the provocation, but he also questions the king's generosity towards a mother who was working to ruin his chief minister who, he vehemently protests, had sought only her elevation.[47]

The cardinal is much more assertive in the rest of the book, where he proceeds to give the king advice for the remaining years of his reign, examining each of the three orders in turn. Richelieu emerges as a practical politician, bent on reform. As befits a prince of the church, the most extensive proposals concern the first order, where he is keen to correct as far as possible abuses in the system of ecclesiastical appointments.[48] The more concise remarks which follow in the chapters on the nobility and the Third Estate portray Richelieu as keen to bring every element of society under the king's authority, but also to present himself as the true defender of the cause of the nobility, whom he calls 'un des principaux nerfs de l'Estat',[49] a class whose fortunes have been needlessly depleted by the expense of life at court. He vigorously argues the case for just reward and fair treatment for deserving nobles and severe punishment for those 'qui manqueront de servir la couronne de leurs espées et de leurs vies avec la constance et la fermeté que les loix de l'Estat requièrent'.[50] He steadfastly advises against compromise where duels are concerned in the interests of the monarchy and the nobility itself.[51] He again appears to have the interests of the true aristocracy at heart when he recommends the abolition of the venality of offices as the main thrust of his programme of reform of the Third Estate. Ever the pragmatist he recognises, however, that he is much more likely to be remembered for the implementation of the policy of sending 'intendans de justice et de finance' to the provinces to control corruption at every level and to bring into line those 'qui estant puissants et riches, oppriment les foibles et les pauvres sujets du roi'.[52]

One of the principal themes of the *Testament* is the importance of appointing the right man for the right job, and the need to refer as many decisions as possible to him. The more polished and abstract chapters offer a defence of the position and authority of the chief minister. The chapter entitled 'Du Conseil du prince' lists the many virtues of the ideal counsellor: solid judgement, probity, strength, resolve, and above all application which is defined as 'la perfection d'un conseiller d'Estat, le concours de toutes ses actions'.[53] Whilst it is admitted that such virtues are rarely to be found in one man, Richelieu clearly realises that he may be as closely identified as any with this portrait of the perfect royal adviser. When considering the subject of the ideal number of Councillors of State, he writes:

> J'ajoute qu'il n'en peut avec fruit avoir plus de quatre et qu'encore faut-il qu'entre eux il y en ayt un qui ayt l'authorité supérieure et qui soit comme le premier mobile qui meut tous les autres cieux sans estre meu que de son intelligence.
>
> J'ay peine à me résoudre à mettre en avant cette proposition, parce qu'il semblera que j'y veuille soutenir ma cause.[54]

Among the most telling of the arguments by analogy which he uses to prove his point is one that casts some doubt on the king's own application:

> S'il est vray que le gouvernement monarchique imite plus celuy de Dieu qu'aucun autre,[...] on peut dire hardiment que, si le souverain peut ou ne veut pas luy mesme avoir l'oeil sur sa [carte] et sur la boussole, la raison veut qu'il donne particulièrement la charge à quelqu'un par-dessus tous les autres. [55]

Part Two makes abundantly clear that *raison d'état* is the tenet of Richelieu's central philosophy of government. Prefaced by the reminder 'que le premier fondement du bonheur d'un Estat est l'establissement du règne de Dieu', successive chapters identify reason, public interest, and foresight as the principles of good government, leaving no room for the emotions. It is argued that reason and passion are as incompatible as women and politics:

> S'il est vray que la raison doit estre le flambeau qui esclaire les princes en leur conduite et en celle de leur Estat, il est encore vray que, n'y ayant rien au monde qui compatisse moins avec elle que la passion, qui aveugle tellement qu'elle fait quelquefois prendre l'ombre pour le corps. Un prince doit surtout éviter d'agir par un tel principe qui le rendroit d'autant plus odieux qu'il est directement

contraire à celuy qui distingue l'homme d'avec les animaux ...
Les femmes paresseuses et peu secrettes de leur nature sont si peu propres au gouvernement, que si l'on considère encore qu'elle sont fort sujettes à leurs passions et, par conséquent, peu susceptibles de raison et de justice, ce seul principe les exclud de toute administration publique ...

Lest Richelieu's misogyny be in doubt he adds:

Il y a peu de règles qui ne soient capables de quelque exception. Ce siècle mesme en a porté quelqu'une qu'on ne sçauroit assez louer, mais il est vray qu'ordinairement leur molesse (sic) les rend incapables d'une vertu masle, nécessaire à l'administration et qu'il est presque impossible que leur gouvernement soit exempt ou de la bassesse ou de diminution, dont la foiblesse de leur sexe est la cause, ou d'injustice ou de cruauté, dont le dérèglement de leurs passions qui leur tient lieu de raison est la vraye source.[56]

On the need for the exercise of the strictest punishment regardless of sentiment, Richelieu reminds the king with an insistence not found in the less finished chapters which follow:

Je l'ay souvent représenté à V.M. et je la supplie encore de s'en ressouvenir soigneusement, ... V.M. a besoin d'estre divertie d'une fausse clémence plus dangereuse que la cruauté mesme, puisque l'impunité donne lieu d'en exercer beaucoup qu'on ne peut empescher que par le chastiment.
    La verge, qui est le symbole de la justice, ne doit jamais estre inutile. ... En matière de crime d'Estat, il faut fermer la porte à la pitié, mespriser les plaintes des personnes intéressées et les discours d'une populace ignorante qui blasme quelquefois ce qui luy est le plus utile et souvent tout à fait necessaire. ... Il faut, en telles occasions, commencer quelquefois par l'exécution, au lieu qu'en toutes autres, l'eclarcissement du droit par tesmoins ou par pièces irréprochables est préalable à toutes choses.[57]

Where the *Testament* bans women and the emotions from the political stage and favours execution with no questions asked when necessary, La Rochefoucauld identifies a jealous love for the queen and an appetite for revenge as the the main motives behind the cardinal's insistence on a triple policy which inevitably ended in the spilling of noble blood. Thus, the defeat of the Huguenots and the English at La Rochelle is prefaced by an account of the duke of Buckingham's brief affair with the queen, when she gave him her diamond *ferrets* as a token of her esteem, making the cardinal so jealous that he actively rejoiced in the news of Buckingham's assassination on his return to England. La Rochefoucauld notes: 'Le

Cardinal triompha inhumainement de cette mort; il dit des choses piquantes de la douleur de la Reine et il recommença d'espérer.'[58]

The Day of Dupes, which the *Testament* does not mention by name, is presented in the *Mémoires* as the signal demonstration of the vengeful cruelty which characterises his relations with the nobility. As the queen mother angrily accuses him of betrayal before her son, the cardinal is shown begging her forgiveness in an obsequious Tartuffian pose: 'Il se jeta à ses pieds et essaya de la fléchir par ses soumissions et par ses larmes.'[59] The list of the dozen dupes who backed the wrong horse, many of whom paid for their disloyalty with their lives, includes almost all the names that we find in the long litany of erring nobles in the *Succincte narration*. The *Mémoires* give a rather different interpretation of the impact on Richelieu's public image of this striking example of the implementation of *raison d'état*:

> Tant de sang répandu et tant de fortunes renversées avaient rendu odieux le ministère du cardinal de Richelieu; la douceur de la régence de Marie de Médicis était encore présente, et tous les grands du Royaume, qui se voyaient abattus, croyaient avoir passé de la liberté à la servitude.[60]

La Rochefoucauld, who tells us that his father also fell from favour at this time, carefully monitors his own increasing hatred of the cardinal:

> J'avais été nourri dans ces sentiments, et je m'y confirmai encore par ce que je viens de dire: la domination du cardinal de Richelieu me parut injuste, et je crus que le parti de la Reine était le seul qu'il fut honnête de suivre.[61]

In the final section of Part I, covering the campaign against the House of Austria and the Spanish question, La Rochefoucauld makes the declaration of war against Spain the principal folly and fault of the cardinal. He also gives a fascinating account of the interrogation tactics which Richelieu practised on him, following Mme de Chevreuse's highly suspicious flight to Spain, for which he tries to deny direct responsibility. Having by his inaction allowed his mistress to be sent a red signal instead of the green which would have confirmed that it was in fact safe for her to stay in France, La Rochefoucauld recounts his brief interview with Richelieu about his own role in the affair:

> Je le vis, et il me parla avec beaucoup de civilité, en exagérant

néanmoins la grandeur de ma faute, et quelles en pourraient être les
suites, si je ne la reparais par l'aveu de tout ce que je savais; je lui
répondis dans le même sens de ma déposition, et comme je lui parus
plus réservé et plus sec qu'on n'avait accoutumé de l'être avec lui, il
s'aigrit et me dit assez brusquement que je n'avais donc qu'à aller à
la Bastille.62

It is his short stay in prison, which curiously enough La
Rochefoucauld insists on noting did give cause for concern to the
King of Spain, which imprints the most terrible image of the
cardinal in his mind, by allowing him to witness at first hand the
suffering of the long-term prisoners. He writes:

Ce peu de temps que j'y demeurai me représenta plus vivement que
tout ce que j'avais vu jusqu'alors l'image affreuse de la domination
du Cardinal. J'y vis le maréchal de Bassompierre, dont le mérite et
les agréables qualités étaient si connues; j'y vis le maréchal de Vitry,
le comte de Cramail, le commandeur de Jars, La Fargis, Le Coudray-
Montpensier, Vautier, et un nombre infini de gens de toutes
conditions et de tous sexes, malheureux et persécutés par une
longue et cruelle prison. La vue de tant d'objets pitoyables
augmenta encore la haine naturelle que j'avais pour l'administration
du cardinal de Richelieu.63

As the resentful young man patiently awaits the cardinal's decline in
exile refusing, for the sake of the queen, an attempt to win him over
to the enemy side by offers of military promotion, the execution of
Cinq-Mars and his accomplice, the historian de Thou, following the
discovery of a rather more substantial Spanish plot, is given as the
final illustration of the swiftness of the cardinal's retribution. Having
himself unexpectedly escaped punishment in this instance, La
Rochefoucauld records the minister's death at the very moment of
his greatest triumph when, 'la conquête de Roussillon, la chute de
Monsieur le Grand et de tout son parti, la suite de tant d'heureux
succès, tant d'autorité et tant de vengeances avaient rendu le cardinal
de Richelieu également redoutable à l'Espagne et à la France'.64
The shock to which his sudden death gave rise, which is related at
the beginning of Part II of the *Mémoires* dealing with the first years
of Mazarin's ministry, seems also to have inspired the off-quoted
piece of literary encomium at the end of Part I, apparently the last
words La Rochefoucauld wrote in his account of his life and times.
As we have seen, Richelieu's one-time arch enemy, making the
national interest paramount, suddenly laments, in keeping with the
spirit of the *Testament,* that the minister did not live longer. 65
    Both the *Testament* and the first part of La Rochefoucauld's
Mémoires have contributed their part to what is now termed the

myth of Richelieu, based partly on the notion that the cardinal was a dominant and domineering minister who led the king by the nose, and somehow stood apart from his contemporaries who reacted to him as a homogeneous group.[66] Yet if the *Testament* is still widely quoted by scholars sceptical of its authenticity, it is partly because this text, for all its foibles in financial and other matters, supports much current thinking on the duumvirate or 'two-headed monarchy' and Richelieu's relations with the grandees.

Modern historians reject the idea that Richelieu attempted to function as an autonomous political entity. Lloyd Moote suspects a closer intellectual collaboration on policy between Louis XIII and his chief minister, and suggests that their relationship was an 'on-going campaign of mutual indoctrination'.[67] Robin Briggs presents him as 'a team man, who operated through multiple circles of friends, allies, and dependents'.[68] He portrays his role as advisor to the king as akin to the tutorial relationship,[69] for which the *Testament*, possibly a work of multiple authorship, might well have made an excellent set text. It has also recently been argued that as a member of the warrior caste nominated to army command as the king's lieutenant-general, no less keen to trace his family back to the mists of time than La Rochefoucauld,[70] Richelieu saw himself as an integral part of the aristocracy.[71]

Although there will always be something of the Alexandre Dumas about La Rochefoucauld's view of politics, the portrait of Richelieu in the *Mémoires* reminds us of the complexity of aristocratic opposition to this most powerful minister. In this much underrated example of his literary virtuosity, La Rochefoucauld, the master of paradox, has yet again left us with '"the sting in the tail" in the last paragraph which obliges us to reassess all that has gone before'.[72]

Notes:

1   P. Erlanger, *Richelieu* Perrin, 1970, III, pp. 356–8.
2   See also R.J. Knecht, 'The reputation of Cardinal Richelieu: classical hero or romantic villain', *Seventeenth-Century French Studies*, XV (1993), 5–24, 15.
3   C.J. Burckhardt, *Richelieu and his Age*. London: George Allen and Unwin, 1970, iii, p. 460.
4   *Monsieur de Pourceaugnac*, in Molière, *Oeuvres complètes*, ed. G. Couton Gallimard, 1971, II, p. 609.
5   La Rochefoucauld, *Oeuvres complètes*, xliii.
6   Ibid.
7   On the question of Richelieu's will, see J. Bergin, *Richelieu: Power and the Pursuit of Wealth*, New Haven: Yale University Press, 1985, pp. 259–263.
8   La Rochefoucauld, *Oeuvres complètes*, pp. 703–708.
9   Ibid., p. 769.
10 J. Bergin, *Richelieu: Power and the Pursuit of Wealth*, p. 256. F. Hildesheimer, *Testament politique de Richelieu*, Société de l'histoire de France, 1995, pp. 14 and 19, gives the date 1668 without explanation. Unless otherwise specified, references and quotations have been taken from

this edition.
11   See Richelieu, *Testament politique*, ed. L. André, Robert Laffont, 1947, p. 458.
12   Richelieu claims: 'Je me contente de ne rien mettre en avant qui ne soit si certain et si clair que toute personne bien censée en trouvera la preuve en son raisonnement.' *Testament politique de Richelieu*, p. 288.
13   See Richelieu, *Testament politique*, ed. André, pp. 65-66 and *Testament politique de Richelieu*, pp. 11 and 35, n. 2.
14   Four manuscripts are dated 1639. Only one or two references to later dates occur in the text.
15   Ibid., p. 201.
16   Ibid., p. 204.
17   Ibid., p. 220.
18   M. Bertaud, 'Le Conseiller du prince', d'après les *Mémoires de Richelieu* et son *Testament politique*', *Les Valeurs chez les memorialistes*, Klincksieck, 1979, 111-129.
19   A 'fault' much criticised by Voltaire. See Richelieu, *Testament politique*, ed. André, p. 55, and H. Weber, ' "Une bonne paix". Richelieu's foreign policy and the peace of Christendom', in *Richelieu and his Age* ed. J. Bergin and L. Brockliss, Oxford: Clarendon Press, 1992, pp. 45-69.
20   *Testament politique de Richelieu*, p. 373.
21   A. Lloyd Moote, *Louis XIII: Louis the Just*, University of California Press, 1989, pp. 161-4.
22   Quoted, Richelieu, *Testament politique*, ed. André, p. 458.
23   Quoted ibid., p. 462.
24   See E. Wirth Marvick, *The Young Richelieu. A Psychoanalytic Approach to Leadership*, Chicago and London: University of Chicago Press, 1980, pp. 24 and 214-5.
25   C. Jouhaud, *La Main de Richelieu*, Gallimard, 1991, p. 115.
26   See Lloyd Moote, *Louis XIII: Louis the Just*, p. 334, n.2.
27   Ibid., p. 16.
28   La Rochefoucauld, *Oeuvres complètes*, p. 47.
29   Ibid., p. 736.
30   Ibid., p. 4.
31   See N. Hepp, 'Idéalisme chevaleresque et réalisme politique dans les *Mémoires* de La Rochefoucauld', in *Images de La Rochefoucauld*, PUF, 1984, pp. 125-140.
32   See H. Weber, 'Richelieu théoricien politique', in *Richelieu et la culture*, CNRS, 1987, pp. 55-66, p. 59.
33   The cardinal's mother came from the *noblesse de robe* and the family territories had only recently been elevated to a *duché-prairie*.
34   See La Rochefoucauld, *Oeuvres complètes*, p. 47.
35   Ibid., p. 30.
36   See Hepp, 'Idéalisme chevaleresque et réalisme politique', p. 140, n. 38.
37   La Rochefoucauld, *Oeuvres complètes*, p. 39.
38   See Hepp, 'Idéalisme chevaleresque et réalisme politique', p. 132.
39   La Rochefoucauld, *Oeuvres complètes*, p. 58.
40   *Testament politique de Richelieu*, p. 132.
38   Jouhaud, *La Main*, p. 8.
42   *Testament politique de Richelieu*, p. 248.
43   The absence of a date in the title of this introductory chapter is thought to be a sign that the text is unfinished.
44   *Testament politique de Richelieu*, p. 43.
45   'Richelieu n'est pas un acteur de l'ombre. Il dissimule ou tient en retrait sa présence pour mieux préparer l'exhibition de la force et l'ostentation de sa puissance.' Jouhaud, *La Main*, pp. 118-9.
46   *Testament politique de Richelieu*, p. 49.
47   Ibid., p. 59.
48   See J. Bergin, 'Richelieu and his bishops? Ministerial power and episcopal patronage under Louis XIII', in *Richelieu and his Age*, pp. 175-202.
49   *Testament politique de Richelieu*, p. 149.
50   Ibid., p. 150.
51   Ibid., p. 158.
52   Ibid., p. 174.
53   Ibid., p. 226.

54 Ibid., p. 229.
55 Ibid., p. 230.
56 Ibid., pp. 246 and 248.
57 Ibid., pp. 259–261.
58 La Rochefoucauld, *Oeuvres complètes*, p. 44.
59 Ibid., p. 45.
60 Ibid. p. 46.
61 Ibid.
62 Ibid., p. 54.
63 Ibid.
64 Ibid., p. 57.
65 Louis André cites a final allusion to the form of a testament in Part Two, ch. 9, end of section 7: 'Si Dieu fait la grâce à votre Majesté d'avoir bientôt la paix, et de la conserver à ce royaume avec ses serviteurs [...], au lieu de laisser cet avis par Testament, j'espère de le pouvoir accomplir'. Richelieu, *Testament politique*, ed. André, p. 70.
66 See Lloyd Moote, *Louis XIII: Louis the Just*, p. 5.
67 Ibid, p. 164; see also D. Parrot, 'Richelieu, the *Grands*, and the French Army, in *Richelieu and his Age*, pp. 135–173.
68 See R. Briggs, 'Richelieu and reform: rhetoric and political reality', in *Richelieu and his Age*, pp. 71-97, p. 73.
69 Ibid., p. 82.
70 See Wirth Marvick, *Richelieu: A Psychoanalytic Approach*, p. 33.
71 See Parrot, 'Richelieu, the *Grands*, and the French Army', pp. 140 and 142
72 D.A. Watts, *La Rochefoucauld: Maximes*, University of Glasgow, 1993, p. 79. See also Hepp, 'Idéalisme chevaleresque et réalisme politique', pp. 139–140.

CHAPTER SIX

Considérations morales et politiques autour d'Henri II de Montmorency: Une polyphonie discordante

NOEMI HEPP

Gaston d'Orléans, outré par la politique de Richelieu que dictaient des vues à long terme et à grande échelle et qui avait amené Louis XIII à se séparer complètement de sa mère et à tenir en suspicion son frère, voulut, dix-huit mois plus tard en 1632, susciter une contre-journée des dupes. Il en escomptait le rétablissement de l'ordre ancien grâce à l'élimination du terrible Cardinal. Il eut recours pour cela à un filleul d'Henri IV, grand seigneur s'il en fut, maréchal de France et gouverneur du Languedoc. L'affaire était de dimension internationale; l'Espagne—à laquelle Marie de Médicis et Gaston lui-même avaient demandé refuge dans leurs exils volontaires—et la Lorraine à laquelle Gaston s'était lié en épousant secrètement la princesse Marguerite, sœur du duc Charles IV, y étaient mêlées. Le projet était d'ordre militaire; Gaston devait descendre de Bruxelles vers le sud-ouest du royaume avec une armée assez composite et rejoindre des troupes levées par Montmorency dans son gouvernement, l'Espagne fournissant des troupes d'appoint et de l'argent. Dès le printemps de 1632, la Cour fut informée des desseins de Monsieur, mais ceux de Montmorency furent tenus secrets jusqu'au 22 juillet, date à laquelle le gouverneur du Languedoc réunit à Pézenas les Etats de sa province et contraignit les participants à signer une déclaration qui les associait à sa rébellion. C'était le moment où Monsieur et son armée arrivaient en Languedoc vers où descendaient en même temps deux armées royales; le choc eut lieu le 1 septembre, tout près de Castelnaudary, la déroute des rebelles fut complète et presque immédiate. Montmorency fut blessé et capturé et, quelques semaines plus tard, il était jugé et condamné à mort par le Parlement de Toulouse—ville capitale de la province sur laquelle il avait eu autorité—puis aussitôt décapité, le 30 octobre, dans une cour de l'Hôtel de Ville. Dénouement sanglant qui apporta la plus grande satisfaction au ministre acharné à établir l'autorité de l'Etat et le plus grand désespoir à Gaston d'Orléans ainsi qu'à une part importante de la haute noblesse. Au lieu d'une contre-journée des dupes s'était produite une confirmation violente et une considérable amplification de ce que cette journée avait représenté.

L'enjeu, on le voit, était énorme. Que Montmorency eût été fautif, personne, après coup, n'en douta. Mais où était la faute? Choisir le parti du frère du Roi contre un roi que beaucoup considéraient comme la victime de son ministre, était-ce une faute morale, ou seulement une erreur politique? Agir par animosité, par ressentiment contre ce ministre qui avait cruellement décapité la noblesse de France, au figuré et—plus d'une fois—au propre, était-ce condamnable? Attendre un secours espagnol, était-ce trahir sa patrie, ou n'y avait-il qu'une faute de jugement dans le fait de s'y être mal pris? Et, si faute il y avait, était-il juste de la faire payer au coupable au prix de sa tête? Ou encore, Montmorency était-il seulement la victime de circonstances qui s'étaient coalisées contre lui? C'est ce carrefour d'idées morales et d'idées politiques—les unes n'étant pas toujours distinctes des autres, d'ailleurs—qu'il nous faut maintenant essayer d'explorer. Nous le ferons à partir de quelques *Mémoires* écrits après coup par des contemporains de l'événement, mais, avant d'en venir à eux, nous présenterons la version officielle des faits telle que le *Mercure Français* de 1632—rédigé à l'époque sous l'œil vigilant du Père Joseph—l'offrait à qui voulait la lire.

Dans le *Mercure*, donc, qui rapporte ce qui concerne Montmorency à l'intérieur d'un récit de la rébellion où d'abord Monsieur seul est impliqué et mis en cause, les pièces essentielles sont la déclaration royale datée de Cosne le 23 août et le récit du procès et des dernières heures du condamné. Dans la première sont énumérés les chefs d'accusation contre le gouverneur du Languedoc jugé coupable d'infidélité et de félonie. Les griefs d'ordre politique sont la préméditation de la révolte, le détournement des pouvoirs qui lui avaient été confiés pour le service du Roi et qu'il a utilisés pour gagner à sa propre cause des villes et des personnes de son gouvernement, le détournement de fonds publics à l'usage de cette même cause, l'emploi de la contrainte à l'égard de députés des Etats de la province et en particulier à l'égard de l'archevêque de Narbonne, fidèle au Roi, enfin la recherche active de l'assistance espagnole. C'est là ce qui constitue le crime de lèse-majesté. Mais il semble fortement aggravé par les deux reproches d'ordre moral qui enserrent l'énumération: au début, celui d'ingratitude envers un souverain qui l'avait comblé de bienfaits, à la fin celui d'hypocrisie puisque, dans le temps même où il travaillait contre lui, Montmorency a protesté de sa fidélité au·Roi. Notons qu'à cette aggravation des griefs ne répond la mention d'aucune circonstance atténuante.

Avant de donner le texte de la déclaration royale, le *Mercure* n'avait pas manqué de préciser que plusieurs villes du Languedoc—des villes protestantes en particulier—avaient refusé de se laisser séduire par la rébellion et que le duc d'Epernon avait pris l'initiative d'écrire au Roi qu'il lui était parfaitement loyal. C'est le même esprit, consistant à montrer qu'au milieu du Mal, le Bien est aussi en action, qui va présider au récit du procès. Le Bien sous toutes ses formes: en avouant son crime de rébellion contre le Roi, en rétractant spontanément une déclaration faite la veille, comme quoi il n'avait pas signé le texte subversif du 22 juillet, en se reconnaissant digne du châtiment suprême, Montmorency avait satisfait à la fois à la morale et à la politique. En se préparant très pieusement à la mort et en abordant sa dernière heure dans la plus grande sérénité, le condamné avait satisfait à toutes les exigences du christianisme. Le Roi, de son côté, en permettant à Montmorency de faire un testament, bien que l'arrêt du Parlement de Toulouse portât confiscation de tous ses biens, et en allégeant quelque peu les modalités de l'exécution—non pas sur une place publique mais dans un lieu clos—avait traité le coupable avec magnanimité et satisfait à l'ordre des personnes aussi bien qu'à celui de l'Etat. Si bien que le long récit du *Mercure* pouvait se conclure sur un portrait flatteur de Montmorency—'Qui ôtera de sa vie le 22 juillet, le premier de septembre et le trentième octobre 1632 trouvera qu'elle est toute pleine de gloire, de bonheur et de sagesse'— et sur l'évocation, prudente dans le style mais non ambiguë, de la valeur politique du châtiment:

> Il y en eut qui écrivirent en ce temps-là que cet exemple de la Justice du Roi en la personne du Duc de Montmorency rendrait sages les plus mauvais, les retenant dans le devoir et obéissance qu'ils doivent à leur Roi.

Politiquement, moralement, religieusement, tout s'achevait au mieux selon le *Mercure*; si l'autorité de l'Etat triomphait, les vieux idéaux ne se trouvaient pas purement bafoués.

On ne s'étonnera pas que nous n'ayons pas rencontré de mémorialiste qui partage cette vision des choses. A l'extrême opposé, nous trouvons dans les *Mémoires* que Monsieur fit écrire par l'un de ses secrétaires, Lasseré, non pas le langage de l'Etat tel qu'était en train de le modeler Richelieu, mais celui de la société féodale où les grands peuvent, sans crise de conscience aucune, agir pour faire prévaloir leurs propres valeurs. Dans leur système, tout service mérite récompense et donc Montmorency qui, au début de l'automne 1630, avait 'porté hautement les intérêts du cardinal de Richelieu contre la Reine-mère pendant leur brouillerie de Lyon' avait le droit de s'attendre à se voir gratifié de la citadelle de Montpellier et le droit—peut-être même le devoir—de se révolter contre l'ingrat. Ce même système comporte l'importance primordiale des liens de parenté: le duc a d'autant plus de raisons de passer du service du Cardinal à celui de la Reine-mère qu'il y est poussé par 'Madame sa femme' qui est d'origine italienne et lointaine cousine de Marie de Médicis. Pour le faire prévaloir, ce système, le recours à l'étranger n'est nullement interdit et les *Mémoires* dont nous parlons affirment tranquillement que 'le projet de cette guerre était fondé ... sur le secours étranger que les Espagnols avaient promis'. La bonne conscience est donc parfaite. Elle est encore renforcée par une caution ecclésiastique de haut rang: l'évêque d'Albi—Alphonse d'Elbène—avait fait valoir à Montmorency que sa rébellion 'n'était chose qui fût sans exemple' et que le duc d'Epernon ayant, au temps du ministère de Luynes, travaillé à délivrer la Reine-mère, captive au château de Blois, tout s'était très bien passé: le Roi avait fait bon visage à sa mère libérée et Epernon avait été absous. (On voit au passage pourquoi le *Mercure* signalait en 1632 la profession de loyalisme de ce duc ...) D'après les *Mémoires* de Gaston d'Orléans, en somme, la seule faute que l'on pourrait, si l'on y tenait, reprocher à Montmorency serait d'avoir mal évalué le changement de système qu'impliquait l'établissement du pouvoir de Richelieu. Encore cela n'est-il pas dit et Montmorency nous est-il représenté, ainsi que Monsieur, blanc comme neige.

Pas plus que la thèse du *Mercure*, nous n'avons vu celle de Gaston d'Orléans reprise par un autre mémorialiste. Ceux dont nous voulons parler à présent sont bien conscients qu'en 1632 on n'est plus en 1619. Mais ils ne sont pas, pour autant, convaincus que l'ordre nouveau soit le meilleur possible ni que Richelieu ne mérite que louanges. Parmi eux, nous citerons d'abord Pontis de qui P. Thomas du Fossé a rédigé les *Mémoires*. D'après ce texte, conçu dans une perspective catholique, monarchique, mais plus encore, peut-être, aristocratique, le seul motif de rébellion de Montmorency a été le souci du bien public: il ne pouvait

> supporter la domination violente de celui qui s'était rendu en quelque sorte maître de l'esprit et de la personne du Roi [et] se ligua avec M. le duc d'Orléans pour délivrer la France, tous les grands et le Roi même de l'oppression sous laquelle ils gémissaient. Tel fut son dessein dans lequel il ne paraissait rien que de louable.

Opposer Richelieu au Roi—ce que Pontis est loin d'être seul à faire—permet de jouer entre les systèmes de valeurs. Pontis peut ainsi tout à la fois, dans l'ordre de la morale politique, louer Montmorency et le blâmer, 'n'étant jamais permis de prendre les armes contre son prince pour quelque sujet que ce puisse être'. Par ailleurs, sur un plan plus terre-à-terre, il le blâme d'une erreur de jugement, celle de s'être engagé avec un prince qui, trop haut placé pour risquer lui-même quoi que ce soit, était voué d'avance à abandonner ses complices en cas d'échec. Mais, passant rapidement de ces préalables au récit de la campagne militaire qui aboutit au désastre de Castelnaudary, Pontis évite de donner sur la désobéissance au Roi le moindre détail: elle est adoucie par ce silence. Tandis que sont mis en lumière l'animosité de Richelieu à l'égard de Montmorency et le formidable passe-droit que constitua, voulue par le Cardinal, la tenue du procès à Toulouse alors que, pair de France, le gouverneur du Languedoc ne relevait que du Parlement de Paris. Le 'service de l'Etat' était-il autre chose que le service des passions du Cardinal? Pontis, sans le dire, suggère que non.

Dans le récit du procès, sur lequel il ne s'étend pas beaucoup, Pontis met en lumière seulement quelques points. Le premier est la déposition d'un témoin qui,

> interrogé s'il avait connu M. de Montmorency dans le combat ... répondit en pleurant que, l'ayant vu tout couvert de feu, de sang et de fumée, il eut d'abord de la peine à le reconnaître, mais qu'enfin, lui ayant vu rompre six de leurs rangs et tuer quelques soldats dans le septième, il jugea bien que ce devait être M. de Montmorency ... ,

hommage à l'éclatante valeur militaire de l'accusé. Le second est que celui-ci impute à son seul 'malheur' et à son 'mauvais conseil' un engagement 'pour lequel il ne voulait point chercher d'excuses sur la personne de Monsieur', en quoi il se montre pleinement homme d'honneur. Le troisième est qu'il nie 'toute intelligence avec les étrangers sur la frontière' et déclare 'qu'il n'avait jamais eu intention de nuire à l'Etat', contre-vérité sans doute, que justifie le désir de paraître loyal sujet du Roi, selon la commode dissociation du souverain et de son ministre. Toutes les valeurs aristocratiques sont là, assorties de 'tant de modération et d'honnêteté et d'un ton de voix si charmant que les juges ont avoué qu'ils eurent une peine extrême à se contenir, voyant ce grand homme dans un état si touchant'.

De la fin chrétienne de Montmorency, le *Mercure* a déjà parlé, nous n'y reviendrons pas avec Pontis, sinon pour dire que celui-ci ajoute des nuances qui font conclure à la sainteté du condamné. Un noble motif de rébellion, un combat marqué par une éblouissante bravoure, une déposition généreuse et sereine devant un tribunal qui n'était pas celui que son rang lui assignait, la mort d'un saint martyr, victime de la haine de 'l'homme rouge', tels sont les traits par lesquels Pontis, peu soucieux de politique mais attentif aux valeurs morales de l'aristocratie pour autant que ce sont aussi des valeurs chrétiennes, héroïse 'le grand duc de Montmorency' et vilipende le Cardinal: le point de vue s'oppose tant à celui du *Mercure* qu'à celui de Gaston d'Orléans.

Il y a moins de faste, mais plus d'émotion vraie, dans le récit que fait Puységur du procès et de l'exécution de Montmorency, la seule partie de cette sombre histoire sur laquelle il s'exprime sans laconisme. Officier loyal entre tous qui, sollicité par Monsieur de commander les troupes levées pour lui en Flandre, n'a pas songé un instant à accepter cette offre, Puységur ne recourt pas à la dissociation facile du Roi et de son ministre. S'il ne parle d'eux que fort peu, il est clair pourtant que son loyalisme ne va pas jusqu'à se mettre par le cœur de leur côté dans ce drame; le Cardinal est évoqué dans une seule phrase du texte comme 'celui qui voulait qu'il mourût' et le seul dans tout le royaume qui n'aimât pas le duc de Montmorency; le Roi est montré froid, silencieusement irrité contre les larmes qu'il voit répandre par tous autour de lui, et inflexible aux supplications qui montent vers lui. Mais l'attention du lecteur est surtout orientée vers l'opposition entre le désespoir de ceux qui ont affaire à l'inculpé puis au condamné—ses juges y compris—et la tranquille fermeté de celui qui s'applique à consoler ceux que submergent les larmes, à se charger lui-même, à faire au Roi une parfaite amende honorable et enfin, à l'approche du supplice, à imiter Jésus-Christ dans sa Passion.

Consoler ceux qui pleurent et se charger lui-même, c'est ce que fait Montmorency dans la première scène de ce court récit, où il est confronté aux deux officiers qui l'ont capturé sur le champ de bataille. Le rapporteur du procès

> lui demanda s'il les connaissait; il répondit que oui, et qu'ils étaient gens d'honneur, braves et de ses amis. Il les embrassa tous deux qui pleuraient. Le rapporteur lui demandant s'il n'avait aucun reproche à faire contre eux, il dit que non, si ce n'est qu'ils avaient trop d'amitié pour lui, qu'il était au désespoir de les voir pleurer comme ils faisaient, qu'il les priait de se consoler; que pour lui, il avouait qu'il méritait la mort, puisqu'il avait été assez malheureux pour prendre les armes contre son Roi. Le rapporteur leur demanda s'ils l'avaient pris ayant l'épée à la main et combattant contre les troupes de Sa Majesté, mais, ne pouvant répondre dans les sanglots qu'ils poussaient et les larmes qu'ils répandaient, il dit lui-même au rapporteur: Monsieur, il suffit que je vous le dise, qu'il est vrai qu'ils m'ont pris ayant l'épée à la main, et combattant contre les troupes de Sa Majesté.

Cet admirable Montmorency qui console ceux qui pleurent sur lui, on le retrouvera tout à la fin du récit en face du chirurgien qui l'avait soigné de ses blessures pendant les mois de septembre et d'octobre: '... consolez-vous, Lucante, je vous veux embrasser et vous dire adieu pendant que j'ai les bras libres'. Entre temps, il y aura eu, la condamnation une fois prononcée, l'amende honorable au Roi à qui le condamné fait dire que le déplaisir qu'il a de l'avoir offensé lui est plus fâcheux que la mort qu'il va subir. Quant à la volonté d'imiter Jésus-Christ dans sa Passion, omniprésente en sourdine, elle apparaît surtout au moment où, apprenant que le Roi lui accorde 'que le bourreau ne le toucherait point, ne lui mettrait point la corde sur les épaules', Montmorency proteste: 'Non, je ne veux point cela, je suis criminel et désire être traité comme tel. Dieu a été traité de même et a eu la corde au col, et si, il était très juste'.

Montmorency coupable? Pour Puységur, la réponse est oui, certainement. Mais si grand, si noble que personne d'autre que lui-même n'est digne de parler contre lui. Ce n'est pas le mémorialiste qui l'accusera, qui expliquera en quoi il était coupable, ni d'ailleurs qui le défendra. Refus d'entrer dans les affaires politiques qui ne sont pas de son ressort, refus de s'ériger en juge, intime sensibilité morale et profonde chaleur affective à travers une expression contenue, telle est l'attitude, très différente de toutes les précédentes, que nous venons de voir se manifester.

Après avoir vu défendre des thèses par le *Mercure*, Gaston d'Orléans et Pontis, après avoir senti chez Puységur une sensibilité blessée au plus vif, nous avons gardé pour la fin de ce parcours le texte le plus intelligent et le plus moderne que nous ayons rencontré chez les mémorialistes, celui de Nicolas Goulas. Gentilhomme ordinaire de la chambre de Monsieur, Goulas ne pouvait ni ne voulait accuser de plein fouet son maître—ni donc le principal bras armé de sa rébellion—ni l'approuver. De ce dilemme, dont Puységur s'était échappé par le cœur, il allait, lui, s'échapper par la réflexion psychologique, en essayant de comprendre de l'intérieur le drame vécu par Montmorency et en le présentant comme une pure tragédie, celle d'un homme qui 'fut extrêmement malheureux et fut l'artisan de son malheur'. Ce drame n'est évoqué que de façon sporadique et incomplète, car le but du mémorialiste est de raconter l'ensemble de l'épisode du point de vue de Monsieur et de sa suite, non de prendre pour centre le gouverneur du Languedoc; de celui-ci, il n'est presque plus rien dit après le désastre de Castelnaudary. Mais, entre l'arrivée de Monsieur et des siens dans le territoire qui relevait de Montmorency et le terrible combat, c'est bien sur lui qu'est concentrée l'attention, lui que Goulas dépeint 'avec toute l'audace du dieu Mars sur le visage'.

Les raisons qu'avait eues Montmorency de 's'embarquer' avec Monsieur? Goulas répond ici comme avaient fait les *Mémoires* de Gaston d'Orléans: l'influence de son épouse et le ressentiment contre le Cardinal qui avait trompé ses espérances. 'Cette âme grande et généreuse avait embrassé de bon cœur cette occasion de se venger, en servant la mère et le frère unique de son Roi.' Goulas ne le blâme donc pas à l'origine. Mais, dès l'arrivée de Monsieur en Languedoc, la tragédie se profile. Montmorency fait dire par un messager qu'il n'est pas prêt; on lui avait promis du temps jusqu'à l'automne et on arrivait au début de l'été: 'lui manquant en tout, il n'était obligé à rien'. Et Goulas de méditer, se mettant à la place du malheureux, sur tout ce en quoi on lui avait manqué: on lui avait promis que le duc de Lorraine, combattant contre les troupes du Roi, les retiendrait loin du Languedoc 'et il s'était accommodé, on lui avait fait voir l'Espagne armée et personne ne branlait de ce côté'. En outre, Monsieur lui avait envoyé comme bras droit le duc d'Elbeuf dont il ne voulait pas. Et puis une ombre sinistre s'étendait sur lui car il avait raconté quelques semaines plus tôt à des proches 'que le temps approchait qu'un astrologue avait prédit à M. le Connétable, son père, que les astres le menaçaient d'un grand malheur et qu'il l'avait figuré tel qu'on en pouvait conclure une mort par main de bourreau'. Sans entrer dans le détail des déconvenues qui survinrent dans les semaines suivantes, on les voit déjà comme programmées dans une phrase qui les précède:

> Enfin le projet était bien pensé, et il y avait de quoi donner dedans, mais on le trompa, ou les rencontres des choses le firent tromper, et je suis fort trompé ou, s'il eût pu se dédire et se débarrasser de nous en levant les soupçons que la Cour avait justement conçus de lui, il l'aurait fait volontiers et nous aurait plantés là.

Que faudrait-il de plus pour nous assurer qu'aux yeux de Goulas la précipitation de Montmorency au combat de Castelnaudary malgré ceux qui tentaient de le retenir ne fut pas autre chose qu'un suicide? Et pour amener le lecteur à penser que, bien plus que 'la bravoure étourdie et emportée' du duc, le responsable en est le sort?

Aux questions que nous posions au début de ces pages, on voit combien les réponses des uns et des autres divergent. Certaines de ces questions n'ont d'ailleurs été abordées que par un ou deux mémorialistes, ce qu'explique aisément le fait que tous ne traitent pas la même partie de l'histoire. Il y a cependant unanimité dans l'admiration pour Montmorency et, au-delà de sa personne, dans une certaine idée de ce qui fait la grandeur d'un gentilhomme. Mais si la fidélité est une part de cette grandeur, celui qui la pratique est-il libre d'en choisir l'objet?—C'est le nœud de la question. Et, sur ce point, en dehors du *Mercure* qui répond non et de Monsieur qui répond oui, personne n'est tout à fait clair. Il n'y a pas de clarté, en particulier, quant au recours à l'étranger; même la déclaration royale du 23 août n'en fait pas le grief principal contre celui que, dans une perspective moderne, nous appellerions un traître. Ailleurs, elle est ou avouée tranquillement, ou admise sans remarque particulière, ou passée sous silence. On ne trouverait personne, par contre, pour admettre aussi calmement la désobéissance à l'égard du Roi: c'est pourquoi plusieurs de nos textes n'en parlent pas. A certains égards, on a l'impression d'être dans un *no-man's-land* de la morale politique. Mais, qu'ils aient ou non répondu à nos questions, chacun des textes sur lesquels nous nous sommes arrêtée reflète tout un monde de pensées—souvent aussi d'arrière-pensées—et de sentiments qui nous semble valoir d'être connu pour lui-même.

CHAPTER SEVEN

Medicine and Statecraft in the *Mémoires* of the Cardinal de Retz[1]

COLIN JONES

> Toutes les humeurs de l'Etat étoient si émues par la chaleur de Paris, qui en est le chef [noted Retz in August 1648, reviewing the turbulent state of the capital over the previous year] que je jugeois bien l'ignorance du médecin ne préviendroit pas la fièvre, qui en étoit comme la suite nécessaire.[2]

Written breathlessly, with inspired elan and as if in a series of long, intense spurts, Retz's *Mémoires* show surprisingly few substantial text revisions and erasures.[3] It is thus worthy of note that in the citation above, he had first written the word 'ministre' before replacing it with 'médecin'.

In what senses was a minister also a physician? The verbal replacement—or maybe Freudian slip?—highlights the presence in the *Mémoires* of what Derek Watts has characterized as 'families of images'[4]—in this case a metaphorical equation between bodily medicine and statecraft. Though noted by critics, the medical and body imagery found in the *Mémoires* has not, to my knowledge, been systematically explored. My aim in the present essay is to do that, paying close attention to the text of the memoirs and to the context of their production, setting Retz's writings against the broader background of politics, political thought and medical ideas.

If a minister could be equated with a physician, this was essentially because the body of the state was sick. Retz's medico-political diagnosis of the ills of France on the eve of the Fronde is well-known:

> Le dernier point de l'illusion, en matière d'Etat, est une espèce de léthargie, qui n'arrive jamais qu'après de grands symptomes. Le renversement des anciennes lois, l'anéantissement de ce milieu qu'elles ont posé entre les peuples et les rois, l'établissement de l'autorité purement et absolument despotique, sont ceux qui ont jeté

originairement la France dans les convulsions dans lesquelles nos
pères l'ont vue (GEF, i, pp. 289–90).

The figuring of French society as a physical body was in fact a well-
established trope of political analysis. Insofar as France was thought
to have a 'constitution' in the seventeenth century, it was conceived of
as a bodily constitution.[5] This highlighted an often unreflective
organicism about society which had Aristotelian roots and a strong
medieval pedigree.[6] The cosmos was viewed anthropomorphically as
a human body—or alternatively as a plant, a tree—and by extension,
the state too was figured as an organic entity. As Montaigne had
noted,

> Il se trouve une merveilleuse relation et correspondance en cette
> universelle police des ouvrages de nature, qui montre bien qu'elle
> n'est ny fortuite ny conduyte par divers maistres. Les maladies et
> conditions de nos corps se voyent aussi aux estats et polices: les
> royaumes, les républiques naissent, fleurissent et fanissent de
> vieillesse, comme nous. Nous sommes subjects à une repletion
> d'humeurs inutile et nuysible: soit de bonnes humeurs, ... soit
> repletion de mauvaises humeurs, qui est l'ordinaire cause des
> maladies. De semblable repletion se voyent les estats souvent
> malades et l'on a accoustumé d'user de diverses sortes de purgation.[7]

Similarly, at the heart of the Wars of Religion in the late sixteenth
century, the humanist Jean Bodin had seized the metaphor of bodily
purgation as a means of re-establishing the state's balance of humours
in his reference to vagrants and vagabonds: 'Il n'y a donc moyen de
nettoyer la république de telle ordure que de les envoyer en guerre qui
est comme une médecine purgative et fort nécessaire pour chasser les
humeurs corrompues du corps universel de la république'.[8]

By the middle decades of the seventeenth century, as we shall see,
the languages of the body had developed into a characteristic idiom of
constitutional opposition to the political programme associated with
Richelieu, then Mazarin. The building up of centralized authority, the
development of a state bureaucracy, and the imposition of substantial
tax increases and other financial expedients so as to allow the state to
pursue an aggressive foreign policy were widely viewed as imposing
excessive burdens on the body social.[9]

Yet one of the beauties of the body metaphor as an ingredient in
political debate was its versatility. Supporters of strongly authoritarian
monarchical policies and their underlying philosophy of *raison d'état*
used the metaphor too, so as to place emphasis on the need to avoid
the hydra-like proliferation of heads associated with democracy: 'le
corps politique aussi que le naturel', noted royal chaplain Ceriziers in

his *Le Tacite français* (1648), 'doit avoir plusieurs membres, [mais] un seul chef'.10 The propagandists of royal absolutism prioritized the need for a single mind (the monarch's) in bringing under control and back to pristine health a body politic which was wracked by rebellions and turbulence—'peccant humours' in the political language of the body. Richelieu himself compared the French people (and more specifically, tax-payers) to a pack-animal which responded to whipping, but also ruefully noted that 'Jamais médecine ne fut agréable au goût d'un malade' (Ibid., p. 353). Guez de Balzac, who served as one of Richelieu's press team, evoked the 'fièvre chaude de rébellion', and compared early seventeenth-century France to 'un vieux débauché qui a fait ce qu'il a pu pour mourir, et qui vit en dépit des médecins'—with the clear enough corollary that Providence and good monarchical physic were essential for the re-establishment of this unruly patient. A governmental pamphlet which appeared in 1632, *L'Hellébore pour nos malcontents, cueilli au jardin d'un Anti-Machiavel* even attacked the opponents of absolutism for utilizing body metaphors as a means of exaggerating the putative ills of France to which they could thus pose as able physicians.11

It was not unknown for a government propagandist to pose, as here, as an 'Anti-Machiavel': another, author of the anonymous *Le Jubilé d'un Espagnol, d'un Jésuite et d'un bon Français* in 1626, for example, targeted the Jesuits as quintessential machiavellians. Yet this charge was more normally levelled against the style of government which Richelieu and Mazarin had popularized. *Raison d'état* was held to consist in the separation of political interests from religious and from wider moral considerations—Richelieu's diplomatic alliance with Protestant princes was a particular problem here, notably with the *dévot* interests who were urging a Catholic Bourbon–Habsburg alliance in order to extirpate protestantism throughout Europe. Machiavellianism also signified a 'tyrannical' lack of respect for established forms of authority (the so-called 'fundamental laws of the kingdom'), a penchant for violent remedies and a predilection for governmental secrecy.12

Richelieu and Mazarin were also heavily criticized for treating the state organism as a machine. Government propagandists did indeed have recourse to a language of political mechanism: the universe was for one 'un ouvrage artificiel et une Machine', the state for another 'cette grande et merveilleuse machine qui est composée de tant de ressorts différents'.13 Non-organicism thus tended to be equated by the government's opponents with the nefarious practices of *raison d'état*. This mechanical imagery was viewed as proceeding less from the new science of Copernicus and Galileo, moreover, than from machiavellianism, which seemed to offer a set of decontextualized mechanical techniques for political control. Mazarin was, Scarron jested, 'un faiseur de machines', and the opponents of the cardinal ministers accused them of turning politics into a base 'mechanical art'. The machiavellian procedures of the cardinal ministers were thus delegitimized under a witheringly patrician *cascade de mépris*.14

During the Fronde, the *mazarinades* continued the tradition of using the name of Machiavelli as an 'ideological projectile'.15 Mazarin in particular was portrayed as a faithful disciple of the Florentine sage, and was alleged to have set out to import from the city-states of the Italian peninsula (the xenophobia of the *mazarinades* was flagrant) a quest for tyranny quite out of keeping with French mores: Italian 'fourberie' was contrasted with 'cette aimable candeur de nos aïeux'.16 In his *Mémoires*, Retz echoes and amplifies these sentiments, portraying the cardinal ministers as poor servants of the public interest. Furthermore, he also emphasized the fact that both Richelieu and Mazarin had in their different ways not only neglected France's health, but had also by their incompetence and their duplicitous love of violent methods aggravated the state's ills and produced new 'maladies d'Etat':

> Le cardinal de Richelieu la vint traiter comme un empirique, avec des remèdes violents, qui lui firent paroître de la force, mais une force d'agitation qui en épuisa le corps et les parties. Le cardinal Mazarin, comme un médecin très-inexpérimenté, ne connut point son abattement. Il ne le soutint point par les secrets chimiques de son prédecesseur; il continua de l'affoiblir par des saignées; elle tomba en léthargie, et il fut assez malhabile pour prendre ce faux repos pour une véritable santé. ... Si cette indolence eût été ménagée, l'assoupissement eût peut-être duré plus longtemps; mais comme le médecin ne le prenoit que pour un doux sommeil, il n'y fit aucun remède. Le mal s'aigrit; la tete s'éveilla; Paris se sentit, il poussa des soupirs; l'on n'en fit point de cas; il tomba en frénésie (GEF, i, pp. 289–90).

As we can see, medical metaphors came quite easily to Retz. His portraits of the main *dramatis personae* of the Fronde also owed much to conventional humoral theory. The four humours were present in the major actors of the Fronde—including the Paris crowd, credited with quasi-personal agency. Individuals' humoral organization formed their 'temperaments' which, again, helped explain their behaviour. Thus Anne of Austria's excess of bile produced a certain 'aigreur' in the cast of her personality, while the indecisive Gaston d'Orléans could be marked out as phlegmatic.17 Choler too was a constant leitmotiv, and, like the other humours, risked producing acts of frenzy and folly when carried to excess. Madness is not the attribute of a particular individual or group in the *Mémoires*, it represents an extreme to which all were prone if their temperament were thus predisposed, and if their humoral imbalance became too extreme. 'La folie entraîne chacun dans un aveuglement', Michel Foucault has noted, 'où il se perd'.[18] This was the case with the Maréchal de La Meilleraie at the height of the crisis of August 1648: 'tout pétri de bile et de contretemps, il se mit en colère jusques à l'emportement et même jusques à la fureur' (GEF, ii, p. 21). The people of Paris was particularly prone to such 'emportements', but so was the royal court, while the *noblesse d'épée* or even that most prosaic of bodies, the *parlement*, could also on occasion be affected by transports of frenzy.[19]

Retz's resort to medical metaphors is more than an unreflective use of a common idiom of political discourse. His humoral analysis links with his insistence on the role of irrationality in human affairs and his finely-attuned concern for psychological analysis.[20] 'Je connoissois le cardinal', he notes disdainfully of Mazarin on one occasion, for example, 'pour un esprit qui n'eût pas pu s'empêcher de croire qu'il n'y eût une arrière-boutique partout où il y avoit de la place pour en bâtir; et c'est presque jeu sûr, avec les hommes de cette humeur' (GEF, iii, p. 211). Retz's perennial enemy, Mazarin, was moreover the key target in one of Retz's most insistent medical themes—namely the contrast between his own politico-medical philosophy and the 'empirical' bent of the 'machiavellian' cardinal minister.

By 'empirical' medicine, Retz's contemporaries understood less medicine informed by experiment and observation, than unlicensed medicine practised by medical irregulars: rather than scientific method, the term denoted the sheerest quackery. An *empirique*, Richelet's dictionary noted, was 'celui qui tient que la médecine ne consiste que dans l'expérience', and it went on to observe, 'On dit aussi *faire l'empirique*, C'est à dire, le charlatan'. Furetière was broadly in agreement: 'Les médecins de la faculté de Paris traitent tous les autres d'Empyriques, de charlatans'.[21] Such practitioners were familiar—if much excoriated and harassed—figures in seventeenth-century Paris, despite the Faculty's best efforts to drive them out. Often haunting the Pont-Neuf—also the major pitch for the sale of *mazarinades*—these figures sometimes set up small stages on which to practise their patter and stagecraft, bedecking their shows with betasselled tumblers, acrobats and assorted zanies. 'Opérateur' was another term used for such individuals—a social type defined as 'Médecin empyrique, charlatan qui vend ses drogues et ses remèdes en public et sur le théatre'.[22]

A representative figure here was the Italian Christophe Contugi, eponymously nicknamed 'L'Orviétan' on account of the 'wonder-drug' he retailed, with its putative virtues as an antidote against poisoning and, it was claimed, plague. Contugi managed to keep at arm's length the Paris medical faculty, which poured scorn on his kind of panacea, and even obtained royal permission to sell his brand of Orvietan, whose secret recipe he jealously guarded. By the late 1640s, he had set up his colourful stall on the Pont-Neuf, and was soon a well-enough-known Parisian figure to appear as himself in one of Molière's plays, and to feature as a character in a number of *mazarinades*: the 1649 pamphlet, *Dialogue de Jodelet de l'Orviatan* [sic] *sur les affaires de ce temps* had him chatting over the problems of the day with the well-known *farceur*, another Parisian stock figure.[23]

The charlatan *empirique* was a figure who cropped up in a number of other pamphlets during the Fronde. In *Le Fidèle Empirique, ou le Puissant Ellébore d'un Anti-Machiavel*, the author offered to 'contenter les malcontents de l'Etat et affermir la liberté des peuples'.[24] More colourfully, in the *Agréable Récit de ce qui s'est passé aux dernières barricades de Paris* (1649), the rhymester-author depicted another denizen of the Pont-Neuf, 'Carmeline l'Opérateur' providing defensive fortifications for the bridge including false teeth, herniary trusses, buckets, ostrich eggs, a stuffed crocodile and other objects of his charlatanesque art.[25] Significantly, the charlatan-cum-empiric was often depicted as an Italian. Contugi was only the most famous of a string of Italian showmen-healers who hawked their own brand of Orvietan and other antidotes and remedies. They were linked in the popular imagination too with Italian theatre troupes and entertainers—indeed, the public exhibitions of medical quacks on the Pont-Neuf owed far more to burlesque farce and the *commedia dell'arte* than to the orthodox Galenic medical philosophy espoused by the Paris medical faculty.

For Retz and for the authors of the *mazarinades*, to brand Mazarin an *empirique* was to associate him with all the vices which French xenophobes had long attributed to Italians. For two hundred years, one medical writer was to note at the end of the seventeenth century, Italy 'a fourni la France de musiciens, de comédiens, de charlatans, de devins, d'astrologues, d'empoisonneurs, de partisans, de banquiers, de favoris, de capitaines'[26]—which was only to omit, of course, hardened machiavellians. In fact machiavellians had a particular point of comparison with empirics, in the attachment of both to secrecy: the *remèdes secrets* of the latter matched the notorious penchant of the former for *secrets* and *remèdes d'Etat*.

Labelling Mazarin an 'empirical' practitioner was putting him on a level with street hawkers wheedling their living from the public, practising without a proper medical (read, political) philosophy, trusting in the violent impact of a single drug and ignoring the general temperament and humoral disposition of the patient. It is amusing and instructive to observe Retz drawing on this panoply of Italianophobe prejudices in his depiction of his arch-rival: Mazarin was a social outcast ('Sa naissance étoit basse et son enfance honteuse'), a rootless condottiere ('Il fut capitaine d'infanterie en Valteline'), a crook ('un escroc'), an inveigler, possibly a homosexual, a crawler and so on— and 'l'original de *Trivelino Principe*', the Harlequin-like figure famous in Italian burlesque theatre (GEF, i, pp. 283–6). Such a list recalled the equally and comprehensively dismissive verses of Scarron in his *Le Passeport et l'adieu de Mazarin* which appeared in 1649:

Adieu donc, pauvre Mazarin,
Adieu mon pauvre Tabarin,
(Tabarin was, like Trivelino, a stock character of burlesque farce.)
...
Adieu peste du carnaval,
Adieu, beau, mais méchant cheval,
...
Adieu, maître des Trivelins
Adieu faiseur de machines
Adieu, cause de nos ruines.[27]

These were themes, moreover, which were repeated and diffused in numerous *mazarinades*. Some authors styled themselves 'Médecin politique' or some similar title, but far more than these were keen to offer medico-political prescriptions.[28] For many, Mazarin was not simply a machiavellian and a Pont-Neuf quack, he was also the poison in the body politic which required an antidote. For Scarron, a 'peste du Carnaval', for Dubosc Montandré, in *Le Nœud de l'affaire* (1651), he was 'ce mal contagieux, la peste mazarine'.[29] Just as with bubonic plague, physicians sought to expel the noxious poisons from within the body, so the physician-statesman should seek to purge this source of pollution from the state so as to restore a pristine purity.[30]

If it was the role of a statesman to offer solutions to ailments in the body politic, then it seemed clear in the *Mémoires*, that Mazarin was part of the problem rather than part of the solution—a disease rather than a healer. Retz accused his arch-rival of spreading the disease he embodied: highlighting Mazarin's trickery ('filoutage') as minister, he noted how this caused the spread of disdain ('le mépris') for the people—'qui est la maladie la plus dangereuse d'un Etat et dont la contagion se répand le plus aisément et le plus promptement du chef dans les membres' (GEF, i, p. 287).

A particular line of contrast which Retz made between himself and Mazarin was precisely over that most machiavellian—and Italian—theme, violence. The latter is often figured in the *Mémoires* as a kind of contagion. With aristocratic hauteur, Retz strongly rejected the 'violent remedies' in which both the nostrum-seller and the machiavellian specialized, and which exuded the spirit of the 'mechanical arts'. In December 1648, he recoiled from using 'le grain de catholicon d'Espagne'—by which he meant military aid from Spanish troops—to fortify the Frondeur cause (GEF, ii, p. 117). 'Catholicon', 'le premier des remèdes purgatifs', had been invoked metaphorically in the *Satire Ménippée* during the League in 1593—Spanish military aid to the Catholic League was compared to this quack-remedy peddled by Spanish charlatans.[31] Violence was always, for Retz, 'jamais qu'un remède empirique' (GEF, ii, p. 269). Hence military aid from Spain, he later noted, should be seen 'comme un remède à nos maux, mais comme un remède que nous convenions d'être dangereux et empirique, [et qui] seroit infailliblement mortel à tous les particuliers, s'il n'étoit au moins un peu passé par l'alambic du Parlement' (GEF, ii, p. 245; cf. ibid., p. 248). The support of the *Parlement*, bastion of order and legality, was thus necessary to convert a popular, empirical medicine, into a worthwhile and appropriate remedy. Support from the *Parlement* was, he told Anne of Austria in July 1651, 'l'unique et souverain remède' (GEF, iii, p. 387). A quick fix, such as the ill-advised use of Spanish military might or (in 1652) the popular purging of hostile elements within the *Parlement*, would cause as much harm as good (Cf. GEF, ii, pp. 275–6).

Retz viewed the projects of Mazarin (and even some of his own allies) as lacking in both legitimacy and likely efficacy. Just as for the physician there was, as the saying went, 'hors la faculté, point de salut', so no durable solution to France's political problems would be found which did not incorporate the Paris *Parlement*, symbol of constitutionality, and, in Retz's almost Montesquieuian words, a 'sage milieu' between 'the licence of kings and the libertinage of peoples' (GEF, i, p. 272).[32] In Retz's political universe, law always has priority over force of arms: and the machiavellian Italian Mazarin lay accused of reversing maxims deeply embedded in French constitutional practice.

Retz thus looked down on both his rival 'médecins politiques' and on the Italian empiric Mazarin for their dangerous belief in one-shot, violent remedies. It was the same kind of disdain that a physician of the Paris medical faculty would reserve for the street-corner huckstering of a Pont-Neuf charlatan. In much the same way, he would also hold, his background and qualities of character put him loftily above those fellow memorialists and historians of the Fronde: these were individuals who wrote for money or influence—'âmes serviles et vénales'—or who lacked the social background to understand high politics—'ces auteurs impertinents qui, étant nés dans la basse-cour et n'ayant jamais passé l'antichambre, se piquent de ne rien ignorer de tout ce qui s'est passé dans le cabinet' (GEF, III, p. 353–4. Cf. iv, pp. 85–6). Retz numbered among those of his contemporaries who felt that it was solely to *les Grands* 'qu'il appartient de raisonner'.[33]

Retz differentiated himself from other 'médecins politiques' too by grounding his programme in a more complete and sagacious medico-political philosophy than such lowly figures could manage. While others could offer only one remedy—the exile of Mazarin— for Retz this step formed merely part of a long and complex recovery plan for France's sorely-taxed 'constitution'. In his *Mémoires*, Retz laid out for his reader the prescription he had urged on the ailing state, based on a diagnostic gaze *sans pareil* and the soundest of medical judgements. The body of the state did not require violent remedies or radical surgery,[34] only a return to the *status quo* ante the health-damaging incursions of the cardinal ministers. What was required was not the incompetence of inexperienced, empirical and 'mechanical' practitioners like Richelieu and Mazarin but the prudence and the expectant medicine of the sage physician. Only the latter had the training in medico-political philosophy to predict as well as to cure ill health: 'un des grands défauts des hommes', he noted in March 1649, 'est qu'ils cherchent presque toujours dans les malheurs qui leur arrivent par leurs fautes des excuses devant que d'y chercher des remèdes; ce qui fait qu'ils y trouvent souvent trop tard les remèdes qu'ils ne cherchent pas d'assez bonne heure' (GEF, ii, p. 383).

Prescience was indeed one of the principal criteria by which this semiologist of the body politic differentiated himself from other 'médecins d'Etat'. The barricades in August 1648 had been utterly unexpected by all but he: 'il est pourtant vrai qu'il n'y avait pas un seul courtisan ni un seul ministre qui n'eût déjà vu des signes infaillibles de la révolution' (GEF, ii, p. 281). Foresightedness and lucidity were, moreover, in short supply at times of political crisis: 'les hommes', he noted, 'ne se sentent pas dans ces sortes de fièvre d'Etat, qui tiennent de la frénésie' (GEF, IV, pp. 307–8). It required a physician-statesman with a thorough experience in the course and complications of diseases and attuned to the potential of the irrational in human affairs:

civil war, he acknowledged in March 1649, 'est une de ces maladies compliquées dans lesquelles le remède que vous destinez pour la guérison d'un symptôme en aigrit quelquefois 3 ou 4 autres' (GEF, ii, p. 395). He knew when 'maladies d'Etat' were reaching their critical point—the term 'révolution' which he used on several occasions had a medical denotation as well as the better-known political and astronomical meanings.[35] In political as in medical revolutions, moreover, only the sagacious and prudent had a sense of the timing which was, he regarded, essential to cure. In politics as in medicine, 'certains moments sont capitaux et décisifs' (GEF, iv, p. 21)—the secret, Retz says elsewhere was 'd'en savoir discerner et prendre les instants' (GEF, iii, p. 425).[36]

A good physician also had the epistemological modesty to accept that certain illnesses were incurable: thus what he calls 'la démangeaison de la négociation' was an irremediable epidemic—a 'maladie populaire'—among the duke of Orleans's party in 1651–2 (GEF, iv, pp. 212, 233). He could do little about this—any more than he could cure 'la peste' of royal courts—flattery, which 'l'infecte toujours au point qu'elle lui cause un délire incurable' (GEF, iii, p. 386). Unlike a medical charlatan, Retz offered no panaceas, and freely acknowledged the role that providence played in human affairs. What he called 'le chapitre des accidents' (GEF, ii, p. 436) could thwart the best-laid plans for recovery. Even—perhaps especially—the good physician knew his limits. Those limits were all the more important in something like the Fronde—'ce corps monstrueux et presque incompréhensible même dans le genre du merveilleux historique' (GEF, iv, p. 131).

For Retz, acting the part of 'médecin politique' during the Fronde, and writing its history after the event were two equally heroic ways of struggling hand-to-hand with this 'corps monstrueux et presque incompréhensible'. The epic dimension of the challenge ruled out petty considerations of success or failure by the normal rules of run-of-the-mill practitioners. He ascribed his behaviour to a certain sublimity—which may be tracked back to his readings of Longinus—and which was, in his eyes, the preserve only of *âmes d'élite* such as his own (GEF, iv, pp. 65, 298).[37] In a passage which Retz is likely to have known, Quintilian states:

> A pilot will wish to bring his ship safe to harbour, but even if he is swept out of his course by a storm, he will not for that reason cease to be a pilot. ... So too the doctor seeks to heal the sick; but if the violence of the disease or the refusal of the patient to obey his regimen or any other circumstance prevent his achieving his

purpose, he will not have fallen short of the ideals of his art, provided he has done everything according to reason.[38]

A remark such as this extends not just to navigation, oratory and medicine, but also, for someone like Retz, to statecraft—that medicine of the body politic. Playing according to the rules of the art might, in the case of medicine, be subjected to merciless satire by a Molière, but it was an essential requirement for all who engaged in these pursuits.

At this point, however, we seem to be reaching the limits of the utility of the medical metaphor as a form of political analysis and action. Retz proved adept, in his *Mémoires*, at using this established political idiom to colour, to persuade, to appeal, and (not least) to blacken the record of his arch-rival Mazarin. It also had a strongly heuristic bent, allowing Retz to uncover, establish and refine what he regarded as key principles of political life and action. Yet medical imagery is only one among a range of metaphorical systems which Retz adopts. Indeed, it is probably not the most heavily-used or most significant form to be found in the *Mémoires*: military and theatrical imagery has a higher profile.[39] Furthermore, Retz the organicist is occasionally crossed by Retz the mechanicist: he could view the state, for example, as a broken-down clock ('horloge') with a disordered mechanism (GEF, ii, p. 203); and if organicist metaphors distinguish his constitutional *prises de vue*, his discussion of tactical and especially party-political matters is rife with mechanicist imagery. The 'bon chef de parti' had to be a mover of wheels and levers rather than a life force.[40]

Though medical, organicist imagery had its uses, therefore, it also had its limitations. A further domain in which this boundary may be detected relates to the social status of the physician in early modern France in general—and in Retz's *Mémoires* in particular. Medical imagery allows Retz to highlight the distance which separated a Paris faculty physician from an Italian quack-cum-adventurer, and to demonstrate his own erudition and science. He also got on well with his own physician Vacherot: the latter, 'homme de mérite et de réputation dans sa profession' (GEF, iv, pp. 458–9) cured him of venereal disorders, looked after him and even suggested ingenious escape plans when his master was in prison, and generally proved a model of fidelity—Retz admitted shedding tears at his death.[41] All the same, a physician was only a physician—and belonged more in the ranks of honoured bourgeois clients than in the entourage of *les Grands*, with whom Retz depicts himself allying, competing and jousting during the Fronde.[42] Retz palpably thrilled to his own phrase, 'Je sors d'une maison illustre en France et ancienne en Italie'—and his hauteur as regards physicians comes clearly into focus in his comment on Fabio Chigi, the future pope Alexander VII: 'sa physionomie était basse', Retz noted, 'et sa mine tenoit beaucoup du médecin, quoiqu'il fût de bonne naissance' (GEF, v, p. 35). The disdain is somewhat breathtaking. It highlights one of the major limitations for a personality like Retz casting himself as a political physician. For a statesman and a writer who had fashioned himself in the spirit of the epics of Antiquity, Plutarch's *Lives* and the romances of *L'Astrée*, he felt more at home as one of Corneille's tragic heroes than as the butt of Molière's satire.

Notes:

1   I would like to thank J.B. Shank, who worked as research assistant on this project, for guiding me around the ARTFL database and for numerous invaluable suggestions.

2   GEF, II, pp. 5–6, A. Feillet, J. Gourdault, R. Chantelauze (eds), *Œuvres du Cardinal de Retz*, 'Grands Ecrivains de France' edn, Paris, 11 vols, 1870–1920, ii, pp. 5–6. Other good editions of Retz's works include M.-T. Hipp & M. Pernot (eds), *Cardinal de Retz. Œuvres*, 'Bibliothèque de la Pléiade', Paris, 1984, and S. Bertière (ed.), *Cardinal de Retz. Mémoires*, 2 vols, Paris, 1987. S. Bertière is also the author of the best current biography of Retz, *La vie du Cardinal de Retz*, Paris, 1990. [Note: in the interests of space, I will wherever possible give volume and page-number references to the 'Grands Ecrivains de France ('GEF') edition in the text rather than in the footnotes.]

3   For *ratures* generally, see A. Bertière, *Le Cardinal de Retz mémorialiste*, Paris, 1977, pp. 532–3. For the example at issue here, see GEF, ii, p. 6, footnote.

4   D.A. Watts, *The Cardinal de Retz. Ambiguities of a Seventeenth-Century Mind*, Oxford, 1980, p. 70. Cf. A. Bertière, *Cardinal de Retz*, esp. pp. 354–64.

5   Cf. R. Cotgrave, *A Dictionarie of the French and English Tongues*, London, 1611, art. 'constitution': 'the constitution, temper, complexion of the bodie'.

6   Cf. R. Mousnier, 'Comment les Français du XVIIe siècle voyaient la constitution', *XVIIe siècle*, 1955 for an interesting discussion of this point. Valuable too in general terms is L. Barkan, *Nature's Work of Art. The human body and the image of the world*, New Haven & London, 1975. For the medieval background, cf. E.H. Kantorowicz, *The King's Two Bodies: a study in medieval political theology*, Princeton, NJ, 1957, esp. pp. 209–10, 218ff.

7   P. Villoy (ed.), *Les Essais de Montaigne*, reprint edn, 2 vols, Paris, 1965, i, p. 682.

8   Cited in M. Fosseyeux, 'La taxe des pauvres au XVIe siècle', *Revue d'histoire de l'Eglise de France*, 1934, p. 410.

9   On this, R. Bonney, *Political Change under Richelieu and Mazarin, 1624–61*, Oxford, 1978; O. Ranum, *The Fronde: a French Revolution, 1648–52*, New York & London, 1993, esp. chapters 1, 2. For political ideas, the key secondary work is E. Thuau, *Raison d'état et pensée politique à l'époque de Richelieu*, Paris, 1966.

10   E. Thuau, *Raison d'état*, pp. 36–7.

11   Cited in ibid., pp. 50–1, 259, 227.

12   Ibid., pp. 196–7 and passim. See too the excellent discussion of these points in F.E. Sutcliffe, *Politique et culture, 1560–1660*, Paris, 1973.

13   Thuau, *Raison d'état*, p. 386.

14   For Scarron, see below, quotation on p. 96. The barb was probably also partly aimed at the complex stage mechanisms which certain charlatans, 'opérateurs' and showmen utilized. For the epistemological and social stakes involved in 'mechanical' accusations, see the excellent discussion in M. Biagioli, *Galileo, courtier: the practice of science in the culture of absolutism*, Chicago & London, 1993, p. 6 and passim. As is noted below, however, Retz himself on occasion used a strongly mechanicist imagery: see page 101.

15 Ibid., p. 60. Cf. H. Carrier, 'Machiavel dans les pamphlets de la Fronde', *Studi francesi*, 12 [special number], 1968.
16 For the *mazarinades*, see two highly different works: H. Carrier, *La Presse de la Fronde (1648–53)*. *Les Mazarinades.I . La Conquête de l'opinion*; *II. Les Hommes du livre*, 2 vols, Geneva, 1989, 1991; and C. Jouhaud, *Mazarinades: la Fronde des mots*, Paris, 1985. There is still a great deal to be gleaned too from the classic C. Moreau, *Bibliographie des mazarinades*, 3 vols, Paris, 1850–1; and see too idem, *Choix des mazarinades*, 2 vols, Paris, 1853. The citation is from *L'Anatomie de la politique du coadjuteur*: see the edition of this in C. Jones, *Contre Retz: sept pamphlets du temps de la Fronde*, Exeter, 1982, p. 28.
17 B. de Mendoza, *Le Cardinal de Retz et ses mémoires. Etude de caractérologie littéraire*, Paris, 1974. This work is far more convincing when it considers Retz in the light of contemporary humoral theory rather than linking it in to twentieth-century psychometrics. Cf. O. Temkin, *Galenism*, Ithaca, New York, 1977.
18 M. Foucault, *Folie et déraison. Histoire de la folie à l'âge classique*, 2nd edn, Paris, 1972, p. 24.
19 For the Parisian crowd, see e.g. GEF, ii, p. 528; for the court, ibid., iv, p. 363; for high nobles, ibid., ii, p. 513 and iv, p.412; for the Paris *Parlement's* impetuosity, ibid., ii, p. 64 (and for the Bordeaux Parlement ibid., iii, p. 59). For Mazarin, cf. ibid., iii, p. 42. On the question of madness, cf. S. Bertière, 'La Fronde: un temps de folie? D'après les *Mémoires* du Cardinal de Retz' in R. Duchesne & P. Rouzeaud (eds), *La Fronde en questions*, Paris, 1989.
20 See Watts, *Cardinal de Retz*, esp. chapter VII, 'Weaklings and heroes'.
21 P. Richelet, *Dictionnaire françois*, Paris, 1680 and A. Furetière, *Dictionnaire universel*, The Hague, 1694. For confirmation on this point, see Cotgrave, *Dictionarie*, art. 'Empyricke'.
22 Furetière, *Dictionnaire*, art. 'Opérateur'.
23 Moreau, *Bibliographie*, no. 1080, reprinted in H. Carrier, *La Fronde. Contestation démocratique et misère paysanne. 52 mazarinades*, 2 vols, Paris, 1982. 'L'Orviétan' also appears in Moreau, *Bibliographie*, nos. 2470 and 3548 and in Molière's *L'Amour Médecin* (1665). Cf. C.S. Le Paulmier, *L'Orviétan. Histoire d'une famille de charlatans du Pont-Neuf aux XVIIe et XVIIIe siècles*, Paris, 1893. For the Pont-Neuf as distribution centre for the *mazarinades*, see Carrier, *La Presse de la Fronde*, i, p. 356 and ii, pp. 177–8. For a fuller exploration of relations between the Paris medical faculty and charlatan-empirics, see L.W.B. Brockliss & C. Jones, *The Medical World of early modern France* (forthcoming).
24 Moreau, *Bibliographie*, no. 1387.
25 Pp. 13–14 (Moreau, *Bibliographie*, no. 56). The pamphlet is reprinted in Carrier, *La Presse de la Fronde*, ii, no. 46.
26 de Vigneul-Marville, *Mélanges d'histoire et de littérature*, 2 vols, Rouen, 1699, 1700, i, p. 43. Retz had to defend himself in his memoirs over the Italian origins of his own family: for how authors of *mazarinades* utilized this, cf. Jones, *Contre Retz*, p. xvii.
27 Moreau, *Bibliographie*, no. 2730.
28 See esp. *Le Médecin politique, ou, Consultation pour la maladie de l'Etat* (1649: Moreau, *Bibliographie*, no. 2438); *Le Médecin politique, qui donne un souverain remède pour guérir la France, malade à l'extrémité* (1652: Moreau, *Bibliographie*, no. 2439). Cf. too *Consultation et ordonnance des médecins de l'Etat pour la purgation de la France malade* (1649: Moreau, *Bibliographie*, no. 780), and the pamphlets beginning *Avis salutaire ...* (Moreau, *Bibliographie*, nos. 345–52).)
29 Carrier, *La Presse de la Fronde*, ii, pp. 59–60. Cf. Moreau, *Bibliographie*, no. 2531.) Two other pamphlets, *L'Antidote pour guérir la France* (1649) and *Le Vin émétique, l'unique antidote et le dernier remède pour les maux dont la France est menacée* (1652) called for Mazarin's exile. (Moreau, *Bibliographie*, nos. 89, 4028. On similar lines, see too nos. 88, 672, 791, 1088, 1392.).
30 It would be interesting and instructive to analyse the *mazarinades* in the light of the perspectives opened up by Mary Douglas' celebrated *Purity and danger*, London, 1966. Some medical recipes took a frankly scatological turn—as with *Le Constipé de la cour avec une prophétie burlesque* (1649) or *Paris débloqué, ou les Passages ouverts, en vers burlesques* (1649)—or became crudely anatomical in other ways—*Le Tempérament amphibologique des testicules de Mazarin, avec sa médecine* (1651), for example. (Ibid., nos. 778, 2692, 3758.)
31 See the comments in footnote 1 in GEF, ii, p. 117.

32 For discussions on this point, cf. C. Jones 'The organisation of conspiracy and revolt in the *Mémoires* of the Cardinal de Retz', *European Studies Review*, 11, 1981. Cf. too GEF, i, pp. 278, 318–19; ii, 102–3; etc.

33 J. Ferrier, *Le Catholique d'Etat*, cited in M. de Certeau, *L'Ecriture de l'histoire*, Paris, 1975, p. 163.

34 On this point, contrast, for example, *Le Point de l'Ovalle, faisant voir que pour remédier promptement aux maladies de l'Estat*, et... (Moreau, *Bibliographie*, no. 2808), p. 4: 'Et sans nous amuser à languir dans les douleurs d'une fièvre-lente, hastons nostre guérison, par un remède qui soit un peu plus violent mais qui soit infaillible', etc ... (Reprinted in Carrier, *La Presse de la Fronde*, i, no. 20).

35 The medical aspect of the term emerges—alongside the cyclical astronomical and political meanings—in the *Dictionnaire de l'Académie française* (1694): 'Révolution d'humeurs, mouvement extraordinaire dans les humeurs, qui altère la santé'.

36 On questions of timing, see esp. GEF, i, p. 164 (where the medical equivalent is particularly evident); ii, pp. 477–8; iii, pp. 84, 424–5; v, pp. 21, 202–3, 211; etc.

37 On the sublime, see the brilliant article of Marc Fumaroli, 'Apprends, ma Confidente, apprends à me connaître'. Les *Mémoires* de Retz et le traité *Du Sublime*', *Versants. Revue suisse des littératures romanes*, 1, 1981.

38 Quintilian, *The Institutio Oratoria*, 4 vols, London, 1921, i, pp. 334–7.

39 D.A. Watts, 'Le Sens des métaphores théâtrales chez le cardinal de Retz et quelques écrivains contemporains', in *Mélanges offerts au professeur René Pintard*, Paris, 1975. See too A. Bertière, *Cardinal de Retz*, pp. 354–64.

40 See esp. GEF, i, p. 152; and for other examples of mechanicist imagery, see GEF, ii, pp. 347–8; iii, pp.186, 316, 343, 460–1; iv, pp. 223, 235, 508, 513; etc.

41 GEF iv, pp. 465, 506–7; S. Bertière, *Vie*, pp. 417, 484, and passim.

42 On the rhetoric of the heroic in the memoirs, see now J. Delon, *Le Cardinal de Retz orateur*, Paris, 1989, esp. pp. 16ff.

CHAPTER EIGHT

The Fouquet–Colbert Rivalry and the 'Revolution' of 1661

RICHARD BONNEY

A work on the theme of ethics and politics in seventeenth-century France can scarcely fail to address the issues of Mazarin's fortune, the legitimacy of the perquisites of office, and (by implication at least) what Cardinal de Retz might have gained in worldly wealth had he achieved his ambitions in 1651–2 and secured the coveted post of chief minister. Would Retz have been able to sustain that 'haughty refusal to accept gifts of money, even when he was in dire financial straits'? Would he not, like Mazarin, have sought to recoup his 'enormous debts'?[1] If not, then what was Retz's motivation for seeking the highest office, and why was his ethical position so different from that of Richelieu or Mazarin?[2] Did any of the politicians of seventeenth-century France have a monopoly of virtue, or were statesmanship and ruthless careerism compatible? When surveying the evidence of ministerial wealth, and comparing it with ministerial statements of selfless service to monarch and country, one is reminded of Retz's comment: 'L'on y trouve des faits si opposés les uns aux autres, qu'ils en sont incroyables; mais l'expérience nous fait connaître que tout ce qui est incroyable n'est pas faux'.[3] This is where the evidence of the Fouquet–Colbert rivalry towards the end of Mazarin's ministry, and the significance of the changes inaugurated by Louis XIV in 1661 are worth reconsideration.

We look in vain for a recent account in the biography of Mazarin;[4] instead, we find a version of events from the prolific pen of Daniel Dessert. For Dessert, the writings of three of the four principal actors—Louis XIV, Fouquet and Colbert—cannot be taken at face value; while the fourth, Mazarin, deliberately obscured the evidence for his own reasons ('dans une certaine mesure, le roi est la dupe de son ministre ...').[5] The evidence of Mazarin's personal fortune at his death—the largest personal fortune created under the *ancien régime*, and on the size of which Dessert focuses much of his argument—

reveals a chief minister 'maître des destinées du royaume [qui] nage dans la plus inexplicable opulence'. Certainly, Mazarin had always sought to promote his personal fortune. Yet, during the Fronde, his first fortune had been shattered: 'Il s'est donc refait à une vitesse stupéfiante, et, dans de telles proportions, qu'on ne peut s'empêcher d'avoir des doutes sur la pureté du miracle'.6 Mazarin's argument, of course, was that his wealth proceeded from the king's generosity; but the insufficiency of this argument was clear from his 'peur panique'— Dessert's description—lest there should be any inventory of his wealth on his death: 'Colbert devra centraliser tous ses papiers sans qu'il y ait inventaire et ne pourra les communiquer à personne, excepté au roi'.7 Colbert was thus made an accessory to any malpractice, but there was no choice in the matter, since from June 1651, when he was recruited from Le Tellier's service, Colbert was Mazarin's *intendant de la maison*: he alone knew the mechanisms by which the fortune of the Cardinal had been rebuilt after the disasters of the Fronde.8 Colbert seems to have commenced his cabal in 1657, during the lifetime of Servien, the finance minister appointed jointly with Fouquet in 1653; but with the death of Servien in February 1659, and the appointment of Fouquet as sole *surintendant des finances*,9 criticism came to the fore. The intrigues of Colbert and Hervart against Fouquet in 1659 were thus a trial run for the *coup* of September 1661: the arrest and trial of the finance minister, the establishment of the *chambre de justice*, the abolition of the *surintendance* and the creation of the *conseil royal des finances*. For Dessert, 'Colbert praticien dément Colbert théoricien': 'Dans ses actes, rien ne le différencie de la conduite des surintendants ... Le combat entre la maxime de l'ordre et celle du désordre n'est plus qu'un artifice pour masquer une ambition dévorante ...'10 Fouquet was thus no more than an archetypal sacrificial victim to affirm the sovereign's authority at the beginning of Louis XIV's personal rule.11 This is a fundamental revision of the traditional interpretation of the reforms of 1661, 'très largement inspirées par Colbert', in which the king's jealousy of Fouquet's ambition, and his desire to bring about institutional changes and to exercise the *métier du roi* are seen as the *primum mobile*.12

Dessert argues that Fouquet was the victim of a 'système fisco-financier de la monarchie en crise'.13 Fouquet's self-justification to Le Tellier after his arrest provides a compelling picture of Mazarin's (lack of) system:14

On ne pouvoit pas avoir d'une règle certaine avec M. le Card[inal] en matière d'argent. Il ne don[n]oit jamais d'ordres précis. Il blasmoit et permettoit. Neantmoins, il désapprouvoit tout. Après que l'on avoit convaincu de l'impossibilité de réussir autrement, il approuvoit tout ...

Fouquet completely failed to comprehend why the 'revolution' of 1661, including his own arrest, was necessary. Had the king wanted his resignation as *surintendant des finances*, he could have had it, since it had been offered. Why was there need for such 'extremitez', when he could have been placed under house arrest in Brittany under the tutelage of La Meilleraye, the lieutenant-general and former finance minister, who was no friend of his? Above all, his ethical self-justification was that of *force majeure*. He had done what had been necessary, and no more:[15]

> Je puis avoir fait des fautes. Je ne m'en excuse pas rien. J'ay fait qu'il a fallu faire et c'est par là que j'ay soustenu les affaires et que je n'aurois peu faire sans cela ...

The problem was Mazarin's lack of system. 'M. le Cardinal ... faisoit recevoir presque le total de l'argent comptant du Royaume pour divers usages', yet the chief minister brought confusion 'dans les formes et le défaut de fournir les décharges à point nommé ...' Above all, the size of Mazarin's personal fortune was Fouquet's best defence:[16]

> il est nottoire que si les deniers sont trouvez au profit et à l'usage particulier de quelqu'un dans le Royaume, c'est au proffit du mesme M. le Cardinal qui s'en est encore trouvé saisy au moment qu'il es[t] mort ...

Against this self-justification, the royal commissioners prosecuting Fouquet attempted to mount a case—dare we call it a 'modern' definition of the distinction between the public and private spheres in financial administration?—that had the minister been prepared to live in an 'honneste parcimonie' he would not have had to steal from the king. The *malversations au fait des finances* of which Fouquet was accused included the charge that he had authorized unnecessary royal borrowing and while *ordonnateur* he had lent the king money. It was claimed that he had made no distinction between his own and the king's money, and had drawn up the royal accounts at his private residence. He was accused of participating in the revenue farms and tax contracts under assumed names and of taking pensions and other illicit payments from tax farmers and tax contractors. (In any case, the former intendant of finance, Le Tellier, admitted in May 1664 that Mazarin himself had done so.)[17] Fouquet was blamed for, and alleged to have profited from, the abuse of treasury bills.

In answer to the argument that a finance minister as *ordonnateur* should never lend personally to the crown, Fouquet replied that he had been asked to do so by Mazarin and the king, and that the interest he had charged for his services was lower than the rate usually charged by financiers who in any case had been unwilling to lend. He specifically denied the allegations concerning participation in the revenue farms and tax contracts. Nor had he taken pensions or other gifts from tax farmers and tax contractors. The attempt to prove from his personal accounts that he had stolen the king's money appears to have broken down, largely because of the way in which the accounts were kept.[18] Personal expenditure of 36.9 million *livres* exceeded income of 35.9 million between February 1653 and August 1661. With disarming frankness, Fouquet accepted that he had been extravagant, but denied the charge of peculation. On the charge of financial maladministration, he stated simply that his objective had been to satisfy Cardinal Mazarin and ensure that there were sufficient revenues to meet royal expenditure. Certainly, much money had been borrowed—this had been his principal task when in office—but the loans were necessary and had been authorized either by Mazarin or by the king. On his deathbed, Mazarin recognized that most of his orders to Colbert concerning his private fortune had been given orally. Yet most of Mazarin's orders to Fouquet had also been given orally. If Fouquet and Colbert disagreed, which, given the inherent rivalry and the long-running conflict between them, they were bound to do, whose version of events would be accepted by the king?[19] There was no written request from Mazarin that Fouquet's word be accepted without question. If the king refused to honour his debts to the finance minister, Fouquet could conceivably have taken civil action for redress against Mazarin during his lifetime. Indeed, he had retained a letter written by the chief minister on 20 October 1659 precisely for this purpose: 'je promets de le faire rembourser par le Roy.'[20] With Mazarin dead, and his probate records covered with a cloak of secrecy and immunity, this course of action was no longer open. Fouquet claimed there were outstanding loans to him of 12 million *livres*.[21] Though it is doubtful whether the prosecution proved the case of corruption, the *chambre de justice* found Fouquet guilty on this charge. On 20 December 1664, his property was ordered to be confiscated, and he was sentenced to exile abroad for life. The crown immediately intervened to convert the punishment of life exile to life imprisonment, 'veu la connaissance particulière qu'il avoit des affaires les plus importantes de l'estat'.[22]

What was the significance of the Fouquet–Colbert rivalry and the 'revolution' of 1661? For Daniel Dessert, 'la forme a très rapidement pris le pas sur le fonds, ce qui a fragilisé un régime qui pensait se fortifier par la manifestation et l'autoproclamation de sa force'. 'Roi justicier et roi solaire', Louis XIV 'ne s'affirme en fait que roi-machine.'[23] From 1662, Louis XIV appropriated the image of the Sun King[24] and such imagery, it has been suggested, was 'obviously incompatible with the mechanical universe of Descartes and Galileo'.[25] In fact, the Copernican revolution led to the multiplication of the number of Suns in the universe, which was conceived as a patchwork of separate regions, each dominated by its own Sun, rather than a single empire loosely ruled by a single emperor. Absolutism and the Copernican Revolution thus co-existed harmoniously in a rearranged universe.[26] There was no contradiction between a *roi-machine* and a *roi soleil*: the one affirmed the other, just as Colbert's programme for the codification of legislation affirmed the principle of undivided legislative sovereignty.[27] Colbert's initiative in both the construction of the king's public image and the codification of legislation suggests a common purpose which Fouquet sorely lacked. Colbert was merely the instrument for the king's advancement; by advancing the king, the minister advanced himself. Fouquet had made a critical mistake by appearing to advance himself before the king's own image had been constructed. Peter Burke writes that 'between about 1655 and 1660 Fouquet virtually replaced the king as the kingdom's leading patron ... Colbert intended to re-establish the king's dominance ...'[28] What was true of the arts was true of politics and financial management. Fouquet's downfall was secured because he could not demonstrate that he advanced the king's service more than he had advanced his own, any more than he could show that he had been specifically authorized by Mazarin to lend money to the crown. That lack of care with his personal papers, which thus fell entirely into the hands of his adversaries,[29] betrays also a lack of political acumen. How should a minister deal with a young king of twenty-three years of age who, given Mazarin's poor health, might at any moment embark on his personal rule? Fouquet never seems remotely to have considered the possibility that the king might wish to rule personally, rather than remaining a figurehead under a continuation of the *ministériat*. Worse, he seems to have been remarkably self-confident that the Lionne–Le Tellier–Fouquet triumvirate would not endure, and that just as Mazarin had displaced Chavigny and Sublet des Noyers in 1643 so he would emerge as chief minister within a few months of the new regime.[30] It therefore mattered not that the king should ask him to surrender his office of *procureur général* at the *Parlement* of Paris, because higher office than this was expected.[31] Because of excessive self-confidence, he was seriously outmanoeuvred by Colbert, who as intendant of finance held the register of expenses and revenues for him between March and September 1661.[32] Certainly, Dessert is correct in arguing that Fouquet was not the originator of the perverse 'système fisco-financier de la monarchie en crise'[33] and that Colbert was vindictive to an extraordinary extent: the future controller-general of finance had much to hide so that the permanent incarceration of the former finance minister was essential if his execution could not be secured. From the point of view of the king, the loyalty of Fouquet in 1652 at the end of the Fronde was forgotten, and what mattered most was the potential rebel who had drafted the *projet de Saint-Mandé* to cover the eventuality of his fall from power. To Louis XIV, Fouquet's plan must have seemed a plan for resurrecting the Fronde.[34] Dessert comments that 'en choisissant Colbert, il n'est pas du tout certain que Louis ait fait le choix le plus judicieux';[35] but Colbert was never foolish enough to draft a document which could lay him open to a charge of *lèse-majesté*. Under Richelieu, there can be little doubt that this sort of evidence would have been sufficient to secure prompt conviction and execution. Fouquet was saved by the scrupulousness of the trial judges, especially Lefèvre d'Ormesson.[36]

The moral of the story is surely that Fouquet was no hero, but his own worst enemy—his ambition, extravagance and above all, his political miscalculations, had contributed to his own downfall.[37] At his trial, Fouquet admitted that he had lacked sufficient 'exactitude et précaution' in keeping the registers of the royal finances.[38] Colbert learnt the lesson and his accounting changes and the dramatic reduction in secret expenditure (*ordonnances de comptant*) were intended to exemplify the personal rule of a king who, as depicted in the imagery of Le Brun, had reformed his finances in 1661.[39] It has recently been argued of the Fronde that 'the failure or success of revolution ought not to be measured by the criterion of permanent change'. 'The fact that millions of peasants and city-dwellers paid substantially lower taxes, or no taxes at all for two or three years', it has been contended, 'must be considered an important revolutionary accomplishment'.[40] 'Revolutions in government' are difficult phenomena to characterize, since it may be argued that government is inherently non-revolutionary. And yet that criterion of permanent change which is absent from the Fronde, it may be argued, is present in the governmental 'revolution' of 1661: the accounting changes and the reduction in secret expenditure were permanent, at least for the lifetime of the king, which proved to be fifty-four years. There was no serious increase in secret expenditure until almost the end of the *ancien régime*.[41] Daniel Dessert argues that 'la monarchie n'a rien gagné à la chute de Fouquet'[42] yet government without a chief minister was a cheaper option than the continuance of Mazarin's system. A change in attitudes arose in 1661, which the similarities between the events in that year and those of 1715, with the fall of Desmaretz, cannot obscure. Desmaretz lost favour under the Regency, but was never prosecuted by the *chambre de justice* of 1716. The move towards more precise accounting under Colbert initiated a growing distinction between public and private, between royal service and private gain. The assets of Fouquet were evaluated at in excess of 15.4 million *livres* at the time of his arrest in 1661. The driving force behind his prosecution, Colbert, certainly acquired a fortune for himself in his long twenty-two-year ministerial career: but it was much smaller than Fouquet's, amounting to less than 6 million *livres* by whichever method the fortune is calculated.[43] The objective evidence of the relative size of the fortunes of the two ministers suggests that the events of 1661 were indeed a turning point in ethical attitudes. Huge though they seem, the perquisites of office and illegal gains of finance ministers were as nothing compared to the 22 million *livres* acquired by Richelieu and the 35–37 million acquired by Mazarin as chief minister. Standards of probity in French public life had to start at the top, and it was one of the permanent achievements of Louis XIV's personal rule drastically to reduce the potential for illicit gain. Law made an enormous fortune under the System but then lost most of it when the System collapsed. After 1720, ministerial gains from office were small beer indeed compared to the situation before 1661. Calonne (1783–7) was considered a corrupt finance minister by the standards of his time; but his gains from office were minuscule in comparison with his predecessors in the first half of the seventeenth century.[44]

Louis XIV is supposed to have said to Fouquet: 'Oui, je vous pardonne ...' The minister claimed after his arrest that 'sa parole doibt avoir quelque effect, donnée à un subject dans un temps de paix, sans contrainte ...'[45] Perhaps by 1661 there was a higher ethical requirement in politics than that a king should keep his word to his minister. The higher requirement was that the minister should keep the king's financial affairs in such good order that no pardon was ever necessary. Fouquet admitted that perhaps what he had done was wrong; certainly it was 'contre l'ordre'. The 'maxim of order' was Colbert's solution, placating the king while at the same time providing for the minister's security in office. Thus it was that Colbert enjoyed the fruits of twenty-two years in office, while his displaced rival suffered three years of imprisonment in Paris until December 1664 and a further fifteen years of incarceration at Pinerolo until his death in March 1680. At the centre of all the attacks against Fouquet we certainly find Colbert; but, crucially, behind Colbert we find the support of Louis XIV. And why? Because Colbert was never a chief minister, nor did he lay any claim to such a post. Louis criticized the 'dérèglement' of Fouquet's ambition, and the attempt to make himself 'l'arbitre souverain de l'Etat'.[46] He did not suspect such ambitions in Colbert; but even if such ambitions were latent, the rapid rise of Louvois acted as a check on them.[47] The balance of ministerial cliques was the norm during the personal rule.[48] The king had learnt that 'singulier paradoxe' of absolutism—Dessert's phrase—that 'ceux-là même qui incarnent parfaitement l'absolutisme, en raison de leur réussite et à cause de leur génie, l'annexent à leur profit et en dérivent finalement les fruits'.[49] If 'le pouvoir n'existe que par et pour celui qui l'exerce par délégation, en son propre nom',[50] then the important thing was to halt such delegation and halt it permanently: 'Sa Majesté a supprimé pour toujours la commission de surintendant de ses finances et toutes les fonctions qui y sont attachées'.[51]

The king did not become at a stroke, by the ruling of 15 September 1661, 'le seul ordonnateur des fonds',[52] since real problems remained with regard to the spending powers of ministers: after Colbert's death, there was almost invariably a conflict of interest between the expenditure plans of the secretary of state for war and his colleague charged with the responsibility for the navy; both might be at odds with the controller-general of finance. Yet, crucially, prior royal authorization to spend had to be secured, while the symbolic abolition of the *surintendance des finances* was only momentarily reversed for John Law in 1720[53] and otherwise remained a permanent change under the *ancien régime*. This was a profound reversal of Mazarin's system under which, in Fouquet's own words, 'M. le Cardinal Mazarin ... estoit le véritable et souverain ordonnateur et consommateur', making use of 25 or 30 million *livres* a year 'comme il vouloit'.[54] One of the 'maximes fondamentales du royaume', that 'le Roy et le conseil soient ordonnateurs des despenses', was at stake in the Fouquet trial, at least in the view of Denis Talon, the royal prosecutor. 'Où sont escrites ces maximes fondamentales du royaume?', Fouquet asked. The king could exercise such powers himself, or he could exercise them by delegation, through a chief minister and a *surintendant des finances*.[55] When pressed by Fouquet to give him better written guarantees, Mazarin had always contended that his powers as *surintendant* and 'les ordres continuels qu'il donnoit et verballem[ent] et par billets escritz' were sufficient.[56] With Mazarin dead, Fouquet's main defence was fifty years' practice by previous *surintendants*.[57] It was precisely this tradition of financial administration, including the burning of the records of the secret expenses (*comptants*),[58] which the 'revolution' of 1661 brought to an end.

BIBLIOGRAPHY

Antoine, M., *Le dur métier du roi. Études sur la civilisation politique de la France d'ancien régime,* Paris, 1986.

Apostolidès, J.-M., *Le roi machine. Spectacle et politique au temps de Louis XIV,* Paris, 1981.

Bergin, J.A., *Cardinal Richelieu. Power and the Pursuit of Wealth,* New Haven and London, 1985.

Bonney, R.J., 'The secret expenses of Richelieu and Mazarin, 1624-1661', *English Historical Review,* 91, 1976, pp. 825–36.

—*The King's Debts. Finance and Politics in France, 1589–1661,* Oxford, 1981.

—*Society and Government in France under Richelieu and Mazarin, 1624–61,* Basingstoke, 1988.

—and Bonney, M.M., *Jean-Roland Malet: premier historien des finances de la monarchie française,* Comité pour l'histoire économique et financière de la France, Paris, 1993.

Bosher, J.F., *French Finances, 1770–1795. From Business to Bureaucracy* , Cambridge, 1970.

Bourgeon, J.-L., *Les Colbert avant Colbert. Destin d'une famille marchande,* Paris, 1973.

Burke, P., *The fabrication of Louis XIV,* New Haven and London, 1992.

Clément, P., *Lettres, instructions et mémoires de Colbert ...,* 10 vols, Paris, 1861–82.

Corvisier, A., *Louvois,* Paris, 1983.

Dessert, D., 'Pouvoir et finance au XVIIe siècle: la fortune de Mazarin', *Revue d'histoire moderne et contemporaine,* 23, 1976, 161–81.

—'L'affaire Fouquet', *L'histoire,* 32, 1981, 39–47.

—*Argent, pouvoir et société au Grand Siècle,* Paris, 1984.

—*Fouquet,* Paris, 1987.

—*1661. La mémoire des siècles. Louis XIV prend le pouvoir. Naissance d'un mythe?,* Brussels, 1989.

Duchêne, R. and Ronzeaud, P. (eds), *La Fronde en questions,* Aix-en-Provence, 1989.

Fouquet, Nicolas, *Les œuvres de Mr Fouquet ministre d'estat contenant son accusation, son procez et ses défenses contre Louis XIV, roy de France,* 16 vols, Paris, 1696.

Goubert, P., *Mazarin,* Paris, 1990.

Harris, R.D., *Necker and the Revolution of 1789*, Lanham, New York, London, 1986.

Hutchinson, K., 'Towards a Political Iconography of the Copernican Revolution', *Astrology, Science and Society. Historical Essays*, ed. P. Curry, Woodbridge, 1987, 95–141.

Mousnier, R.É. (ed.), *Le conseil du roi de Louis XII à la Révolution*, Paris, 1970.

Mousnier, R.É. (ed.), *Un nouveau Colbert. Actes du Colloque pour le tricentenaire de la mort de Colbert*, Paris, 1985.

Ranum, O.A., *The Fronde. A French Revolution, 1648–1652*, New York and London, 1993.

Villain, J., *La fortune de Colbert*, Paris, 1994.

Watts, D.A., *Cardinal de Retz. The ambiguities of a seventeenth-century mind*, Oxford, 1980.

Wolfe, K.W. and Wolfe, P.J. (eds), *Considérations politiques sur la Fronde. La correspondance entre Gabriel Naudé et le Cardinal Mazarin*, Paris–Seattle–Tübingen, 1991.

Notes:

1   Watts (1980), p. 63.
2   Dessert (1976); Bergin (1985).
3   Watts (1980), p. 50.
4   Goubert (1990), p. 434, accepts Dessert's account 'même si Colbert y est fort maltraité — assez justement d'ailleurs'.
5   Dessert (1989), pp. 45, 51–2, 62–3.
6   Ibid., p. 67. On the details of the fortune: ibid., pp. 72–3; Dessert (1976); Dessert (1987), p. 207.
7   Dessert (1989), pp. 69–70.
8   Bonney (1981), p. 229; Wolfe and Wolfe (1991), p. 25 n. 3, on a financial memorandum sent by Colbert to Brühl on 26 Oct. 1651, shortly before his return from exile. Naudé was convinced during the Fronde that Colbert should issue a statement of Mazarin's debts, and the reasons for their having been contracted; but he was unable to secure Colbert's compliance: ibid., p. 78. Dessert (1987), p. 237, stresses the recent acquisitions of wealth by Mazarin. Cf. Dulong, 'Mazarin, ses banquiers et prête-noms', in Duchêne and Ronzeaud (1989), p. 89. For Colbert in Le Tellier's service: Bourgeon (1973), pp. 225–6.
9   Bonney (1981), pp. 255, 286; cf. Dessert (1987), p. 233. Dessert, p. 113, comments: 'La présence équivoque et intéressée du Cardinal, et la surveillance médisante et envieuse de Colbert, qui ne désarme pas, limitent le champ d'action de Fouquet.'
10   Dessert, 'Colbert contre Colbert', in Mousnier (1985), p. 118. Fouquet argued the same at his trial: 'le sieur Colbert en possession de la surintendance des finances qu'il exerce sous un autre titre et pour laquelle il avoit deslors une sy grande passion qu'il y avoit desja donné des atteintes à la mort de Monsieur Servien ...' A[rchives] N[ationales] 144 ap 68 Dr. 2, f. 219.
11   Dessert (1989), p. 94.
12   Antoine, 'Colbert et la révolution de 1661', in Mousnier (1985), p. 105; on the theme in general: Antoine (1986).
13   Dessert (1987), p. 258.
14   B[ritish] L[ibrary] Add. MSS. 39,673, f. 74; Clément (1861–82), vii, pp. 399–401.
15   Ibid.
16   AN 144 ap 69 Dr. 4, f. 239; Fouquet (1696), xiii, p. 69.

17   A[rchives des] A[ffaires] E[trangères, Mémoires et Documents,] France 913, f. 163v–164r: Mazarin 'avoit fait des prêts, et que pour son remboursement il avoit pris des receptes sur lesquelles on luy donnoit des remises comme aux traitans; que Monsieur le Cardinal sousfermoit et donnoit peu de remises et ainsi gagnoit beaucoup'. Fouquet said similar things at his trial: AN 144 ap 60 Dr. 2, f. 38v; ibid. Dr. 3, f. 38.

18   Bonney (1981), p. 268, pp. 322–5.

19   Most damagingly of all, Fouquet claimed at his trial that his loans after Mazarin's death had been registered 'dans le registre de la surintendance tenu par le sieur Colbert. Le Roy l'a veu & leu luy même toutes les semaines ...'

20   Bonney (1981), p. 262; Fouquet (1696), viii, pp. 279, 290. The loan was only for one million *livres* for four months.

21   BL Add. MSS. 39,673, f. 77. He claimed that he had loaned 'environ 20 millions en six mois' at 10 per cent interest between the death of Mazarin and his arrest: Fouquet (1696), viii, pp. 297–8.

22   Bonney (1981), p. 269; Fouquet (1696), vii, pp. 271, 273.

23   Dessert (1989), p. 137.

24   Apostolidès (1981), p. 47.

25   Burke (1992), p. 130.

26   Hutchinson (1987), p. 108. The author is grateful to Dr Alex Keller for this reference.

27   Boulet-Sautel, 'Colbert et la législation', in Mousnier (1985), p. 123.

28   Burke (1992), pp. 49–50.

29   Dessert (1987), p. 242.

30   He claimed precedence over Le Tellier and Lionne as 'le premier en rang comme estant le plus ancien conseiller d'estat et le plus ancien dans la qualité de ministre': Fouquet (1696), xi, p. 136.

31   Bonney (1981), p. 265; Dessert (1987), p. 240. The evidence for the expectation of higher office is clear from Fouquet himself, who recalled Mazarin's deathbed words: 'j'avois beaucoup de connoissance de la justice & des finances par mes charges, mais qu'il estoit obligé de dire à Sa Majesté de plus, que j'estois capable de luy donner de très bons conseils sur tous les autres affaires de l'estat, de quelque nature qu'elles fussent.' Fouquet (1696), xi, p. 134. Less favourable words are reported in Bonney (1981), pp. 262–3.

32   Bonney (1981), pp. 261–2; Fouquet (1696), xi, p. 136.

33   Dessert (1987), p. 258: 'Nicolas n'est pas responsable de ce système vicié. Il n'a fait que le gérer au mieux, étant données les circonstances ...' But could Fouquet prove this?

34   Bonney (1981), p. 271; Dessert (1987), pp. 354–64, reproduces the *projet de Saint-Mandé* but is extremely generous to Fouquet in diminishing its importance: ibid., pp. 241, 254–5. Evidence of his earlier loyalty in 1648–52 is clear: Bonney (1981), p. 20 n. 2.

35   Bonney (1981), p. 342.

36   Ibid. pp. 268 n. 1, 269 n. 8.

37   Ibid. p. 269.

38   Ibid. p. 268.

39   Cover illustration to Bonney and Bonney (1993); ibid., p. 37, p. 41, for the accounting changes. For the secret expenses: Bonney (1976); Bonney (1981), p. 309.

40   Ranum (1993), p. 345.

41   Bosher (1970), pp. 119, 194; Harris (1986), pp. 745–7.

42   Dessert (1987), p. 343.

43   Bonney (1981), p. 181, pp. 324–5; Meyer, 'Louis XIV et Colbert ...', in Mousnier (1983), p. 73 n. 6 quotes the erroneous figure of some 10 million; Dessert (1981), 40; Dessert (1987), pp. 152, 348–53. Villain (1994), pp. 322, 334, 336, corrects all earlier interpretations, and provides various estimates of 4.95, 5.8 and 5.75 million. Louvois gained a fortune of some 8 million in a career spanning some twenty years (1672-91). Bullion, Richelieu's finance minister (1632-40), gained a fortune of 7.8 million in just eight years in office.

44   Since the fortunes of finance ministers in the eighteenth century await investigation the received wisdom could yet be revised.

45   Bonney (1981), p. 263 n. 2; BL Add. MSS. 39,673, f. 75v.

46   Quoted by Dessert (1987), p. 11; ibid., p. 12, Dessert dismisses this statement as 'pour une grande part composé et inspiré par un canevas préparé par Colbert'.

47   Corvisier (1983).

48 Engrand, 'Clients du roi. Les Colbert et l'Etat, 1661–1715', in Mousnier (1985), pp. 85–97; Bérenger, 'Charles Colbert, marquis de Croissy', in Mousnier (1970), p. 173.
49 Dessert (1989), p. 45.
50 Ibid. p. 46.
51 *Règlement* of 15 Sept. 1661: Clément (1861–82), ii, pt i, p. 749; Bonney (1988), p. 77; AN E 1713, f. 173; AAE France 911, f. 166.
52 Antoine (1986), p. 43.
53 Bonney (1981), pp. 286–7.
54 Fouquet (1696), v, pp. 148, 165, 196.
55 AN 144 ap 69 Dr. 4, fos 253v–254v; Fouquet (1696), xiii, pp. 89–90.
56 AN 144 ap 69 Dr. 4, fos 348v; Fouquet (1696), xiii, pp. 241–2.
57 AN 144 ap 69 Dr. 4, fos 257-8; Fouquet (1696), xiii, p. 95.
58 Fouquet denied that he had practised this: AN 144 ap Dr. 4, fos 258–9; Fouquet (1696), xiii, p. 96.

CHAPTER NINE

Crescit ut aspicitur
Condé and the Reinterpretation of Heroism, 1650–1662

MARK BANNISTER

The 'fabrication' of Louis XIV—the creation of an image of the monarch as the very incarnation of the state and its *gloire* through painting, sculpture, medals, literature and public spectacles—has been the subject of much scholarly analysis in recent years.[1] For the most part, the analysis has concentrated on the period from 1661 onwards when Louis emerged very clearly as the major force in the process, but in fact the ideological groundwork had been laid throughout the 1650s, from the point when Louis de Bourbon, le Grand Condé, had been identified by Mazarin as the chief enemy of the concept of monarchy that was emerging from the Fronde. Condé's role and position within the state and his public image were such that, if the monarchy were to impose its authority through a redefined relationship between state and subject, it was essential that he be brought into line. The 1650s therefore saw an effort on the part of the servants of the crown to reduce him to the appropriate position in the national consciousness.

A major factor contributing to Condé's place in that consciousness was his enormous reputation as a military leader. As a result of his series of outstanding victories over the Spanish and Imperial forces from Rocroi (1643) to Lens (1648), he had become the living embodiment of the concept of heroism which so fascinated the French mind in the 1630s and 1640s. Playwrights and novelists presented military heroes who prized above all their moral independence and who pursued personal *gloire* even while fighting on behalf of their king; extraordinarily charismatic, they could inspire their troops to recover from seemingly the most desperate positions and displayed the qualities of both general and foot-soldier at the same time. Condé's military style, a mixture of careful assessment of the enemy's strengths and weaknesses and a flamboyant willingness to take risks, was the perfect expression in real life of the literary ideal, much more so than the prudence and tactical correctness of a Turenne. In particular, the *topos* of *capitaine et soldat en même temps* fitted him perfectly and the panegyrists had no difficulty in depicting him as the new Alexander, driven ever onward by the thirst for *gloire*. One of their favourite images of him was the eagle, soaring majestically above the rest of the world, solitary in his outstanding *vertu*, though the whole range of homeric similes had been used by the time the victory at Lens had been celebrated.[2]

It was not, however, Condé's heroic status alone that made him a threat to the ideology of the centralized monarchy. As *premier prince du sang*, he was the senior member of the *noblesse d'épée* outside the immediate royal family and consequently focused the aspirations of the hundreds of nobles who based their claim to a privileged position on service to the state associated with a centuries-old right to moral autonomy within the law. As Governor of Burgundy and Bresse, he illustrated the principle that the provinces of the kingdom were governed by *les grands* on behalf of the king whose interests, it was argued, coincided with theirs. Charismatic, strong-willed, independent of mind, noble in every sense of the word, he was the incarnation of the old aristocratic values which had always sat uneasily with the concept of subservience to a king and he was inevitably a prime target when it came to a confrontation between old and new in the Fronde. If the king were to be the focus of the aspirations of all orders in the state, all *gloire* had to attach to him and only by reflection to those who had served him; all government had to be understood to be under his direct control. During the years of the Fronde and of his exile, therefore, the systematic reinterpretation of Condé's reputation and the radical redefinition of his role within the state were priorities for the crown.

The questioning of the nature of Condé's heroism in fact began as a result of his own actions in the year following the outbreak of the parliamentary Fronde. His support for the royal cause at that time was dictated not by any sympathy for Mazarin, with whom he had been at loggerheads since the beginning of his military career, but by a conviction that the demands of the *Parlement* represented a threat to his own status within the aristocratic structure. His haughty and sarcastic manner alienated the parliamentary delegates during the conference of Saint-Germain in September 1648 and the mass of the population in and around Paris gained first-hand experience of what military heroism meant in human terms when he used the royal troops to blockade Paris in 1649. The Parisians saw themselves putting up a heroic resistance to the tyranny of Mazarin and therefore inevitably identified Condé with that tyranny, though their attitude towards him combined respect, which was totally lacking as regards Mazarin, with puzzlement that he could treat loyal Frenchmen in such a way. Many of the *mazarinades* urged him to abandon Mazarin in order to save his *gloire*, preferably retiring to distant battlefields to fight the foreign enemy.[3] For some, eager to spread accounts of the atrocities the great 'hero' had allegedly committed in the countryside around Paris, it was already too late to salvage his reputation, and the history of the Condé family was held up as evidence of his natural propensity towards ambition and greed.[4]

When Condé showed his opposition to Mazarin openly and was consequently imprisoned, his heroic status became a major political issue. The *Lettre du roy* which provided the court's justification for arresting him set out to show that the external manifestations of glory were no guarantee of genuine heroic virtue. Motivation was all-important. Condé was driven by ambition and greed, it was again argued, and approached all his military ventures with the primary aim of increasing his own power and wealth, loyalty and *générosité* being largely a mask: 'il a fait voir clairement que le bien de nostre service n'a iamais eu en son intention que la moindre part dans les actions de guerre qu'il a entreprises'.[5] The argument was developed in supporting pamphlets. Lionne asserted that Condé's victories had dazzled many people but that those who were capable of looking beyond the surface could see 'que l'esprit qui le portoit dedans les batailles n'estoit pas le vray genie de la pure generosité, & qu'il y avoit beaucoup d'interest & beaucoup d'ambition meslez parmy son courage. ... Il a servy l'Estat & son Roy, mais son premier motif estoit de se servir soy-mesme.'[6] In the face of such a blatant attempt to deny Condé's heroic status, his supporters could only reassert the purity of his motives and hope that their readers still believed in the sublimity of human endeavour. Those who accuse Condé of self-interest are capable of operating only at the level of machiavellian cynicism, they claimed: 'Pernicieuse façon de raisonner & de laquelle si on se sert, il n'y a point de belles actions qui ne reçoivent des interprétations dangereuses'.[7] Let the world consider his great deeds: 'Et puis l'on iugera par là si Condé qui avoit arboré les trophées de son Roy, gravé ses lys & planté si loing ses estandars, auroit eu l'ame si lasche & si effeminé, pour loger chez luy un Demon si pernicieux, que le monstre dont [sic] il est accusé d'avoir produit au iour'.[8]

The civil war of 1652 was essentially fought out around the same conflicting views of the role of the morally independent aristocrat within the state. Condé's propagandists constantly stressed the fact that the king's power was limited by the *lois fondamentales* which ensured that that power could only be used for the good of the state. A vital check was the royal council made up of the *princes du sang*: 'Le Roy ne peut rien faire sans conseil; ce conseil ne doit estre composé que de ses Princes, ou de ceux qui y sont appellés par leur participation'.[9] Each prince had his networks of authority and influence which allowed him to administer parts of the country on behalf of the king and Condé certainly assumed he had the right to sign treaties with foreign monarchs in his own name.[10] To Mazarin, any form of government that did not depend entirely on the decisions of one person was a republic with all the overtones that the word carried of the regicide and oligarchic rule seen in England: 'M. le Prince ... n'a jamais souhaité autre chose, pour exercer une entière autorité sans aucun obstacle, que réduire le ministériat en république, comme il l'est à présent'.[11]

The events of early July 1652 reveal in microcosm the nature of the confrontation between the two ideological positions. Condé's exploits at the battle of the Faubourg Saint-Antoine were presented by his supporters as further evidence of the sublime heroism of which he was capable, general and soldier *à la fois*, exposing his life for the good of the people, and many who were not partisans of his were prepared to admire the man and his deeds. After the massacre of the Hôtel de Ville two days later, it was apparent to all who had any doubts about the Prince's motives that the kind of régime he claimed to be fighting for—aristocratic but with popular support and a largely figurehead monarch—would not bring the order and discipline they longed for above all else.

With the king's authority restored and the Parlement stripped of most of its traditional functions, Condé became the object of an exercise designed to show the correct relationship between the monarch and the aristocracy. In 1654, he was tried for treason *in absentia*: many of the charges concerned actions that implied the usurpation of the king's sovereignty such as the receiving of homage and the granting of commissions and it was felt to be so important that the nobles should digest the message that they must not presume to exercise power in their own right that the *Maître des cérémonies*, Sainctot, was sent to the houses of all the *ducs*, *pairs* and *maréchaux* who had failed to present themselves at the *Parlement* to summon them to the trial. Condé was stripped of all his honours, privileges and functions within the state and condemned to death.

At the same time, the process of building up the myth of the king as a quasi-divine figure, maintaining the state by virtue of his superhuman qualities, began to get under way. Although it was to symbolize Louis's entire reign after his assumption of personal power, the image of him as the sun dispelling the dank mists of discord and dispensing its warmth and energy to the earth and the other planets surrounding it had actually been used since his majority in 1651.[12] In 1653, Louis danced in the *ballet de la nuit* as the rising sun, symbolizing his victory over the Fronde. Three years later, his *devise* in the *carrousel* held at the Palais Cardinal was *ne piu ne pari*, none greater nor equal, with again the *emblème* of the sun, 'à quoy l'on compare iustement nostre grand Monarque, qui n'a rien au dessus de luy, & qui n'a pas son pareil en excellence'. Equally significant was the fact that two of the nobles who took part, the marquis de Soyecourt and the marquis de Mancini, wore *emblèmes* and *devises* showing the eagle, the classic symbol of Condé's heroic greatness, in a subordinate position to the sun: 'Con mirar illustra: cet Aigle represente une personne que la naissance & le merite approchent du Soleil de l'Estat, dont les rayons le rendent encor plus illustre, aussitost qu'il le regarde'.[13]

The development of a teleological interpretation of history stressing Louis's role as the major figure ensuring that the destiny of both himself and France was fulfilled was also evident. In 1654, when the royal authority was barely re-established, the *prévot des marchands* had already commissioned a statue of 'Louis XIV terrassant la Fronde', showing the boy king with his foot on the head of a subjugated rebel.[14] He was credited with having insisted that his coronation should take place against the advice of his counsellors who feared the danger from his enemies,[15] and the triumphal arches erected for the occasion in Rheims stressed the voluntary submission of his people who considered themselves fortunate to be able to submit to his authority.[16] In 1656, Puget de la Serre, who only five years earlier had been praising Condé in the most extravagant manner and comparing his career to that of Alexander the Great, published his *Panegyrique de Louis quatorziesme* in which the history of the previous fifteen years is reinterpreted on the assumption that Louis had been aware of his destiny since early childhood and had been personally responsible in some undefined way for the sequence of victories from Rocroi to Lens. None of his generals is mentioned by name. After his coronation, we are told, his personal military career began, revealing his extraordinary aptitude for the heroic conduct of a battle, which apparently justified the *topoi* and comparisons with Alexander previously attached to Condé.[17]

While he was in exile, Condé's reputation inevitably faded as the king became the sole focus of the nation's identity. The other members of his family and many of his supporters had accepted an amnesty and were certainly not inclined to sing his praises in public.

The official *Gazette* made only a very occasional reference to his having attended some function in Brussels: otherwise he was eclipsed from the public consciousness. In June 1658, the *Gazette* mentioned Condé in its reports on the Battle of the Dunes, in which he was seen to have thrown himself into a virtually impossible situation with his customary *fougue*, only in negative terms: his horse was killed beneath him, he was almost taken prisoner, he was forced to withdraw and his army fled in disarray. Turenne, on the other hand, was 'comme l'ame de toutes ces belles Actions', sure in the knowledge that he was near 'un Roy, dont la presence rend presque tousjours les bons succez inséparables de la justice de ses Armes'.[18] In the quasi-official *Relations de guerre*, La Mesnardière likewise reduces the role of Condé to that of merely another Spanish commander, defeated after so many victories, 'non sans deplaisir de se voir battu par des Armes dont il eprouve le pouvoir avec douleur, & qu'il pourroit encore commander avec gloire'.[19]

From July 1656, negotiations were held in Madrid over a possible peace-treaty between France and Spain and the terms on which Condé would be received back into the good graces of the French king formed one of the major sticking-points. Mazarin was determined that Condé should be made to symbolize the new order in which all subjects, however elevated their status in the hierarchy, were seen to be qualitatively different from the monarch and had no right to any function or power within the mechanisms of state except in so far as the king chose to require service of them. The King of Spain, on the other hand, pressed on behalf of Condé for the complete restitution of his *charges* and appointments, that is, in effect for the recognition of the quasi-hereditary basis that Condé had always claimed for his governorships and other offices.[20] So great was Mazarin's determination that it was eventually he who won at the cost of a few minor concessions. Article 79 of the Treaty of the Pyrenees, written in the cardinal's own hand, declares that Condé has expressed his great sorrow at having worked against the interests of his sovereign and that, if Louis will only restore him to his favour, he will serve him with inviolable fidelity:

> il ne pretend rien en la conclusion de cette paix, pour tous les interests qu'il y peut avoir, que de la seule bonté et du propre mouvement dudit Sgr. Roy son Souverain Seigneur; et desire mesme qu'il plaise à S. Mté. de disposer pleinement et selon son bon plaisir en la manière qu'Elle voudra de tous les dedommagemens que le Sgr. Roy Catholique voudra luy accorder, ... qu'il remet tout aux pieds de S. Mté.

In subsequent articles, it is made clear that Louis in his magnanimity will forgive Condé, allow him back into France, restore his privileges as *premier prince du sang* and deign to grant him the governorship of Burgundy and Bresse with some other offices. When Louis and Condé met for the first time since the Fronde, it was in private at Aix-en-Provence, but judicious 'leaks' let it be known that Condé had knelt humbly before his sovereign. The moral and political autonomy of the individual, however heroic, was no longer legitimate.

Though Condé was welcomed back to the kingdom by his peers, it is clear that none of them saw him as anything more than a leading subject.[21] During the time of his exile, the national ethos had changed so rapidly that any reappearance of the exaltation of Condé's heroism would have seemed like a revolutionary attempt to return to the chaos of the Fronde. His admirers were reduced either to making no reference to the previous ten years or to adopting positions of extraordinary ingenuity. Caillière, for instance, explains that destiny required that France should unite with Spain through a royal marriage. If Condé had continued to fight for France, Spain could only have ended as a humiliated vassal. It was therefore necessary for him to be used to balance the two nations' forces more evenly for a time and now that the union with Spain has been brought about, Louis, who was aware of the divine plan and realizes that Condé has fulfilled his role, is happy to welcome him back.[22]

Nor was Condé allowed to avoid being involved in the process of royal mythogenesis. He was required to take part in functions at which his status as a servant of the monarch, albeit an honoured one, was stressed. In particular, the *carrousel* of 5–6 June 1662 was used to show how Louis had imposed himself on the aristocracy. The king himself led the *quadrille des romains*, the largest and most magnificent of the five *quadrilles*; he wore as his *emblème* the sun dissipating the clouds and the ten knights supporting him each had an *emblème* and *devise* on the theme of the sun and its power over the earth, e.g. a sundial exposed to the sun ('sans toi je ne suis rien') or a lion looking at the sun ('de tes regards vient mon ardeur'). Condé led the third *quadrille*, the Turks, certainly a warlike nation but still the enemies of christendom, and appropriately had the crescent as his *emblème* with the accompanying *devise: crescit ut aspicitur*, 'il augmente selon qu'il est regardé'. Perrault's commentary in the sumptuous official record of the occasion makes clear for the benefit of posterity the significance of this choice: 'Comme le Croissant augmente de plus en plus en lumière selon qu'il est regardé du Soleil, ainsi le Prince qui le prend pour sa Devise veut faire entendre que tenant du Roy toutes ses grandeurs & tout son éclat, il reconnoit que sa gloire augmentera à proportion des regards favorables qu'il recevra de sa Majesté'.[23] The rest of Condé's life was to be lived on those terms.

The *réinsertion* of Condé and the reinterpretation of his heroism as no more than an exemplary manifestation of the model of service required of all subjects was a political necessity for the monarchy if it was to impose the idea that the king was qualitatively different from all other human beings. It was to be some years before the general adulation of Louis reached the level offered by Bauderon de Sénécé:

> Ce que le Soleil est dans l'Univers, le Roy l'est dans son Royaume; tous deux sont les images visibles de Dieu & ses Lieutenants sur Terre; tous deux contiennent les perfections réunies de toutes les Creatures; tous deux ont une puissance indéfinie & indépendante de tout autre que de leur Createur.[24]

However, the treatment of Condé and, equally significant, his voluntary submission to it represented an important move in that direction. At the same time, the process was reinforced by the important ethical change taking place in France, the re-evaluation of human nature, particularly in terms of the role of free-will. Panegyrists were to claim that Louis had changed the character of the French: 'Dans le mesme pays & sous les mesmes visages on trouve d'autres hommes; Il s'est fait une Revolution morale, un changement de l'esprit, un passage doux & agreable du mal au bien'. For François Faure, the change was entirely for the better: 'les François ne sont plus inconstans, mal disciplinez, ni emportez, comme l'estoient leurs Peres'.[25] He was right in his observation of the change but the conclusion drawn by Antoine Adam is arguably more accurate:

> C'est la vieille France, austère, stoycienne, libérale, qui a été vaincue. Une France nouvelle apparaît, plus vive sans doute et plus riante, mais moins forte et moins fière, moins défendue contre les périls de la tyrannie.[26]

It was not that Louis had forced the French into a different ethical mould: rather, he was able to benefit from the major changes taking place.

In the years immediately preceding the Fronde, when Condé's military triumphs were admired as manifestations of the sublimity of personal endeavour, the expression of *gloire* in its purest form, the belief in the moral autonomy of the individual and the power of the will which had its roots in the stoicism of earlier decades was already declining rapidly. By the time Condé returned from exile, the role played in human behaviour by the passions, now viewed as essentially irrational and perhaps even uncontrollable forces, was beginning to be widely recognized and the moral ideal was no longer the heroic individual who imposed himself on the world around but the *honnête homme* who showed self-restraint in the interests of social harmony and thought more about the sensibilities of others than about the effect he himself was making. Condé's great deeds were remembered and respected, certainly, but, as a moral being, he had to take his place in a new world in which he rejoined the mass of his fellow-men and looked up to a monarch who had gathered all heroic qualities unto himself.

Notes:

1   See especially N. Ferrier-Caverivière, *L'Image de Louis XIV dans la littérature française*, Paris, 1981; J. Apostolidès, *Le Roi-machine: spectacle et politique au temps de Louis XIV*, Paris, 1981; P. Burke, *The Fabrication of Louis XIV*, New Haven and London, 1992.
2   For attempts at the epic style, see particularly Chapelain, *Ode pour Monseigneur le Duc d'Anguien*, Paris, 1646, and Louis Le Laboureur, *Les Victoires de Monseigneur le Duc d'Anguyen*, Paris, 1647.
3   See e.g. Brousse, *Lettre d'un religieux envoyée à Monseigneur le Prince de Condé*, Paris 1649; *Au Prince du sang, surnommé la cuirasse* (s.l.n.d.); *Très-humble remonstrance d'un gentihomme bourguignon à Monseigneur le Prince*, Paris, 1649; *Lettre du chevalier Georges de Paris à Monseigneur le Prince de Condé*, Paris, 1649.
4   See, e.g. *Les Impietez sanglantes du Prince de Condé* (s.l.n.d.); Portail, *Discours sur la deputation du Parlement à Mr le Prince de Condé* (s.l.n.d.); *L'Ouy-dire de la cour* (s.l.n.d.).
5   *Lettre du Roy sur la detention des Princes de Condé et de Conty et duc de Longueville*, Paris, 1650, p.8.
6   Lionne, *Discours et considerations politiques et morales sur la prison des princes de Condé, Condy et duc de Longueville*, Paris, 1650, p.8.
7   *Lettre de Monsieur Brun, ambassadeur pour sa Majesté Catholique en Hollande, envoyée à Messieurs du Parlement de Paris*, The Hague, 1650, p. 5.
8   *Lettre de Monseigneur le Prince de Condé à Messieurs de Paris*, Paris, 1650, p. 5.
9   Dubosc-Montandré, *La Decadence visible de la royauté, reconnue par cinq marques infaillibles*, s.l., 1652, p. 7.
10   The first of these, signed in Madrid on Condé's behalf, was dated 15th February 1651 when Condé had barely emerged from prison.
11   M. Ravenel (ed.), *Lettres du Cardinal Mazarin à la reine, à la princesse palatine, etc. écrites pendant sa retraite hors de France en 1651 et 1652*, Paris, 1836, p. 71.
12   See *Imagines regiae et heroicae* (s.l.n.d.), seemingly published in January 1652, and François de Bretaigne, *Le Roy mineur ou panegyrique sur la personne et l'éducation de Louis XIV*, Paris, 1651.   A later edition of this latter work, presumably pirated since it gives no details of the author's name or the place and date of publication, contains an added section attacking the queen mother and praising Condé.
13   Gissey, *Les Emblesmes et devises du Roy, des Princes et des Seigneurs qui l'accompagnerent en la cavalcate royale et course de bague que sa Majesté fit au Palais Cardinal 1656*, Paris, 1657.
14   This statue is now built into the wall of the château at Chantilly.
15   Cériziers, *L'Année françoise ou la premiere campagne de Louis XIV*, Paris, 1658, p. 22.
16   N. Lescalopier, *Douze tableaux du Roy Tres-chrestien Louis XIV Auguste*, Paris, 1655.
17   Puget de la Serre, *Panegyrique de Louis Quatorziesme Roy de France et de Navarre* (s.l.n.d.). The date of publication, 1656, can be assumed from the point at which the account of Louis's career stops.
18   *Recueil des gazettes nouvelles ordinaires et eztraordinaires, relations et recits des choses avenues tant en ce royaume qu'ailleurs pendant l'année mil six cent cinquante-huit*, Paris, 1659, pp. 573-84.

19 La Mesnardière, *Relations de guerre, contenant... le siege de Dunkercke en l'année 1658*, Paris, 1662, p. 208.

20 The best illustration of Condé's view of the quasi-hereditary rights he enjoyed is the short note he sent to Mazarin when his brother-in-law, the Amiral de France, was killed at Orbitello: '...vous saves qu'il n'avoit rien de plus proche que mon fils et que c'est son seul heritier. ...ie m'asseure que vous aures la bonté de demander ses charges et gouvernements pour moy et pour mon fils.' (Musée Condé, Chantilly, MS 1539, J IV, 28th June 1646).

21 The Condé archives contain more than two hundred letters welcoming him back in early 1660.

22 Caillière, *Lettre heroique sur le retour de Monseigneur le Prince*, Saint-Lô, 1660.

23 Charles Perrault, *Courses de testes et de bague faites par le Roy et par les princes et seigneurs de sa cour en l'année MDCLXII*, Paris , 1670, p. 44.

24 Bauderon de Sénécé, *L'Apollon françois*, Mâcon, 1684, pp. 385-86.

25 François Faure, *Louis le Grand. Panegyrique*, Paris, 1680, p. 104.

26 *Histoire de la littérature française au XVIIe siècle*, 5 vols., Paris, 1948-56, II, 400.

CHAPTER TEN

Love, Marriage and a Disputed Sentence in *La Princesse de Clèves*

JOHN CAMPBELL

La Princesse de Clèves is a short novel about a young woman who, after the death of her husband, continues to reject the only man she has passionately loved. These bald facts have been controversial for three centuries. Discussion has naturally focused on the motives and behaviour not just of the heroine but also of her mother, since it was Mme de Chartres who provided her daughter's moral education. The heart of the matter is both women's attitudes to love and marriage. We seek to know why Mme de Clèves acted in the apparently wayward manner that she did, and to what degree her mother was responsible. It cannot be the province of a short paper to attempt to resolve complex ethical issues which have engendered myriad persuasive interpretations. This article will consider a single sentence, what Roger Duchêne calls 'la fameuse phrase de Mme de Chartres'.[1] It concerns the mother's reaction to the interest shown in her daughter by the Prince de Clèves: 'elle ne craignit point de donner à sa fille un mari qu'elle ne pût aimer'.[2]

If this sentence is 'famous', it is because it is both central to the ethical debate yet notoriously ambiguous. As so often in *La Princesse de Clèves*, its structure owes nothing to the supposed classical virtues of clarity and simplicity. This tortuousness may well be, in Cave's words, 'part of the expressive means by which the reader is led through the psychological labyrinth'.[3] Subordinate to the negative verb *craindre*, itself in the negative, is a verb clause containing an indirect object and a direct object qualified by a relative clause with an incompletely negated verb, *pouvoir*, in the subjunctive. Two crucial ambiguities present themselves. The first relates to the negative *craindre* and Mme de Chartres's lack of worry. Is the mother unconcerned by the fact that her daughter is embarking on a marriage without love, or is she (like any caring mother) happy that with a husband such as Clèves this loveless eventuality is not something she need fear? A second ambiguity concerns the interpretation of the term *aimer*. Does this indicate *amour/passion* or *amour/amitié*?

These ambiguities are reflected in the variety of ways the sentence has been interpreted. Hirsch speaks of its 'ambiguous negative constructions' and the 'ambivalence' of the mother, and Scott of 'the textually ambiguous nature of the mother's response'.[4] Stewart asks whether the information we are given about Mme de Chartres means 'that she failed to exercise proper caution, or that she was confident her daughter would come to love Clèves, or that she thought it didn't matter?'[5] It should be said that many critics express no doubts as to the meaning of the phrase. Unfortunately, they differ in their certainties. Some see the sentence as further evidence of the mother's repressive role, of what Charron calls a 'lavage de cerveau' or Bérouti, more clinically, sees as 'une vigilance surmoïque répressive sur les désirs de sa fille'?[6] An example is Niderst: 'Au fond, c'est Mme de Chartres la première responsable des malheurs où ce couple sera plongé. Mme de Lafayette veut-elle simplement nous dire qu'un mariage sans amour est toujours condamné?'[7] Venesoen views the phrase as proving the 'mauvaise foi' of a mother who had earlier told her daughter that happiness for a woman was in a loving relationship with a husband.[8] For Vigée, the sentence is unambiguous proof of the narrator's disapproval of the mother: 'on ne saurait être plus clair'.[9] Opposed to these views hostile to Mme de Chartres we can set the recent discussion of the sentence reported in *Littératures Classiques*. Here Mme de Chartres is absolved from the desire to starve her daughter of love, as can be seen from Duchêne's reading of the sentence: 'elle donna sa fille à M. de Clèves sans crainte, persuadée qu'il était possible que sa fille se mette à l'aimer'.[10] In this debate the disagreement is over the meaning of *aimer*.

In recording such critical reactions it seems fair to mention the dog that didn't bark. The most common reaction to 'la fameuse phrase' has been silence. Translations have, as they must, kept the reader's options open.[11] In annotated editions of *La Princesse de Clèves*, some loaded to the gunwales with glosses, there is no attempt to clarify the sentence.[12] More curiously, perhaps, many articles specifically dealing with Mme de Chartres and her ethic make no mention of this phrase's ambiguities and the disagreements it has occasioned.[13]

Our interpretation of the sentence will obviously influence to some degree our understanding of the ethical basis of Mme de Chartres's actions, and thus of her daughter's silent submission. In the context, only the context can help us. The phrase occurs after Clèves has managed to talk to Mademoiselle de Chartres about his love for her, and has sought to know what her feelings are for him.

> Elle rendit compte à sa mère de cette conversation, et Madame de Chartres lui dit qu'il y avait tant de grandeur et de bonnes qualités

dans Monsieur de Clèves et qu'il faisait paraître tant de sagesse pour son âge que, si elle sentait son inclination portée à l'épouser, elle y consentirait avec joie. Mademoiselle de Chartres répondit qu'elle lui remarquait les mêmes bonnes qualités; qu'elle l'épouserait même avec moins de répugnance qu'un autre, mais qu'elle n'avait aucune inclination particulière pour sa personne.

Dès le lendemain, ce prince fit parler à Madame de Chartres; elle reçut la proposition qu'on lui faisait et elle ne craignit point de donner à sa fille un mari qu'elle ne pût aimer en lui donnant le Prince de Clèves.

The first interpretation of *craindre* has Mme de Chartres locking her daughter unhesitatingly into a loveless marriage.[14] The contextual basis for this reading is that Mme de Chartres, who has earlier praised married love and shown her distaste for the sexual adventures common at Court, has agreed to this marriage even though her daughter has clearly shown she is not in love with Clèves. The mother therefore seems to be placing her daughter into a situation which would not be recommended by her own rules.[15] This sentence, indeed, has been quoted as evidence that Mme de Chartres was glad that her daughter had taken on board her lessons about the dangers of falling in love.[16] This seeming insensitivity to the affairs of the heart seems to be compounded by Clèves's insistence, fully reported by daughter to mother, that the young woman he loves must also love him, and that he would be 'éternellement malheureux si elle n'obéissait que par devoir aux volontés de madame sa mère'.[17] A further item on the charge-sheet is that the mother is using marriage for social ends: 'Mme de Chartres, qui était extrêmement glorieuse, ne trouvait presque rien digne de sa fille' (p. 15). She has already tried to arrange a socially advantageous marriage for her daughter. One failed attempt provides some insight into her motivation: 'le dépit qu'elle eut lui fit penser à trouver un parti pour sa fille, qui la mît au-dessus de ceux qui se croyaient au-dessus d'elle' (p. 25). For many this has been evidence enough to convict Mme de Chartres of acting without any regard for her daughter's feelings. It is unsurprising that this apparent indifference should colour their reading of the sentence at issue.

This interpretation is enticing. It has, however, the disadvantage of overlooking other important pieces of evidence. First, if Mme de Chartres does seem to act as though marriage was primarily a social contract, she is behaving no differently from any other member of Court society. The historical sources exploited in *La Princesse de Clèves* provide its author with a wealth of material all indicating to what extent marriage in this society is viewed essentially as a social or political bargaining counter (e.g. pp. 9–10). These matrimonial arrangements are not highlighted as something outlandish. The irrelevance of love to marriage is a natural part of the social fabric.

Having said this, Mme de Chartres *is* paradoxically different from her peers, if only because, however conscious of the social dimension of marriage, she does stress the importance of a loving married relationship. One of the fundamentals in the education she dispenses is that her daughter should 's'attacher à ce qui seul peut faire le bonheur d'une femme, qui est d'aimer son mari et d'en être aimée' (p. 15). The solemn and absolute nature of the language hardly suggests a throwaway line or a rule which such a prudent and principled mother would lightly forget. This is emphasized, in the passage from which our sentence is taken, when Mme de Chartres, impressed both by the rank and character of Clèves, asks her daughter 'si elle sentait son inclination portée à l'épouser'. There is no evidence, in the novel, of such solicitousness on the part of any other parent, nor any evidence at all that Mme de Chartres, stung by previous failures, acts in 'haste and near-panic'.[18] This suggests a much more sympathetic reading of the sentence at issue. It is true that Mlle de Chartres declares that she has no feelings one way or the other. But it is reasonable to suppose that the 'bonnes qualités' she had noticed in her suitor, and the absence of negative reaction to him, constitute fertile enough ground for her mother not to worry that love couldn't develop. An important element in the sentence is the subjunctive *pût* rather than the possible *pouvait*. Mme de Chartres is dealing not with fact but with hypothesis.[19] At the moment of the proposal no fear crosses her mind (and thus the past historic *ne craignit point*) that she is giving away her daughter to the *type* of husband whom she wouldn't be able to love, 'un mari qu'elle ne pût aimer'. In the context, this reading of *craindre* seems by far the more plausible of the two.

That leaves the interpretation of what exactly is meant by *aimer*. The uncertainty here carries over from the initial ambiguity of the mother's exhortation to her daughter 'd'aimer son mari et d'en être aimée'.[20] Is Mme de Chartres now happy to see her daughter married to a man with whom she could fall passionately in love? Or does she hope for the development of respectful affection, what Biet calls 'un amour tranquille'?[21] Could the mother be ready for either, or any amalgam of the two? For Duchêne, Mme de Chartres believes the prospective husband is 'digne d'être aimé et capable de susciter de l'amour'. Biet on the other hand maintains that this 'phrase difficile' means that the mother 'donne sa fille au duc de Clèves, et sa fille, au cours du temps, pourra développer un amour tranquille pour lui, mais elle ne pourra pas l'aimer passionnellement'.[22]

The 'passionate' reading of *aimer* is based to some extent on the fact that Mme de Chartres knows, from the very tenor of phrases such as 'éternellement malheureux' that Clèves has used, that he is deeply and violently in love. If she accepts this situation, in defiance of a traditional moral teaching which tried to exclude passion from husband–wife relations, surely she would be willing to accept similar concupiscence from her daughter?23 In Leblanc's words, Mme de Chartres 'espère ... que la vertu du prince et la force de sa passion viendront à bout de la froideur de sa fille'.24

Once again, however, this interpretation of *aimer* comes hard against a wall of evidence, constituted to a large extent by the openly anti-sexual nature of Mme de Chartres's general discourse on love. Between the initial education she dispenses (pp. 14–15), and the chilling death-bed speech on the dangers of passionate love (p. 66), the mother charts the dangerous territory of love. On her bleak *Carte du Tendre*, all manifestations of passion are marked as regions to be avoided by the traveller. Unlike other mothers, Mme de Chartres was not afraid to talk about love, nor did she pretend it was unpleasant. However, this rhetoric served only to show what the appearance of pleasure concealed:

> elle lui montrait ce qu'il y a d'agréable pour la persuader plus aisément sur ce qu'elle lui en apprenait de dangereux; elle lui contait le peu de sincérité des hommes, leurs tromperies et leur infidélité, les malheurs domestiques où plongent les engagements.

The charm of love is seen as a trick, as an allurement, involving hypocrisy and deception, and leading inevitably to unhappiness. The absolute nature of *hommes* leaves little room for optimism.

Crucially, the teaching on love is given in the context of a desire to instil *vertu*. The meaning Mme de Chartres gives to this term is much more limited than its definition as 'une habitude de l'âme, qui la porte à faire le bien, et à fuir le mal' (*Dictionnaire de l'Académie*). This *vertu* will allow her daughter to avoid the dangers of sexual relationships, the treachery of the male lover and the breakdown of conjugal life occasioned by love affairs. Mme de Chartres's ideal is the *tranquillité* of what she calls the *honnête femme*, which 'se dit proprement d'une femme et d'une fille qui sont chastes et vertueuses' (Richelet). From this it can be inferred that she sees the institution of marriage as offering her daughter some protection from the assaults of passion.25 Married love is a means, not an end. The end is *vertu*, as the full context of that other much-quoted phrase shows:

> Elle lui faisait voir aussi combien il était difficile de conserver cette
> vertu, que par une extrême défiance de soi-même et par un grand
> soin de s'attacher à ce qui seul peut faire le bonheur d'une femme,
> qui est d'aimer son mari et d'en être aimée.

Mme de Chartres is thus naturally unperturbed when, after the
wedding, she sees that her daughter has remained impervious to
passion, even to passion for her lawfully-wedded husband. The
relationship is to be cemented by other means:

> elle n'admirait pas moins que son cœur ne fût point touché, et
> d'autant plus qu'elle voyait bien que le prince de Clèves ne l'avait
> pas touchée, non plus que les autres. Cela fut cause qu'elle prit de
> grands soins de l'attacher à son mari et de lui faire comprendre ce
> qu'elle devait à l'inclination qu'il avait eue pour elle avant que de la
> connaître et à la passion qu'il lui avait témoignée (p. 35).

It seems difficult to imagine that a woman with such an anti-passion
streak wanted her daughter to fall in love with any man, husband or
no. The sense of *amour-amitié*, suggested here in 'l'attacher à son
mari', points us to the more likely reading of *aimer* in our sentence.[26]

   This understanding of Mme de Chartres's attitude towards her
daughter may seem to bring us back somewhere near the beginning, to
what Delacomptée calls 'une exigence de frigidité sous peine de
sacrilège'.[27] This is to assume that romantic, sexual love is of its
essence 'a good thing'. No such assumption is made in *La Princesse
de Clèves*. On the contrary, it could be argued that Mme de Chartres's
bleak vision of human sexuality is that of the novel as a whole. It is
important to recognize that the idea of passionate love as a blind and
potentially destructive force exists independently of Mme de
Chartres's morality or her daughter's personal experience. It cannot
coexist with a calm, rational relationship built on mutual respect and
affection. Marriage is an act of the will, but in *La Princesse de Clèves*
passion blows where it wills: 'on n'est pas amoureux par sa volonté'
(p. 138). The whole novel shows the absolute incompatibility of
passionate love and marriage. Indeed, Clèves's disorientation springs
from his failure to understand this basic map-reference, as the
repeated opposition between *mari* and *amant* testifies: 'Pour être son
mari, il ne laissait pas d'être son amant' (p. 35), 'J'ai tout ensemble la
jalousie d'un mari et celle d'un amant' (p. 164). It is not only the
'fameuse phrase' but the whole experience of the novel which surfaces
in Mme de Clèves's question to Nemours: 'les hommes conservent-ils
de la passion dans ces engagements éternels?' (p. 256).
   A plausible interpretation of the sentence thus presents itself: Mme
de Chartres has no fear that her daughter will not be able to have a

relationship of respect and affection with a husband possessed of such good qualities as Clèves. In the light of this reading, Mme de Chartres, for so long condemned as the very model of the repressive mother, might reasonably demand a retrial. Some of the condemnations of her ethical perspective seem rooted in a reading of text or context which is open to challenge, and which perhaps springs from a disapproval predicated upon modern expectations of love and marriage.

This is not to pretend that the interpretation of the sentence given here is any more than a hypothesis. Nor does it do away with the fundamental difficulties the sentence presents, if only because these few words point to behaviour which is itself shot through with contradictions. We might ask, for example, how Mme de Chartres could have begun with a coolly rational assessment of the incompatibility of passion and marriage and then given her daughter to a man passionately in love. This leads us to the paradox at the heart of the daughter's education: the cultivation not just of *vertu*, but of *esprit* and *beauté*. A young woman is encouraged to be virtuous and yet asked to frequent and even grace the occasion of sin. On her deathbed Mme de Chartres declares that nothing in life is worse than 'les malheurs d'une galanterie' and tells her daughter to leave Court (p. 66). She is indubitably sincere. Yet she it is who has striven to place Mme de Clèves in a society where *galanterie* is not only accepted but expected. In the words of La Rochefoucauld, 'La plupart des honnêtes femmes sont des trésors cachés, qui ne sont en sûreté que parce qu'on ne les cherche pas'.[28] Even before Nemours bursts onto the scene, many at Court are attracted by the very physical, intellectual and moral qualities which the mother has so assiduously cultivated for this particular milieu (p. 36). She is of course ready to protect her daughter: 'Mme de Chartres, qui avait eu tant d'application pour inspirer la vertu à sa fille, ne discontinua pas de prendre les mêmes soins dans un lieu où ils étaient si nécessaires et où il y avait tant d'exemples si dangereux' (p. 22). This is tantamount to housing her in a sexual *poudrière* while thinking it enough to provide a fire service. After the mother's death, there is no-one to man the pumps. To give her daughter to an emotionally volatile husband, for one who preaches married *tranquillité*, is therefore to continue the contradictory path already begun. If there is to be an indictment of the mother's ethic, it must begin with these fatal contradictions.

La Princesse de Clèves is, famously, a novel of appearances and paradoxes. This one sentence has presented some of them. The various attempts to decipher it remain a salutary warning of the perils involved in any monolithic interpretation of this enigmatic work, be it as a religious fable or as a story of moral conditioning and sexual repression. That a single sentence can pose so many questions shows the difficulty of reaching conclusions on the larger ethical issues raised by the novel as a whole. Is this one of the reasons for its enduring appeal?

Notes:

1   See C. Biet, 'Droit et fiction: la représentation du mariage', *Littératures Classiques (supplément)*, 12, 1990, pp. 33–49. Duchêne's comment comes in the discussion following this paper, pp. 49–54 (p. 52).

2   The edition used is Mme de Lafayette, *La Princesse de Clèves*, Paris: Livre de Poche, 1974. The passage, quoted later, from which this sentence is taken, occurs on pp. 31–32. Other page-references will be given in parenthesis after the appropriate quotation.

3   Mme de Lafayette, *The 'Princesse de Clèves' with the 'Princesse de Montpensier' and the 'Comtesse de Tende'*, translated and ed. T. Cave, Oxford: Oxford University Press, 1992, 'Introduction', p. xxviii. Note the radically different point of view expressed by J. Garapon, *La Princesse de Clèves*, Paris: Hatier, 1988, p. 73, for whom the typically complex, heavy sentence-structure in the novel 'souligne le goût de la romancière, et de l'héroïne, pour la clarté'.

4   M. Hirsch, 'A Mother's Discourse: Incorporation and Repetition in *La Princesse de Clèves*', *Yale French Studies*, 62, 1983, pp. 67–87 (p. 75); J. Scott, Mme de Lafayette: *La Princesse de Clèves*, London: Grant and Cutler, 1983, pp. 55–56.

5   P. Stewart *Re-readings: eight early French novels*, Birmingham, Alabama: Summa, 1984, p. 80.

6   J. Charron, 'Mme de Clèves ou la création d'une non-femme', in *Actes de Davis*, ed. C. Abraham, Paris–Seattle–Tübingen: PFSCL, 1988, pp. 47–53 (p. 47); R. Bérouti, 'Douleur narcissique et douleur du narcissisme. L'amour ... dans *La Princesse de Clèves*', *Revue française de psychanalyse*, 50, 1986, pp. 749–773 (p. 757).

7   A. Niderst, '*La Princesse de Clèves*: le roman paradoxal', Paris: Larousse, 1973, p. 91.

8   C. Venesoen, *Etudes sur la littérature féminine au XVIIe siècle*, Birmingham, Alabama: Summa, 1990, p. 107.

9   C. Vigée, '*La Princesse de Clèves* et la tradition du refus', *Critique*, 16, 1960, pp. 723–754 (p. 729).

10   See note 1 above.

11   For example, by R. Burns, London: Penguin, 1992, p. 39: 'not fearing that, in giving her daughter to the Prince de Clèves, she was giving her to a man whom she could not love'; Compare Cave, p. 20: 'She accepted it, and was troubled by no fear that she was giving her daughter, in the Prince of Clèves, a husband whom she could not love.' Cave, in a note on the sentence, points to its 'sinister undertones' (p. 208).

12   In twelve editions consulted, published between 1946 and 1990. Adam, in his edition of *La Princesse de Clèves* in *Romanciers du XVIe siècle*, Paris: Gallimard, Pléiade, 1958, does once speak of an ambiguous sentence, but it concerns the identity of the king (note 1, p. 1479).

13   For example, G. Forestier, 'Mme de Chartres, personnage-clé de *La Princesse de Clèves*', *Lettres Romanes*, 34, 1980, pp. 67–76 (p. 69), merely quotes the sentence along with Niderst's judgement on Mme de Chartres's culpability (see note 6); D. Haase-Dubosc, 'La filiation maternelle et la femme-sujet au 17e siècle: Lecture plurielle de *La Princesse de Clèves*', *Romanic Review*, 1987, pp. 432–60 (p. 448), while declaring that Mme de Chartres 'impose à sa fille sa volonté', does not refer to the sentence itself.

14   For this sense of *craindre* with *de* and the infinitive, see Littré ('hésiter, ne pas oser'), who quotes Bossuet: 'Ne craignons pas de parler en cette circonstance.'

15   The suggestion of M. Greenberg, *Subjectivity and Subjugation in Seventeenth–Century Drama and Prose*, Cambridge: Cambridge University Press, 1992, p. 190.

16   Charron, p. 48.

17   This seems to be badly misconstrued by Haase-Dubosc, for whom (p. 448) 'le prince de Clèves comprend très bien que si Mlle de Chartres l'épouse, c'est qu'elle "n'obéissait que par devoir aux volontés de madame sa mère" '.

18 As suggested by J. Todd, 'The Power of Confession: The Ideology of Love in *La Princesse de Clèves*', in *An Inimitable Example: the Case for the 'Princesse de Clèves'*, ed. by P. Henry, Washington: Catholic University of America Press, 1992, pp. 225–34 (p. 230).

19 For this use of the subjunctive, see M. Grevisse, *Le Bon Usage*, Gembloux: Duculot, 1975, section 1013b. Note in particular the example given from Boileau's *Art Poétique*: 'Faites choix d'un censeur ... / Que la raison conduise.'

20 M. Moriarty, 'Discourse and the body in *La Princesse de Clèves*', *Paragraph*, 10, 1987, pp. 65–86 (p. 73): 'The language of love is here ambiguous. No doubt by "aimer son mari" Mme de Chartres means a different kind of love from the "amour" here referred to, but it is crucial, indeed perhaps tragic, that the same signifier covers both kinds of feeling, because of the possibility of conflicting interpretations of an apparently shared value.'

21 Biet, p. 52.

22 See A. Cantillon, *La Princesse de Clèves*, Paris: Nathan, 1989, p. 22: 'Le seul bonheur possible étant d'aimer son mari, il faut épouser quelqu'un que l'on puisse aimer un jour, dont le mérite puisse susciter l'estime, et les bons procédés la reconnaissance.'

23 Biet, p. 44: 'Cette morale, élaborée par les théologiens, enseignée par les directeurs de conscience et traduite en de nombreux catéchismes, exclut formellement la passion des relations entre époux: aimer sa femme de passion, c'est commettre le péché d'adultère.' Note that the evidence presented by Biet contradicts the point of view of W. Leiner, 'La Princesse et le directeur de conscience. Création romanesque et prédication', in *La Pensée Religieuse*, ed. M. Tietz and V. Kapp, Tübingen, Biblio 17, 1984, pp. 45–68 (p. 51), who sees Bourdaloue and the author of *La Princesse de Clèves* in agreement 'pour considérer le mariage comme le résultat d'une passion qui explique et rend légitime l'amour à l'intérieur du mariage.'

24 P. Leblanc, 'Le bonheur conjugal d'après *La Princesse de Clèves*', in *Mélanges d'Histoire Littéraire (XVIe-XVIIe siècles) offerts à Raymond Lebègue*, Paris: Nizet, 1969, pp. 293–303 (p. 296).

25 See Hirsch, p. 75: 'I would suggest that the marital *amour* Mme de Chartres has in mind could naturally grow out of the Princess's feelings of "respect" and "gratitude"; its function is not to disturb or move her in any way, but to guard her against the danger of extramarital affairs.'

26 This would rule out of court the remark by W. Goode, 'A Mother's Goals in *La Princesse de Clèves*', *Neophilologus*, 56, 1972, pp. 398-406 (p. 398): (quoting the sentence) 'The irony in the use of the verb *pouvoir* in this statement is obvious; one has no control over whom one loves, as later events will prove.'

27 J-M. Delacomptée, 'Rivalités amoureuses et pouvoir politique dans *La Princesse de Clèves*', *Stanford French Review*, 12, 1988, pp. 205–230 (p. 227).

28 La Rochefoucauld, *Maximes et Mémoires*, Paris: Union Générale d'Editions, 1964, maxim no. 368. For a recent and very reliable exposition of this writer's thought, see Derek Watts, *La Rochefoucauld, 'Maximes et réflexions diverses'*, Glasgow: Glasgow French and German Publications, 1993.

CHAPTER ELEVEN

Marie de Villars: A Political Woman?

WENDY PERKINS

In October 1679 Marie de Gigault de Bellefonds, marquise de Villars, left Paris to join her husband, Pierre de Villars, who in May of that year had taken up the post of *ambassadeur ordinaire* to the court of Carlos II in Madrid. Her position automatically conferred on her the title of *ambassadrice*. A collection of her letters, first published in 1759, is headed *Lettres de Madame la marquise de Villars, Ambassadrice en Espagne*, and, as is clear from an allusion in the opening letter to 'les autres Ambassadrices', she accepted this designation and used it when mentioning women of the same status.[1] The function of ambassador had two main elements, namely gathering often sensitive information to be relayed to the king, and conducting negotiations; a third, seemingly trivial but in fact equally crucial task was to fulfil 'tous les actes de la politesse internationale'.[2] For this delicate and complex job, he received briefing instructions from the king, but little training, while the ambassadress had even less preparation: it was assumed she would be engaged mainly in running the ambassadorial home and in hosting or attending social events. Tradition notwithstanding, it seems reasonable to ask whether she might sometimes have performed political duties, in the strictest sense of the term, and to examine the extent to which social tasks had a political value.

In general, women had long been held unsuited to politics. Deemed by nature fickle, indiscreet, incapable of sustained—indeed any—thought, they were considered by definition devoid of the qualities essential to affairs of state. In France, opportunities to wield political power at the highest level were particularly limited for women, since under salic law, they could not inherit the throne. Nevertheless, despite theories about their abilities and strictures concerning their 'natural' role as executive head of a household, many women in fact, at all levels of society, were involved in political activity, especially in protests over the imposition from the centre of new laws or taxes.[3] Moreover, thinking about what constitutes history generally, and therefore also political history, together with the use of new or neglected sources and new ways of looking at known sources by historians of women, have tended to open up significant areas for investigation and suggest that women were not unimportant as historical actors.[4] The worlds of the court and international diplomacy are obvious 'arenas' in which aristocratic women might have had a real political role and the letters of Mme de Villars are an invaluable document in the assessment of that role at one particular, rather difficult, historical moment.

Like many women of her time, she owed her status, in some degree, to a man. Pierre de Villars had entered diplomacy by one of the conventional routes, that is to say he belonged to the old nobility and had been a soldier.[5] In 1670 he had been appointed *ambassadeur extraordinaire* to the Spanish court on the occasion of the birth of Louis XIV's second son, and then *ambassadeur ordinaire* from April 1671 to November 1673. He then served as *ambassadeur ordinaire* at the court of Savoy from May 1676 to January 1679. His appointment to Madrid in that year was therefore his third and testifies to his skill and to the trust which Louis XIV put in him. He owed his advancement, therefore, to his own abilities, but also in part to Marie de Villars. Though neither wealthy nor of particularly illustrious birth, both were members of a small, privileged elite. Mme de Villars was, from 1671, an intimate—probably the most intimate—friend of Mme de Sévigné, whose correspondence indeed offers insight into the nature of Marie de Villars's immediate circle. She appears to have been close to Charlotte Ladvocat, marquise de Vins, whose sister Catherine was the wife of Pomponne.[6] It is not inconceivable that this association was helpful to Villars, since Pomponne seems to have become a kind of protector to him after the death of Lyonne. Marie de Villars was clearly a strong personality in her own right: to a comment in his *Mémoires* that 'Elle était salée, plaisante, méchante' (II, p. 744), Saint-Simon, in the *Addition au Journal de Dangeau*, appends the description: 'Une petite bonne femme sèche, vive, méchante comme un serpent, de l'esprit comme un démon' (II, p. 1136). Pierre de Villars was appointed ambassador at a critical juncture in French–Spanish relations. To seal the Treaty of Nijmegen, Louis XIV's niece, Marie-Louise d'Orléans, was married on 31 August 1679 to Carlos II. This event coincided with the death of Don Juan d'Autriche, Carlos's illegitimate brother, who had, to all intents and purposes, been ruling Spain. A genuine political opportunity thus presented itself, and France might have hoped to use Marie-Louise to bring a degree at least of influence to bear on Carlos as far as foreign policy was concerned, exploiting their union to effect a French–Spanish alliance. In France, Mme de Villars had had no political role in the narrowest sense of that term and as she herself writes 'je n'étois pas ... connue, et considérée au Palais Royal' (p. 121). In Madrid she had immediate and undeniably high status, since she was of the same nationality as the queen. This article will argue that, perhaps because of the particular circumstances pertaining at the time, she also fulfilled an important political function.

The *Lettres de Madame la Marquise de Villars* is a collection of thirty-seven surviving letters to Madame de Coulanges, written between November 1679 and May 1681. A major theme in the correspondence is the political dimension of both the queen's life and Mme de Villars's own role as *ambassadrice* at the Court. It is regularly punctuated with expressions of her desire for a greater degree of detachment from Marie-Louise,[7] but there existed in fact a strong bond between these two women, even if not of their own making. They had both, after all, been thrust into an unfamiliar and unwelcoming environment, with Spain, highly aware of France's increasing, and its own waning, power in Europe, obsessed with French intentions in the Low Countries. Mme de Villars was not without diplomatic experience by 1679, but her time in Savoy, at the court of the regent Marie-Jeanne de Nemours, duchesse de Savoie, whose father, Charles-Amédée de Savoie, duc de Nemours, Pierre de Villars had served as *gentilhomme* much earlier in his career, was quite different from, and cannot have prepared her for, the court of Carlos II. As for Marie-Louise, she was unlikely to have received any real preparation at all for her role: indeed, Mme de Villars's political duties and comments arise out of the position in which Marie-Louise was placed.

The exact degree of political significance to be attached to the letters seems at first difficult to determine, as they are marked by very pronounced parallel discourses, being sometimes cautious, sometimes outspoken and critical. The correspondence as a whole might be said in a sense to reflect both the ambiguity and the elusive character of diplomacy itself. On the one hand, for example, it would appear that Mme de Villars was what might be called a 'natural diplomat'. The letters never take less than seriously the importance of respecting a country's attitudes and observing the 'manières et ... cérémonies ... depuis les moindres choses jusques aux plus importantes' (pp. 8–9). This general philosophy stems from a recognition, based on experience perhaps, that in many instances an appropriate word or gesture demands little effort, while the political ramifications of neglecting an act of courtesy are enormous. Of a journey beyond the city gates, for example, the second letter states:

Il faut soigneusement tirer tous les rideaux du carosse dans la Ville, autrement on passeroit pour n'être pas honnête femme, et par tout pays il seroit fâcheux de se décrier pour un si petit sujet (pp. 11–12).[8]

Her own willingness to conform, so crucial to establishing and maintaining good relations with the Court of Spain, is made explicit in a comment that 'je sçais bien comme il faut louer, et donner des avis à propos, quand je me trouve dans l'occasion de le faire' (p. 113). Whether natural or acquired,[9] this understanding of how important was a kind of social flexibility in court and thus political life, is put into practice from the first occasion on which she was introduced to the royal family and its entourage:

On m'avoit fait donner une Almoade [a kind of 'carreau']. Je m'assis seulement un instant pour obéir, et je pris aussitôt une légere occasion de me tenir debout, parce que je vis beaucoup de Senoras de Honor qui n'étoient point assises, et que je crus leur faire plaisir d'être comme elles (pp. 26–7).[10]

In this and other passages, the correspondence demonstrates a more or less unquestioning commitment on Mme de Villars's part to this major aspect of her role. It is allied to an acute political awareness. At first, admittedly, this quality is obscured by expressions of self-effacement and extreme caution, which are not always easy to comprehend given her experience. Statements in the first letter such as 'Je n'ai pas eu le courage d'aller à Burgos' (p. 6) or 'Je n'ai pas encore voulu recevoir de visites' (p. 8), culminate with the exclamation in the second: 'Que j'appréhende de m'habiller, et de commencer à sortir! Je ne suis point du tout née pour représenter' (p. 15).[11] In addition, prudence manifests itself in her attention to the etiquette which dictates that no-one see the queen before her entrée: 'Je n'ai pas même voulu aller à l'Eglise, où l'on peut la voir d'une tribune, de peur qu'on ne m'accusât de trop d'empressement' (pp. 20–21). In one form or another this sentiment becomes a refrain in the correspondence: one of her reasons for wishing that she be permitted to attend the queen less often is, for example, that 'je voudrois me mettre entièrement hors de portée d'aucun soupçon' (p. 51). Moreover, the letters also request Mme de Coulanges to exercise caution, Letter IV concluding with the words: 'Je ne pense point, quand tout le monde verroit ceci, que je pusse en recevoir ni reproche ni blâme. Cependant, usez-en avec prudence' (p. 35). Similarly, Mme de Villars professes herself alive to the limitations on her writing as far as 'high' politics are concerned in the statement '...je suis toujours sur mes gardes pour ne rien écrire qui vise aux affaires d'Etat' (p. 109); she also professes care in dealing with other diplomats in this observation about the marquis de Grana's attempts to draw her into discussion about the Spanish Court: 'Pour moi, Madame, vous croyez bien que je n'entre dans aucun de ces détails' (p. 119), and even claims to know little about things in any case: 'Voilà tout ce que vous sçaurez des affaires d'Etat. Je n'en sais guère davantage' (pp. 84–5).

No doubt to some extent allusions to her own ineptitude, lack of knowledge and, in effect, her relatively minor political status are rhetorical statements demanded by conventional modesty, and it is not impossible that some are delivered tongue-in-cheek. They surely also point to a considerable degree of political alertness and intelligence. Her observations, for instance, about the inadvisability of discussing certain events, her reference to the discretion necessary with other diplomats and to the fact that her own knowledge is limited, might all be taken as evidence that she was fully aware of the precise political image of herself which should be conveyed to those in France through the correspondence. Equally, her desire to maintain a certain detachment from the queen, her assertion that 'ce que la Princesse fera de bien ou moins bien, ne me doit point être attribué' (pp. 43–4) are not necessarily expressions of cowardice or of an attempt to avoid political responsibility. Rather they can be interpreted as a recognition of the delicacy, even danger, of her position, in a Court where she was surrounded by hostility and suspicion: the letters point to an understanding that caution was essential, both on her own behalf, but more particularly on behalf of Pierre de Villars, whose authority and political mission could be so easily undermined. It can be argued above all that there is proof of Marie de Villars's political sensitivity in the steps she took to secure approval for her conduct. Letter IV shows, for example, a reluctance to accede to the queen's request that they meet daily without an assurance that this had the support of the king and queen mother. Furthermore, Letter VI seeks, indirectly, approval from Louis XIV:

> Vous voyez donc que du côté de cette Cour, tout veut que je sois souvent avec la Reine; mais si je ne sçais que la Cour de France l'approuve, rien ne me peut empêcher de retirer mes troupes, et de laisser penser ici tout ce qu'on voudra; c'est pourquoi je vous supplie encore une fois de tâcher de sçavoir ce que vous pourrez là-dessus (pp. 52–3).

These are the words and actions of a woman aware of her political duty and its importance. They are also, it can be argued, especially in the request put to Mme de Coulanges, the words and actions of a woman who, consciously or unconsciously, attributes to herself a good deal of political significance.

Much else in the correspondence also implies that Marie de Villars had a vigorous political personality. In the first place, despite her caution, she is in fact unafraid to employ wit and irony at the expense of the Spanish and their customs. Letter V, describing the way in which the obligatory receptions are arranged and conducted, observes that 'Toutes ces femmes causent comme des pies dénichées' (pp. 39–40), and offers this comment on the unnaturally early hour at which queen and king retire:

> ils se couchent tous les jours à huit heures et demie, c'est-à-dire, le moment d'après qu'ils sont sortis de table, ayant encore le morceau au bec (p. 46).[12]

On her own account this somewhat sarcastic rhetorical question is put concerning the privilege, accorded only to the *ambassadrices* of France and Germany, of being received in the queen's apartments: 'Avec cette prérogative, peut-on ne pas se trouver heureuse à Madrid?' (pp. 116–17).[13] These attempts to amuse are accompanied, however, by outright criticism, not just of obvious targets such as a bull-fight or an auto-da-fé, but of the life which the queen is obliged to lead. Letter VIII, for example, having stated that she is in good health, adds that 'Il n'est pas moins vrai aussi, avec tout cela, que la vie qu'elle mène, ne lui est guères agreable' (p. 77), and Letter XV states that 'Pour des plaisirs, elle n'en voit aucun à espérer dans cette Cour' (p. 122). Not infrequently, observations such as these are followed by comments on the queen's docility and subservience, as if to underline the unacceptably constricting nature of her existence. This is the case, for instance, with the first of the comments quoted above, and in Letter IX, which having described the drab and unexciting Madrid carnival, adds: 'sa douceur, sa complaisance, et toute sa conduite, sont des choses extraordinaires à dix-huit ans' (p. 83).

In addition, the correspondence portrays Marie de Villars as an important political adviser to the queen, despite disclaimers such as 'Je ne m'entremets de rien ici' (p. 121), or 'je n'ai aucun personnage à faire auprès d'elle' (p. 122). One of the tasks she perceived for herself was the creation of good relations between Marie-Louise and the ladies of the court: 'Je fais tout ce que je puis ... pour la faire souvenir de leur dire tout ce qui est le plus propre à les [les Dames] gagner' (pp. 76–7). Another, rather more important from a political point of view perhaps, was the attempt to persuade her that she now 'belonged' to Spain. This was done partly by changing the subject—'Quand je vois qu'elle croit avoir sujet de s'ennuyer, je change de discours' (p. 199)—

partly by suppressing her memories of France, and partly by emphasizing the need to adapt: 'je lui dis souvent qu'elle n'a pas dû croire qu'on les [usages] changeroit pour elle (p. 122)'. It would also seem that part of the function she fulfilled was to guide the queen through what is presented as a maze of conflicting and deliberately misleading advice; as it is put in Letter IX of 6 March 1680: 'd'abord qu'elle arriva, on lui donna les plus méchans conseils du monde. Elle le connoît bien présentement' (p. 83). Above all, it was clearly part of a joint strategy to convince Marie-Louise that her interests lay in maintaining a good relationship with the queen mother:

> Depuis le moment que la jeune [Reine] est entrée en Espagne, M. de Villars s'est appliqué à la bien persuader qu'il falloit absolument pour son repos qu'elle fût en bonne union avec la Reine sa belle-mère; et qu'elle se gardât bien d'écouter des avis contraires. Je ne fais autre chose aussi que de tâcher à lui mettre cela dans la tête (pp. 214–15).

Thus Mme de Villars's own relationship with the queen appears to have been characterized by the kind of diplomacy, on her side, which she was adept at using with others at the Court. What is striking is that this political conformism exists alongside a marked tendency to challenge the life that had been chosen for the queen, or at least the way in which it had been handled. Two distinct themes emerge here, the first of which concerns the preparation—or lack of it—for her new role: 'il n'auroit pas été plus mal qu'on lui eût donné en France quelque bonne tête en qui elle eût confiance' (p. 44). The second is the need for an official adviser in Spain:

> Entre nous, ce que je ne comprends pas, c'est qu'on ne lui ait pas cherché par mer et par terre, et au poids de l'or, quelque femme d'esprit, et de mérite, et de prudence, pour servir à cette Princesse de consolation, et de conseil. Croyoit-on qu'elle n'en eût pas besoin en Espagne? (p. 122).

As de Courtois points out,[14] the appointment of such a woman would have been politically unacceptable to those in control at the Spanish Court. In effect, of course, it was Mme de Villars herself who fulfilled the function whose importance is so convincingly conveyed here. She therefore acquired a kind of political autonomy and significance through her assessment of the queen's position and her use of the opportunity which it offered. Moreover, despite the 'Entre nous' in this passage, one might argue that she was drawing the attention of those beyond Mme de Coulanges to her role, seeking acknowledgement for her political achievements in relation to Marie-Louise.

On one level, Mme de Villars's letters are the elegant and witty compositions of one *mondaine* to another. Letter XXIV might state that 'je n'aime point du tout à écrire' (p. 180), but Mme de Villars must have been aware that her letters would be read aloud by Mme de Coulanges; indeed Letter X, describing an outing to the River Mencenares, invites her to do so: 'Je vous prie, Madame, de conter cela, comme vous sçavez orner toutes les choses auxquelles vous voulez donner un air' (p. 95). The letters are literary creations and Marie de Villars an author conscious of her audience. That the correspondence was indeed read aloud is clear in a letter from Mme de Sévigné to Mme de Grignan dated 28 February 1680: 'Mme de Villars mande mille choses agréables à Mme de Coulanges; c'est chez elle qu'on vient apprendre les nouvelles' (II, p. 852). Linda Timmermans' suggestion that Mme de Villars 'se servait de son talent épistolaire pour se faire valoir dans le monde' is perhaps in some ways not unduly harsh.[15] Yet the correspondence and Marie de Villars's life in Spain were undeniably political from a number of different points of view, none of them negligible and several of them demanding. The effort involved in acting as adviser to Marie-Louise, for example, seems to lie behind this question: 'Vous la louez du bon goût qu'elle a pour moi; mais sçavez-vous à quelle sausse je me mets pour être trouvée de si bon goût?' (pp. 111–12). The letters do not discuss political theory, nor do they offer lengthy political judgements— Pierre de Villars's despatches to Louis XIV are more focused and detailed, politically speaking[16]—but they do appear to have a certain weight and independence of mind. Indeed, Mme de Villars, together with her husband, was accused of subversive activity and recalled to France.[17] Given the discrepancy between the claims of non-involvement in the queen's life and the quite considerable political guidance offered, it is possible that the letters asserting lack of knowledge and a desire not to interfere were a smoke-screen. It is not clear, however, what the Villars might have hoped to achieve and any political activity not sanctioned by Louis XIV was extremely risky for them, financially dependent as they were on appointments made by the king. It is perhaps as likely that they were victims of Spanish readiness to accuse the French of underhand activity, or the fear in some quarters that they were training the queen to have too great an influence over Carlos.

Two further issues of interest concerning women in politics arise from a consideration of this correspondence. In a letter of 26 January 1680, Mme de Sévigné writes: 'Elle [Mme de Villars] fait des relations fort jolies et fort plaisantes à Mme de Coulanges, croyant bien qu'elles iront plus loin' (II, p. 816), the implication being that they will eventually be seen by Mme de Maintenon, a close friend of Mme de Coulanges. De Courtois argues that Pierre de Villars needed justification 'par avance' (p. 66) for his actions and that Mme de Villars's letters performed a vital task for him here, their addressee having been in fact carefully chosen. Moreover, in response to the request from Marie de Villars discussed above, Louis XIV wrote:

> Continuez toujours de me tenir averti de ce qui se passe, non-seulement pour ce qui concerne le gouvernement de l'Etat, mais même le particulier et domestique du Roi et de la Reine, et comme la marquise de Villars a permission de voir la jeune Reine et qu'elle peut être informée de tout ce qu'elle dit et de tout ce qu'elle fait, comme aussi du traitement qu'elle reçoit, je désire que vous me fassiez savoir toutes choses en détail.[18]

If, as we have seen, it was one of the elements in an ambassador's mission to collect important information, Mme de Villars played a central role during her husband's third term of duty. Not only this, it is quite clear not just that Mme de Coulanges came to have a political role, but that a network of women was functioning here in parallel to the more conventional channels used by the men. In two ways, therefore—in explaining de Villars's actions and in informing the king—all the women involved had a significant political purpose.

The second focus of interest in this correspondence is Marie-Louise. It is a commonplace to state that royal marriages were a matter of high politics, but if, as seems likely, France had a political aim in marrying Marie-Louise to Carlos II, a strange discrepancy existed between that aim and the way in which it was approached. Marie-Louise was unwilling to be used in this way, unprepared for her role, uninterested in politics, and in all likelihood out of her depth at the Spanish Court. Her situation throws into relief the fate of many employed for political ends. Moreover, it can even be argued that this was a political opportunity squandered by the French crown. As for Mme de Villars, it can be said that her actions were motivated by the interests of France, whether it was a question of respecting Spanish customs, requesting royal approval for her conduct, or being instrumental in supplying information to the king. Above all, despite the claims that the advice offered to Marie-Louise was 'pour son repos' (p. 216), it was given in fact with French foreign policy in mind, since an understanding between the new queen and the queen mother might help to effect, through joint influence on Carlos, the alliance sought by France. Unlike the French government, of which she is in a sense indirectly critical, Mme de Villars exploited to the full the political opportunity which emerged in 1679.

Notes:

1   Marie de Villars, *Lettres de Madame la Marquise de Villars*, Amsterdam and Paris, 1759, p. 8. All page references will be to this edition, whose spelling has been retained.

2   C.-G. Picavet, *La Diplomatie française au temps de Louis XIV* (1661–1715), Paris, Félix Alcan, 1830, p. 71.

3   It would appear that women sometimes lead such protests. It is surely legitimate to treat many revolts in the seventeenth century, whatever their cause, as genuine political activity, since they were virtually the only means of registering a reaction to decisions taken by government. See R. Briggs, *Early Modern France 1560–1715*, Oxford University Press, 1977; R. Mettam, *Government and Society in Louis XIV's France*, London and Basingstoke, Macmillan, 1977; C. Dulong, *La Vie quotidienne des femmes en France au grand siècle*, Hachette, 1984. Further research on the precise nature of political activity by women can only be of value.

4   Amongst the many writings here, see B.A. Carroll, ed., *Liberating Women's History*, Urbana, University of Illinois Press, 1976; S.J. Kleinberg, ed., *Retrieving Women's History*, Providence and Oxford, Berg, 1988; P. Burke, ed., *New Perspectives in Historical Writing*, Cambridge Polity Press, 1991; N.Z. Davis and A. Farge, eds, *A History of Women in the West; III: Renaissance and Enlightenment Paradoxes*, Cambridge Mass. and London, England, Harvard University Press, 1993.

5   Accounts of the life and career of Pierre de Villars are in: Louis de Rouvroy, duc de Saint-Simon, *Mémoires*, Y. Coirault, ed., Paris, Gallimard, I, pp. 39–40; A. de Courtois, ed., *Lettres de Madame de Villars à Madame de Coulanges*, Paris, Plon, 1868, pp. 10–33.

6   Mme de Villars and Mme de Vins are first mentioned together in a letter of 19 June, 1675. See Marie de Rabutin-Chantal, marquise de Sévigné, *Correspondance*, R. Duchêne, ed., Paris, Gallimard, 1972, I, p. 736. Thereafter they are linked fairly often, in a way which implies a friendship had formed; see for example, a letter of 29 December, 1679 which states of Mme de Vins: 'vous et Mme de Villars lui manquez' (II, p. 781). The letters suggest Mme de Villars also associated with Mme de Pomponne, Mme de Lafayette, Mme d'Huxelles, Mme de Lavardin.

7   See, for example, this statement: 'quand ... elle recevra mille visites, je me propose ... de lui en rendre moins' (p. 50); see also Letter XXXII, pp. 215–16.

8   Of the 'fête des taureaux' she says: 'je me levois pour m'ôter de dessus le balcon où j'étois, si M. de Villars ne m'eût dit que pour rien du monde il ne falloit faire cette faute' (p. 78).

9   De Courtois suggests that Mme de Villars's affection for Mme de Grignan might have been in reality 'complaisance pour la mère' (op. cit., p. 22). Perhaps it can be suggested that Mme de Villars had always been a 'diplomat'.

10   See also this account in Letter IV of a conversation with the Queen's ladies-in-waiting: 'je dis qu'il falloit apprendre l'Espagnol, et s'empêcher ... de dire un mot de François à la Reine ... Je dis en Espagnol à la Camarera Major, ce que je disois à ces Françoises, elle m'en sçut un très-bon gré' (p. 32).

11   In Letter V she says: 'je suis triste et peinée par avance, d'aller représenter en public' (p. 45).

12   Back-handed compliments are also a feature of the letters; see, for example, Letter VIII: 'Toutes les Dames, généralement parlant, sont honnêtes et civiles, surtout celles qui ont un peu voyagé avec leurs maris' (p. 80).

13   There is, presumably, similar sarcasm in the comment 'elle [the Queen] eut le plaisir ... de voir tuer un sanglier par le Roi son mari' (p. 50).

14   Op cit., p. 278.

15   L. Timmermans, *L'Accès de la femme à la culture (1598–1715)*. Paris, Champion, 1993, p. 194.

16   Some of these are quoted by de Courtois in the introduction of his edition of the letters; see pp. 44, 57–8. There might be an interesting study to be done here comparing the despatches of Villars and Mme de Villars's letters.

17   See Letters XXXIV and XXXV, pp. 225–37.

18   Quoted by de Courtois, p. 56.

CHAPTER TWELVE

Ascendant et déclinaison de la noblesse française dans le système de Boulainvilliers

YVES COIRAULT

> Il possédait extrêmement les histoires, celle de France surtout à laquelle il s'était fort appliqué, particulièrement à l'ancien génie et à l'ancien gouvernement français et aux divers degrés de sa déclinaison à la forme présente.

Dans les *Mémoires* de Saint-Simon,[1] ce bel éloge d'Henri de Boulainvilliers 'surnage' aux multiples critiques formulées par le duc et pair à l'encontre d'un système réduisant la pairie à la portion congrue des responsabilités publiques.

Mais dès la parution de quelques-uns de ses écrits, plusieurs années après sa mort (1722), les thèses historiques, politiques, astrologiques du Comte avaient suscité d'impertinents ou trop pertinents commentaires. Ainsi pouvait-on lire dans le *Journal des Savants* de juin 1731 une plaisante protestation de Charles de La Grange, abbé de Trianon, conseiller-clerc de Parlement et audacieux esprit: Monsieur le Comte, censeur si obstiné des 'légistes' et autres pieds-plats, n'avait-il pas confectionné ses dernières cartouches dans la 'garde-robe des laquais de ses ancêtres'?

> La merveilleuse subtilité de son système l'a fait remonter jusqu'à ces précieuses garde-robes, où il croit avoir découvert que ses ancêtres ont fait apprendre à écrire et un peu de chicane à quelques-uns de leurs petits laquais esclaves, pour en former des secrétaires; que ces petits esclaves sont devenus légistes ... Heureux laquais, heureux système! qui mettent à ses pieds ces compagnies souveraines ... Les fantômes des ancêtres parés de cordons et de bâtons de commandement voltigent continuellement dans le cerveau d'un ancien noble et y produisent nécessairement un gonflement et un dérangement de tous les esprits, qui engendrent des idées fantastiques de grandeur et d'excellence.

Maladie excusable en ce qu'elle 'produit un faux bonheur'.[2] *Beati pauperes* ...

On se gardera de tout diagnostic à l'emporte-pièce. La juxtaposition de deux jugements antithétiques d'écrivains des deux bords et, quoique plus jeunes que lui, contemporains de Boulainvilliers, incite au contraire à de nouvelles réflexions sur sa conception du droit, son idéologie socio-politique et ce qu'on se risquera à appeler sa philosophie de l'histoire—étant bien entendu que les dernières décennies ont vu paraître, pour une meilleure connaissance de l'homme et de l'œuvre, de nouveaux apports critiques qu'il serait présomptueux d'ignorer. S'il est permis de douter que le Comte puisse passer aux yeux d'un historien moderne pour aussi expert en 'sciences humaines' qu'en ce que l'auteur de *Louis Lambert* rangeait apparemment parmi les 'sciences divines', du moins, au seuil d'une brève récapitulation, convient-il de reconnaître d'abord en celui de l'*Histoire de l'ancien gouvernement de la France* un chercheur de bonne volonté et un doctrinaire de bonne foi, tenant honnêtement sa partie entre un P. Daniel, dont la 'prévention' le rebutait,[3] et le P. Mabillon, dont il aurait eu intérêt à pratiquer persévéramment la méthode.

Il ne détestait pas les escalades d'inductions. 'Commençons donc par écarter tous les faits'... Une injonction aussi péremptoire au lecteur, il fallait être Jean-Jacques Rousseau pour la formuler. Il n'empêche que tout l'édifice conceptuel de Boulainvilliers repose sur un ensemble d'images sommaires que postulaient sa pensée et son désir, et dont bien avant la fixation du 'système' était parachevée la cristallisation. Le mythe 'germanique' avait des charmes puissants auxquels des aristocrates n'étaient assurément pas insensibles: les chevaliers chevelus surgis au galop des forêts de Franconie reléguaient le Troyen Francus dans les oubliettes de la Fable et des contes de vieilles; de Pharamond à Clovis, de Childebert Ier à Childéric III, les imaginations françaises se forgeaient à l'envi de belles histoires, promises aux lanternes magiques. Il appartenait à Henri de Boulainvilliers d'en extraire et suractiver l'efficace dans le domaine de la pensée politique et sociale. Paradoxalement (à nos yeux) le vrai libéralisme devait être le fruit d'une conquête à la pointe de l'épée ou au tranchant de la francisque (promise à tout autre avenir).

Non que les 'faits' n'aient point précédé la fiction. Non que des images d'Epinal promues en scènes fondatrices, comme inscrites dans l'éternité, aient été plus dénuées de références objectives, proprement historiques, que les légendes de Thésée, ou de Romulus, ou du roi Arthur. Mais, quoique passablement sauvage, ce paysage choisi de la grande parade mérovingienne, où les 'Français naturels', assemblés en 'champs de mars' (ou de mai), décidaient du sort de toutes les Gaules sans consulter les Gaulois ni les Gallo-romains attachés en pauvres 'roturiers' à la 'glèbe', s'accordait à merveille, comme par une harmonie préétablie, avec la société idéalement hiérarchisée à laquelle aspiraient, avec Boulainvilliers et son disciple Nicolas Fréret (et Fénelon, et le jeune Montesquieu ...), bon nombre de seigneurs gémissant sous les menaces de l' 'horrible marteau' d'un despotisme odieux à Saint-Simon. Le mythe germanique n'eût-il préexisté, le Comte l'eût sans doute inventé de toutes pièces en lui donnant les vives couleurs de l'histoire. Hypothèse qui n'est pas en tout cas impensable. Mais de Tacite à Mézeray, du vase de Soissons au bardit des Francs, des Grandes chroniques de France aux textes polémiques de la Fronde, déjà s'était constituée, documents à l'appui, une sorte de vulgate mythistorique où l'ancienne aristocratie trouvait, très platoniquement, son compte et sa justification.

Rêve idyllique—sauf pour les exclus de l'époque. L'utilité n'en était pas moins évidente que le charme, dès lors que la fable à la fois confortait le goût d'une liberté depuis longtemps foulée par la monarchie absolue, et fondait ses superstructures idéologiques sur l'antiquité des 'monuments': 'Personne n'ignore que les Français [entendons les Francs venus d'outre-Rhin[4]] étant originairement des peuples libres, qui se choisissaient des chefs sous le nom de Rois, pour faire exécuter les lois qu'eux-mêmes avaient établies, ou pour les conduire à la guerre, n'avaient garde de considérer les Rois comme des législateurs arbitraires, qui pouvaient tout ordonner sans autre raison que leur bon plaisir.' Bien révélateur à cet égard l'enthousiasme d'un 'calife de Babilone' voyant dans ces Français un 'peuple de Rois', et par conséquent dans leur chef 'le Roi des Rois', concourant toutefois avec ses sujets ou soi-disant tels à l'administration du gouvernement! Ceux-ci constituaient le premier Parlement, et, en vertu du 'principe fondamental que tous les Français étaient égaux et justiciables de leurs pareils, les dignités accidentelles [duchés, marquisats, pairies, etc.] ne changeaient point le caractère intime formé par la naissance française'.[5]

Qu'il y ait eu en tout pays et à toute époque des *optimates*, des *proceres*, voilà qui ne faisait pas difficulté;[6] et l'on avait depuis beau temps en mémoire certain récit de Menenius Agrippa (*Les Membres et l'Estomac*): un organisme social ne pouvait survivre sans une distinction des fonctions. La véritable question demeurait cependant celle de la légitimité d'une telle distinction en quelque sorte reçue, c'est-à-dire, en la conjoncture, celle d'une antique contrainte par le glaive et la violence. Fallait-il rechercher en amont, dans l'histoire, ou, en deçà de l'histoire et du flux temporel, dans une nature ou une sur-nature, ou encore, par une rupture épistémologique, dans les champs des 'futuribles' et de l'utilité sociable, l'origine, le principe, la caution de nécessaires (fatales ou désirables) inégalités?

Il n'était pas illicite de se satisfaire du principe, apparemment confirmé par un jeu de certitudes objectives et d'inférences, selon lequel la noblesse était parfaitement synchrone de la monarchie héritière de la puissance impériale. Qu'on se souvienne des paroles de Jacques de Silly de Rochefort aux Etats d'Orléans (1560): 'Il faut maintenir la noblesse en ses privilèges, franchises et libertés, aussi antiques que l'institution des Rois'.7 Le problème n'était pas exactement celui de l'existence ou de l'absence d'un primitif contrat:8 pour les réfractaires de tout bord au despotisme 'oriental', ne suffisait-il pas d'une simple imagerie, ménageant un halo d'indétermination, telle que monarque et noblesse, initialement non hiérarchisée (en instance de hiérarchisation), se prêtassent mutuellement appui dans la plus naturelle et profitable des symbioses?

Le fait—ou la stupéfiante image—de la violence non seulement anticipait, mais en quelque sorte authentifiait le droit. *Vae victis*. La supériorité du vainqueur sur le vaincu est une évidence première. 'Il n'y a point réellement de plus véritable noblesse que celle qui est acquise par droit de conquête, comme il n'y a point de plus grande distinction entre les hommes que celle qui naît de la soumission du vaincu.' On lit ailleurs: 'Les nobles étaient de fait et de droit les seuls grands de l'Etat.'9 Et, au temps de Louis XIV, le Tiers Etat—'si disproportionné de la noblesse', écrira Saint-Simon,10 mais qui, selon Voltaire, n'en composait pas moins 'le fonds de la nation'11—se trouvait, en dépit de sa supériorité numérique, soumis et 'à plaît-il, maître' sous la coupe des arrière-neveux, biologiquement légitimes ou historiquement légitimés, des envahisseurs qui avaient mis un terme au déclin de l'Empire romain. La race, mais d'abord l'histoire, cette donnée, opère tout—étant entendu que celle-ci se prête habituellement à toutes les manipulations ... Des lois 'fondamentales' et non-écrites, mais prétendues infrangibles, sont visibles comme des symboles dans les scènes originelles du royaume, reçues par tous sinon pareillement interprétés. 'A la place de Dieu'—mais n'a-t-elle pas la caution divine?—l'Histoire 'est devenue dépositaire du contrat originel, des droits des Français et des secrets du pacte social. Elle est désormais l'instance décisive de légitimation'.12 Ainsi l'ordre se fonde-t-il sur le respect de la tradition, collective réminiscence.

Une objection se présente d'elle-même à l'esprit: pourquoi choisir tel moment de l'histoire? pourquoi cette violence plutôt qu'une autre, ou qu'une période de tranquillité 'sans histoire'? Pourquoi pas une autre 'égalité', en amont de l'amont? La liberté des Gaulois ne fut-elle pas iniquement confisquée par des 'barbares' venus de l'Est? Certes, on pouvait répondre, non sans quelque cynisme: 'Il faut bien s'arrêter dans la rétrodiction'.[13] Boulainvilliers était homme à justifier un tel ancrage: ici commençait l'histoire de la France, de la 'Franco-Gallia'. Dès lors, une histoire plus ou moins événementielle se parait des couleurs de l'éternité, et la violence, initiale et créative, de toute l'*aura* juridique de légitimité qu'impliquait le recours, non moins juridique, à l'argument de la prescription. Ce que disait un marquis d'Argenson de la puissance royale s'appliquait admirablement aux puissances 'collatérales' responsables des textes législatifs: la prescription avait achevé d'en 'canoniser' l'autorité.[14] Qu'importait une 'origine vicieuse'? Selon Boulainvilliers lui-même, l'usage aussi ancien que la monarchie 'a acquis la force d'une loi fondamentale',[15] méritant par là un consentement universel. Ce qui n'est pas sans rappeler certain propos du cardinal de Retz, que dis-je? de Jean François Paul de Gondi (ou de Mascardi?), mis dans la bouche de Verrina[16]: 'Le crime d'usurper une couronne est si illustre qu'il peut passer pour une vertu.' Depuis plus d'un millénaire le crime était largement prescrit de l'invasion franque; confirmée par la voie royale de la continuité et de la gloire monarchiques, la victoire même des conquérants avait fait accéder les descendants des 'Français naturels' au monde des éternelles structures tant éthiques que politiques, au point de rendre acceptable, vénérable même, ce que Derek A. Watts appelle justement, à propos d'un héros en retard et à contre-courant, une 'mystique de l'inégalité'.[17]

Sparte avait remplacé Rome. L'on ne saurait s'étonner, à la réflexion, de certain éloge hyperbolique de la féodalité que les lecteurs découvraient, non sans scandale, dans les textes du Comte publiés en 1727. De quoi s'agissait-il pour notre héros mélancolique faisant mieux que pressentir la fin de sa race et peut-être de sa caste, sinon de rechercher dans la cendre les traces d'une authentique grandeur—'Dans le caveau des miens plongeant mes pas nocturnes', pour reprendre un bel alexandrin de Vigny—et, par un vain désir de la 'révolution' que serait un retour aux sources et de la résurrection des 'anciennes libertés',[18] de recouvrer, sans en abolir la patine, les 'monuments' d'une félicité perdue? Se souvenant de la fière réponse d'Adalbert de Périgord à Hugues Capet ('Qui t'a fait roi?'), il était persuadé avec le bon seigneur que 'la noblesse ne doit à la royauté ni son établissement ni ses droits';[19] et ce qui nous apparaît comme le 'polycentrisme féodal',[20] prélude à une totale anarchie, était perçu par notre historien-astrologue comme une correspondance des cieux, un parfait écho de la musique des sphères. Dans la France médiévale, particulièrement entre l'empire de Charlemagne et les règnes, funestes entre tous, de Philippe le Bel et de Philippe Auguste, l'harmonie caractérisait, à l'exemple du cosmos tel que pouvaient le concevoir

Saint Thomas ou Bérulle, voire Torquato Tasso, auteur d'un traité *De la Noblesse*, ou le juriste et historien Charles Loyseau,[21] un corps social organiquement un—le Roi étant 'empereur en son royaume'— mais intégrant sans en ruiner la relative autonomie les seigneuries d'inféodés eux-mêmes inféodants. Heureuse et exquise symphonie des règles et des libertés agencées en nid d'abeilles! Admirable la police des fiefs, résultant des distributions des terres dont s'étaient vus gratifiés les guerriers fils de guerriers! Mais ce n'était pas la terre, c'était le sang qui, d'âge en âge, conférait, confirmait, maintenait la noblesse.[22]

'Pour le Comte, l'Age d'or [disons: le premier Age d'or] de la noblesse—des vrais Français donc—se situait au Haut Moyen âge, sous les Mérovingiens, lorsque la fonction guerrière qu'elle incarnait eut relégué au second rang la fonction sacerdotale'.[23] Après une courte éclipse, au temps de l'excessive autorité de Pépin le Bref, vint le restaurateur des antiques libertés, Charlemagne, auquel les seigneurs furent redevables d'un splendide renouveau[24] qui perdura plusieurs siècles. Ce fut en effet à partir de la fin du VIIIe siècle qu'aurait commencé cet autre Age d'or de la Gaule française, celui d'une société féodale présentée par notre auteur comme 'idéal type des rapports de la société civile et du roi de France'.[25] En ce temps-là, pour reprendre le vers de *L'Invitation au voyage*, 'tout n'[était] qu'ordre et beauté'. Le Roi régnait. Chaque seigneur, inféodé inféodant, gérait sa seigneurie,[26] rendant à ce pâle Césarion qu'était un roitelet des bords de Seine tout ce qu'il devait, mais seulement ce qu'il devait à un diminutif de César.

Temps radieux où chacun était à sa place, y compris les pauvres serfs appartenant à la 'nation soumise'. *Et quievit terra*, ainsi que le répètent à l'envi les chroniqueurs d'autrefois. Mais il faut citer, comme la formulation la plus remarquable et la plus scandaleusement synthétique (elle indignera en particulier un marquis d'Argenson,[27] et Voltaire, pour ne rien dire de Michelet), les lignes de la *Quatrième Lettre sur les anciens Parlements:*

> Je crois donc pouvoir terminer cette description en disant qu'encore que les philosophes grecs et particulièrement Aristote, n'ayent eu aucune idée du gouvernement féodal, et qu'en particulier le dernier ne l'ait point compris au nombre de ses catégories politiques, on le peut regarder comme le chef-d'œuvre de l'esprit humain dans ce genre, soit qu'on le considère par rapport à la véritable grandeur des Rois, soit qu'on l'estime par rapport à la liberté qu'il assurait aux sujets.

Un tel panégyrique n'était-il pas en contradiction avec ce que le Comte désignait comme 'axiome certain', à savoir que 'tout ce qui est violent ne saurait être durable'?[28] Il faut bien, pensait-il sans doute, anticipant sur des jugements de nos historiens, 's'arrêter dans la rétrodiction'. Afin d'assurer la prescription, ne suffisait-il pas de fixer en bon lieu le bout de la chaîne? L'essentiel restait la perfection d'une société humaine où le moindre district reproduisait comme en abysme la structure d'un groupe englobant, où, par un admirable effet d'équilibre, toutes les unités, quelle qu'en fût la taille, s'interpénétraient et contre-tenaient.

Cela ne signifie pas que la pensée de Boulainvilliers ait cédé au pur caprice. L'opinion, pour nous fantastique, selon laquelle la féodalité réalisait un modèle inégalable de gouvernement, ne reposait pas seulement sur le 'bon plaisir' de l'écrivain aristocrate: celui-ci s'érigeait aussi en moraliste ... rénovateur; anatomiste et historien des mentalités (avant la lettre), il était soucieux de fixer dans l'absolu proprement axiologique une hiérarchie de valeurs conforme à l'éthique inséparable du 'sang bleu'. A cet égard, quelques assertions auraient de quoi surprendre jusqu'à l'indignation bon nombre de nos contemporains, lesquels, projetant en de lointaines époques les horreurs d'un proche passé, et, par incapacité d'éviter les pièges de l'anachronisme, mesurent codes et croyances du XVIIe siècle, voire du premier XVIIIe, à l'aune, s'il en est une, du laxisme moderne. La vertu 'est plus ordinaire dans les bonnes races que dans les autres'; elle 'a besoin de l'éclat de la fortune pour se signaler; et cette fortune, c'est la naissance qui la donne presque ordinairement ... Ainsi une naissance noble est sans contredit le moyen le plus commun de faire valoir et de faire honorer la vertu.'[29] A une maxime dont s'imposait jadis l'évidence, il est en effet tentant d'opposer, truisme des 'Lumières', des vers de la tragédie voltairienne intitulée *Eriphyle* (1732):

Les mortels sont égaux. Ce n'est pas la naissance,
C'est la seule vertu qui fait leur différence ...

Il ne l'est assurément pas moins de formuler une objection que nos aïeux, seigneurs ou gueux, durent méditer aux approches de notre grande Révolution: 'Si la noblesse doit être d'abord vertu, comment la vertu ne serait-elle pas principe?'[30] D'un Boulainvilliers, il est malaisé d'imaginer ce qu'eût pu être la réponse à une telle question: peut-être se fût-il contenté de murmurer que bon sang ne saurait mentir ni dégénérer, que bon chien chasse de race, etc. La *race* en tout cas, autrement dit le lignage, était à ses yeux un critère commode et comme une garantie de très ostensible valeur personnelle. Quant aux objections qui accueillirent en leur temps, ou peu après leur temps, de semblables thèses—celles d'un abbé Du Bos, opposant au 'système' et aux gens des châteaux la thèse dite romaniste, celles du président

Hénault ou de Mathieu Marais, ou d'un marquis d'Argenson rêvant d'un contrat 'conditionnel' entre le 'peuple' et le monarque, et redoutant qu'un gouvernement aristocratique ne vînt 'accabler les roturiers'[31]— elles ne prenaient évidemment en compte ni une assez nébuleuse métaphysique, entant l'éthique sur l'ethnique ainsi que le fera un Gobineau, et évoquant une sorte de jansénisme de la liberté (Dieu ayant d'avance reconnu et marqué génétiquement les siens), ni certaine théologie de l'Histoire qui ne semblait pas incompatible avec l'espoir d'une résurrection en quelque sorte politique.

'Tout est révolution dans le monde', écrivait d'Argenson;[32] 'tout est cercle et période', lira-t-on dans les *Mémoires* de Saint-Simon.[33] Ne parlons pas de Vico, longtemps ignoré en France. Du moins, depuis Polybe, l'idée du grand retour (*anacyclosis*) trouvait-elle grâce auprès de bons esprits, confirmant les uns dans une vue pessimiste d'une histoire répétitive, autorisant quelques autres, tels que Boulainvilliers, à attendre un regain de ce qui leur semblait, quoique le mot ne fût pas encore en usage, un modèle de civilisation. Donnant tout à la noblesse, selon l'observation d'un commentateur de l'époque, le système ménageait une ouverture sur un avenir qui n'écartait pas la probabilité pour les nobles (et les 'anoblis', qu'il ne convenait pas de désespérer) d'une brillante autant que légitime compensation: non seulement la récupération, par la haute noblesse, de son droit de participer à la 'juridiction effective sur les matières de gouvernement et sur la promulgation des lois',[34] mais encore le rétablissement en tous leurs privilèges de ces anciens 'Egaux' qu'étaient les hobereaux possesseurs de colombiers et jouissant d'un banc à l'église paroissiale.

Qualifié par nos contemporains de 'réactionnaire'[35] et comme tel ordinairement noté d'infamie, notre idéologue, qui n'était pas exactement un utopiste, se situe parfaitement au nadir d'un historien d'outre-Manche tel que Macaulay. Au demeurant, 'trois degrés d'élévation du pôle renversent toute la jusrisprudence'.[36] A chaque nation, ou composé de 'nations', son 'génie'. En Angleterre, l'aristocratie héréditaire 'se montrait la moins exclusive et la moins arrogante des aristocraties; elle n'avait rien du caractère odieux d'une caste, elle se recrutait constamment dans les rangs du peuple, et redescendait souvent jusqu'à lui'. Au plus loin de l'étanchéité des 'ordres', par un 'salutaire mélange des classes', il n'existait 'aucune barrière qui séparât, comme dans d'autres pays, le patricien du plébéien.'[37] Héritier de 'rois' dépossédés, le Comte n'inclinait nullement vers les idéologies de substitution. Fidèle à ces valeurs 'dures' qu'étaient le courage et la générosité—contre ces autres valeurs, pétrifiées et pétrifiantes, que sont celles de la Banque et qu'illustre l' 'Enrichissez-vous' de Guizot—mais ayant renoncé, car il était trop tard, au rêve bleu d'une nouvelle Fronde, il souhaitait tout au plus, ou tout au moins, que fût remis en honneur ... l'honneur, âme des belles âmes, spécialité de l'aristocratie; et la qualité; un héroïsme de l'altitude et de la distinction. 'Dieu nous a donné les cieux comme un livre ...'[38] Il a donné aussi l'Histoire, non moins instructive que le grand livre de la Nature, non moins fondamentale et fondatrice du Droit—et des devoirs—que l'analyse de l'Homme en tant qu'être de raison. Conformément à son *Discours sur l'inégalité*,[39] rêvant, pour reprendre les vers étincelants de *La Jeune Parque*, 'que l'avenir lui-même / Ne fût qu'un diamant fermant le diadème', le bon seigneur proposait l'idéal d'un juste équilibre, c'est-à-dire exact et historiquement prouvé, de l'organisme social, respectant ce qu'il croyait être (non sans contradiction intime, car, à défaut d'amalgame, que devenait en son système la Gaule française ou la France gauloise?[40]) l'identité du royaume et le 'génie de la nation'.

Archéologue doublé d'un astrologue, donc philosophe de la tête aux pieds, désireux d'ancrer le temps dans l'immémorial et curieux de toutes maisons, il combinait adroitement et—ne lui marchandons pas cet honneur!—innocemment l'érudition livresque et les élévations vers la transcendance. Sa quête des 'signes' épars dans le passé national visait à consolider une métapolitique élitiste sacralisant un ancien viol des foules réputées autochtones. Survivant à cette quête, il reste le témoignage d'un noble effort en vue de la restauration de valeurs proprement éthiques, le désir ou la nostalgie d'un 'chef-d'œuvre' qu'il ne croyait pas inconnu. Vaine et spirituelle revanche contre une dérive rétrospectivement fatale des institutions, son système répondait du moins à une précieuse exigence: celle de 'se sentir', de penser noblement, de se comporter en gentilhomme, de 'changer la vie' en y restituant on ne sait quel parfum d'authenticité. Adorateur du droit féodal et du ciel constellé, il récusait de toute son âme les fausses valeurs d'une société à demi éclairée, mais toujours trop humaine.

S'il y a des rapports assez manifestes entre politique et histoire, il en est d'autres, dont Henri de Boulainvilliers offre une belle illustration, moins nécessaires et, pour le meilleur ou pour le pire, plus séduisants, entre histoire et poésie.

Notes:

1   Saint-Simon, *Mémoires*, 'Pléiade', t. V, p. 222: à la mi-août 1715, le Comte prédit la mort prochaine de Louis XIV. Aux yeux du duc et pair, le moindre tort de Boulainvilliers n'était pas d'avoir été membre de la cabale, pour ne pas dire le club, du duc de Noailles.

2   Cité dans Renée Simon, *Henry de Boulainvilliers historien, politique, philosophe, astrologue*, Gap, 1940, pp. 110–111. L'auteur consacre un intéressant chapitre (1ère partie, ch. III) à l'accueil fait aux thèses sur la noblesse durant les XVIIIe et XIXe siècles.

3   Dans sa Première Lettre sur les anciens Parlements, Boulainvilliers critiquait à la fois Mézeray, qui n'avait 'presque aucune notion juste sur la première race', et le P. Daniel, esprit prévenu et paresseux, dont l'érudition historique ne dépassait pas la médiocrité.

4   Sous la plume de notre auteur, les mots *peuple* et *multitude* désignent les Francs, libres et égaux (initialement, les *milites* approuvant par acclamations les décisions de leurs chefs). Il est en effet hors de question d'y adjoindre les Gaulois réduits en esclavage. Même un Mably parlera de 'gouvernement populaire' à propos des Francs, de 'nos ancêtres les Germains' (A. Delaporte, 'Les avatars de la légende franque au XVIIIe siècle', dans *Annales de Bretagne et des pays de l'Ouest*, t. 93, 1986, 193-208, pp.194–196). Si l'on ose évoquer ici George Orwell, les Francs étaient infiniment 'plus égaux' que les serfs, artisans ou paysans.

5   *Lettres sur les anciens Parlements de France que l'on nomme Etats généraux*, A Londres, chez T. Wood et S. Palmer, 1753, 2ème Lettre, t. I, pp. 37–38, 41 et 45. Voir R. Price, 'Boulainvilliers and the myth of the Frankish conquest of Gaul', *Studies on Voltaire*, vol. 199, 1981, pp.155–185.

6   Voltaire, *Essai sur les mœurs*, Garnier, t. II, p.26: 'Dans tout pays, il y a eu des distinctions d'état'. Mais Voltaire blâmait toute distinction 'avilissante' (ibid., p. 32).

7   Harangue rapportée par De Thou; citée dans A. Devyver, *Le Sang épuré. Les Préjugés de race chez les gentilshommes français de l'Ancien régime (1580-1720)*, Ed. de l'Univ. de Bruxelles, 1973, p. 67.

8   Selon J.-M. Goulemot ('Questions sur la signification politique des *Lettres persanes*', dans *Approches des Lumières*, Mélanges Jean Fabre, 1974, 213–224, p. 218), ' 'contrat-non-contrat' ne représente pas une opposition pertinente à l'aube du XVIIIe siècle'. Peut-être la notion, qui apparaît souvent dans les discours politiques d'aujourd'hui, de 'courants' et de 'sensibilités' éviterait-elle de se laisser piéger par des vocables donnant en l'occurrence l'illusion d'une science 'dure'.

9   Boulainvilliers, *Mémoire sur la noblesse* (Manuscrit d'Angoulême, no. 23), et *Essais* de 1732, cités dans R. Simon, *H. de Boulainvilliers historien* ..., ouvr. cité, pp.71 et 80.

10   *Mémoires*, 'Pléiade', t. VI, p. 278.

11   *Essai sur les mœurs*, chap. CLXXV.

12   F. Furet et M. Ozouf, 'Deux légitimations historiques de la société française au XVIIIe siècle: Mably et Boulainvilliers', *Annales ESC*, mai–juin 1979, 438–451, p. 439.

13   Ibid., p. 442.

14   *Considérations sur le gouvernement ancien et présent de la France*, Amsterdam, 1764, pp. 124–125.

15   *Dissertation sur la noblesse française*, B.N., F.fr., n.a. *9813*, ff.3–4.

16   *La Conjuration de Fiesque*; cité dans D.A. Watts, *Cardinal de Retz. The Ambiguities of a Seventeenth-Century Mind*, Oxford Univ. Press, 1980, p. 151.

17   Ibid., p.160. Au XVIIIe siècle, une telle mystique devait s'accommoder, assez paradoxalement (la polysémie du vocable prêtant à quelques jeux dialectiques), avec la revendication de l'égalité: les aristocrates recouraient à ce concept ambigu afin de 'conforter la société d'ordres traditionnelle' (A. Delaporte, *L'Idée d'égalité en France au XVIIIe siècle*, P.U.F., 1967, p. 333). Il n'était pas si malaisé de concilier une mythologie de l'enracinement et une éthique de la chevalerie: nul Gide à cadogan ne disputait contre un Barrès à talons rouges.

18   Richelieu ne s'est pas 'effray[é] de tant de marques de l'ancienne liberté' (*Lettres sur les anciens Parlements*, 1ère Lettre; Londres, 1753, t. I, p. 21).

19   *Dissertation sur la noblesse française*, fol. 29.

20   P. Chaunu use de cette expression dans *Histoire et décadence*, Perrin, 1981, p. 274.

21   Voir son *Traité des ordres* de 1610, p. 2: 'Car nous ne pourrions pas vivre en égalité de condition'; p. 37 sur la supériorité des gens 'de bonne race'.

22   'Non la terra era nobile, ma il sangue' (Diego Venturino, 'Feudalismo e monarchia nel pensiero politico di H. de B.', *Annali della Fondazione Luigi Einaudi*, XVIII, 1984, 215–241, p. 224).

23   A. Delaporte, 'Les avatars de la légende franque ...', art. cité, pp.196–197.

24   Charlemagne a jeté 'les semences de la féodalité' (Boulainvilliers, 4ème Lettre, éd. citée, t. I, p. 101).

25 F. Furet et M. Ozouf, art. cité, p. 445.

26 Selon la formule de Philippe de Remi, sire de Beaumanoir, auteur des *Coutumes du Beauvaisis* (XIIIe siècle), chaque baron était 'souverain en sa baronnie'; voir Jacques Krynen, *L'Empire du Roi*, Gallimard, 1994, où sont analysés les projets et les progrès de l'absolutisme à partir de Philippe Auguste.

27 Le droit féodal? Une 'odieuse servitude' importée de Lombardie; la thèse germanique? un 'beau roman qui rend [l'usurpation] légitime'; la féodalité était 'un système bizarre de gouvernement', 'le monstrueux gouvernement féodal' (*Considérations ...*, pp. 119, 114, 116 et 123). Dans le *Catalogue du Siècle de Louis XIV*, Voltaire critiquera l'apologie du régime féodal présentée dans les textes de Boulainvilliers (René Pomeau, *La Religion de Voltaire*, Nizet, 1969, p. 99).

28 4ème Lettre, p.129.

29 *Dissertation sur la noblesse...*, déjà citée, fol. 6. Un La Bruyère avait nettement perçu l'équivoque d'une telle relation: 'Jetez-moi dans les troupes comme un simple soldat, je suis Thersite ...' (*Les Caractères*, 'Des grands', no. 41).

30 G. Chaussinand-Nogaret, *La Noblesse au XVIIIe siècle. De la féodalité aux lumières*, Ed. Complexe, 1984, p.15. Ainsi un marquis d'Argenson, séduit par l'image d'une société 'méritocratique', souhaitait-il que 'chacun fût fils de ses œuvres' (ibid., p. 33), et semblait-il par ailleurs douter, sans trop oser enfoncer la matière, que la naissance eût nécessairement partie liée avec le courage: 'On présumera toujours dans un Etat que les nobles d'extraction sont nés avec des sentiments distingués de courage et de vertu' (*Considérations ...*, p. 5). Mais il est des formulations plus percutantes: 'convenons que les nobles ressemblent beaucoup à ce que les frelons sont aux ruches' (ibid., p.116), comparaison qui manifestement les disqualifie dans la perspective de l' 'arithmétique morale' d'un Bentham.

31 *Considérations ...*, p. 6. Il n'est pas douteux que d'Argenson, dont le sobriquet ('la Bête') paraît aux lecteurs modernes de la dernière injustice, n'était pas homme à goûter la féroce grandeur des paladins ni la tendresse des troubadours.

32 Ibid., p.15.

33 *Mémoires*, 'Pléiade, t. VII, p. 306.

34 Boulainvilliers, *Histoire de l'ancien gouvernement de la France [...]*, La Haye-Amsterdam, 1727 (éd. originale), t. II, p. 317. Dans les rangs de la noblesse, au XVIIe siècle, étaient largement majoritaires les anoblis de plus ou moins fraîche date: si notre auteur regrettait les anoblissements 'monstrueux' qui s'étaient multipliés à partir de Philippe III, il n'en jugeait pas moins indispensable de ne pas séparer au sein du second ordre le bon grain et l'ivraie.

35 Voir Harold A. Ellis, *Boulainvilliers and the French Monarchy [...]*, Cornell Univ. Press, 1988, pp.208–213. Le critique le définit comme un 'aristocratic constitutionalist'.

36 *Pensées*, éd. Philippe Sellier, no. 94.

37 T.B. Macaulay, chap. I de son *Histoire d'Angleterre* (trad. par J. de Peyronet et A. Pichot), R. Laffont, 1989, t. I, p. 25.

38 *Essai de justification de l'Astrologie judiciaire* (Mss. d'Angoulême) cité dans R. Simon, *Boulainvilliers historien ...*, ouvr. cité, 4ème pie, chap. II, p. 640. Cf. p. 645: il faut 'déterminer un ascendant propre à chacun' (*Histoire de l'Apogée du Soleil*).

39 Voir F. Furet et M. Ozouf, art. cité, p. 44. Selon Voltaire, l'égalité est à la fois 'la chose la plus naturelle, et en même temps la plus chimérique' (*Dictionnaire philosophique*, art. 'Egalité'); il y a une 'inégalité nécessaire entre les conditions' (*Essai sur les mœurs*, ch. XCIII).

40 Voir D.Venturino, 'Metodologia della ricerca ... nella concezione storica di H. de B.', *Rivista storica italiana*, XCV, 1983, 2, 389–428.

PART II

THE POLITICS

OF

THEATRE

CHAPTER THIRTEEN

Corneille: Ethic and *Polis*

HENRY PHILLIPS

While a critical consensus exists to suggest that Corneille's early tragedies articulate the passage from the heroic to the political order, no unanimity is evident in the interpretation of that transition. The problem derives from the way in which the heroic ethic comprising a set of values, which legitimate heroic action accruing to the individual's 'gloire', can be adapted to or accommodated by a political order where value is invested in the undisputed authority of the king and where no alternative focus is permitted or possible. I shall navigate my own way through the interpretations now on offer by selecting various elements of the heroic ethic and charting their position in the transformation of the individual's place within the political community.[1] I shall concentrate especially on enactment, recognition, the refusal of dependency and heroic excess, paying attention above all to the role of Auguste in *Cinna*.

Enactment is important to the degree that heroism is not a state of being but is, in the words of Starobinski, a 'création continuée'.[2] The hero can never remain in stasis and must look always to be in action. Hence it is vital that occasions for heroic acts must be grasped: 'l'héroïsme ne saurait se contenter de "voir" et d' "attendre" le danger'.[3] Horace is the character who best expresses this aspect of the hero's situation in his celebrated speech to Curiace on the unique opportunity afforded each of them to reach hitherto unclimbed heroic peaks (lines 432–52). Enactment, that is to say the personal dynamism involved in heroic action, will be crucial to a proper understanding of Auguste.

Horace's remarks also demonstrate the existence of the heroic group which is complementary to royal authority and which exists in an uneasy alliance with it, forming as it does a community in its own right. The heroic group constitutes 'l'univers de la singularité',[4] its autonomy representing a challenge to the success of a centralized state. How can the heroic ethic privileging the action of individuals anxious either to secure or to enhance their reputation be compatible with an authority which is external to the heroic group? A fundamental issue is therefore the nature of the *political* community.

Another element of the heroic ethic relevant to the eventual move towards the political order is recognition which operates in what I shall call an axis of recognition. Doubrovsky underlines the importance of reciprocity in the necessity to be recognized by others of the same status.[5] The axis of recognition is illustrated at its most complete in *Le Cid* where Chimène must prove herself the equal of Rodrigue in terms of the ethical system they share. Clarke asserts that Chimène looks beyond private vengeance and places all her hopes in the king,[6] thus accepting a new political order. Greenberg argues that Chimène obstructs the new order in her constant pursuit of Rodrigue.[7] Neither view is sustainable. In this play each character provides the other with the legitimation of their action, and Rodrigue constantly submits himself to Chimène's judgement, in consequence seeking death, rather than defer to a higher authority (ll. 752–53 and ll. 1480–92). Rodrigue is as firmly placed in the order of Chimène as she is in his. This is not yet the political order.

The most telling evidence of Chimène remaining faithful to the demands of the heroic group is the way in which she expresses her own demand for justice to the king. Certainly she begins by suggesting that her pursuit of Rodrigue is of as much concern to the king's authority (ll. 681–2 and ll. 689–90). Later, the slippage from justice to revenge is apparent: 'Qu'il meure pour mon père' (l. 1365). The heroic ethic rather than royal justice is thus projected onto the king who, in having ultimately no option but to accede to the duel between Don Sanche and Rodrigue (l. 1425), is forced to accept a code which is not part of his political order. Moreover, although Rodrigue has fought the Moors without the king having issued an order (ll. 1217–8), this in no way contributes to a new political order. After his victory, the most important form of recognition comes from the Moorish kings who have fought in the battle and who confer on him the title of 'Le Cid'. Rodrigue remains in this sense outside the sphere of the king.

One of the problems identified by a number of critics in *Le Cid*, notably Prigent and Clarke, is the attitude of the older generation who seem to be estranged from the historical process as it is evolving. Is Rodrigue qualitatively different in the way he acts himself? Does he for example transcend the level of family quarrel to make amends by placing his valour successfully at the service of the state, thereby taking himself out of the heroic group to become absorbed in the political world of the king? This cannot be the case. Rodrigue and the Count of necessity share the same axis, or the Count would not consider Rodrigue worthy of fighting or even worthy of his daughter. Indeed, the Count speaks of 'Ce grand cœur qui paraît aux discours que tu tiens' (1. 419). Rodrigue in one sense imitates the Count, or at least recognizes his behaviour as worthy, in the same way that Rodrigue has come to recognize his own as the right course of action. There can be no qualitative difference in Rodrigue's status, or the status of the group, before and even after the batttle because the heroic impulse that leads him to fight Don Gomès is the same as that which leads him to fight the Moors. This is especially so if he has acted without the king's command. The state hero derives his legitimacy from the hero as defined in the terms of the heroic group. Rodrigue may be a more attractive character than the Count but in political terms he is not necessarily an advance on him. Rodrigue remains resolutely within the heroic group.

If the axis of recognition is intact in *Le Cid*, its decline begins with *Horace*. Horace reminds Curiace, from whom, above all others, he would expect to share this axis of recognition, what is lost if those within the heroic group fail to live up to its values (ll. 484–502). Horace's position is unconditional. Gradually, however, the sources of recognition fade away or are refused. Does he, as Prigent argues, become then a hero of the state? At the end of the play, at the judgement of Horace, the king does indeed include him in the needs of the state but from outside the heroic framework. Horace is not a hero of the state in the sense that he wishes to be so. The autonomy of the heroic situation is clearly established by Horace who makes it clear to Curiace that their combat is unique and that the opportunity is given only to them (ll. 432 et seq.). The state is barely mentioned in this most important speech.[8] The two orders, political and heroic, remain separate. The pull of the hero is still away from the political arena. The real problem is the gradual disappearance of an axis of recognition from those who are in a position to be part of it. Where are the other heroes? That is Horace's tragedy.

The disintegration of the axis of recognition is complete in *Cinna*, especially in a situation where the nature of heroic values has in any case degenerated.[9] In Act II, scene 1 Cinna gives an impression of the *grands* as divided amongst themselves (ll. 577–82). Rivalry may be an element of heroism – indeed it is essential – but not from within the sort of self-seeking coterie that Cinna describes. The implied need is therefore for a *chef* in a situation where the axis of recognition is so fragmented.

Cinna's case illustrates one further aspect of the complexity of the heroic situation as a prelude to a political solution and that is the notion of dependency. Within the heroic group dependency runs counter to the desired autonomy of the hero. It is however the position of kings which illustrates at its most crucial the relation of dependency. Don Gomès knows that Don Fernand's crown would be in jeopardy if he were to disappear, a fact which Fernand acknowledges himself (ll. 642–46). Tulle too has to admit that he needs Horace (ll. 1745–46). This relation of dependency is thus a threat to the king's unrivalled political authority.

The critical debate is perhaps sharpest at this point. Clarke asserts that in *Le Cid* Chimène and Rodrigue invest their hopes in the king in the name of a 'higher and reconciling justice which can fully resolve this conflict rooted in the feudal order which his rule has superseded'. Greenberg seems to ignore Rodrigue's acceptance of Chimène's position in maintaining that Rodrigue accomplishes the subjugation to 'the structure of the new Father' which Chimène refuses.[10] Moreover: 'The act of enunciating a judgement consolidates the king's power. It symbolically marks as a political act the "new beginning" of the State; a new beginning that is a new repression'.[11] My own analysis of *Le Cid* suggests that the grounds for this supersession have yet to be discovered because the king has still to establish his own autonomy. Although Prigent sees Chimène as partly responsible for the degeneration of the heroic position in helping to create 'l'Etat-arbitre et le roi-juge' and that *Le Cid* ends in an heroic universe 'animé par les lois de la monarchie', he at least admits that Fernand does not possess the means to enact his own politics and that he represents a transitional figure: 'l'Etat se construit en dehors de ce roi-juge'.[12]

Within *Le Cid* itself the position of royal authority can only be desired and exists at an ideal level. Don Arias may indeed argue that: 'Jamais à son sujet un roi n'est redevable' (l. 369). But: 'songez que les rois veulent être absolus' (l. 387). The slippage is obvious. The king's image, moreover, is sited in courtly flattery (the words of Don Arias again) rather than in reality:

> Ils [the Moors] savent au dépens de leurs plus dignes têtes
> Combien votre présence assure vos conquêtes. (ll. 621–22)

The reality is that Rodrigue will frighten the Moors in the *absence* of the king. The very opportunism of the king's justice in *Horace* is a sign of his dependence on Horace.

But there are two other problems which kings confront in the face of an ethic existing as complementary if not contrary to the political order. The first is the idea of excess inherent in the heroic act. Heroism is of course by definition 'excessive' because all acts in the present and future must exceed those which have preceded them. Fernand himself seems to legitimate the notion of excess:

Et lorsque la valeur ne va point dans l'excès,
Elle ne produit point de si rares succès. (ll. 1239–40)

In *Horace* it seems even that the legitimacy of excess is unconditional and affects affairs of the family as well as affairs of state. Tulle expresses this dilemma himself:

Je viens de savoir quel étrange malheur
D'un fils victorieux a suivi la valeur,
Et que son trop d'amour pour la cause publique,
Par ses mains à son père ôte une fille unique. (ll. 1453–56)

He even addresses Horace as 'guerrier trop magnanime' (l. 1759). The king admits that the need for excess places Horace 'au-dessus des lois' (l. 1754):

Ta vertu met ta gloire au-dessus de ton crime;
Sa chaleur généreuse a produit ton forfait;
D'une cause si belle il faut souffrir l'effet. (ll. 1760–62)

No limits then can be set to this excess in the name of the state since excess is a condition of heroism and the state has need of heroes. In any case, by its very nature, no real measure of excess can exist. It is excess more than any other aspect of the heroic ethic which the political order must seemingly appropriate, especially since excess can be so harmful to the state in a group which is outside the political order.

The second problem I have referred to above is the focus of admiration in the context of heroism and politics.[13] 'Admiration' can loosely be defined as a sense of awe before the actions of characters who behave as befits their rank and status as heroes. It implies no moral judgement. 'Admiration' thus focuses the attention of the spectator on the hero who becomes the centre of our emotional response. Corneille's 'admiration' could also be regarded as akin to charisma. Max Weber's definition reproduced in the *Supplement* to the OED refers to charisma as setting an individual personality apart from ordinary men by virtue of exceptional powers or qualities. Paul Ricoeur argues that what Weber calls 'le pouvoir charismatique' is 'la grâce personnelle et extraordinaire qui fait de certains individus des "chefs"'.[14]

One of the factors of 'admiration' is that the hero as its source provides a model to be followed or imitated. The hero is undoubtedly the focus of 'admiration' or charisma. This is particularly true of Le Cid who becomes a 'chef' in his own right as recognized by foreign kings and co-exists as such with his own king. The passage from the heroic ethic to the political order will also require the appropriation of 'admiration'/charisma. But charisma is essentially a personal quality. The political order, if it is to stand alone as the supreme authority and value, will therefore have to project 'admiration'/charisma through the *person* of the king rather than through royal authority as simply a function of the State.

Auguste is the eventual focus of all these issues and is promoted as at once the saviour of heroism and of the State. This can only be achieved by the gradual isolation of previous heroes. Horace becomes conscious of his isolation in Act IV, scene 5 and gives the impression of believing that even his father has abandoned him (ll. 1419–26). The isolation of Horace is compounded by the *conditional* response of others to his unconditional demands. All the characters in *Cinna* arrive at a form of isolation. Emilie is abandoned by Cinna, and Maxime rejects Auguste and is rejected by Emilie. Finally Auguste is abandoned by everybody, except of course Livie, who is not herself of any heroic status. Auguste stares at a void from which he must and does emerge.

But the establishment of royal authority as the supreme value has above all to address the person of the monarch, especially since Fernand and Tulle have manifestly lacked any substantial personality, and this must be achieved through the enactment that occurs once Auguste has been confronted with the void which faces him. Hence Auguste's clemency must be a personal decision and not one founded on the 'external' advice of Livie. Moreover without such enactment the state would be deprived of dynamism or at least it would be a dynamism which the king does not control. Prigent is right moreover to suggest that Auguste's clemency gives him a chance to establish his autonomy whereas revenge would simply align him with others.[15] Royal authority should be seen to be acting upon the world and not as subject to it.

The king has also to find his place in the axis of recognition. It emerges in the course of *Cinna* that the axis of recognition has collapsed and that Auguste has no axis of recognition within which to situate himself. Recognition is related directly to the notion of example. It is essential for the king, if he is to convince or convert others, to be the source of recognition and therefore of imitation. His act of clemency ensures that he is the unrivalled focus of recognition. As the supreme model he can then judge the heroism of others. For others to be recognized they depend on him to the extent that all must enter his world. The recognition he dispenses and of which he is the criterion becomes therefore a function of power. Furthermore Auguste represents a single focus of 'admiration' to the extent that there is no longer competition for it. Competition now derives from the need to secure the recognition of the monarch. Charisma is then associated with the real 'chef' and the charisma of others is borrowed. Indeed Auguste's example spreads even more widely than his own kingdom in that he constitutes an example for other kings (ll. 1773–74).

What we have witnessed in *Cinna* is nothing less than the fusion of hero and monarch which, in Clarke's words, enables Auguste to 'reconcile all interests and transcend partisan disunity within the community of men'.[16] This does not entail the disappearance of the heroic ethic. Rather the political solution can only occur on the basis of an appropriation by politics of that ethic. This is not without its problems. In the first place the appropriation of heroic values by the king legitimizes them but at the same time denies access to them by others since the heroic group has in the past been the source of reciprocal recognition. The hero has been designated so precisely because there were other heroes. Now no other individual can be the equal of the king. The legitimation of heroic values seems to be a way of dissolving them. But how can we then judge Auguste as a hero?

Another problem is that of enactment. In the case of Auguste himself, how is enactment possible in the future? Does he retain his heroic status by sole virtue of his act of clemency? Or does Corneille look forward to the cult of image-making where the consecration in history of this new beginning for royal power in the image of the king as hero is a substitute for heroic action itself? For there is a problem for future kings. Certainly Auguste has managed to create himself. Is it therefore necessary for others to do so in the same way, especially when heroism is, so to speak, not transferable? If so, how do they achieve this? Doubrovsky's comment is highly pertinent: 'Après l'insuffisance du héros, on devine celle du monarque, plus cruelle encore, puisqu'elle ne laisse plus, après elle, aucun recours. Alors que la Politique devait éliminer la Tragédie, nous assistons à *la Tragédie même de la Politique*'.[17] There is in any case no going back. Royal authority could not possibly relinquish a position on which its power is so unequivocally founded, to the extent that new forms of control which limit the scope of action and which increase the relation of dependency (like that of Versailles?) may have to be envisaged.

This dissolution of heroic values increases even more in the case of the monarch the isolation which attaches to the heroic group (the latter is not as such a socializing institution). Prigent is right to comment that: 'La solitude héroïque et la solitude monarchique se superposent'.[18] Greenberg speaks of 'his splendid, isolated integrity'.[19] Auguste's isolation is reflected in an axis of recognition where there is no longer a real sense of reciprocity. As Doubrovsky points out: 'Malheureusement, le projet d'Auguste d'être traité à la fois comme "ami" et comme "souverain", ou plus exactement, de retrouver sa souveraineté par le biais de l'amitié est contradictoire. On ne peut établir en même temps des relations de supériorité ou de réciprocité'.[20] It is difficult in these circumstances to see Auguste as a member of a group. Doubrovsky's conclusion that 'le héros renvoie au roi, le roi au héros. Cette circularité semble fonder désormais l'équilibre de l'Etat'[21] would be acceptable if the implication of his statement were that there are no other heroes. By establishing uncontested power, the new system can only work in one direction. The heroic group is absorbed in the monarch.

One of the problems we associated with heroism in *Le Cid* and *Horace* was the apparent legitimation of excess in heroic action by the king. If the monarch has now appropriated the heroic ethic in the political context, what is his relation to the problem of excess? Auguste has shown himself capable of excess in going beyond what might be expected of him after the discovery of the conspiracy, in which case he represents the ultimate legitimation of excess. The question in his case becomes now the limits of excess in the sense that he would seem to be the arbiter of what they might be. If he is the only hero, he is clearly in one sense in excess of others. But will he at the same time be able to impose limits on himself, especially in the light of heroic excess being associated with crime and with the hero being set thereby 'au-dessus des lois'? Auguste's clemency is certainly an excess of virtue but, if kings have henceforward to create themselves, where is the guarantee that they will behave like Auguste?[22]

A paradox in the situation of Auguste might be however that the establishment of political authority based on heroic values and on a reversal of the relation of dependency in particular, finds itself dependent on another perspective. Many critics have pointed to the importance of religion at the end of *Cinna*. Auguste's clemency becomes a 'pardon de Dieu'.[23] It is given to Livie to express this divine consecration:

> [Rome] n'a plus de vœux que pour la monarchie,
> Vous prépare déjà des temples, des autels,
> Et le ciel une place entre les immortels. (ll. 1771–73)

This places a rather different emphasis on the 'conversion' of Emilie who seems to experience a 'road to Damascus' in reverse:

Et je me rends, Seigneur, à ces hautes bontés;
Je recouvre la vue auprès de leurs clartés. (ll. 1713–14)

Doubrovsky registers Emilie's realization as a 'prise de conscience
politique'.[24] Is it not rather an act of faith, since Emilie does not seem
to 'think out' her new-found position, linking it herself to a divine
origin:

Le ciel a résolu votre grandeur suprême;
Et pour preuve, seigneur, je n'en veux que moi-même. (ll. 1721–22)

Furthermore this conversion and act of faith are isolated in time.
Political argument can eventually constitute a form of knowledge
which is transferable in the way that acts of faith are not. But at the
stage we have reached in *Cinna* we have not yet reached the
legitimation of the divine status of the monarch.

Doubrovsky's assertion that *Polyeucte* is not a religious play at all
seems in this context to be quite valid. Clarke points out that for
seventeenth-century *moralistes* little difference existed between the
hero and the saint since the hand of God is at work in all deeds of
exceptional virtue:

both Balzac and Corneille draw on a mystical theory of heroism and
kingship in which this higher and impulsive reason is believed so
suddenly to illuminate individual action that it offers incontrovertible
evidence of heroic rightness and, in the case of the ruler, of royal
legitimacy. In pardoning Cinna, Auguste senses to the full this
passionate spur to action and at last achieves a harmony with the
highest kind of Reason in the grace of a full understanding of God's
providential purpose in the world.[25]

The main problem here is that the religious legitimation of Auguste's
position is asserted rather than demonstrated. *Polyeucte* therefore
takes us one stage further.

Example in the matter of conversion has been seen in the case of
Emilie and Auguste to have been of supreme importance. Pauline's
conversion on the basis of Polyeucte's example is also an act of faith,
but this time according to a faith which is directly focused on the
Christian God. The most important act of conversion however is that of
Félix which resituates the axis of recognition within a Christian
framework. Sévère's lack of hostility to Christianity and his assertion
that service to God is not incompatible with service to the emperor
completes the integration of power within the same framework.
Doubrovsky's comment on *Polyeucte* is of paramount importance for
the passage of the heroic to the political but via the example of the hero:

Le service du monarque terrestre et du monarque divin doit, en fin de compte, être identique. Si Félix, devenu chrétien, reste gouverneur, et s'il prononce les dernières paroles de la pièce, c'est qu'en lui, l'alliance du salut et de l'ordre a le dernier mot: il n'est plus simplement question que Dieu assure le salut individuel ... mais encore le salut de l'Etat.[26]

The constraints of space prohibit any further exploration of the implications of the appropriation of the heroic ethic by the political order. It would however be important to assess the consequences of Auguste's clemency for control of the writing of history which became so vital in the seventeenth century. A precondition of that control might be that the king should himself make history, a further reason for the absorption of the heroic imperative into the political order. The most important realization of Corneille is in the investment of power in the *person* of the king. This is peculiarly suitable for a concept of tragedy based on the dynamics of action through character. In this light it is interesting that so many of the plays following those I have dealt with constitute a prolonged reflection on kingship. But that narrower focus has considerably less dramatic potential than working through the problems of history. The rest of Corneille's theatre provides only footnotes to what has gone before.

Notes

1   The interpretations of Corneille's writings I shall be referring to are: D. Clarke, *Pierre Corneille: Poetics and Political Drama under Louis XIII*, Cambridge, 1992; S. Doubrovsky, *Corneille ou la dialectique du héros*, Paris, 1963; M. Greenberg, *Corneille, Classicism and the Rules of Symmetry*, Cambridge, 1986; M. Prigent, *Le Héros et l'Etat dans la tragédie de Corneille*, Paris, 1986. There is also an essay of Greenberg's entitled 'The Grateful Dead: Corneille's Tragedy and the Subject of History', in *Subjectivity and Subjugation in Seventeenth-Century Drama and Prose: the Family Romance of French Classicism*, Cambridge, 1992, pp. 48–64.
2   Quoted in Prigent, p. 77.
3   Doubrovsky, p. 138.
4   Prigent, p. 76.
5   Doubrovsky, p. 147.
6   Clarke, p. 151.
7   Greenberg, *Corneille*, p. 52.
8   See Doubrovsky, p. 149 and p. 162. For a contrary view, see Prigent, p. 42.
9   See Doubrovsky, p. 191.
10   Clarke, p. 151 and Greenberg, *Corneille*, pp. 52–53.
11   Greenberg, *Corneille*, p. 86.
12   Prigent, p. 183, p. 116 and p. 123.
13   See H. Phillips, *The Theatre and its Critics in Seventeenth-Century France*, Oxford, 1980, pp. 67–70, and Clarke, pp. 101–3.
14   P. Ricœur, 'Ethique et politique', in *Lectures 1: Autour du politique*, Paris, 1991, pp. 233–38, p. 234.
15   Prigent, p. 65.
16   Prigent, p. 65.
17   Doubrovsky, p. 221 (Doubrovsky's emphasis, p. 221).

18 Prigent, p. 57.
19 Greenberg, *Corneille*, p. 115.
20 Doubrovsky, p. 57.
21 Doubrovsky, p. 218.
22 Prigent is aware of this problem (see p. 147).
23 Doubrovsky, p. 221.
24 Doubrovsky, p. 216.
25 Clarke, pp. 227–28.
26 Doubrovsky, p. 258.

CHAPTER FOURTEEN

Sur l'échec des conjurés dans *La Mort de Sénèque*

MADELEINE BERTAUD

Des tragédies de la conspiration composées au XVIIe siècle, celles à sujet romain sont les mieux connues. Très rapprochées dans le temps, elles présentent entre elles suffisamment de ressemblances pour que Roger Guichemerre ait pu parler d'une 'véritable typologie de la tragédie de la conjuration'. Cependant chacune d'elles, remarquait-il aussitôt, a sa tonalité particulière, son 'individualité propre'.[1] On ne peut en effet cerner leur contenu politique et moral en évoquant simplement le thème du tyran, ou l'histoire du règne de Louis XIII, fertile en complots, même si l'un comme l'autre donnent à ce théâtre de la conspiration un air de famille.

Nous nous proposons donc d'adopter, pour *La Mort de Sénèque,*[2] un angle d'observation beaucoup moins ouvert en nous arrêtant à l'échec des conjurés. A la différence de *La Mort de César* ou de *Cinna,* mais semblable en cela à *La Mort d'Agrippine* du libertin Cyrano de Bergerac, la tragédie de Tristan ne met pas en scène un Prince dont le sage gouvernement mérite que l'on oublie le coup d'Etat qui l'a porté au pouvoir, et qu'on lui reconnaisse une véritable légitimité—comme Auguste ou César, présents avec cette image dans la mémoire collective, mais un tyran, et même un de ceux que l'Histoire a le plus résolument désignés comme des monstres. A priori, le traitement d'un tel sujet semble appeler une perspective radicalement manichéenne, amenant à regretter l'échec des conjurés. Sans doute *La Mort de Sénèque* permet-elle une lecture simple: Pison et ses amis tentent de mettre fin au règne de Néron; malheureusement, ils échouent (de même, Agrippine aspire à venger la mort de Germanicus; malheureusement, elle échoue). Cependant un examen attentif des mobiles des différents conjurés, des raisons de leur échec, et aussi de la manière dont leur fin, puis celle, toute différente, de Sénèque, sont présentées, oblige à revenir sur ce schéma.

Les conjurés apparaissent au début de l'acte II, à un moment où leur dessein est formé, et son exécution proche, puisque le fer destiné à Néron est déjà prêt. Cependant leurs motivations sont-elles claires? Sont-elles absolument saines? Le seul Rufus mentionne les siennes, en termes vagues ('un feu de vengeance', II, 2, v. 322) et qui donnent à craindre qu'il ne règle ses propres comptes:

> L'infâme! il apprendra le poignard dans le cœur
> Qu'il devait n'estimer que les hommes d'honneur. (vv. 323–324)

Cette impression sera de fait confirmée par Sénèque un peu plus loin:

> Ce brave Capitaine est jaloux aujourd'hui
> Qu'un lâche Tigillin soit mieux traité que lui. (II, 4, vv. 647–648)

Surtout, on remarquera qu'il faut qu'arrive Epicaris, une femme, et une affranchie, pour que les mots de Parricide, de Tyran, de Monstre, soient lancés (II, 2, vv. 334, 386, 397, 399), et que les crimes de Néron soient rappelés, avec une véhémente indignation ('Avons-nous oublié ...', v. 341; 'Ne nous souvient-il plus ...', v. 349), à ceux qui ont apparemment besoin d'être stimulés pour agir, tandis qu'à Pison même il faut rappeler ses responsabilités de chef (vv. 409–410). La première faiblesse des conjurés tient donc à leur manque de détermination, à ce 'sentiment timide' dont s'inquiète Epicaris (v. 333). Quant au 'zèle ardent' dont parle la jeune femme (II, 3, v. 568), il semble gîter en elle seule. Ou presque – car Lucain est fermement déterminé à aller jusqu'au bout:

> La gloire est d'achever cette belle entreprise ... (II-3, v. 489)

Mais bien qu'il se dise inspiré par la Vertu, et par le Ciel (vv. 490–491), on ne peut s'empêcher de penser que l'amour est son premier moteur ('... Je veux à votre exemple ...', v. 554). Epicaris le chapitre d'ailleurs sur ce sujet:

> ... toute l'amour qu'il faut que l'on explique
> Doit avoir pour objet la Liberté publique. (II, 3, vv. 549–550)

Disons que si Lucain aime vraiment 'la République' (v. 553) et diffère en cela de Cinna, qui doit se faire violence pour adhérer à la cause de sa maîtresse, sa motivation n'est pas politiquement pure.

Trouve-t-on par ailleurs chez les conjurés (chez tous les conjurés) les qualités requises (toutes les qualités) pour mener à bien le projet qu'ils exposent à l'acte II, un de ceux qui permettent d'entrer dans l'Histoire auréolé de gloire, à condition, comme le rappelle Lucain, d'aller jusqu'au bout ?

> Mais il faut faire en sorte, ...
> Qu'à ce digne projet l'événement réponde,
> Et qu'il ne soit pas dit aux siècles à venir
> Qu'on entreprit fort bien ce qu'on ne peut finir. (II, 3, vv. 485–488)

La première, et la plus indispensable, est énoncée par Sénèque, c'est le courage, poussé jusqu'à l'abnégation:

> Qui voudra pour le perdre [Néron] abandonner sa vie
> Pourra facilement contenter son envie. (II, 4, vv. 625–626)

Or on voit Rufus plus disposé à mesurer les risques de l'entreprise que la gloire qu'elle peut procurer (II, 2, v. 455). Cependant le vieillard n'est pas inquiet là-dessus: à l'exemple de ses ancêtres Pison est d'un cœur 'et noble et franc' (II, 4, v. 639), la plupart des autres ont 'l'âme grande et hautaine' (v. 654). Il redoute plutôt la présence, dans un groupe à l'évidence trop nombreux pour avoir une forte cohésion, d'un traître (v. 665), et ne voit qu'un moyen de prévenir ce danger: se hâter.

La hâte, qui est en elle-même un facteur de risque (les préparatifs seront bâclés), est aussi le moyen d'éviter que le secret ne s'évente. Alors que Lucain se méfie—à tort—du naturel féminin, 'enclin à trop parler' (II, 3, v. 495), c'est à Sévinus que songe Sénèque:

> Il s'empêche de tout, de tout il fait mystère,
> Si ses propos mal joints ne donnent des soupçons,
> Il en pourra donner par toutes ses façons. (vv. 658–660)

Que manque-t-il au Sénateur? La discrétion, qui en l'occurrence serait un trait d'intelligence. Nous touchons là à quelque chose d'essentiel: l'intelligence n'est pas moins indispensable à des conjurés que le courage physique, que les qualités morales. Or, tandis que celle de Néron s'impose à l'évidence, seule parmi ses ennemis Epicaris se distingue vraiment par 'la bonté du sens' (II, 3, v. 508), qu'on la verra déployer lorsqu'après son arrestation elle sera confrontée au tyran et à Procule, son délateur.[3] En revanche, comme l'avait compris Sénèque, le comportement de Sévinus sera fatal à tous: non content de faire dérouiller dans sa maison une arme tenue de ses ancêtres, il rédigera son testament, fera préparer baume et bandages ... Tant de mystères intrigueront son affranchi: Milicus n'aurait rien eu à dire à Sabine si Sévinus avait été sage. Cet homme, que très lucidement Néron méprise —N'a-t-il de grands desseins que pour m'assassiner? (III, 2, v. 954) —n'était pas de taille à préparer un coup d'Etat.

Voici un tableau qui n'est pas de bon augure—encore n'est-il pas complet. Les entreprises politiques, et c'est le mérite de Machiavel, si mal compris dans la France d'Ancien Régime, de l'avoir affirmé, ne s'accommodent pas toujours des exigences de la morale individuelle, ni du code de l'honneur en usage dans telle ou telle société. Le sens des réalités, de l'efficacité, doit l'emporter sur le culte de la vertu, et il y a de la grandeur à faire ce choix, quand l'objectif le vaut. C'est ce que n'a pas compris Pison, qui refuse d'inviter le tyran dans sa maison, afin qu'on l'y poignarde:

> Ce trait me fait horreur, je ne suis point capable
> De voir du sang d'un hôte ainsi tacher ma table. (II, 2, vv. 433–434)

Epicaris admettra que ce refus est 'généreux' (v. 446), mais de l'échec des conjurés émane une autre leçon: quand on travaille au bien public, il est des vertus qui deviennent des défauts, et qui loin d'approcher celui qui les cultive de l'abnégation, s'apparentent à l'amour-propre.

Ainsi, avant même que la nouvelle des arrestations d'Epicaris, puis de Sévinus, ne sème le trouble chez les conjurés et ne les oblige à inventer une conduite adaptée à cette situation imprévue, de graves tares, et des insuffisances, marquent leur groupe. On ne peut s'attendre à ce que celles-ci s'évanouissent dans les difficultés. En ce qui concerne le courage physique et l'abnégation, la femme certes ne décevra pas. Elle acceptera, non seulement de sacrifier sa vie, mais de souffrir les pires tourments, répondant ainsi à l'attente confiante de Lucain:

> Elle est toute romaine en grandeur de courage. ...
> Plaignons Epicaris, mais ne la craignons pas. (IV, 1, vv. 1100–1113)

Elle montrera cette 'constance' (v. 1112) dont les contemporains de Tristan, lecteurs de Juste Lipse et de Du Vair, savaient qu'elle était le propre des vrais stoïciens. Cependant, en état d'arrestation, l'enjeu de son sacrifice ne pourra plus être la perte du tyran, mais seulement le salut de ses amis.

Quant à eux, comment se comporteront-ils? Et d'abord, comment réagira leur chef? Par la peur, l'accablement, le désespoir, et par d'inutiles plaintes —' ... tout est perdu', IV, 1, v. 1078—qui sont aussi des lamentations sur lui-même: 'O malheureux Pison!' (v. 1091). Loin de penser à aider ses hommes, il cède au découragement, et de manière durable. Le désespoir, que l'Ecole rangeait au nombre des passions, ne trouvait naturellement pas grâce aux yeux des stoïciens. Mais il n'était pas moins grave dans l'optique chrétienne, puisque désespérer revient à douter de la bonté divine. Et Pison en effet doute de celle-ci:

> Le sort nous est contraire, et le Ciel en courroux
> Pour conserver Néron, prend parti contre nous. (vv. 1081–1082)
> Les Cieux nous ont trahis pour protéger le crime. (v. 1163)

C'est assez dire que ce chef perd dans l'épreuve sa qualité de chef, et le geste de Lucain qui le quitte (v. 1157) a des allures de destitution, tandis que les énergiques leçons de Rufus le soldat montrent l'étendue de sa déception: il lui parle d'honneur, de gloire, de vertu (vv. 1165–1171; 1182–1185), et lui rappelle que le danger faisait partie de l'entreprise, qu'il est inclus dans le prix de la gloire à acquérir; que l'important est d'agir vite et, puisque le plan initialement prévu ne peut se dérouler, d'improviser, de gagner le peuple, de combattre – et de mourir s'il le faut, de 'la main d'un soldat' (v. 1230) plutôt que de celle d'un bourreau. A rien de tout cela Pison ne peut se résoudre: il redoute la garde allemande de l'empereur, il méprise trop le peuple, 'ce Monstre à cent têtes' (v. 1216), pour s'appuyer sur lui. Enfin, il craint que la colère du tyran ne retombe sur sa femme:

> Si dans cet accident on voit que je frissonne,
> C'est de crainte que j'ai pour sa chère personne. (III, 2, vv. 1267–1268)

Un sentiment qui, même si l'on admet son authenticité—car il peut aussi servir à déguiser sa peur—et après son respect inopportun des lois de l'hospitalité, le range définitivement dans le camp des faibles, indignes de servir une noble cause. Un grand Romain comme on se les imaginait à l'époque de Tristan—le Fabricius de Guez de Balzac ou le vieil Horace—n'aurait jamais eu ce genre de préoccupation. Pison quitte la scène, alors que Rufus, résigné, lui lance:

> Si tu viens à périr, meurs sans nous faire tort. (v. 1273)

Cette prière sera la seule entendue—Pison se fera ouvrir les veines dans sa maison.

Sévinus nous occupera moins longtemps; son manque d'intelligence étant connu, il suffira d'y ajouter la lâcheté, que Pison avait prévue:

> Cet homme délicat se voyant à la gêne,
> Abrégera nos jours pour accourcir sa peine. (IV, 2, vv. 1175–1176)

Elle n'éclatera pas sur-le-champ, et Néron perdra un peu de temps à le faire parler. Mais le piège imaginé par Milicus—lui faire savoir, ou lui donner à croire, que son ami Natalis a parlé—ne manquera pas son effet. Sitôt maudit ce perfide supposé, Sévinus se met à table puis, ne saisissant pas le jeu de Rufus qui feint de vouloir le faire parler, trahit celui-ci, par dépit autant que par bêtise. Après 'ces bons offices' (IV, 4, v. 1360) rendus à Néron, il suffira à Sabine de laisser miroiter un pardon, une grâce, la vie sauve enfin, au lieu des tourments attendus, pour que le digne Sénateur, qui n'oublie pas qu'il a donné sa foi de ne pas parler, lui remette ... un papier, une liste. On retrouvera l'homme à l'acte V, dans un rôle plus répugnant encore, lorsqu'il essaiera de faire parler Epicaris en lui promettant le pardon de César, juste avant que cette 'passionaria', cette 'Vierge de la Révolution', selon les expressions de Jacques Scherer,[4] n'aille à la mort en bravant Néron et sa compagne:

> Tyran, je t'apprendrai que je sais bien mourir. (V, 3, v. 1750)

Quant à Lucain, deux vers suffisent à nous le donner à voir, tel que les *Annales* l'ont montré: il

> Nomme tous ses Amis qui trempent dans le crime
> Des tourments préparés redoutant la rigueur. (V, 3, vv. 1696–1697)

Comment, devant un tel tableau, se dire que le dramaturge n'a pas voulu porter un jugement sur ses personnages de conjurés? Jacques Scherer a souligné que ceux-ci étaient 'traités beaucoup plus sévèrement par Tacite que par Tristan';[5] cela va de soi, et nous ne reviendrons pas sur le parallèle qu'il a esquissé entre le livre XV des *Annales* et notre tragédie, d'autant que les notes de l'édition de Jacques Madeleine parlent d'elles-mêmes. Mais il n'est peut-être pas superflu de considérer les deux types de transformations apportées par Tristan aux figures que lui fournissait l'historien. Pour les hommes, rien n'est conservé de ce qui touchait aux mœurs relâchées de Sévinus, à l'épicurisme de Pison, qui n'était vertueux qu'en apparence. Comme l'a noté le savant éditeur, la discrétion du dramaturge leur donne plus de 'dignité tragique'[6] qu'à leurs modèles, c'est-à-dire qu'elle fait d'eux des personnages propres à évoluer dans une tragédie, telle que l'avait définie Aristote. Les gommages ici n'ont pas de signification politique, ils sont simplement imposés par le genre pratiqué. En revanche, tout ce sur quoi Tristan a mis l'accent—le manque d'intelligence des conjurés, qui explique à la fois l'insuffisante préparation du complot et les indiscrétions commises, leurs carences morales, la vertu au sens premier du terme, cette force de l'homme qui leur fait si lamentablement défaut—semble bien indiquer qu'il n'avait aucune sympathie à l'égard de ces personnages, et que leur échec ne lui inspirait pas d'indulgence. Quant à Epicaris, dont Tacite assurait qu'avant qu'elle n'entrât, on ne sait comment, dans leur secret, 'rien d'honnête ... n'avait occupé sa pensée', l'héroïsation dont elle est l'objet, si contraire aux préjugés qui s'attachaient aux rôles d'affranchis, s'explique moins par le mythe du Romain évoqué ci-dessus, que par la volonté de l'auteur de faire ressortir davantage encore, en saluant le courage d'une femme, l'insuffisance des hommes. Le respect de l'histoire ne permettait naturellement pas de transformer Epicaris en une nouvelle Judith, mais elle est bien plus qu'une égérie telle que l'époque de Louis XIII en connut. Elle est déterminée, intelligente, vertueuse, prête à mourir pour le bien public; et quand on l'entend, alors qu'elle vient de subir la torture, braver Néron et Sabine, on songe aux vers de Corneille, qui étaient encore à écrire:

> Le débris de l'Empire a de belles ruines,
> S'il n'a plus de Héros, il a des Héroïnes ... (*Attila*, I, 2, vv. 253–254)

L'analyse qui vient d'être faite pourrait induire en erreur: si Tristan brosse des conjurés ce tableau peu flatteur, c'est sans doute qu'il ne blâme pas celui qu'ils rêvent d'abattre. Mais la mise en scène d'un être tel que Néron rend l'hypothèse aberrante; et ce serait une perte de temps que de démontrer ce qui est évident: l'empereur qui a fait assassiner sa mère et incendier sa Ville, celui qui 'désole Rome aux yeux de tout le Monde' (II, 2, v. 338), est un monstre. Et notre auteur n'a pas fait le choix scandaleux du monstre contre ses adversaires.[7] C'est dans un autre débat qu'il a pris, nous semble-t-il, position. Pour ce faire, il a choisi pour héros un personnage extérieur à la conjuration, un Sage, et en même temps une victime de Néron. Et il l'a fait parler, agir, mourir.

Sénèque occupe parmi les personnages une place tout à fait à part, et qu'il faut se garder de commenter hâtivement: le vieil homme ne peut entrer dans la conjuration, puisque Néron est son 'nourrisson' (v. 680). Certes cette raison n'est pas sans valeur, pas plus qu'il ne faut compter pour rien sa reconnaissance à l'égard d'un maître généreux. Mais les propos que le philosophe tient à son neveu, qui est aussi son disciple, et qui ne se trouvent pas chez Tacite,[8] contiennent des leçons qui ne valent peut-être pas que pour lui. Sénèque n'a aucune hésitation sur la nature de Néron: l'empereur est devenu un tyran. Du tyran il a la cruauté et la bassesse morale, la démesure et la faiblesse (voir II, 4, vv. 585–590). Pourtant le vieillard refuse de rejoindre les conjurés:

> Je m'en lave les mains, et je n'y trempe point. (II, 4, v. 696)

Quoique la formule fasse—un peu fâcheusement—penser à Pilate, elle n'indique ni démission, ni lâcheté. Sénèque a du tyran une conception qui transcende le plan simplement humain, et de l'Histoire une vision tout à fait providentielle:

> C'est un fléau des Dieux;
> C'est la punition de nos fautes passées:
> C'est un présent fatal de leurs mains courroucées,
> Qu'ils pourront retirer selon notre souhait
> Quand leur juste courroux se sera satisfait. (II, 4, vv. 612–616)

L'idée d'un châtiment envoyé par le Ciel était présente chez Tacite (L. XVI, 16), mais elle se trouvait aussi dans *La Cour Sainte*, bien connue de Tristan, qui s'en était déjà copieusement inspiré pour sa *Mariamne*, et qui y revint encore pour *La Mort de Crispe*. Du long chapitre du P. Caussin intitulé 'Saint Paul et Sénèque à la cour de Néron', le dramaturge ne retint guère que cela, et l'hypothèse d'un Sénèque chrétien, converti par l'apôtre (voir II, 4, vv. 703–709). Ces emprunts, alors qu'à la même époque l'avocat Mascaron, qui fournit également à Tristan quelques détails, ne croyait pas à la conversion du philosophe, ni d'ailleurs à de possibles rencontres ou échanges épistolaires entre les deux hommes,[9] donnent à penser. Car c'est précisément le jour où il s'apprête à se rendre chez Paul, et où il découvre à Lucain cette nouvelle loi 'de respect, de justice et d'amour' (v. 708), que le vieillard refuse de se joindre aux conjurés, et donc de faire sienne la doctrine selon laquelle,

> Pour punir les Tyrans dans le siècle où nous sommes
> Les Dieux le plus souvent se sont servis des hommes. (vv. 617–618)

Tristan prenait ainsi position sur une grave question politique, à laquelle les assassinats d'Henri III et d'Henri IV avaient donné une actualité brûlante qu'entretenaient, même s'ils ne visaient pas la personne du Roi, les complots qui marquèrent le règne de Louis XIII. Pour les théoriciens de la monarchie de droit divin, le tyran est certes un fléau, mais un fléau envoyé par Dieu, et dont le châtiment est l'affaire de Dieu. Le tyrannicide est donc interdit, puisqu'en le pratiquant les sujets se substituent à Dieu dans l'exercice de sa justice. Cette doctrine fut, à la fin du XVIe siècle et dans les décennies qui suivirent, l'objet de graves attaques.[10] Or, de Néron, Sénèque parle en précepteur, mais aussi en simple sujet lorsqu'il considère que le tuer serait pour lui commettre un 'parricide' (v. 678). Il suffirait d'ailleurs de changer le dernier mot des propos qui suivent (de remplacer 'nourriture' par 'père'), pour qu'ils deviennent une exacte profession d'adhésion au principe de la monarchie de droit divin:

Mais voyant de l'Etat la ruine éclater
Sénèque doit le plaindre et non pas l'assister;
Il croirait irriter le Ciel et la Nature
S'il attentait ainsi contre sa nourriture. (vv. 691–694)

Quant au procès du monstre, il ne réunit pas, pêle-mêle, tous les meurtres ordonnés par Néron. Ceux qui sont rappelés par Epicaris (I, 2) appartiennent au passé de la tragédie. Mais, dans le temps de l'action, le crime de Néron n'est pas de faire mettre à mort les conjurés: peu de chefs d'Etat ont imité Auguste, et l'Histoire ne les a pas pour cela montrés du doigt; Biron n'a pas été gracié par Henri IV, ni Bastien-Thiry par De Gaulle. En fait, seule la torture infligée à Epicaris ajoute, dans cet épisode de la conjuration, à la noirceur du tyran. Le crime de Néron, c'est comme le titre l'indique d'avoir ordonné la mort d'un innocent, à qui il devait tant. Injustice, cruauté, cupidité, ingratitude, faiblesse d'un homme que Sabine manœuvre à sa guise, voilà les fautes capitales dont le dramaturge laissera entendre, en le montrant en proie à la folie (détail présent dans *La Vie des douze Césars* de Suétone ainsi que chez Caussin et Mascaron, mais que l'on ne trouve pas chez Tacite), que Dieu le châtiera terriblement, tout comme il a châtié Hérode après la mort de Mariamne.

Ces remarques n'auraient pas lieu d'être faites à propos d'un Corneille, ou d'un Scudéry, dont l'attachement aux principes monarchiques, et pour le second à la personne de Richelieu, est notoire. Mais sur Tristan, l'on a moins de certitudes. Il a longtemps appartenu à la maison de Monsieur, et le monde des conspirateurs ne devait pas lui être inconnu, même s'il ne pouvait en observer que les dehors, et l'agitation. Il semble s'en être fait une piètre idée. Trouvant chez Tacite un tableau qui s'accordait à ses propres impressions, il n'eut pas envie de l'adoucir. Il tenait ainsi compte du changement qui était en train de s'amorcer dans la manière d'écrire l'Histoire, moins événementielle, plus attentive aux hommes, et qu'on allait retrouver mûrie, un peu plus tard, chez Saint-Réal. Mais, surtout, il fournissait un indice non négligeable aux historiens de la littérature et aux biographes, qui s'interrogent sur ses attaches avec le libertinage, pour y croire, comme Adam et Mongrédien, pour les nier, comme Lachèvre et Lebègue, ou pour soutenir, comme Daniela Dalla Valle, la thèse d'une évolution, depuis une jeunesse libertine, jusqu'à la dévotion qui se manifeste dans l'*Office de la Sainte Vierge*, de 1646:[11] quand, en 1643, Tristan composa *La Mort de Sénèque*, il y tint un langage semblable à celui que l'on entend dans *Les Juives*, écrites par le très catholique Garnier. Néron a le même statut que Nabuchodonosor; il est comme lui, dans sa tyrannie, l'agent de Dieu. Face à ses exactions, il faut prier le Ciel, et non prendre les armes; les sujets n'ont pas à sortir de leur condition de sujets pour entrer en sédition contre le maître que le Tout-Puissant leur a donné. Sans doute la leçon est-elle moins appuyée que dans *Les Juives*, puisque les fautes des Romains ne sont pas précisées, alors que celles du peuple juif le sont. Elle n'était d'ailleurs pas appelée par l'actualité: la régence d'Anne d'Autriche ne commençait pas sous le signe de la tyrannie ... Mais cette leçon est assez explicite en ce qui concerne Tristan qui, associant à la mise en scène d'un odieux tyran la condamnation du tyrannicide, faisait à la fois profession de soumission à l'Eglise et au Trône. S'il avait dans sa jeunesse écouté Théophile, il s'en était bien éloigné. Il resterait à estimer la part de la conviction dans ce changement ... l'homme était prudent, il en donna la preuve pendant la Fronde, qui ne le vit dans aucun camp. Mais les curiosités biographiques autorisent-elles à sonder les cœurs? Nous nous en tiendrons pour notre part à ce que le texte dit.

Notes:

1   R. Guichemerre, 'A propos de *La Mort de Sénèque*: les tragédies de la conjuration', in *Cahiers Tristan L'Hermite*, IV, 1982, pp. 5 et 13.
2   Edition critique par J. Madeleine, Paris, S.T.F.M., 1984 (2e tirage). *La Mort de Sénèque* figure aussi au t. II du *Théâtre du XVIIe siècle* de J. Scherer et J. Truchet, Paris, Gallimard, 'Bibliothèque de la Pléiade', 1986.
3   Epicaris parvient d'abord à convaincre Néron qu'elle est accusée à tort (voir III, 1, v. 789); puis, 'adroite et subtile' (v. 835), 'rusée' (v. 839), maniant habilement la rhétorique (voir v. 856), elle fait si bien qu'il reste sans certitude sur la réalité d'un complot. S'il décide de l' 'applique[r] à la gêne' (v. 908), ce n'est pas parce qu'elle a échoué à se défendre, mais par prudence de monarque —autrement dit ... par intelligence (voir v. 906).
4   Ed. citée, p. 1339.
5   Ibid., p. 1339.
6   Loc. cit.
7   D'ailleurs, s'il a reconnu au premier l'intelligence qu'il a déniée aux seconds, il s'est empressé de montrer combien l'utilisation de cette intelligence, au service du mal, était perverse. Voir I, 1, vv. 127–136.
8   Tacite précise seulement, à propos de la condamnation à mort de Sénèque, que rien ne prouvait qu'il eût comploté (L. XV, 60).
9   Mascaron, *La Mort et les dernières paroles de Sénèque*, 1637.
10 On trouvera un bref rappel de la question dans ma thèse: *La jalousie dans la littérature au temps de Louis XIII*, Genève, Droz, 1981, pp. 208–221.
11 Voir D. Dalla Valle, *Il Teatro di Tristan L'Hermite*, Turin, 1964, pp. 15–17.

CHAPTER FIFTEEN

'Le Poids d'une couronne': The Dilemma of Monarchy in La Calprenède's Tragedies

GUY SNAITH

In the dedication of his tragedy *La Mort des enfans d'Herodes* to Cardinal Richelieu, La Calprenède apologizes for depicting 'les malheurs de Mitridate, d'Elisabeth, & d'Herode' rather than celebrating France's good fortune under the cardinal. He writes:

> J'ay toujours bien jugé qu'il m'estoit plus facile d'exposer la generosité de Mitridate qu'un rayon de la vostre, & de traicter les maximes d'Estat d'Elisabeth, & d'Herode que d'escrire les eminentes vertus de celuy qui possedant toutes les bonnes qualitez que ces deux ames politiques ont possedées est exempt de toutes les mauvaises.[1]

All of La Calprenède's tragedies deal with the dilemmas monarchs face in ruling. Rebellions, crowns in jeopardy, threats to the security of the state form the constant background to all of his tragedies but *Phalante*. In such plays La Calprenède's monarchs are called upon to resolve a political crisis. More often than not they find themselves forced to resort to their *maximes d'Estat*. La Calprenède explores both the public and private faces of monarchy in his scrutiny of humanity under pressure.

Spanning the years 1635 to 1643, La Calprenède's nine extant plays alternate between the two most popular genres of the time. His tragedy *La Mort de Mitridate* (1637) is followed by two tragi-comedies, *Bradamante* (1637) and *Clarionte* (1637), before he returns to a series of three tragedies with *Jeanne, Reyne d'Angleterre* (1638), *Le Comte d'Essex* (1639), and *La Mort des enfans d'Herodes* (1639). Then, after turning one last time to tragi-comedy with *Edouard* (1640), he finishes off this stage of his career with the tragedies *Phalante* (1642) and *Herménigilde* (1643).[2]

Political situations and themes recur throughout the plays, whether tragedy or tragi-comedy. Six of the nine deal with sedition, either actual or presumed (Mitridate, Jeanne, Essex, Hérode, Edouard, Herménigilde). In three this leads to a trial of the rebels (Jeanne, Essex, Hérode). Five reveal upheavals in the royal family itself (Mitridate, Clarionte, Hérode, Edouard, Herménigilde). Six depict relations between counsellors and the monarch (Jeanne, Essex, Hérode, Edouard, Phalante, Herménigilde). And in six the traditional *clémence/rigueur* debate exercises the sovereign's heart and mind (Clarionte, Jeanne, Essex, Hérode, Edouard, Herménigilde). Whether set in England at the time of the usurpation of Lady Jane Grey or the rebellion of the Earl of Essex, or in Judaea at the court of Herod the Great twenty two years after the death of Mariamne, the archetypal tragedy of La Calprenède takes the form of a rebellion which threatens the welfare of the state and often the life of the monarch, a trial, the hesitation of the monarch torn between those in favour of the ostensible rebel and those against, and the decision finally being taken that for the good of the state the miscreant must be put to death. The similarity of plot throughout his career, however, points to a desire on La Calprenède's part more to repeat earlier successful formulae than to re-explore a similar political theme from a different angle. The decor changes, the approach remains the same.

Therefore, despite the recurring political colour of the plays, it must be said that La Calprenède could not be called a political dramatist. That is, he is not, to use Gillian Jondorf's definition,

> A dramatist who is making a statement of political views, or airing political problems in his works, and whose dramatic technique can best be understood in the light of its connection with this political content.[3]

La Calprenède is not politically *engagé*. His plays are in no way political propaganda. They proclaim no political message. Speeches dealing with general political issues are conspicuous by their rarity.[4] Those issues—usurpation, rebellion, regicide—remain grave problems, but it is the dramatic possibilities of such subject matter which constitute their attraction. The *clémence/rigueur* discussion between Elizabeth and Mary Tudor in *Jeanne* is memorable for the liveliness of the clash of temperaments and the suspense of Jane Grey's fate hanging in the balance rather than for insights into the issue of clemency (IV, 1). Far from indulging in political debate at his trial, Essex refuses even to defend himself, and the scene is marked by the emotional rhetoric of the clash between Cecil and himself (III). In *Herménigilde* tempers flare between father and son and are more thrilling than any ultimate answer as to whether a king should ever break his word (II, 1). Such encounters between sisters, enemies, or father and son are dominated by the personal rather than the political. Truchet posed himself the question 'de savoir si la tragédie est politique par nature'.[5] His answer was unequivocally affirmative. War, peace, sedition, clemency, the problems which face La Calprenède's monarchs, constitute the traditional subject matter of tragedy, providing powerful stories of conflict between human beings of the highest of ranks with opportunities for confrontation, spectacle, pathos, and rhetorical display. Therefore, from the first scene, if not from the first lines, of every tragedy but *Phalante* we are thrown into a world in political crisis. The play becomes a working-out of that initial political problem, but always pursued on the personal level. Politics constitute the framework within which personal relationships are explored. Those relations centre on the opposition between the protagonist—the title role—and the character who is the instrument of his fate. But this does not allow one to talk in unqualified terms of hero and villain. As the pursuer, torn between two courses of action and wracked by doubts, the antagonist too gains our sympathy. It is worth noting that aside from *Mitridate*, where Pharnace acquires his crown only in the last scene, the antagonist is the monarch. As head of state, it is predominantly around the antagonist that the political themes eddy.

In his first play La Calprenède begins the fifth act with stances in which Mitridate soliloquizes on what it is to be king. Despite the 'Gloire, grandeurs, Sceptres, victoire' (l. 1363) he has known, Mitridate begins by saying:

> Mais si tous avaient comme moi,
> Senti le poids d'une couronne,
> Un berger craindrait d'être Roi. (ll. 1360–62)

In the last play Lévigilde cries out: 'ô malheur inseparable de la Couronne!' (*Herm*, II, 2). These two cries from the first and last of his extant plays summarize La Calprenède's major political obsession: the burden of monarchy.

The theme of 'le poids d'une couronne' rather mechanically introduced into *Mitridate* develops into a more integral part of the tragedies to follow. It is at the same time a theme which La Calprenède's audiences would have recognized as synonymous with the plight of the ruler in tragedy. Such laments are both traditional and natural. Such is one of the eternal paradoxes to fascinate dramatist and public alike: the hollowness of grandeur, the loneliness of the great, the magic that evaporates, the disenchantment which shadows the obsession. A commonplace stretching from the Agamemnon of Euripides to the cinematic cliché of the emptiness of stardom, it is an obvious way of dramatizing life at the top, as sixteenth and seventeenth-century dramatists realized. From the beginning of the tragic revival in the sixteenth century such had invariably been the case for the monarch. The chorus in Garnier's *Cornélie* had chanted about how much safer is life 'caché dessous un toict de chaume'.[6] And Montchrestien's Elizabeth would undoubtedly have agreed, as she opens *La Reine d'Escosse* declaring:

> Un corps sous le Soleil n'a jamais plus d'une ombre;
> Mais tant et tant de maux qu'ils surpassent tout nombre,
> Acompagnent le Sceptre, envié des humains,
> Lourd fardeau toutesfois de l'esprit et des mains
> Qui croist de jour en jour, puis à la fin accable
> Son possesseur superbe encor que miserable.[7]

When La Calprenède's *Mitridate* reaches the point of his stances, therefore, he becomes a member of a chorus of royals whose threnody reverberates from one French classical tragedy to the next. The tone can be one of sudden realization as is the case of Garnier's Créon: 'Que ce bandeau royal est un heur deceptif!'.[8] An accusatory note can filter in as when Guérin de Bouscal's Agiatis concludes their catalogue of woes by rhetorically asking ex-King Cléomène: 'Voy, si pour estre heureux, il suffit d'estre Roy?'.[9] Weariness marks the state of mind of Corneille's Auguste, as he talks of the crown:

> Dans sa possession, j'ai trouvé pour tous charmes
> D'effroyables soucis, d'éternelles alarmes,
> Mille ennemis secrets, la mort à tous propos,
> Point de plaisir sans trouble, et jamais de repos.[10]

A note of warning can sound as Rotrou's *Venceslas* describes the thankless nature of ruling to his son Ladislas: 'Mais, comme les douceurs, en sçavez vous les peines'.[11] Such laments form part of a literary tradition of kingship, a tradition in which 'the office of the king subjugates the man', as Baudin put it.[12] But the man need not let his subjugation pass without comment.

'Douceurs ... peines': La Calprenède's drama does not dwell on the magic of the crown. Although he offers classic cases of the lure for those outside the throne room, he stresses more the burden of those within. 'Le bonheur seulement d'un trône l'a charmé' (l. 1032) Mitridate says of his son, but disenchantment accompanies Pharnace's first moments as king. 'Et l'appas des grandeurs est un charme puissant' (*JdA*, IV, 1) says Gloucester, and Jane was human enough to fall briefly victim to the superficial charms of the crown, but the glamour proved illusory. Mary's claim to the throne was legitimate, her ideals praiseworthy; disillusionment sets in with the first act of her reign. Elizabeth, Hérode, Hélène, Lévigilde, having all reigned longer, know the demands monarchy makes and carry the scars. In keeping with the pessimism which informs his drama, it is the responsibility of the crown which La Calprenède emphasizes. 'Douceurs' are either exhausted or have never been tasted at all.

La Calprenède's approach to the traditional dichotomy of kingship is the clash between the ideal and the reality of monarchy. Without necessarily being exclusive to him, without his having been specifically influenced by anyone else, this approach represents a personal trait of La Calprenède, one he makes his own by the consistency with which he treats it.

The ideal of monarchy is twofold. It can be the superficial one of the trappings of royalty, or it can be a vision of how to rule, an ideal of just government which one tries to turn into a reality, or indeed it can be a combination of both. Whether one is entranced by the appearance or devoted to the essence of monarchy, neither is as it seems. The realities of wars, conspiracies, civil unrest, or higher duties to the state often involving life or death decisions put the tragic monarch to the test as ruler and as human being.

In his *examen* of *Clitandre* Pierre Corneille writes of the three ways in which a king can appear on the stage: as king, as man, as judge. He concludes:

> Il peut paraître comme roi et comme homme tout à la fois quand il a un grand intérêt d'Etat et une forte passion tout ensemble à soutenir ... et c'est, à mon avis, la plus digne manière et la plus avantageuse de mettre sur la scène des gens de cette condition.[13]

Of La Calprenède's monarchs only Charles in the tragi-comedy *Bradamante* appears as judge alone, Corneille's least impressive category. Otherwise, they are torn between a variety both of national interests and of passions, for La Calprenède's monarchs do not function in isolation. Wives, children, lovers, and courtiers crowd around them, each character having his role to play in the political world. Aristotle recommended close ties of birth or affection as subjects highly suitable for tragedy and Corneille comments:

> C'est donc un grand avantage, pour exciter la commisération, que la proximité du sang et les liaisons d'amour ou d'amitié entre le persécutant et le persécuté, le poursuivant et le poursuivi, celui qui fait souffrir et celui qui souffre.[14]

Ties of blood and affection will all be turned to good account by La Calprenède as he tests the mettle of his monarchs.

From his first play, La Calprenède realized the dramatic value to be had from 'la proximité du sang'. In *Mitridate* La Calprenède's use of the theme exposes the father behind the regal façade, as we are presented with the picture of a great warrior king confronting a son who refuses to follow in his footsteps, indeed who is turning his back on his father's beliefs and betraying him to the other side. In *Hérode* we witness a family in the final stages of disintegration as the heirs to the throne are schemed against by their half-brother, aunt and uncle. Their father, who ruthlessly attained power through sheer force of will, is now old and battered, bedevilled by counsellors, and, caught between the calls of vengeance and love, justice and pity, is no longer in control and is forced into sacrificing his own family to the very policies he has lived by. In *Herménigilde*, caught between his love for his son, his passion for his scheming wife, and his duty to the state, Lévigilde finds himself in that perennial opposition between his duty as king and his role as father and, as he contemplates having to order his son's execution if he wants to ensure peace in his kingdom, he asks himself the same question as La Calprenède's monarchs have pondered in play after play: 'Faut-il que j'affermisse mon Throsne par la perte de ce que j'ay le mieux aymé et que je cimente de mon propre sang les fondemens de ma Monarchie?' (II, 2).[15]

For two of La Calprenède's queens, the 'forte passion' is their love for a subject. Elizabeth's love of Essex and Hélène's of Phalante continually expose the human being lurking beneath the 'pourpre éclatante' (*CdE*, l. 1705) of their office. Behind the splendid and ruthless exterior Elizabeth presents to the world is the figure of a world-weary unloved woman just capable of maintaining her principles to the end, but ultimately crumbling once the truth is known, reason finally giving way to love:

> Ah! je devais forcer d'un pouvoir absolu
> Ton esprit obstiné, t'absoudre de tes crimes,
> Oublier ma naissance, oublier mes maximes,
> Oublier ma Couronne et ce pays ingrat,
> Et pour te conserver me perdre avec l'Etat. (ll. 1688–92)

Both Elizabeth and Hélène suffer from the dilemma of being a human being with emotional needs as well as a monarch with the duties and restrictions that such a position imposes. To the outside world Hélène is a paragon of beauty and virtue, and yet her surface calm barely hides the turmoil of her love for Phalante. Not strong enough to combat the force of emotion, Hélène surrenders to the power of love by telling Phalante how she feels. Rebuffed, she thereafter feels that she has failed as queen by allowing the personal to interfere with the official. It is difficult consistently to live up to the high standards monarchy sets as an ideal. It is difficult to be both woman and queen. For once putting herself first, Hélène slips from her former heights into a kind of moral twilight. Her final purifying gesture is to take her life.

In his first appearance Hérode is seen chasing off his brother, sister, and son, crying after them: 'Conseillers inhumains qui bourrelez ma vie,/Qu'on me laisse en repos, allez monstres d'envie' (ll. 129–30). All of La Calprenède's tragedies but *Mitridate* are set in a royal court, where La Calprenède can also explore the theme of the monarch at the mercy of his or her counsellors. In a world of rebellions, trials and executions, court factions form, and conspiracy theories flourish. The denunciations of counsellors from Mary through Elizabeth and Hérode to Lévigilde all bear witness to the difficulty monarchs experience within their own courts in finding out the truth, in knowing whom to believe, and whom to trust.

La Calprenède's are not rulers who are introduced in the last act to tidy up. They are husbands, fathers, and lovers we see struggling throughout the full five acts of the play. By means of the situations of domestic tragedy, love tragedy, or milieu tragedy, La Calprenède reveals the interplay of private personality and public personage. The humanity of his monarchs is constantly set off against their social roles and responsibilities. The duality of their existence is summed up in a series of oppositions. It is the clash of the reality of their life and the ideals their position sets for them. It is the difficulty of satisfying one's personal desires and goals when they conflict directly with the welfare of the state. It is the sway of emotion as opposed to the voice of reason. It is the call of Nature versus the *raison d'état*, the need to reconcile the call of *père* with that of *roi*, of woman with that of queen. Through these dualities, La Calprenède chronicles the anguish that the man and woman suffer trying to achieve that elusive reconciliation. Monarchs find themselves at centre stage. The exploitation of their dilemmas and conflicts is also conceived hedonistically. kings and queens carry with them a built-in theatricality, as Truchet himself comments: 'rien de plus théâtral que la royauté' (p. 97). Like Corneille and his other fellow dramatists, La Calprenède is interested in the pleasure to be had from the spectacular clash of opposing forces and the confrontation of great men and women.

Although La Calprenède deals with the traditional political themes of tragedy, there is also a coincidence between his drama, the preoccupations of contemporary theorists and the reality of Louis XIII's reign. Cardinal Richelieu himself appears to have been no stranger to the kind of problem which occupies the minds and emotions of La Calprenède's rulers, as we see him urging Louis XIII:

> Il est arrivé tant de maux aux princes et à leurs Etats, lorsqu'ils ont plutôt suivi leurs sentiments que la raison et qu'au lieu de se conduire par la considération des Intérêts publics, leurs passions ont été leurs guides, qu'il m'est impossible de ne supplier pas V. M. d'y faire souvent réflexion pour se confirmer de plus en plus en ce qu'Elle a toujours pratiqué au contraire.[16]

Transposed into La Calprenède's terms, the clash of reason and emotions is that of the monarch versus the human being, an opposition which Richelieu himself does not neglect when he makes reference to the different conduct expected of 'un grand Roi' and 'un particulier' (p. 276). Richelieu was under no illusions as to the essential humanity of monarchs, despite their high office and their divine inspiration. Kings and counsellors, he realizes, 'considérés comme personnes privées, sont sujets aux mêmes fautes, comme tous les autres hommes' (p. 452). The eternal dichotomy of the ruler, of the 'roi' and the 'particulier' in one body, is what La Calprenède explores, laying bare the 'personne privée' behind the 'personne publique'.[17] Richelieu's terms betray the same polarities as La Calprenède exposes. The ideals of government the Cardinal praises are constantly juxtaposed with the reality of the near impossible implementation of such ideals in the real world. When he writes: 'Il est certain que les Etats les plus heureux sont ceux où les princes et leurs Conseillers sont les plus sages' (p. 288), one senses that he too knows such an ideal is rarely going to be met outside theoretical writings and tragicomedies like *Bradamante*.

La Calprenède's plays, in their emphasis on the reason of state, also treat a subject which was of major political importance throughout the latter half of Louis XIII's reign, and one which Church sees as 'the most important contribution of Cardinal Richelieu's generation to the growth of political thought in France'.[18] The keystone of Richelieu's political beliefs, the reason of state, which envisaged the need for a morality of the state separate from that of the individual, had become common political currency by the mid 1630s, and La Calprenède uses it to explore the psychology of men and women under pressure, as tragedy traditionally seeks to do. Although Richelieu may think that the occasional abuse of power can be forgiven because it is only individuals who suffer and their interests cannot be compared to those of the state (p. 344), in La Calprenède it is the fate of those individuals which is played out before our eyes. The welfare of the state may hang before us, but it is individuals we have known through four acts who are sent to their deaths in the fifth, and it is monarchs we have watched agonizing throughout the length of the play who have been called upon to make the decision.

The names of Chalais, Boutteville, Marillac, Montmorency and others all bear witness to the factions of the time, the conspiracies, the rebellions, to the continual plots against the cardinal's person, and to the ruthlessness with which justice was meted out once he had come to power. All were sacrificed for the good of the state, in the name of the *raison d'état*. So are the heroes of La Calprenède. Indeed, the pattern of a typical La Calprenède tragedy—rebellion, trial, condemnation, vain appeals, execution—is repeated in the case of each of the noblemen mentioned above. La Calprenède's drama reflects not only the theoretical preoccupations but also, like the *Testament of Richelieu*, the political realities of the age.

Endowed with a sacred office, touched by the hand of God, physically attractive, morally virtuous, equipped with a transcendent power enabling one to be victorious in war, just in peace, and to provide security, prosperity, and happiness to subjects who love, respect, and obey one, such are the qualities of the ideal monarch which can be pieced together from references scattered throughout the plays of La Calprenède. Such is the perfect reciprocity between monarch and people recommended by Richelieu himself:

> Le roi sera puissant par la possession du Cœur de ses sujets, qui, considérant le soin qu'il aura de leur bien, seront portés à l'aimer par leur propre intérêt. (p. 450)

Such an image is thus both conventional and shared by contemporary theorists. It is rarely attained.

Justice under Hérode is a mockery; Hélène shows little feeling for the future of her subjects; Lévigilde breaks his word: La Calprenède's monarchs falter as ideals of just government come into contact with the reality of their existence. It is easy to be just, honourable, dignified and charming if one inhabits a world like that of the tragi-comedy *Bradamante*, where justice for Charles involves arranging tournaments and marriages. In the world of real wars and rebellion, however, the justice to be meted out deals in human life. Even this need not cause the monarch undue concern, but, by binding them with ties of affection or blood to the subjects they must punish, La Calprenède has stacked the cards against them. It is their humanity which causes them their grief. With ideals of justice, of protection, of the welfare of the state shimmering before them, monarchs set out to solve problems. They stagger away from the encounter bruised and scarred, their moral principles more often than not in tatters.

The ethical dilemmas of two of La Calprenède's monarchs demonstrate the point. In *Jeanne, Reyne d'Angleterre*, Mary Tudor represents a classic case of a sovereign suffering from the disparity between an ideal of monarchy and the reality of ruling. She arrives on a throne just wrested from the hands of a usurper and in the midst of civil unrest. She comes armed with her 'bonté si rare' (II, 1), with ideals of peace and clemency, with a dream of ushering in 'un siecle d'or' (II, 1), of turning England into the promised land. Such an ideal is only reinforced by the memory of her father Henry VIII's 'Empire de fer', the main characteristic of which she sees as 'le sang si souvent respandu' (IV, 1). A golden vision of monarchy dances in her head:

> Et je croy que le Ciel sousmet un peuple à nous,
> Pour recevoir des Roys un traittement plus doux. (IV, 1)

The welfare of the people is paramount for Mary. As the main conspirator, Northumberland must die, as must his son Guilford, but must Jane too be sacrificed for having simply obeyed? Is the golden age to have its birth in innocent blood? Mary desperately shies away from such realities, but a throne requires that one dirty one's hands. Everything demands Jane's death: the state, justice, Mary's safety; everyone clamours for her death: the barons, Norfolk, Elizabeth. Mary's goodwill is not enough to be a guiding principle for ruling a state. Other 'moyens de regner' are necessary (IV, 1). And yet she shrinks from this kind of politics:

> Ah! c'est trop acheter les biens d'une Couronne,
> Je ne puis recevoir les conseils qu'on me donne,
> Et j'ayme mieux déchoir de ce superbe rang
> Qu'establir ma grandeur au prix de tant de sang. (IV, 1)

Jane follows Northumberland and Guilford to the block. Mary is forced into bespattering her bright new reign with the blood of both the guilty and the innocent. The ironies are all too clear. History repeats itself. Peace is bought by the shedding of blood and by the sacrifice of the monarch's peace of mind. Her ideals questioned, her principles compromised, Mary, in the first official act of her reign, succumbs to the tyranny of monarchy.

In La Calprenède's last extant play *Herménigilde*, the theory of the inviolability of the royal world is tested. It is a theme which has threaded its way throughout the plays. Lines on the subject even echo from tragi-comedy to tragedy. When Essex, clinging to the ring given him by Elizabeth, tells Lady Cecil it was confided,

Avec cette promesse inviolable et sainte,
Cette Royale foi qui ne peut être enfreinte (ll. 1253–54),

Léon's words to Charles in *Bradamante* are recalled:

Sachant que la parole inviolable et sainte
D'un si grand Empereur ne peut pas être enfrainte. (V, 2)

In the last play Lévigilde succeeds in ending a rebellion which has
divided Spain for two years by promising his rebellious son a pardon.
No sooner has Herménigilde surrendered than Lévigilde breaks his
word and has him imprisoned. Recarède, the king's second son,
berates his father:

Quelle honte à la Royale maison d'Espagne, quel oprobre à la
dignité de tous les Rois, et quelle leçon pour jamais à tous ceux qui
s'asseurent à leur parolle. (II, 1)

We are shown what is expected of a monarch by witnessing the very
opposite of that expectation. Recarède's outrage forcefully underlines
the feeling that there is an unwritten code of behaviour for princes
corresponding to an ideal vision of the prince, at the same time as
demonstrating that in reality the ideal often shatters under the
pressure. Recarède is the spokesman of the ideal of kingship;
Lévigilde is the one who bears the burden of finding the solutions,
knowing that in the world of men, war, and rebellions one often has to
compromise one's high ideals. His expertise in the dirty dealing of
politics is proved by his ending the rebellion with this one manoeuvre
of using Recarède to capture his brother and then breaking his word.
Before Recarède's indignation Lévigilde's reaction may seem cold-
blooded, but he is secure in having done what is right. He replies to
Recarède:

Je me suis servy de vous comme d'un subjet pour en remettre un
autre en son devoir, et pour espargner le sang de beaucoup
d'honnestes gens qui seroient peut-estre tresbuchés pour la querelle
de ce révolté. (II, 1)

Elsewhere he mentions his anxiety over 'des desordres et des revoltes
generales' and the importance of ensuring 'le repos de mes Estats' (IV,
1; IV, 2). He has sacrificed the ideal of monarchy to the greater good
of the welfare of the state. He has sacrificed the moral principle to
expedience. To his daughter-in-law Indégonde he reiterates that it was
'une parolle donnée pour espargner le sang de mes subjets' and he
goes on to end the discussion with:

> Ceux qui sont plus sçavans que vous dans les maximes d'un Estat
> ne trouveront pas ma procedure estrange, et me blasmeroient si je
> vous en rendois un plus grand conte. (II, 4)

Lévigilde is in fact right. In 1597 Pope Clement VIII absolved
Henri IV from having to stand by his word to a heretic, Queen
Elizabeth. The greater good at stake there was the preservation of the
Catholic Church.[19] Montaigne had earlier theorized:

> Le Prince, quand une urgente circonstance et quelque impetueux et
> inopiné accident du besoing de son estat luy faict gauchir sa parolle
> et sa foy, ou autrement le jette hors de son devoir ordinaire, doibt
> attribuer cette necessité à un coup de la verge divine; vice n'est-ce
> pas, car il a quitté sa raison à une plus universelle et puissante
> raison, mais certes c'est mal'heur.[20]

Once again, political theory, historical reality, and the world of La
Calprenède's drama conjoin. The literary tradition coincides too. In
1637 Du Ryer had introduced the breaking of a king's word into his
tragedy *Alcionée*. The hero put his faith in the royal word only to
discover that the king had had no intention of keeping it. Of the two
kings, only for La Calprenède's Lévigilde does the action cause any
emotional strain. Du Ryer's monarch sets about clearing up the matter
without a second thought; in La Calprenède one cannot forget that the
pendant to Lévigilde's defence of his actions in the first scene of Act
II is his regret of his actions in the following scene.

Cries are still raised against the abuse of power. Spilt blood is the
mark of the despotic monarch from Mitridate's treatment of his
subjects (32) to the 'sanglante memoire' of Mary Tudor's predecessors
(*JdA*, II, 1), to Elizabeth thinking of Mary Queen of Scots and still
haunted by 'le sang qui crie encor d'une innocente Reine' (*CdE*, l.
1710), to Hérode and his 'regne de sang' (111). From their subjects'
point of view, nothing can hinder such monarchs. Southampton warns
against an Elizabeth who has trampled underfoot 'l'honneur, et le
droit, et le sang' (*CdE*, l. 288) in order to cement her position. Rulers
walk a tightrope, trying to maintain a delicate balance between laxity
on the one hand and abuse of power on the other. And one thinks of
Richelieu advising Louis XIII:

> La verge, qui est le symbole de la justice, ne doit jamais être
> inutile. Je sais bien aussi qu'elle ne doit pas être si
> accompagnée de rigueur qu'elle soit destituée de la bonté. (p. 341)

Somewhere in between falls the good, strong rule. It also depends
upon one's perspective, for in *Jeanne* Mary condemns Henry VIII as

virtually a tyrant, while Elizabeth can admire him for the firmness of his rule (IV, 1). Indeed, in the dedication of *Essex*, La Calprenède mentions that Elizabeth inspires both horror amongst the French and veneration amongst others (p. 205). And in the play itself we see how Elizabeth is congratulated for the single-mindedness of her rule, which has resulted in greater security for England (II, 1). In breaking his word, Lévigilde offends the high ideals of Recarède but he has saved many lives. Monarchs are often forced into positions of arbitrary use of power by the realities of ruling. A series of cries reverberates from one play to another, from Mary's 'Dure raison d'Estat que tes loix sont barbares' (*JdA*, IV, 2), to Hérode's 'Dures raisons d'Estat, esloignez vous de moy' (l. 1164), and to Lévigilde's 'O Inhumaines raisons d'Estat! ô impitoyables maximes!' (*Herm*, II, 2). It is the lot of La Calprenède's monarchs to be forced into ways of ruling that contradict their personalities.

'C'est un fâcheux destin que le destin des Princes', comments Elizabeth's maid of honour (*CdE*, l. 1413). Even if the trappings of ruling are attained and enjoyed, they remain insubstantial and hollow. For Mitridate or Jane their ephemeral charms do not counterbalance the sheer weight of responsibility involved. For Elizabeth or Hélène no amount of royal purple can fulfil emotionally. In trying to put into practice their aims and ideals, rulers find that the sacrifices are indeed great. Ideals of just government are jettisoned in the headlong rush for political expedience. At the beginning of her reign Mary is forced to compromise morally; at the end of hers Elizabeth too comes to realize the moral price of politics. For some rulers any illusions about monarchy are long past. Hérode recognizes the price one pays. Lévigilde is resigned to the dirty business of ruling. Nevertheless, both balk at the blood sacrifices ostensibly demanded of one's own family if one is to move even haltingly towards a world of peace and security essentially along the same lines as Mary's vision, albeit much more workaday. Mary refused to believe the work had to be dirty; Lévigilde does the dirty work but does not have to like it. The price remains the same.

In La Calprenède's tragedies we are, therefore, interested in two fates. Of course, we want to know whether Jane, or Essex, or Hérode's children, or Herménigilde will indeed be executed, but we are interested as much in the fate of 'celui qui fait souffrir' as 'celui qui souffre'[21]. The tragic burden is shared. Locked together by bonds of suffering, protagonist and antagonist are dependent upon each other, and the tragedy is the result of both their alienation and their interdependence. The estrangement of father and son, of husband and wife, of lovers, the increasing isolation of two people related by bonds of family or affection, all underscored by the failure of dialogue, constitute the basis of La Calprenède's dark vision. And yet, an essential difference exists between La Calprenède's *persécutants* and his *persécutés*.[22] Torn by internal forces, antagonists find themselves opposite protagonists who know no real division within themselves. Their traits fixed in their first scene, they remain true to this posture to the end, rising nobly to their fate, earning our admiration and our pity, but without reaching the point of awareness which is ideally granted to the antagonists. Those antagonists, human in their vulnerability, caught between duties and personal desires, experiencing ambivalence and doubt, but ultimately forced to make a choice, face the future alone, having to bear the weight of the decision they have taken. No matter where they may flee, there will be no balm for their conscience, no escape from their solitude.

Gillian Jondorf classifies Garnier's use of the theme of the lure and burden of kingship as 'rhetorical rather than political' (p. 72). The same is true of all the political themes La Calprenède introduces, whether rebellion, usurpation, regicide, or justice. Yet, in his own modest way La Calprenède, through the rhetorical and the personal, succeeds in revealing political truths of a general kind. Through the constancy of his vision, even if due to the reworking of similar situations, he succeeds in making a comment on the tragic nature of power: the compromises made for it; the difficulty of reaching unpopular decisions, of knowing whom to trust; above all, the lonely world that exists for the monarch behind closed doors. It can be said of La Calprenède, as of his fellow creators of French classical tragedy from *c.* 1550 to the Revolution:

> En dehors de tout engagement, de toute allusion, une méditation fondamentale sur l'Etat, la souveraineté, la justice se poursuit de tragédie en tragédie.[23]

Notes:

1   La Calprenède, *La Mort des enfans d'Herodes*, ed. by G.P. Snaith, Textes littéraires, LXIX, Exeter: University of Exeter, 1988, p. 2.
2   The dates given are those of publication. The dates of first performance appear to have been one or two years earlier. After this series of plays La Calprenède turned to writing the long historical romances for which he is most famous. A final play, *Bellisaire*, of 1659 has been lost.
    Modern editions of three of his plays exist: *La Mort de Mithridate* and *Le Comte d'Essex* are included in the second volume of *Théâtre du XVIIe siècle*, ed. by Jacques Scherer and Jacques Truchet, Bibliothèque de la Pléiade, 1986; *La Mort des enfans d'Herodes* is in Exeter's Textes littéraires series (see Note 1). For the other plays, references will be to the original edition.
3   Gillian Jondorf, *Robert Garnier and the Themes of Political Tragedy in the Sixteenth Century*, Cambridge, 1969, p. 7.

4   Recarède's set piece on the horrors of civil war is impressive but remains rooted in the dramatic context (*Herm*, I, 3).

5   Jacques Truchet, *La Tragédie classique en France*, Paris, 1975, p. 89.

6   Robert Garnier, *Cornélie* (IV, ll. 1297–1302), in *Porcie, Cornélie*, ed. by Raymond Lebègue, Les Textes français, Paris, 1973.

7   Antoine de Montchrestien, *La Reine d'Escosse*, ed. by Joseph D. Crivelli, Paris, 1975, I, ll. 5–10.

8   *Antigone* (V, l. 2663), in *La Troade, Antigone*, ed. by Raymond Lebègue, Les Textes français, Paris, 1952.

9   *La Mort de Cléomènes, Roy de Sparte*, Paris, 1640, II, 4.

10   *Cinna*, II, 1, ll. 373–76.

11   Jean Rotrou, *Venceslas*, ed. by Derek Watts, Textes littéraires, LXXIX, Exeter: University of Exeter, 1990, I, 1, 32.

12   Maurice Baudin, *The Profession of King in Seventeenth-Century French Drama*, Johns Hopkins Studies in Romance Literatures and Languages, 38, Baltimore, 1941; reprint, New York and London, Johnson, 1973, p. 15.

13   In *Writings on the Theatre*, ed. by H.T. Barnwell, Oxford, 1965, p. 85.

14   'Discours de la tragédie', in *Writings on the Theatre*, p. 38.

15   Derek Watts points out that the title of the Spanish play that was the main source of Rotrou's *Venceslas* is *No hay ser padre siendo rey* or 'On ne saurait être père en même temps qu'on est roi', a proverb La Calprenède's kings would no doubt agree with (Textes littéraires ed., p. IX).

16   *Testament politique*, ed. by Louis André, 7th edn, Paris, 1947, p. 271.

17   The terms are Richelieu's (pp. 276, 454).

18   William F. Church, *Richelieu and Reason of State*, Princeton, New Jersey, 1972, p. 11.

19   Church, p. 55.

20   In 'De l'utile et de l'honneste', in *Essais*, ed. by Maurice Rat, 2 vols, Paris, 1962, II, pp. 216–217.

21   The terms are Corneille's; see p. 187.

22   The terms are again Corneille's; see p. 187.

23   Truchet, p. 96.

CHAPTER SIXTEEN

African Temptresses and Roman Matrons: Female Roles on the Paris Stage, 1634–1643

DAVID CLARKE

It was unfortunate that the emergence of female 'stars' on the Paris stage of the 1630s—stars who rivalled and even outshone male leads like Mondory and Bellerose—coincided with ministerial encouragement of a more programmatic and educative political tragedy based on subjects drawn largely from Roman history. These simultaneous developments posed obvious difficulties for contemporary dramatists anxious to satisfy both their audiences and His Eminence, since the literary conventions of political tragedy demanded a historical subject while social conventions, whether ancient or modern, rarely accorded women a significant role in politics. After Mlle Lenoir's triumph in late 1634 in the title role of Mairet's *Sophonisbe*, dramatists sought out other episodes of Roman history which offered similar opportunities for an actress to display her qualities.[1] However, these subjects were few and far between, with the consequence that, in the next few seasons, a crop of rival plays appeared using identical, or very similar, subjects. With these doublets the two troupes sought to outdo each other as popular actresses such as Mlles Villiers, Beaupré, and Beauchâteau at the Marais competed for applause with Mlles Bellerose and Lenoir at the Hôtel de Bourgogne. Examination of the ways in which these rival history plays give greater importance to female performers offers an interesting vantage point from which to appreciate the skill and originality with which Corneille re-worked pre-existent stereotypes in catering for the actresses at the Marais.

With the revival of tragedy in the mid-thirties, and after an initial flush of legendary subjects, the most popular choice was to find in Roman history a 'Death of the Hero' attended by a sufficiency of women.[2] This had the advantage of increasing female representation while preserving the traditional prestige of male leads like Bellerose and Mondory, and also presented a reassuringly conventional—and marginal—view of woman's place in a man's world of political decision. The alternative strategy was to imitate Mairet's *Sophonisbe* and record the fortunes of a central female figure, as recounted in the few episodes in Roman history or legend where a woman played a decisive role in political events. Thus two rival tragedies on the subject of Cleopatra appear, a tragedy on Dido and two tragedies based on the history of Lucretia's rape by Sextus Tarquinius.3 Only the first three plays provide truly substantial, because pro-active, female roles, while the plays on Lucretia, though centred on a heroine who is never more than a passive victim, offer fine opportunities for pathos and a celebration of the actress's beauty. To this list of plays on a hero's death or with eponymous heroines we should add two rival history plays, first performed in 1638, which centre on Coriolanus but record how the Roman matron, Volumnie, intervened to persuade her son to abandon his war on Rome.4

Once a suitable subject had been found it was simple enough to invent new parts, major and minor, when history failed to provide the requisite number of women. Thus La Calprenède's *La Mort de Mithridate* contains a plethora of female roles, both historical and invented, in order to accommodate the exceptional strength in starring ladies which resulted from Bellerose's first acquisition of actors and actresses from the Marais in mid-December 1634.5 Chapoton, not content with the two Plutarchan roles of Volumnie and Verginie for his *Le Véritable Coriolan*, invents a sister, Porcie, to cater for a third experienced actress, and Chevreau's *La Lucresse romaine* increases female representation with Tarquin's wife, Tullie. We may also observe a proliferation of minor roles or even decorative walk-on parts. For instance Scudéry's Didon, in addition to the Virgilian role of her sister Anne, also has a 'dame d'honneur' and two daughters, and Chapoton—with what must be the least subtle instance of the gentle art of getting more ladies on stage—provides for a veritable beauty parade of non-speaking 'vestales, dames romaines, et suivantes', all apparently grieving at Rome's plight in Act IV of his *Le Véritable Coriolan*.

To exploit fully his abundance of actresses in *La Mort de Mithridate*, La Calprenède closes the action with a spectacular scene in which Mithridate kills himself surrounded by his dead womenfolk, all of whom have already taken poison in order to avoid being taken in triumph to Rome (V, 3). Such spectacular set pieces, whether tableaux or scenes of formal eloquence, are often used to show the ladies to good advantage. Accordingly Chapoton appeals to the eyes and ears by giving to each of his three actresses a 'harangue' (variously in the name of piety, love, or nature) so giving each lady the opportunity to compete in grace and eloquence before an appreciative audience at the Hôtel de Bourgogne, (*Le Véritable Coriolan*, IV, 7). For the Marais's lesser resources Chevreau's rival version respects the historical number of women but invents more for them to do, multiplying conventional scenes of deliberation, apprehension, or lamentation. Accordingly the celebrated interview with Coriolanus becomes two scenes, the first of which contains the women's pleas and the second their lengthy responses to the hero's decision. Perhaps the most spectacular of such showcase scenes are to be found in Benserade's *La Cléopâtre*, written 'pour l'amour de la Bellerose'. Here Cléopâtre, 'vesteue de deuil, & dans une chambre tenduë de deuil', makes a long farewell to wealth and power (IV, 5). The end of the play is no less spectacular with a curtain drawn back to reveal Cléopâtre dead 'sur un beau lit ... Eras à ses pieds'. Charmion then crowns the dead Cléopâtre, embraces Eras' body, and dies herself (V, 7). This protracted finale suggests another less impressive,—and happily less common—device, the add-on suicide. Scudéry, for instance, writes into the end of his *Didon* a cameo for his second actress, giving Anne a final scene (V, 7) in which to kill herself in remorse for having encouraged her mistress to woo Ænée.

As in the two Lucretia plays, the female roles in tragedies concerned with the death of a hero are almost all entirely passive and contribute very little if anything to the action. Powerful actresses like Mlle Villiers and Mlle Bellerose must have found such parts unrewarding in comparison with the meatier roles which had been available to them in the tragedies of legendary atrocity written for the 1634/5 season.[6] Like Shakespeare's Portia, excluded from Brutus' deliberations with an 'angry wafture of [the] hand' (*Julius Caesar*, II, 1), these heroines are there to encourage, experience fear or premonitory dreams, or offer warnings which are invariably ignored by the menfolk. Thus Guérin's Porcie is kept well away from the action until her last-act suicide, which deed constitutes her only independent initiative and justifies her inclusion in the play's title. This typical passivity leaves little room for distinctive characterization of these parts: at best they are stereotyped in terms either of 'manly' bravery or 'womanly' timidity—a characteristic occasionally interestingly developed as a dislike of warmongering. Chevreau's Tullie, for instance, expresses distaste for men's dangerous pursuit of military glory and is at once reproved by Tarquin (*La Lucresse romaine*, II, 2). It is clear however that this supposed 'timidity' of her sex is being used to point up the excessive belligerence of her husband, a 'superbia' which will bring about his dynasty's expulsion from Rome. Elsewhere in the play Lucresse expresses similar fears for

Collatin, but mawkishly occupies more stereotypical ground in lamenting the difficulty of looking her best when so worried for a husband who alone gives meaning to her life:

> C'est de luy seulement que depend mon plaisir,
> Il fait toute ma peur comme il fait mon desir. (ibid., II, 3)

Through her Chevreau suggests that a woman's duty is to be brave, and not to oppose the manly valour that prompts Collatin's absences on the battlefield:

> Je le voudrois coupable, & luy serois rebelle
> Si je le retenois quand la gloire l'appelle; ...
> Quoy qu'on entende dire à ces esprits infames,
> L'homme est fait pour la gloire & non pas pour les femmes.
> (ibid., II, 6)

It is truly a man's world in these tragedies, where men are the primary source of any strengths that their womenfolk prove capable of displaying. Scudéry, whose plays voice with particular emphasis the theme of 'frailty thy name is woman', includes in his *Didon* observations on how easily women fall for an attractive male, and in *La Mort de César* creates a Porcie whose defining quality is above all to have inherited her father's courage and political convictions:

> *Porcie*: La fille de Caton ne peut estre timide.
> *Brute*: O d'un pere excellent, excellente heritiere! (ibid., I, 1)

In much the same spirit, she admits to Brute that she is capable of courage only because she draws upon his strength:

> Vous reveillez en moy la constance endormie. (ibid., II, 4)

Guérin's Porcie is little different, as she rehearses her Republican pedigree to the greater glory of the menfolk:

> Toutesfois banissons ce mouvement de femme,
> Ma naissance suffit pour instruire mon ame. ...
> C'est assez que je suis la fille de Caton.
> (*La Mort de Brute et de Porcie*, I, 1)

Finally, in a case where history actually guarantees the womenfolk a decisive political role, Chevreau's Verginie nonetheless sums up the insipid characterization of so many of these female roles when, on hearing of the death of Coriolan, she announces her intention to commit suicide:

Coriolan est mort! la cause de ma vie
Sans qu'on m'ait fait mourir, m'a donc été ravie?
N'atens plus rien du sort, voy que tout est pery,
Et que tu n'as plus rien n'ayant plus de mary. (*Coriolan*, V, 8)

In the very different case of more energetic, and so more dangerous, temptresses at the centre of the few tragedies which imitated the subject of *La Sophonisbe*, the problem of the heroine's morality led to more varied characterization. The official desire for public 'utilité' on the stage was at some odds with the way in which Mairet's two doomed lovers, after breaking marriage vows and political loyalties, still won the sympathy of the audience as they fell victim to Scipion and the ruthless advance of Roman military power. Clearly any imitation of Mairet's play, if it were to meet the Cardinal's approval, would need to correct such a moral impact. One way of doing this was to invent a female role to counterbalance that of the dangerous *femme fatale*. Thus Mairet introduces Octavie, Antoine's first wife and sister of Octavius Caesar, to provide an improving counter-illustration of marital fidelity. True to the ineffective stage destiny of other Roman matrons, she appears in Act II to give advice to Antoine (which is ignored) and re-enters in Act IV to plead too late for her husband (who is already dead). However a rectified characterization of the heroine was more effective, and the theme of fidelity in love, especially if combined with maternal solicitude, serves greatly to refurbish the image of Cléopâtre in both Benserade's and Mairet's plays. In a striking reform of Sophonisbe's conduct, both temptresses are unwaveringly faithful despite Antoine's cruel mistrust, and only reluctantly obey his dying wish that, for their children's sake, they make overtures to Caesar. Similarly Scudéry's Didon may be weak in falling for Ænée, but she redeems herself as queen by expressing remorse for a failure of political responsibility. As she prepares for death, Didon admits that it was not political prudence but 'une folle amitié' which inspired her to woo Ænée, and that she now deserves her fate for having sacrificed her people's interests to following her heart:

Malheureuse Didon, ton esprit maintenant,
Est touché des forfaits d'un perfide inconstant.
Mais il le falloit estre alors que ta foiblesse
Mit ton Estat aux mains de celuy qui te laisse.   (*Didon*, V, 1)

The 'moral tone' of these plays is also improved by attributing similar regrets to the heroes who are ruined—or risk being ruined—by the seductions of the eponymous *femme fatale*. So Mairet's Antoine bitterly regrets his days of wine and roses:

> J'ay dormy trop longtems dans le sein des delices,
> La peste des vertus, & la source des vices.
> Enfin j'ay trop aymé ce qui ne m'aymoit pas
> (*Marc Antoine ou la Cléopâtre*, IV, 1)

More powerfully still, the very subject of Dido's abandonment offers the improving spectacle of a hero who actually escapes from his temptress's enchantments. Once the lovers have fallen for each other in Act II, the last three acts of Scudéry's play develop into a tragedy of providentially authorized ingratitude in the interests of the hero's higher destiny:

> Ænée: Je voy qu'elle [Didon] a raison, & que je la trahis
> Mais les Dieux apres tout, veulent estre obeis.
> (*Didon*, IV, 3)

Such intimations of a noble austerity of conscience, once coupled with suicide in expiation of earlier failings, become a powerful means to the redemption of the temptresses themselves. Thus Benserade's Cléopâtre envisages suicide as a punishment for having 'betrayed' Antoine by trying to soften César with her charms, and for weeping for herself rather than for his death:

> Mes yeux pour le flechir ont employé leurs charmes,
> Ils ont lancé des feux, il ont versé des larmes,
> J'ay trahy mon Antoine, & j'ay donné les pleurs
> Deubs à son souvenir à mes propres malheurs,
> A de foibles attraits mon ame s'est fiée,
> Cesar m'a fait faillir, & m'en a châtiée,
> Et comme je voulois qu'il devint mon amant,
> Le sujet de mon crime en est le châtiment. (*La Cléopâtre*, V, 5)

Similarly the heroine's sense of personal worth, as dynastic pride prompts a suicide qualified as 'digne ... de sa majesté' or 'genereuse et belle' (Benserade, *La Cléopâtre*, V, 8), legitimately earns the spectator's sympathy. Following the example of *Sophonisbe*, both Cleopatras escape the humiliation of figuring in a Roman triumph, just as Dido's death ends the humiliation of being sacrificed to Rome's destiny. As Benserade's César observes of Cléopâtre's language in expressing her desire for death: 'C'est la vertu qui parle & non pas le peché' (*La Cléopâtre*, V, 3). And Mairet's heroine actually lays claims to an exemplary moral quality:

Il est temps desormais, que je donne à mon tour
Un exemple de cœur, de constance & d'amour.
(Marc Antoine ou la Cléopâtre, V, 6)

And indeed, in these final scenes of Mairet's tragedy, her fearlessness
before death even prompts César reluctantly to accord her the status of
an 'honorary man':

> Cæsar: ... se ravir par elle [la mort] aux triomphes de Rome,
>   Plustost que d'une fâme est l'ouvrage d'un homme.
> Mæcene: Sophonisbe pourtant ne le fit pas trop mal. (ibid., V, 8)

When compared with these several paragons of marital fidelity and
repetitive, if spirited, temptresses, Corneille's female roles show a
remarkable diversity, even when it is clear that they derive from a
common currency of accepted tragic stereotypes. Not that he was any
more successful at first in integrating secondary female roles into the
action, as Scudéry was quick to point out of *Le Cid*: 'on voit
clairement que D. Urraque n'y est que pour faire jouer la
Beauchâteau'. But Mlle Villiers's Chimène served notice of the
originality with which Corneille's future political tragedies would
refresh the received stage stereotypes of female conduct. Dependent
though she might be upon male decision in the larger world of
national interest, Chimène scandalously attributed equal importance to
her twin identities of lover and daughter. So, while looking to the
menfolk for justice, she refused to pay the price of their political
accommodations (*Le Cid*, V, 7). Where Sophonisbe's infidelities had
hardly raised an eyebrow three seasons earlier, the violence of the
controversy precipitated by the conduct of 'cette fille dénaturée'—to
use Scudéry's terms—is very evidence that such critics were not only
jealous of Corneille's success, but also recoiled from the disquieting
implications of so unstereotypical a characterization.[7]

In contrast, *Horace*, Corneille's first exercise in the new Roman
political tragedy, contains female roles which, superficially at least,
seem to return to the conventional characterization of attendant
womenfolk as passive observers and victims. But Camille, in her
unsuccessful attempt to subvert Curiace's loyalty to country (II, 5) and
suicidal scorn for the Roman 'vertu' of the menfolk (IV, 4),
interestingly renews the temptress figures of other history plays. So
again Sabine, like Porcie, is constantly shut out of the action.
However, unlike the Infante, as Corneille observes in his *Examen* of
1660, she is closely involved in the action as wife and sister, and
functions as a primary moral conscience consistently ignored by
patriots who dare not listen to the voice of humanity.[8]

But only with Emilie in *Cinna* does Corneille indisputably emancipate his heroine from the ineffectual company of so many other noble daughters, creating a heroine who, until the very final moments of the play, takes a commanding role at the very centre of a political crisis. The role's dramatic brilliance and central importance to the action result from its paradoxical conflation of two traditionally distinct identities, as her identity as virtuous daughter and avenger of a noble father is combined with the role of a temptress who will lead her lover against the Roman Imperium and nearly cause his ruin. Furthermore the secondary role of Livie echoes many previous characterizations of the Roman matron as loyal confidant and source of advice, but with the interesting variation that her advice is rejected as 'des conseils d'une femme', a machiavellian counsel of weakness which has no place within the idealist political lesson of the play (IV, 3). *Polyeucte*, the overtly Christian counterpart of *Cinna*, is a marital drama as well as a tragedy of conscience of major political importance and presents yet another refreshment of the available stereotypes in its one major female role. Pauline's response to Sévère unsurprisingly renews the image of the faithful wife but, extraordinarily, she also acts as temptress to her husband as she seeks to dissuade him from the road of higher virtue. As Didon discovered of Ænée, she finds that Polyeucte is 'insensible à ces tristes appas' (IV, 3) and that her beauty and love are insufficient to turn him from his providential destiny and a martyr's glory (V, 2).

In the following season of 1643, Corneille's *La Mort de Pompée* displays what is perhaps his most telling use of the available models of heroines from Roman history. Here he offers a definitive treatment of both temptress and matron in the twin roles of Cléopâtre and Cornélie and, in comparison with Chaulmer's treatment of the subject in 1638, displays his extraordinary superiority in the creation of two female roles sufficiently impressive to satisfy the most demanding of actresses and audiences.[9] Chaulmer's play looked back to tragi-comedy, with its *romanesque* stereotypes in a love affair between a fictional Sexte, jealously coveted by Cléopâtre, and a fictional Léonie. His vapid inventions pale before the severity of Corneille's recreation of the final collapse of Republican legitimacy, the realism and breadth of the political argument and, not least, the complex characterization of the two major women's roles. Both are decisively involved in the unfolding of the political action and provided with scenes of exceptional dramatic brilliance, Cléopâtre as a politically adept temptress and proudly independent queen of Egypt, and Cornélie as the supreme illustration of a Roman matron's high-minded fidelity to honour and justice. Thinking of such striking creations Saint-

Evremond rightly observed that: 'Corneille n'a pas moins d'égard au caractère des femmes illustres qu'à celui de ses héros'. In particular he admired Cornélie, observing, with a characteristically jaundiced glance at a certain widowed Trojan princess, 'de toutes les veuves qui ont jamais paru sur le théâtre, je n'aime à voir que la seule Cornélie, parce qu'au lieu de me faire imaginer des enfants sans père et une femme sans époux, ses sentiments tout romains rappellent dans mon esprit l'idée de l'ancienne Rome et du grand Pompée'.[10]

Once we set these heroines against their contemporary counterparts, it is not hard to see how Corneille's dominance of the tragic stage in the 1640s owed not a little to his ability to create so distinctive a series of roles for the talents of Mlles Villiers, Beaupré and Beauchâteau. He himself would seem to have been well aware of this—if the 'Marquise' of his *Stances* was indeed the rising young star, Mlle Du Parc. As he reminded the young lady in his poem, the homage which she received with such indifference came from a poet whom her kind had always found well worth cultivating:

Pensez-y belle Marquise,
Quoi qu'un grison fasse effroi,
Il vaut bien qu'on le courtise
Quand il est fait comme moi.[11]

Notes:

1 W. Deierkauf-Holsboer, *Le Théâtre du Marais*, 2 vols, Paris, 1954–1958; W. Deierkauf-Holsboer, *Le Théâtre de l'Hôtel de Bourgogne*, 2 vols, Paris, 1968–70.

2 G. de Scudéry, *La Mort de César, tragédie*, Paris, A. Courbé, 1636: played first at the Marais with Mondory as Brutus; G. de C. de la Calprenède, *La Mort de Mithridate, tragédie*, Paris, A. de Sommaville, 1636: given its first performance date in the season of 1635/6, its cast numbers and the nature of the female roles, almost certainly written for the Hôtel de Bourgogne; G. Guérin de Bouscal, *La Mort de Brute et de Porcie ou la Vengeance de la mort de César, tragédie*, Paris, T. Quinet, 1637: certainly performed in the season 1636/7, but it is not certain where; C. Chaulmer, *La Mort de Pompée, tragédie*, Paris, A. de Sommaville, 1638.

3 I. de Benserade, *La Cléopâtre, tragédie*. Paris, A. de Sommaville, 1636: first performed in 1635 at Hôtel de Bourgogne and specifically written as a star vehicle for Mlle Bellerose; J. Mairet, *Marc Antoine ou la Cléopâtre, tragédie*, Paris, A. de Sommaville, 1637: first performed late 1635 at the Marais, and specifically written for Mondory and Mlle Villiers; G. de Scudéry: *Didon, tragédie*, Paris, A. Courbé, 1637: dedicated to the comte de Belin, protector of the Marais, so probably performed there. This play was 'rectified' in 1643 by Boisrobert's *La Vraie Didon*, the preface of which simply sets aside Virgil's 'erroneous' narrative and presents the heroine as an unswervingly chaste princess: F. de Boisrobert, *La Vraie Didon, chaste tragédie*, Paris T. Quinet, 1643; P. Du Ryer, *Lucrèce, tragédie*, Paris, Antoine de Sommaville, 1638: first performed 1637, probably at the Hôtel de Bourgogne; U. Chevreau, *La Lucresse romaine, tragédie*, Paris, T. Quinet, 1638: first performed early 1637 probably at the Marais; the recent T.L.F. edition of Du Ryer's play unaccountably settles for both troupes: P. Du Ryer, *Lucrèce, tragédie (1638)*, éd. J. F. Gaines et P. Gethner, Genève, Droz, 1994, pp. 7 and 17.

4 Chapoton, *Le Véritable Coriolan, tragédie*, Paris, T. Quinet, 1638: first performed early 1638 by the Hôtel de Bourgogne (see frontispiece, 'representée par la Troupe Royalle'); U. Chevreau, *Coriolan, tragédie*, Paris, A. Courbé, 1638: first performed 1638 at the Marais.

5   These women's roles are well matched to the different ages of the four lady 'stars' of Bellerose's troupe in September 1635. For the aging Mlle Valliot there was Mithridate's wife Hypsicratée. In a splendid variant on the breeches roles with which this actress had long been associated, Hypsicratée enters dressed in full armour (*La Mort de Mithridate...*, II, 1) to fight beside her husband on the battlefield where later:

> Cette forte Amazone atterre de ses mains,
> Et les Bithyniens et les soldats Romains. (ibid., II, 5)

Mlle Lenoir and Mlle Beaupré (who were to move to the Marais at the end of the season) are well suited to the roles of Nise and Mithridatie, daughters of Mithridate, and Mlle Bellerose would have completed an impressive family group in the important role of Bérénice, wife of Pharnace. According to the author, this part was a major reason for the play's success: 'Les actions de cette femme ont donné à ma Tragédie une grande partie du peu de réputation qu'elle a, et ... celle qui les a représentées dans les meilleures compagnies de l'Europe a tiré assez de larmes des plus beaux yeux de la terre' (ibid., Au Lecteur).

6   J. Rotrou, *Hercule mourant, tragédie*, Paris, Sommaville et Quinet, 1636: first performed early 1634 at the Hôtel de Bourgogne (Déjanire, Iole).

P. Corneille, *Médée, tragédie*, Paris, F. Targa, 1639: first performed in the season 1634/5 at the Marais (Médée, Créuse).

I. de Benserade, *La Mort d'Achille, tragédie*, Paris, A. de Sommaville, 1636: first performed in 1635 (Hécube, Polyxène, Briséide).

7   G. de Scudéry, 'Observations sur *Le Cid*', in P. Corneille, *Œuvres complètes*, ed. G. Couton, 3 vols, Paris, Bibliothèque de la Pléiade, 1980–7, I, pp. 787 and 789.

8   D. Clarke, 'Plutarch's Contribution to the invention of Sabine in Corneille's *Horace*', *Modern Language Review*, 89, i, 1994, pp. 39-49.

9   C. Chaulmer, *La Mort de Pompée, tragédie*, Paris, A. de Sommaville, 1638.

10   C. de M. de Saint-Evremond, 'Dissertation sur *Le Grand Alexandre*' (1668), in *Œuvres en prose*, 4 vols, Paris, 1962-69, II, pp. 73 and 97-98.

11   P. Corneille, 'Stances' in *Œuvres complètes...*, III, 107-8, p. 108.

CHAPTER SEVENTEEN

How Quinault uses Political Commonplaces

WILLIAM BROOKS

In his edition of Rotrou's *Venceslas*, Derek Watts shows how political themes constitute the essence of the play.[1] Plays of the period commonly used extensive political subject matter. However, after Corneille's first retirement playwrights preferred, on the whole, to dramatize sentimental emotions such as love and jealousy. Yet Quinault, for example, used political material in twelve of his sixteen conventional plays, written between 1653 and 1671.[2] I shall suggest that while his use of politics is merely episodic and ornamental in his early plays, and his political subject matter hardly rises above the commonplace, political themes gradually develop into an organic element of the action.

Les Coups de l'amour et de la fortune (1655) features a political predicament. Is the rightful heir the legitimate Stelle, or her sister Aurore, conceived illegitimately but born after their parents' clandestine marriage? How sensible is Aurore's willingness to share the throne? How important is her unpopularity? Was her upbringing at another court designed to prepare her for the throne or to distance her from it? A grand debate (I, 3) recalls the council scenes of Pierre Corneille, but how does Quinault develop such potentially rich material? He doesn't. After a maxim voiced by Stelle, dazzling by its ordinariness ('On brise une Couronne alors qu'on la partage'), the political interest disappears between Acts 1 and 5, where it re-surfaces briefly. It is simply a pretext for the hero to distinguish himself in Aurore's service.

Le Fantôme amoureux (1656)[3] includes the commonplace theme of whether the ruler is above the law, and the related question of whether he is a good ruler. When the duke kills Fabrice, Fabrice's father declares:

Il est mon prince encor malgré sa tyrannie,
Le destin des Sujets dépend des Souverains.
Un crime devient juste en partant de leurs mains.
(*Le Fantôme amoureux*, II, 4; ll. 538–40; Cicero edition, p. 62)

The duke later meets Fabrice, whom he believes to be a ghost, and apologizes (V, 5; ll. 1634–50), admitting that 'plus ta perte est injuste, & plus mon crime est noir'. When finally this murderous tyrant is tricked into approving Fabrice's marriage, he accepts defeat and declares:

> Vous trahissiez ma gloire à ne me pas trahir;
> A qui commande mal, on doit mal obeïr;
> Aux injustes desseins on peut justement nuire.
> (V, 7; ll. 1745–47; Cicero edition, p. 126)

There is no question of a serious political message. In neither play does the political material constitute a political plot; moreover, it lacks cohesiveness and is conventional and episodic.

Ornamental and episodic political material reappears in most of Quinault's early plays, but although commonplace, it gradually becomes more evenly distributed and better integrated into the action. For example, Clodésile's conspiracy, which serves to introduce *Amalasonte* (1657),[4] is not, as in *Les Coups*, just a pretext, but resurfaces from time to time and helps to mislead both Amalfrède and Amalasonte about Théodat's feelings. Amongst other political themes there is, for example, an illustration of flatterers at court. These flatterers are also the conspirators. Clodésile states how they should treat the queen's favourite, and intended husband, Théodat:

> Il n'est plus nostre égal puis qu'il va s'agrandir,
> La Fortune le flate, il luy faut applaudir,
> Et puis que cette Aveugle à l'élever s'engage,
> Il faut aveuglément respecter son ouvrage.
> (*Amalasonte*, I, 1; ll. 15–18)

When Théodat is disgraced, and they show their vindictiveness, the fallen favourite muses upon their fickleness (I, 5; ll. 169–76).

The acquisition of a crown justifies any means. Plotting to murder Théodat, Clodésile declares:

> Si [ce crime] peut me couronner il sera glorieux,
> Tous les moyens sont beaux lors que la fin est belle,
> La Couronne rend pur ce qui s'approche d'elle,
> Et quand un crime noir mène au Trône où l'on tend,
> Par l'éclat qu'il y trouve il devient éclatant.
> (III, 1; ll. 754–58)

Another commonplace is the dilemma facing a father in the queen's service when his son appears to be a traitor (II, 1).

In *Le Feint Alcibiade* (1658), a conspiracy occupies much of Acts 1 and 5, as well as part of Act 4. There is discussion of kingship and the balance between the king's personal concerns and public duty, the question of flatterers is aired, and there is a council scene and a further episode in which the king seeks advice (I, 2; I, 4; IV, 2; V, 9). Préxaspe's conspiracy, which colours the opening of *Le Mariage de Cambise* (1658), provokes reflections on flatterers (I, 2, ll. 31–40) which echo Théodat's remarks. Once again, there is discussion of kingship in both personal and public terms (I, 5; IV, 1). Other political discussions colour parts of III, 2 and IV, 1.

Gradually, politically motivated characters also participate directly in the central action. In *La Mort de Cyrus* (1658–59), Odatirse's ambition to marry Thomiris directly threatens the lovers' happiness. Moreover, by rousing the army, he puts pressure on Thomiris to agree; finally, a military rising to avenge his murder forces Thomiris to condemn Cyrus to death. Thus, political ambition and the ruthless use of power drive the plot forward. Although the army's hostility recalls that of the people in *Les Coups*, this time the army influences events whereas Aurore's subjects are mentioned and then ignored. Other commonplaces also occur: Odatirse declares that 'Mon crime seroit beau s'il estoit couronné' (I, 2), and also voices the ruler's supremacy over the law (I, 5).

Odatirse was also in love with Thomiris, but in *Stratonice* (1660),[5] Barsine's political ambition totally subordinates her love. Barsine loves Antiochus, the heir to the throne, but his father, Séleucus, is about to marry Stratonice. Barsine is acutely aware of the likely outcome:

> Le Prince est en peril de n'estre jamais Roy,
> Et le Roy peut donner, pour comble de miseres,
> Des Maistres à son fils, en luy donnant des Freres.
> [Moreover, Stratonice's father]
>   soûtiendra sa fille, & mettra ses enfans,
> Après la mort du Roy, dans le Trône où je tends,
> Et je seray . . .
> Toûjours femme d'un Prince, & jamais d'un Monarque.
>   (*Stratonice*, I, 2; ll. 92–94, 99–102)

Barsine's conclusion is that she must prevent the proposed marriage and replace Stratonice with herself as Séleucus' wife (I, 2, ll. 107–8). Elsewhere, she makes general remarks on political themes and on her ambition, which she calls 'le soin des grands cœurs' (whereas 'l'amour, des cœurs oisifs n'est que l'amusement') (V, 1; ll. 1454–56; see also I, 1).

Stratonice, on the other hand, loves Antiochus but her uncle, Philippe, refuses to postpone her marriage to Séleucus and adds a comment which could have been spoken by Barsine:

Songez qu'il faut regner, & que l'ambition
Doit estre des grands cœurs l'unique passion,
Qu'il ne faut rien haïr que ce qui peut vous nuire,
Qu'il ne faut rien aimer à moins que d'un Empire.
(II, 1; ll. 419–22)

In the final scene, Séleucus' abdication, enabling his son to marry Stratonice, reminds spectators that, however prominent political considerations may become in Quinault's plays, they never motivate the majority of his characters.

In these plays of Quinault's middle period, there are plotters, flatterers, favourites, and commonplaces about the rights of kings and the duties of subjects. Political material no longer disappears after Act 1, to re-emerge briefly in Act 5. It is in Act 3 of *Amalasonte* that Clodésile tries to murder Théodat and that Theudion has his son arrested, in Act 4 that Clodésile's anger starts the chain of events that leads to the truth, and between Acts 4 and 5 that Theudion determines to kill his son. These are politically motivated actions, however mundane. It is in Act 2 of *Le Feint Alcibiade* that the political disgrace of the real Alcibiade is revealed. In Act 3, Lisandre admits to political ambition and there are reminders of Agis's duty to kill the monstrous boar; in Act 4, Charilas's plot is overheard by Cléone-Alcibiade, and this influences the events of Act 5. In Act 3 of *Le Mariage de Cambise*, the disgraced Préxaspe's arrival delays Darius's search for Aristonne and indirectly causes the events which ensue when he fails to find her in time; in Act 4, Préxaspe's exile is discussed and Darius expresses his loyalty to Cambise instead of asking for Aristonne's release. In short, political material increases in variety and prominence, and begins to impinge upon the love plot which forms the essential problem of the play.

In three of Quinault's last four tragedies, political themes of considerable dramatic potential occur: in the first two, the problem of usurpation, and in the third, that of a great commander threatened by a politically motivated conspiracy. Moreover, although the political action could still never be described as weighty, there is for the first time in Quinault's plays a dilemma for the central characters between their love and their political interests. In *Agrippa* (1662), Agrippa-Tibérinus must not reveal his identity to Lavinie, because if it were known, he could not continue to occupy the throne. Consequently, he must accept and even encourage her hatred. This clash between love and political imperative is much discussed between father (Tirrhène) and son (I, 5; III, 2; IV, 4). In *Astrate* (1664–65),6 Astrate loves Elise and she loves him, but neither realizes that he is the missing son of the king she has murdered: her interests are to eliminate him, and his duty is to be her mortal enemy.7 The clash is not at once perceived because Astrate's identity is unknown, but political tension arises early in the play from a situation Quinault has used before, that of a queen reigning alone (Amalasonte and Thomiris are the other examples). He adds a dimension to what was formerly merely a static situation by making the people impatient for the queen to marry. This impatience is revealed by Sichée, who encourages Agénor to seize the throne:

> La Cour qui veut un Maistre, à regret suit ses Loix . . .
> Un Roy sied mieux enfin au Trône qu'une Femme . . .
> Tout est pour Vous, le Peuple, & l'Armée, & la Cour.
> Rien n'est pour Elle.
> (*Astrate*, I, 3; ll. 161, 164, 169–70)

Such political comment would have been intended merely to ornament the action in earlier plays, and we might assume that Quinault has included it just to underline the tension between the urgency of marriage and Elise's decision to postpone it; but we gradually realize that it hints at much more, for it emerges that Sichée is a participant in some mysterious conspiracy, of which 'desunir la Maison des Tyrans' (v. 186) is part. Moreover, behind Elise's postponement of the marriage, itself a preliminary to her rejection of Agénor, there is a coherent and astute piece of reasoning. Agénor is related to her and shares the opprobrium attaching to the usurping and murderous royal family. Therefore, Elise plans to marry Astrate instead. She reminds the dismayed Sichée that 'le Peuple irrité' are on the point of rebelling in support of the missing rightful heir to the throne, and concludes:

> [Agénor], en m'épousant, loin d'asseurer ma Teste,
> N'aideroit qu'à grossir l'orage qui s'appreste;
> Et le Peuple seroit encor plus mutiné,
> S'il voyoit des Tyrans tout le Sang couronné.
> J'ay besoin d'un Espoux Illustre, & Magnanime,
> Qui m'alie à la Gloire, & me tire du Crime.
> (I, 5; ll. 295–300)

Although, as ever, the people are sketchily represented, they do influence events. By the end of Act 4, Sichée's own partisans have entered the royal palace; soon even Sichée, who knows they want

Elise's death, cannot promise to control them (V, 2).[8] A messenger brings a brief moment of hope:

> Le Peuple sur ce point, encor ne presse pas.
> Il reserve sa vie, & c'est une Victime
> Qu'il croit devoir garder à son Roy legitime:
> Mais il veut voir son Maistre . . .
> (V, 4; ll.1590–93)

Realizing there is a chance of saving Elise, Astrate presses Sichée to reveal publicly who he is, and Sichée relents (V, 4). It is too late. Elise has taken poison.

There also occurs in both plays a political commonplace that Quinault has not used before, namely the question of the over-mighty subject. It arises in *Agrippa* (I, 2); more strikingly, in *Astrate*, Sichée tries to disunite the royal family by suggesting to Elise that Agénor constitutes a threat (I, 5; ll. 211–14). Kings and queens are again above the law. Sichée tells Agénor:

> [Elise] pretend qu'en tous lieux, & qu'en toutes saisons
> Les volontez des Rois tiennent lieu de raisons.
> (I,3; vv. 141-42)

Likewise, reasons of state can be invoked to justify any desire. Agénor claims that his marriage to Elise is 'un hymen à l'Estat necessaire' (I, 3; l. 131), whereas in reality he is personally ambitious. Elise admits that,

> . . . les Raisons d'Estat qu'on m'a veu mettre au jour,
> N'ont servy que de voile à des Crimes d'Amour.
> (II, 3; ll. 575–76)

Flattery is discussed, too. When Sichée warns that Agénor has 'des Partisans qui soûtiendront ses droicts' (that is, his apparent right to marry Elise), the perspicacious queen responds:

> On court à sa Fortune, & non à sa Personne:
> L'espoir de le voir Roy le fait suivre aujourd'huy,
> N'ayant plus cet espoir, il n'aura rien pour Luy;
> Ce qui suit la Fortune, avec elle s'écoule,
> Et son moindre revers écarte bien la foule.
> (I, 5; ll. 248–52)

In *Agrippa* and *Astrate* the main threat to the lovers arises from their own political interests, perceived or not. The threat posed by a rival in love, much more important in the early plays and here given to the self-effacing Mézence and the bumptious Agénor, is of little consequence, as neither possesses the means, as Odatirse did, of forcing the issue; but their very existence constitutes a political obstacle. The main politically motivated character, whose dramatic importance has developed from the simple villain Clodésile to the powerful Tirrhène and the resourceful Sichée, is central, influencing events from start to finish.

As ever, there is no coherent political philosophy. *Agrippa* shows a usurper being established as the rightful king, whereas *Astrate* concerns the destruction of a usurper. The usurper Agrippa is a virtuous and gentle man, compelled to pretend that he is a heartless, murderous tyrant; Elise is a benevolent ruler who nevertheless has had the rightful king and his sons murdered. Quinault's lack of interest in making political statements is illustrated by his portrayal of usurpation in a different light in each play and by his customary reluctance to explore other political problems latent in the situation. We are twice reminded of the anguish experienced by Agrippa, who cannot reveal his identity lest his occupancy of the throne be jeopardized (I,5 and IV,4), but he takes no political decisions as a consequence of this anguish, even though there are piquant consequences for the love interest. Astrate's discovery of his identity causes scarcely a moment's hesitation before he determines to defend Elise against his own supporters.

In his two remaining plays, Quinault brings the development we have been tracing to its logical conclusion by fusing the political and love threats. In respect of its political themes, the more striking is unquestionably *Pausanias* (1668).[9] The Spartan general Pausanias wavers between, on the one hand, marrying Démarate and retaining the supreme command of the Greek forces and, on the other, abandoning Démarate, honour, command, and perhaps even country, for the love of Cléonice, a captive enemy princess. The chief political plot concerns the conspiracy of the Athenian Aristide to wrest command of the Greek army from Pausanias and gain it instead for his own compatriot Cimon. Aristide takes advantage of Pausanias's love for Cléonice, who is to be awarded to one of the victorious generals. Cimon (who does not appear) wants Cléonice himself, but the astute Aristide supports Pausanias's claim, justifying himself thus to his confidant Sophane:

Ce n'est pas qu'en effet à vous parler sans fard
La Politique ici ne prenne un peu de part ...
Son soin [de Cimon] pour Cleonice est un peu trop pressant ...
Tout est perdu pour lui si cet amour ne cesse;
Cleonice est d'un sang odieux à la Grece ...

Tout doit estre suspect de qui cherche à lui plaire.
J'étouffe en mon Ami de dangereux soûpirs,
Je consulte sa gloire & non pas ses desirs.
                                        (*Pausanias*, I, 5)

Much better to let Pausanias have her. Aristide hopes that Sparta will repudiate Pausanias, because its people have chosen Démarate to be Pausanias's bride and expect their choice to be respected (III, 1). He expounds his plan to Démarate (III, 2), thus alerting her to the political threat to Pausanias. Démarate is passionately in love with Pausanias, and from this moment the political and love threats are fused: when she warns Pausanias of Aristide's plan (IV, 3), she is also preparing her personal vengeance.

The army resents Pausanias's command, and Aristide focuses its resentment on his impermissible love. Eurianax soon warns Pausanias of Aristide's influence over the malcontents (I, 3); subsequently, Pausanias rebukes Aristide for:

Vostre adresse à flatter l'aigreur des mécontens,
Vostre douceur maligne autant qu'ingenieuse
Pour rendre de mon rang la hauteur odieuse,
Vostre art à colorer l'orgueil de vos desseins. (I, 4)

Aristide's reply convinces neither Pausanias nor the audience. Pausanias knows he is plotting a mutiny. Later, Sophane tells Aristide that,

On n'attend que vostre ordre & pour cette entreprise,
Seigneur, selon vos vœux tout est prest sans remise.
Au camp, dans nos vaisseaux, par tout, sans hesiter,
Contre Pausanias on brûle d'éclatter . . .
Nos alliez sont las de son humeur hautaine . . .
Vostre douceur adroite a gagné tous les cœurs. (III, 1)

Eventually the army rises in support of Cimon and against Pausanias and Cléonice; this recalls both *La Mort de Cyrus* (where the army rises in protest at the favoured treatment of a captive enemy) and *Astrate* (where the rebels seek to replace an unpopular leader with one who is more acceptable, incited by a plotter who has pretended to support the former). News of the 'Trouppe mutine,/Maistresse de la Ville, [qui] au Palais s'achemine' (V, 1) emerges early in Act 5, but Pausanias, no coward, scorns the threat until he realizes that the rebels threaten Cléonice. Only then does he renounce his command in return for Aristide's promise to protect her.

As a political calculator, Aristide is a worthy successor to Tirrhène and Sichée. The unproductive love threat to the hero emanating from a rival (Mézence, Agénor) who is spurned by the heroine is relegated to the wings by being given to Cimon, whilst the political threat from the same quarter, extinguished in *Agrippa* and *Astrate* by the convenient deaths of the characters in question, is paramount. Furthermore, the abandoned and jealous Démarate uses it to further her own personal interests. The threat posed by a rebellious army is used constructively by a calculating political operator; it is certainly not just an ornament, and indeed, ornamental commonplaces have disappeared. *Pausanias* lacks reflections on the rights of kings and their standing above the law (save in the conflict, never examined, between Sparta's choice and Pausanias's own preference); it does not consider flatterers and favourites, the duties of subjects, or an over-mighty subject. There is, however, a major political plot and a subsidiary political dilemma (should Pausanias defect to the Persians?), and the play shares with *Agrippa* and *Astrate* the direct involvement of the hero in the political action. Although the variety of comment is less great, there is tighter organization and the political material is fully integrated into the love action.

So well integrated is it into Quinault's last play, *Bellérophon* (1671), that Etienne Gros can identify no political content whatever.[10] This is an instructive mistake. In fact, what Quinault does is to fuse political themes into the play in such a way that they arise from the machinations of the principal villain, and can no longer be called part of the subject matter. I have identified elsewhere three themes: the over-mighty subject, the proper ambition of a princess, and the role of the people. The first two are inventions supporting an illusion created by the consummate deceiver Sténobée, whilst the third, which she initially uses for the same purpose, later ironically becomes a reality which menaces her plans and finally provides a pathetic coda.[11]

To sum up. An evolution in Quinault's use of political themes may be measured by the steady increase in the quantity of political material and its ever more thorough integration into the action, but just as there is no depth to the political considerations because the material hardly rises above the commonplace, so too there is no political philosophy, because both the implicit and explicit political views in his theatre are fortuitous.[12] Quinault is uninterested in political material for its own sake. How else are we to explain the omissions, unexplored questions, and contradictions which arise even within this shallow political framework? He does not examine Amalasonte's alleged injustice towards Clodésile's father, despite the evident analogy, also unexamined, of her unjust decision to order the death of Théodat; he creates no conflict between Theudion's duty to the queen and his love for his son. He does not explore the relationship between monarch and adviser as seen in the roles of Theudion and Lisandre. Agis and Cambise act dishonourably in pursuit of their personal interests, but the same Agis follows his duty to rid his land of a terrible monster and seeks advice before taking political decisions, and the grateful Cambise heaps honours upon a loyal subject, seeks his advice, and hesitates to defy the law by marrying his own sister. Thus, Quinault's purpose is to set up resonances and dilemmas within the love interest of his plays: the political posturings of the characters are defined simply by his need to place them in situations that will create, sustain, complicate, or resolve problems pertaining to that love interest.

None the less, after scattered comments in the early plays, the political material is given a more appropriate context in *Amalasonte* and succeeding plays because they are more serious and, ostensibly at least, historical. More and more, such material, however commonplace and contradictory, not only serves as a pretext for the action but is found throughout the play, where it is not only relevant but increasingly affects the action. Characters whose actions in pursuit of love have a political dimension which is virtually accidental (Lothaire in *Les Coups*, the duke) give way to politically motivated secondary characters (Clodésile, Charilas), whose actions in pursuit of their political ends impinge also upon the love plot; these, in their turn, are replaced by politically motivated central characters (Odatirse, Barsine) who are also lovers and who therefore, for both political and amatory reasons in different contexts, constitute a direct threat to the happiness of the lovers. At the same time as the political interest moves nearer to the centre of the action, political commonplaces are spread throughout the play, so that the audience is repeatedly reminded that a political aspect underlies and shapes the sentimental action. In the last few plays, politically motivated characters remain (Tirrhène, Sichée, Aristide), but the lovers are also given political interests inimical to their love (Agrippa, Astrate and Elise, Pausanias; potentially Lavinie and Cléonice); politics as an ornament all but disappears; and in the final play, the political matter is consciously invented by a criminal lover who employs political pretexts in the service of her passion.

Boileau was probably thinking of *Stratonice* when he wrote the *boutade* which has encapsulated Quinault's theatre ever since: 'Jusqu'à "je vous hais", tout s'y dit tendrement'.[13] Perhaps it is appropriate, then, that the same play should contain the articulation of a dilemma which becomes more acute with each succeeding play. An alternative epigraph for Quinault's theatre lies in the words of Séleucus, whose love for Barsine confronts him with:

> le peril ...
> De renoncer à tout pour me donner à vous,
> De trahir mon devoir, ma gloire, & mon empire.
> (*Stratonice*, III, 3; ll. 1007–9)

Quinault's heroes and heroines may do everything for love, but their political shortcomings and miscalculations also threaten and sometimes encompass their downfall.

Notes:

1 Jean Rotrou, *Venceslas*, ed. Derek A. Watts, Exeter: University of Exeter, 1990, pp. xxiii–xxv.

2 I exclude the eleven libretti from the present study, though my argument, *mutatis mutandis*, applies to those as well. Dates are those of first performance. Plays not available in modern editions may be consulted in any of the commonly available eighteenth-century editions of Quinault's *Théâtre* (5 vols, 1715, 1739, and 1778; the last was reprinted by Slatkine, Geneva, 1970). The textual differences are negligible, though in the 1739 edition most scene numbers differ.

3 *Le Fantôme amoureux*, introd. by Manuel Couvreur, [Paris]: Cicero, 1992.

4 *Amalasonte* in *Théâtre du XVIIᵉ siècle*, vol. 2, ed. J. Scherer and J. Truchet, Paris: Gallimard, 1986.

5 *Stratonice*, ed. E. Dubois, Exeter: University of Exeter, 1987.

6 *Astrate*, ed. Edmund J. Campion, Exeter: University of Exeter, 1980.

7 Even before the revelation of his identity he experiences a clash between his love and his duty to his supposed father, who has revealed that he is the chief conspirator against Elise and a supporter of the rightful heir to the throne.

8 La Bruyère writes of 'un tissu de jolis sentiments, de déclarations tendres, d'entretiens galants, de portraits agréables, de mots doucereux ... suivi à la vérité d'une dernière scène où les mutins n'entendent aucune raison, et où, pour la bienséance, il y a enfin du sang répandu, et quelque malheureux à qui il en coûte la vie' (*Les Caractères*, 'Des ouvrages de l'esprit', 51), and he adds the footnote, 'Sédition, dénouement vulgaire des tragédies'. There is no evidence that he had in mind *Agrippa* or *Astrate* rather than other plays, but his sceptical comments do seem appropriate to these and other plays by Quinault.

9 *Pausanias*, ed. William Brooks and Edmund J. Campion. (In preparation.)

10 E. Gros, *Philippe Quinault, sa vie et son œuvre*, Paris: Champion, 1926, p. 344.

11 *Bellérophon*, ed. William Brooks and Edmund J. Campion, Geneva: Droz, 1990, pp. xxvii–xxix; William Brooks, 'Quinault criticism, Boileau, and the problem of Racine', in *Actes de Las Vegas*, ed. M.-F. Hilgar, Paris, Seattle, Tübingen: Biblio 17, 1990, pp. 37–48.

12 Some years ago, John Van Eerde suggested a consistent condemnation of king and court, flatterers and favourites, and gave examples ('Quinault, the court, and kingship', *Romanic Review*, 53, 1962, pp. 174–86); but Quinault's adverse comments constitute such a small part of his political material, and so many situations show monarchs in a good light, that it seems to me that no consistent philosophy can be derived.

13 Boileau, *Satire* III, in *Œuvres complètes*, ed. F. Escal, Paris: Gallimard, 1966, p. 24.

CHAPTER EIGHTEEN

Politics and Tragedy:
The Case of the Earl of Essex

C. J. GOSSIP

Sedition, real or alleged, provides the starting-point, if not the main tragic focus, of the three seventeenth-century French plays dealing with the trial and execution of Robert Devereux, second Earl of Essex.[1] The facts of the case were available in Camden's *Annales rerum anglicarum et hibernicarum regnante Elizabetha* and in Paul de Bellegent's 1627 French translation of it, as well as in de Thou's *Historiarum sui temporis* and various diplomatic papers.[2] French interest in England, and the desire to dramatize one of its most startling and tragic recent events despite the absence of historical or geographical distancing, can be traced back to earlier stage versions of the deaths of Mary, queen of Scots and Lady Jane Grey.[3] It is more difficult to explain the timing of the appearance of the two groups of plays on Tudor subjects, but the mid to late 1630s, as tragi-comedy in France gave way to tragedy, highlighted the deaths of other victims such as Mithridates, Mariamne and Lucretia, while the late 1670s and early 1680s perhaps called for non-traditional subject matter to fill the void left by the departures of Corneille and especially Racine.

Although the political niceties of the Essex case are no more respected by La Calprenède, Thomas Corneille and Boyer than were those of ancient Greece and Rome by other playwrights, a study of the link between reason of State and personal desire, especially love, and of the different emphases given to public and private interests by the three writers may help to define the limitations as well as the possibilities of politics as a basis for successful tragedy. Unusually derivative though it may be in that it lifts passages of text more or less verbatim from La Calprenède, even Boyer's play, written to compete with Thomas Corneille's, offers variations on the interplay between Elizabeth, her favourite, her rivals and the factions at Court.[4]

Both in their structure and their character-count, the three plays contain important differences. In the earliest, probably performed in 1637, La Calprenède adopts the strategy of opening with a make-or-break encounter between the queen and Essex, their only face-to-face meeting in the five acts. Elizabeth is later given two substantial monologues (I, 4, and II, 2 where, despite an unwelcome headache, she prevents her as yet unknown rival from getting a word in edgeways), while the said Lady Cecil, unhistorical wife of Sir Robert Cecil, also has two soliloquies (II, 3 and IV, 7). Essex is present in only nine of the twenty-seven scenes in all: as the queen tells him in I, 1, l. 141, 'Vous pouvez à loisir prouver votre innocence'. Time is thus left for the accused and the queen to reveal their respective attitudes before and after the set-piece trial which occupies the sole, long scene of Act III. The pardon granted to Essex's friend and co-defendant the Comte de Soubtantonne (Henry Wriothesley, Earl of Southampton) immediately after the judgement (IV, 1, l. 1025) allows La Calprenède to focus his last two acts on his central couple. The ring guaranteeing a Royal pardon is introduced early enough (IV, 5) to cause the Earl concern when it does not produce the expected result (V, 1).

By its distribution of characters La Calprenède's tragedy focuses on Elizabeth, to the relative exclusion of Essex and the sidelining of the rival for the favourite's affections, Lady Cecil, at least until the dénouement. The execution of Essex is reported at the beginning of V, 3, very soon after his last appearance, leaving two hundred and fifty lines in which are recounted Madame Cécile's remorse (V, 5 and 6) and, at considerable length, the assumption of guilt by the queen (V, 7). Other figures, too, play unexpectedly small parts—not just Southampton, who disappears after IV, 4, or the Comte de Salisbery, whose eloquent defence of Essex is contained in a single speech (II, 1, ll. 355–79), but the accusers Cécile, Raleg and Popham, although their case is put in single-scene interventions from II, 1 to V, 1. Forty years later, Thomas Corneille's rather shorter *Comte d'Essex* (1600 lines) offers a substantially different pattern of scenes. Again there is only one meeting between Elizabeth and her favourite and that is a *tête-à-tête* (II, 5) held in the silent presence of a *confidente* and of the duchesse d'Irton. But the queen's entrance is delayed until Act II, with the opening act devoted to Essex and his friend the Comte de Salsbury, his love of the duchesse d'Irton, and Cécile, described in the cast list as 'Ennemy du Comte d'Essex'. The trial, consigned to the second interval, is reported on briefly by Cécile in III, 1, while the rest of that act and Act IV are occupied by the successive attempts of Salsbury, the duchesse and the queen's *confidente* Tilney to bring about Essex's reprieve. Unlike his predecessor, Thomas Corneille leaves less than one hundred lines after the news of the Earl's execution, devoting part of it to an account by Salsbury of the victim's last words and emotional death. But Elizabeth had had the first four scenes of Act V to prepare herself for the event, and a mere sixteen lines allow her to conclude the play with plans to bury the corpse and prepare herself for death.

The play which Boyer provided for the Guénégaud's attempt to upstage the Hôtel de Bourgogne early in 1678 is slightly shorter again (1582 lines) but has thirty-nine scenes compared with Thomas' twenty-four. The queen's same two *confidentes* as in La Calprenède's play appear rarely, but the Madame Cécile/duchesse d'Irton figure, here called the duchesse de Clarence, is on stage more frequently than Essex himself. Elizabeth and her favourite have three meetings *sans suite*, each quite substantial: one of them immediately follows the trial which is staged in III, 1 with Raleg, Salysbery and Popham and with Coban, a *seigneur anglois*, replacing the erstwhile Cécile, and the last encounter comes as late as the middle of Act V. The roles of Coban, who opens the play with Raleg, and of the duchesse are filled out, the former in particular contributing to an atmosphere of menacing evil which heightens the oft-proclaimed innocence of the title character.

The detail of the political machinations of England in its relations with Ireland at the turn of the century must have been as unfamiliar to all three dramatists as the names and offices of some of the personalities, mangled into picturesquely inconsistent forms. None of the three playwrights fully succeeds in focusing the audience's attention on the public and private issues involved. Rather they prefer the scattergun technique of listing multiple motives for the arrest of Essex (and, in La Calprenède, of his trusty friend Soubtantonne) and referring to various ones at different times. The confusion is compounded by the range of adversaries and their division into two, not entirely distinct groups: on the one hand the queen herself and her supporting *demoiselles* (La Calprenède), *confidente* (T. Corneille) and *suivantes* (Boyer), on the other the several Court factions.

If we examine the latter first, we note that La Calprenède's Cécile, in the first of his five appearances, talks generally about *un crime si grand, son attentat, ce crime exemplaire*, Essex's un-English *lâcheté* by which 'il livre à l'ennemi sa Reine et sa patrie' (II, 1, ll. 313, 320, 330, 317, 325). Raleig, three scenes later, merely reacts politely to Essex's bitter words. The dramatist is keeping the specific accusations back for the trial (III, 1), conducted by the Lord Chief Justice Sir John Popham with a superficially scrupulous attention to propriety ('avec toute équité je ferai mon devoir'; 'd'aucun intérêt mon âme n'est touchée', ll. 808–9). The charges relate to *des complots contre cette Couronne, intelligence avec ses ennemis*, and a catch-all *beaucoup d'excès que vous avez commis* (ll. 814–6). Supernumerary staff (l. 818), unusual military guests, and an attempt to sequestrate Royal visitors are mentioned ahead of an armed entry to London (ll. 822–5).

A letter written to the Comte de Tiron (Hugh O'Neill, Earl of Tyrone) proves the desire to deprive Elizabeth of both sceptre and life (ll. 831–4). Popham's incisive, carefully modulated attack, moving from general to specific and from minor to major charge, reduces the angry Essex to passing his defence to Southampton, who burbles on about *honneur* and *gloire* (l. 865), the citizen's right to bear arms (ll. 875–6), the lack of public order in the streets (ll. 881–4), the desire to welcome, not detain, the queen's representatives (ll. 885–90) and—not least, but last—the prevalence of 'lettres contrefaites,/De témoins apostés' (ll. 894–5). Raleig brushes off his and his colleagues' involvement, as does Cécile, while Essex unwisely addresses the latter as 'peste de tous les hommes' (l. 914) and hints at the Secretary's jealousy (ll. 917–8). Then, claiming sole responsibility, the Earl provokes Southampton into a weak defence of their mutual friendship and shared destiny. Popham has little hesitation in convicting both of *lèse-majesté* (l. 984).

The self-restraint of the official accusers,[5] the momentary fairness of Cécile, and Essex's typically haughty refusal to amplify Southampton's words[6] provide a telling contrast with the queen's view of the situation. For her, the favourite's *manquement de foi* and *félonie* coincide with her *ardente amitié* (I, 1, ll. 20, 21, 25); the Tyrone letter and Essex's attempt to overturn both herself and the State clash with her realization that 'je t'aime encor, tout perfide et tout traître' (I, 1, ll. 107, 112, 22). While the text surely does not support the argument that she has yielded her virginity to the Earl,[7] the strong, early admission of her passion is paralleled by an unchanging desire, if not intention, to pardon what she sees as clear-cut guilt. Strictly private confession of his political betrayal will lead to an Auguste-like comprehensive pardon (I, 1, l. 50); and she is shielded from the jealousy which later dramatists introduce, since the deathbed confession of her rival Madame Cécile leaves her but the final scene in which to doubt the strength of Essex's interest. Even there (V, 7) it is self-blame which occupies her most. Thus La Calprenède succeeds in bringing into sharp focus a consistently active queen and a clinically efficient team of accusers of Essex, leaving the Earl himself to cope with his political actions and his other woman.

The charges in Thomas Corneille also mention *cabales* and *ligues*, the *pratiques avec l'Irlande* and the *révoltes publiques*. Reduced to Cécile, with no Raleig or Popham, the critics first find expression in Essex's friend Salsbury (I, 1) and in the woman he loves, the duchesse d'Irton (I, 2), who both give voice to the allegations and wait for a response. Salsbury, however, also brings up the very recent armed attack on the Court, which Essex willingly confirms: 'J'allois sauver un bien qu'on m'ostoit par surprise,/Mais averty trop tard, j'ay manqué l'entreprise' (I, 1). The duc d'Irton there married his young Henriette, but Elizabeth still believes the Earl is in love with 'la Sœur de Suffolc', a sham interest to divert attention. The charges laid by friend and foe alike thus combine love and politics, and the predominant role of the duchesse in the play keeps the former topic to the fore. But Thomas's Cécile is much more active in his opposition to Essex than was La Calprenède's: 'On eust dit, à le voir plein de sa propre estime', the Secretary insists in III, 1, 'Que ses Juges estoient coupables de son crime'. The trial has been conducted offstage—Thomas Corneille may not have wanted to be seen copying his predecessor—but this gives added power to Cécile to twist and strengthen the case which he presents to the queen.

The latter's conviction that Essex scorns her but loves and wishes to marry, then 'crown' 'la belle Suffolc' is sufficient explanation for the Palace attack (II, 1). This invasion of her Court cannot, like the Tyrone letters, be open to challenge; it convicts him 'du plus grand, du plus noir de tous les attentats' (II, 5). Jealousy of her rival is all the more striking and incongruous since Elizabeth has already stated that all she seeks from the Earl is a Platonic relationship, 'la douceur de voir, d'aimer, de soûpirer' (II, 1). But the ever-present resentment, allied to the sentence passed on Essex, explains even if it does not fully excuse the queen's repeated changes of mind in Act III, the complete pendulum swings which lead Madeleine Bertaud to remark tartly: 'Il aurait fallu beaucoup de talent pour rendre crédible un personnage aussi versatile'.[8] The options Elizabeth considers include yielding Essex to Suffolk, to allow him to live (III, 4), but news about the duchesse d'Irton's involvement increases her feeling of abandonment. The Earl, too, is a prey to jealousy, unable to comprehend his lover's argument (I, 2) that, while he is not forced to 'bruler pour une autre', she is duty bound to stifle her passion and give herself to a husband she does not care for.

Compared with La Calprenède, then, Thomas Corneille, through skilful use of the Court attack, draws attention away from the political crimes in Ireland to the private lives of Essex and the queen. As the latter says in one of her more realistic moments,

> Sur le crime apparent je sauveray ma gloire,
> Et la raison d'Etat, en le [Essex] privant du jour,
> Servira de prétexte à la raison d'Amour.(III, 4)

In his treatment of the subject, Claude Boyer adds two further strands: Coban's carefully concealed passion for Elizabeth ('Par des soins empressez j'y travaille en secret/Sans laisser échapper un amour indiscret', I, 1) and the role of the duchesse de Clarence's brother, feared by Coban, in stirring up revolt among the people (IV, 1). Coban's motive is less genuine affection than a desire to become Elizabeth's consort ('C'est par là que la Reine a des charmes pour moy', I, 1), and knowledge of the Essex–duchesse affair is a further lever in this search for power. His chances, however, are slim: Elizabeth dismisses an early comment of his on Essex with a curt 'Je sçauray bien sans vous punir sa perfidie' (I, 3), later suspecting both his and the duchesse's motives (I, 9), and although he serves her later in the play, his death at the hands of the crowd leaves Elizabeth complaining that, along with 'Raleg et ses complices', he has avoided deserved torture.

Popham, in the public part of the trial shown in III, 1 before the queen's intervention, lays the standard general charges—witnesses' depositions, criminal plots, 'toutes ces veritez'—but controls proceedings less firmly than La Calprenède's 'Chancelier d'Angleterre', leading one of the judges, Essex's friend Salysbery, to challenge the fairness of the proceedings and withdraw. Only then does Popham reassure the accused of his total impartiality (III, 2). Elizabeth, as in the 1637 play, shows Essex the Tyrone letter, talks of intercepted messages and 'témoins trop fidelles' (I, 7), but mentions specifically the Earl's decision to 'venir jusqu'en ces lieux m'arracher la couronne' (I, 4), when he could have been satisfied with reigning in her heart (I, 7). Apprised in IV, 2 of his affair with the duchesse, Elizabeth reacts not with hurt pride but with expressions of worldweariness and guilt for *ma noire politique* and its bloody consequences (IV, 3). The jealousy comes later, culminating in the third encounter with Essex just over one hundred lines before the final curtain.

In all three plays, the basic desire of the queen and response from the Earl are the same. In recognition of her *bonté* (La Calprenède, I, 1, ll. 15, 38) or to satsify her *gloire* (T. Corneille III, 4), her *fierté* (Boyer, I, 9), the accused should confess, in private, and she will forgive and forget (La Calprenède, I, 1, l. 50; T. Corneille, III, 2; Boyer, I, 9). Essex relies on his record, his glorious past deeds (especially in the first two plays, less so in the third), to which Cécile, however base his motives, rightly replies that former actions have been duly, indeed perhaps excessively, rewarded (La Calprenède, III, 1, ll. 750–2, 768–74; T. Corneille, II, 3). Indeed, La Calprenède's queen earlier makes the very point (II, 1, l. 347–8). The Earl further affirms his *innocence* (a key term used by accused and friends in all three tragedies), guaranteed by the patent *imposture* of his attackers symbolized in the *lettres contrefaites* used in evidence against him. The overweening pride of 'a man like me' (La Calprenède III, 1, 1. 732; T. Corneille, I, 1; Boyer, III, 1), mentioned by all the characters and asserted in Essex's highly-charged, self-absorbed speeches, together with the confusing array of charges laid, make it difficult to assess the guilt or otherwise of the title-figure. For all the claims that English law will try him fairly, the *parti pris* of his judges, especially Cécile and the equivalent Coban, is obvious, despite the inclusion in Boyer's version of his friend Salysbery, a character who, in La Calprenède's play, preaches the *juste milieu* and disappears before the trial is held.[9] Elizabeth herself is racked with misgivings: as the person who condemned Mary Stuart to death, she now reigns over a peaceful kingdom but is not at peace with herself. Love for someone of lower rank has been an unkind blow of Fate (e.g. La Calprenède, I, 4). In any case, her political ambitions are said to be still alive (La Calprenède I, 5, 1. 280; T. Corneille, II, 5: 'Ce comble de pouvoir où l'on sçait que j'aspire').

Essex's attitude to Madame Cécile in La Calprenède reveals further conflicts of interest. For all his talk of *joie, fers, amitié, obligation* and *foi* (II, 5, ll. 549, 557, 577, 582, 584), there is no proof that the *quelque reste de flamme* he begs for (II, 5, ll. 618) signifies genuine interest any more. Madame Cécile's dismissive asides would appear only to confirm the absence in him of true love.[10] When, in prison, the Earl reveals the ring and asks her to use it to save him, the *lien éternel* which he promises her (IV, 5, 1. 1284) contrasts with his much more open (and self-interested) statement 'Tu pourras à ton gré disposer de mon sort,/Et donner à l'ingrat ou la vie ou la mort' (IV, 5, ll. 1271–2). The ring which the first and last of our texts introduce is indeed well integrated into the action, signifying the emotional hold which Essex has over Elizabeth but also the queen's political influence over the Earl.[11] But its use is discreet: when, for instance, La Calprenède's monarch dispatches Madame Cécile with the words 'il sait bien le moyen pour obtenir sa grâce' (II, 2, 1. 458), the specific reference is only to the request 'que sa repentance implore ma bonté' (II, 2, 1. 456). And just as Elizabeth interprets his sending of the ring as proof of his innocence, so his decision represents no admission of guilt, no sign of repentance, but simply a reaffirmation of his ambition, a chance to survive.

Boyer exploits the ring more openly: Essex refers to it and appears to show it to Elizabeth (III, 5) after the trial has been interrupted and before the verdict is announced, affirming however that 'estant innocent, je ne veux point de grace'. This, too, is the only play which contains a final comment by Essex's accuser. As he dies in a pool of blood, Coban 'de sa barbare joye étale le transport' and says:

Ma mort ... au moins pour la souffrir sans honte
Precede mon suplice & suit celle du Comte,
Il estoit innocent, je suis un imposteur,
Son indigne rival d'amour & de grandeur:
Trop heureux de porter aussi loin que sa gloire
De mon nom odieux l'execrable memoire.   (V, 11)

Is this surprisingly frank statement the truth or just the ultimate revenge of an evil, disappointed man? Both Carrington Lancaster and Madeleine Bertaud, in judging the character of Essex in La Calprenède, conclude that he is innocent, at most merely hostile to his accusers.[12] Elliott Forsyth is more circumspect: Essex is 'un être vaniteux qui n'est peut-être pas entièrement innocent du crime dont il est accusé'.[13] The remorse of Elizabeth in all three versions and her desire to atone for the *mort injuste* of her favourite appear to contribute to the view that a mistake has been made, especially since the Earl's supporters admit that he has acted out of *promptitude* rather than *dessein* or *ingratitude*, showing *quelque imprudence* and a 'fier emportement,/Pardonnable peut-être'.[14] What is clear is that this political subject, while still bearing strong traces of its Irish element, is, for the purposes of dramatic presentation, gradually reduced to a physical invasion of the English Court in conjunction with a possible attempt to seize political power and that this attack contributes to the close link playwrights wish to make between political action and personal passion. The one Elizabeth out of three who does not immediately contemplate death at the end of Act V sums it up well: Boyer's queen is so lovestruck still ('A tout ce que j'aimois j'ay fait perdre le jour,/Ce que j'aimois n'est plus & j'ay tout mon amour') that she calls on the crowd to avenge the Earl's execution:

Et toy peuple mutin acheve sa vengeance.
Ennemy de la Reine, & rebele à ses loix,
Vange une mort injuste & sois juste une fois. (V, 11)

Notes:

1   La Calprenède, *Le Comte d'Essex* (first printed Paris, no publisher, 1639), as in *Théâtre du XVIIe siècle*, vol. 2, ed. J. Scherer and J. Truchet, Paris, 1986; Thomas Corneille, *Le Comte d'Essex* (Paris, Ribou, 1678), as in *Le Théâtre de T. Corneille*, Amsterdam, H. Desbordes, 1701, vol. 5; Claude Boyer, *Le Comte d'Essex*, Paris, Osmont, 1678. In my text, line numbers as well as act and scene numbers are given for La Calprenède's play.
2   See L.A. Hill, *The Tudors in French Drama*, Baltimore, 1932; A. Lefèvre, 'Les sources des tragédies sur le Comte d'Essex (XVIIe siècle) en France et en Angleterre', *Revue de littérature comparée*, 40, 1966, pp. 616–24.

3   On Montchrestien's *L'Escossoise* (1601), La Calprenède's *Jeanne, Reyne d'Angleterre* (1638) and Regnault's *Marie Stuard* (1638), see C.J. Titmus, 'The influence of Montchrétien's *Escossoise* upon French classical tragedies with subjects from English history', *French Studies*, 10, 1956, pp. 224–30.

4   On La Calprenède, see H.C. Lancaster, 'La Calprenède dramatist', *Modern Philology*, 18, 1920–1, pp. 121–41 and pp. 345–60; four studies by G. Snaith ('The portrayal of power in La Calprenède's *Le Comte d'Essex*', *Modern Language Review*, 81, 1986, pp. 853–65; 'La Calprenède —anti-cornélien?', *Seventeenth-Century French Studies*, 8, 1986, pp. 65–74; 'Plaisir à La Calprenède', *Seventeenth-Century French Studies*, 9, 1987, pp. 55–73; 'Suspense as a source of theatrical pleasure in the plays of La Calprenède', in A. Howe and R. Waller (eds), *En marge du classicisme. Essays on the French Theatre from the Renaissance to the Enlightenment*, Liverpool, 1987, pp. 95–121), and two by M. Bertaud: 'Deux ans après *La Mariane*, *Le Comte d'Essex* de La Calprenède', *Travaux de Linguistique et de Littérature*, 25, 1987, pp. 49–64 and 'D'un *Comte d'Essex* à l'autre, La Calprenède et Thomas Corneille', in M. Bertaud and A. Lapetit (eds), *Amour tragique, amour comique, de Bandello à Molière*, Paris, 1988, pp. 99–133. On T. Corneille, see G. Reynier, *Thomas Corneille, sa vie et son théâtre*, Paris, 1892, and D.A. Collins, *Thomas Corneille, Protean Dramatist*, The Hague, 1966. On Boyer, see C.C. Brody, *The Works of Claude Boyer*, Morningside Heights, 1947.

5   Snaith, 'Suspense', p. 106, writes that Cécile 'is shown poisoning the Queen's mind against him [Essex]', revealing his 'malevolence'. Raleigh, too, ensures 'that the condemnation to death holds'. This is true; but it is noticeable how restrained the presentations are. Raleig, for instance, relies on two facts: Essex has just been tried and found guilty, and he has not bothered to answer the accusations (IV, 3, ll. 1135–6).

6   Despite Cécile's concession that Essex has greater *vaillance* than he himself possesses (III, 1, ll. 942–3).

7   Bertaud, 'D'un *Comte d'Essex* à l'autre', p. 102, interprets *mes propres faveurs* (I, 1, l. 8) as meaning that 'elle ne s'est pas montrée sourde à l'appel de la chair' and mocks Lancaster's naïvety ('La Calprenède dramatist', p. 138) in believing that the *gages* of I, 5, l. 266 refer to the ring. J. Truchet, *La Tragédie classique en France*, Paris, 1975, p. 41, also believes that 'elle s'était donnée à lui'.

8   Bertaud, 'D'un *Comte d'Essex* à l'autre', p. 121.

9   He is not part of the trial (Lancaster, 'La Calprenède dramatist', p. 138; cf. the same author's *History of French Dramatic Literature in the Seventeenth Century*, II, Baltimore, 1932, p. 183), for he does not appear in the list of characters in III, 1 and, in II, 1, 367, says to Elizabeth: 'Que vos Juges surtout ne précipitent rien'.

10   Bertaud, 'D'un *Comte d'Essex* à l'autre', p. 110, believes that Essex's words 'ne sont sans doute pas feintes'.

11   Snaith, 'The portrayal of power', p. 861.

12   Lancaster, *History*, II, p. 181: 'Essex was bitterly hostile to Cecil and Raleigh, felt that they were seeking to keep him out of power, and used unlawful means to become, under the queen, the leading person in the government'. Bertaud, 'Deux ans après *La Mariane*', p. 50, n. 4: 'un Essex grand serviteur de l'Etat, et justement fier de l'être, innocent de toute faute politique, exempt des nombreux défauts qu'eut Robert Devereux', and again (p. 55) 'l'Essex mis en scène est innocent de tout crime politique', for the letters produced are indeed forged.

13   E. Forsyth, *La Tragédie française de Jodelle à Corneille (1553–1640). Le thème de la vengeance*, Paris, 1962, p. 377.

14   La Calprenède, IV, 3, ll. 1109–10 (Soubtantonne); T. Corneille, III, 3 (Salsbury) and 4 (Duchesse d'Irton). There are many more examples.

CHAPTER NINETEEN

'Je commence à rougir'
Shame, Self-Esteem and Guilt in the
Presentation of Racine's Hippolyte

EDWARD FORMAN

The problem about Euripides's Hippolytos is not that he is too innocent, but that he feels too proud of his innocence. The problem about Racine's Hippolyte is not that he is guilty, but that he feels too ashamed of his innocence. Even if we reject Racine's characterization of the former as 'un philosophe exempt de toute imperfection' and of the latter as 'un peu coupable', points of contrast outweigh similarities between them, as agents and as victims of tragedy, and the relationship cannot helpfully be analysed without acknowledging the fact that Hippolyte faces political complexities and ethical dilemmas which Hippolytos—not necessarily innocent, but secure in a value system for which he has both parental and divine support—need not consider. This difference in situation affects the way in which audiences, in all ages, have responded to the characters, and to the plays. It is no longer necessary to rescue Hippolyte from the charges of inadequacy by which he was long dogged, or to defend his status as a tragic character: Jean-Louis Barrault on the stage and Louis-Léonard Naneix in the study, amongst others, have done that.[1] But a close look at how Hippolyte's sense of self-esteem is affected by the relationships he forms and the problems he faces, and at the ways—appropriate or otherwise—in which he feels and expresses shame and guilt, under our gaze, may help to shed light on his tragic status and more generally on Racine's conception of the tragic.

It is difficult to pin down the tone of Hippolyte's opening speech. Apparent self-confidence in the first two lines —

> Le dessein en est pris: je pars, cher Théramène,
> Et quitte le séjour de l'aimable Trézène—(ll. 1–2)

is undermined by the agitated doubt of line 3 and the shame expressed in line 4—shame at once associated with the absence of his father:

Dans le doute mortel dont je suis agité,
Je commence à rougir de mon oisiveté.
Depuis plus de six mois éloigné de mon père ... (ll. 3–5)

This contradiction mirrors the more widespread polarization of attitudes for and against the young man: 'fuyard' in the eyes of many, he is defended—at times a little too defensively—by others on the grounds that his initial urge to depart is rational and purposeful. The reality seems to encompass both points of view. Hippolyte is indeed running away, from Aricie, from Phèdre, from his upbringing and vocation (as previously perceived), and even from himself, and his claim to decisive action is at best a sort of fidgetiness. Nevertheless he has a positive sense that the goal of his quest is Thésée—the elusive father, hidden, absent but worshipped ('cacher', l. 7; 'éloigné', l. 5; 'chère', l. 6) through whom alone he can identify himself and give meaning to his personality and existence. We can interpret the opening speech in such a way as to inhibit sympathy for Hippolyte—the stated reason for his departure (to reassure himself and everyone else as to Thésée's safety and well-being) is a mere rationalization of his restlessness and insecurity; or in such a way as to invite sympathy—his self-doubt and shame epitomize the repressive and destructive attitude of autocratic parenting which has left him unable to face maturity. In either case, the initial presentation does not invite clear censure, but focuses on an area of moral ambiguity. A sense of guilt is expressed, in l. 4, but it is met with a positive response (ll. 1–2) and an excuse is hinted at (l. 5).

This does not fit at all well with Racine's categorical claim in the *Préface* to have made Hippolyte 'un peu coupable envers son père'. Since that guilt is particularly associated with Aricie, it is curious to note the moral assumptions behind Théramène's initial presentation of his pupil's feelings:

Et vous mettant au rang du reste des mortels,
Vous a-t-elle [Vénus] forcé d'encenser ses autels?
Aimeriez-vous, Seigneur? (ll. 63–5)

Through his contrived circumlocution and ungainly interrogative, Théramène seems as willing as Phèdre to cast the blame on Venus who, responding spitefully to Hippolyte's proud scorn [l. 61], has calculatedly inflicted an inappropriate love on a helpless human. This is reflected by Hippolyte himself:

Et les dieux jusque-là m'auraient humilié? (l. 96)

and by Racine's own use in the *Préface* of the phrase 'malgré lui', in referring to Hippolyte's love for Aricie. A feeling inflicted in this way does not turn Hippolyte from a man into a villain, but from a superman into a man, 'au rang du reste des mortels' (1. 63—compare too his description of himself as 'asservi sous la commune loi', 1. 535). Hippolytos' superhuman self-control alienated audience sympathy, making him too good to be true, or at least too good to be likeable. By causing his Hippolyte to fall in love, Racine brings him down to the level of the audience—sinful man, perhaps, in a conventional sense, but not man obsessed with inadequacy—and thus allows the normal operation of human sympathy on which tragedy depends. In short, Racine may be justified in arguing that it is the invention of Aricie that turns Hippolyte into a tragic hero, but he seems most unfair in calling his love for her a 'faiblesse' and in going on to use the adjective 'coupable' to describe this weakness and its victim.

Other textual evidence underlines the conflict between Racine's portrayal of Hippolyte and his description of him in the *Préface*. Although fully aware of Thésée's likely disapproval of his feelings towards Aricie, Hippolyte refers to himself as 'l'innocence' in 1. 996, and the word is repeated by Phèdre and Œnone, both before (ll. 893, 903) and after (1. 1238) they discover the truth about Aricie. The final scene, although it does not really deserve the label of 'Phèdre's confession' since she still diverts responsibility from herself towards Vénus and Œnone (ll. 1625–6), is at least categorical in its exculpation of Hippolyte:

> Il faut à votre fils rendre son innocence.
> Il n'était point coupable. (ll. 1618–19)

Can we even say that Hippolyte *feels* guilty about his love for Aricie? Racine has taken pains to ensure that in this as in other respects, his position reflects Phèdre's own. Both suffer from a passion which sympathetic observers might understand and condone, but which fills them with unease. Phèdre's feeling towards her step-son is never incestuous, and in Act II it is not knowingly adulterous, yet she obsessively applies both these terms to herself, and this generates in her a sense of guilt, a loss of self-esteem, which clearly strikes a deep chord of sympathy in western humanity. Hippolyte suffers a similar loss of self-esteem as a result of the uncomfortable and unfamiliar experience of adolescent love, undermining his self-image as a public-school type, brought up in manly virtue—'le gymnaste végétarien vaguement orphique', as Stalloni described him.[2] Racine seems to make a decision to play down Hippolyte's priestly dedication to Artemis, which in Euripides is a fundamental aspect of his virtuous character; and we cannot be sure whether this decision is based on a deliberate desire to change the character, or on Racine's assumption that his well-informed audience would take it for granted. The characteristics associated with Artemis are alluded to by Racine only in so far as Hippolyte manifestly fails to live up to them:

> ... depuis quelques jours,
> On vous voit moins souvent, orgueilleux et sauvage,
> Tantôt faire voler un char sur le rivage,
> Tantôt, savant dans l'art par Neptune inventé,
> Rendre docile au frein un coursier indompté;
> Les forêts de vos cris moins souvent retentissent ... (ll. 128–33)

Here as elsewhere, Neptune has replaced Artemis as the divinity with whom Hippolyte (like Thésée) is principally associated. Théramène, it seems, has been rather slow to observe these changes: Hippolyte himself has been uncomfortably aware of an emotional upheaval, not for 'quelques jours' but for 'près de six mois' (l. 539):

> Moi-même, pour tout fruit de mes soins superflus,
> Maintenant je me cherche, et ne me trouve plus;
> Mon arc, mes javelots, mon char, tout m'importune ... (ll. 547–9)

and Ismène has also noted the contrast between the young man's reputation and the reality (ll. 405–414). Hippolyte, then, disorientated and uneasy about these feelings, suffers from a sense of self-betrayal (Naneix, p. 48, talks of his concern for 'la préservation de son individualité'); but he does not refer to himself as guilty. There is an element of defiance in his self-righteousness, but we are more likely to blame his parents and upbringing for generating in him an inability to cope with tenderness, than to blame him for reacting against that upbringing.

The strength of Hippolyte's reaction to Théramène's first suggestion of his love does suggest that a raw nerve has been touched:

> Aimeriez-vous, Seigneur?
>   – Ami, qu'oses-tu dire?
> Toi qui connais mon cœur depuis que je respire,
> Des sentiments d'un cœur si fier, si dédaigneux,
> Peux-tu me demander le désaveu honteux? (ll. 65–8)

His chastity may not have been based, in Racine's presentation, on religious dedication, but it was innate:

> ... avec son lait une mère amazone
> M'a fait sucer encor cet orgueil qui t'étonne. (ll. 69–70)

It was valued, in a rather prim way:

Je me suis applaudi quand je me suis connu. (l. 72)

And it was associated with a complex sense of guilt about his relationship with his father:

Heureux si j'avais pu ravir à la mémoire
Cette indigne moitié d'une si belle histoire! (ll. 93–4)

Presumably this speech is the first time Hippolyte has attempted to articulate his difficult feelings: at this stage he is unable to make any distinction between appropriate and inappropriate sexual desires, equating sexual gratification of any sort with the verb 'faillir', and falling far short of political correctness in his analysis of the circumstances under which such shortcomings can be exonerated:

Dans mes lâches soupirs d'autant plus méprisable,
Qu'un long amas d'honneurs rend Thésée excusable,
Qu'aucuns monstres par moi domptés jusqu'aujourd'hui
Ne m'ont acquis le droit de faillir comme lui! (ll. 97–100)

I have always wanted those lines to be followed by a long reflective (introverted) pause, so that Théramène—who must also bear a share of the blame for any difficulties attributable to Hippolyte's upbringing—might have the opportunity to respond to his pupil's unhealthy sexism, but fail to take it. Théramène is perhaps equally unhelpful—albeit in an understanding as well as understandable way—in minimizing his pupil's discomfort as a 'farouche scrupule' (l. 121). The counsellor must always tread a difficult tightrope: if he takes the client's worries too seriously, he reinforces the client's self-image as a freak; if not seriously enough, he suggests that the client is making a fuss about nothing. Here Théramène strays in the latter direction with his somewhat dismissive 'Enfin':

Enfin, d'un chaste amour pourquoi vous effrayer? (l. 119)
...
Mais que sert d'affecter un superbe discours? (l. 127)

—to which Hippolyte responds with an icy concision (l. 138) which forces Théramène to change the subject.

It is not hard in such ways to defend Hippolyte by counter-accusing Thésée and Théramène. Since the former is a philandering he-man, he can be blamed for encouraging his son by example to adopt similar attitudes: if you want it, go for it; if you don't get it, fight for it. But paradoxically, he can be blamed almost as much for failing to indoctrinate Hippolyte firmly enough with this message. Hippolyte longs to emulate his father's military heroism, and hints, as we have just seen, at a feeling that to do so would be some sort of passport to selfish sexual gratification, but neither Thésée nor Théramène has given him a coherent code of conduct with which he feels at ease. On the contrary, they both contribute to his confusion about his values, which makes him susceptible to the embarrassment which (in part) prevents him from responding in the most appropriate way to Phèdre's advances and then to Thésée's return. What is it that makes a man feel so uncomfortable about disobeying his father, even if he knows that his father's commands are irrational, even immoral? That is a question for a psychoanalyst or a priest, but the value of tragic literature in helping us to address it should not be overlooked. 'Sans doute la stérilité d'Hippolyte est dirigée contre le Père', says Roland Barthes,[3] and although Hippolyte might defend his right to love, even to love Aricie, he will never stop feeling shifty about his defiance of Thésée. He is governed at first less by love of Aricie than by fear of Thésée, not very convincingly disguised as filial respect:

> Quand même ma fierté pourrait s'être adoucie,
> Aurais-je pour vainqueur dû choisir Aricie?
> Ne souviendrait-il plus à mes sens égarés
> De l'obstacle éternel qui nous a séparés?
> Mon père la réprouve ... (ll. 101–5)

We may indeed blame Thésée further for endowing Aricie with this enticing quality of forbidden fruit. His decree that she should not marry, lest her offspring revive the claim of the descendants of Pallas to the throne of Athens, is neither illogical nor criminal, and it is certainly less inhuman than the wholescale slaughter of her brothers, but it is widely seen as unjust, even vindictive, and it may be classed as an error of judgement. Hippolyte describes his feelings for Aricie as 'un feu que sa [Thésée's] haine réprouve' (l. 993), Aricie charges Thésée with 'votre injuste haine' (l. 1420), and although Théramène implies that Thésée's action against the Pallantides was justified, he makes a distinction between the male line and Aricie herself:

> Jamais l'aimable soeur des cruels Pallantides
> Trempa-t-elle aux complots de ses frères perfides? (ll. 53–4)

Aricie herself is quite understanding about what she describes in a matter-of-fact way as 'ce soin d'un vainqueur soupçonneux' (l. 432), and admits that before catching her first glimpse of Hippolyte,

Je rendais souvent grâce à l'injuste Thésée,
Dont l'heureuse rigueur secondait mes mépris. (ll. 434–5)

There is, however, an aspect of the logic of Thésée's position that seems to be overlooked by everyone in the play, including the most directly interested parties. Why shouldn't Hippolyte marry Aricie? The purpose of Thésée's interdiction is summed up in a colourful conceit by Aricie:

On craint que de la sœur les flammes téméraires
Ne raniment un jour la cendre de ses frères. (ll. 429–30)

Any male children born to Aricie might challenge the descendants of Thésée for the throne of Athens. But if the descendants of Aricie and the descendants of Thésée were the same, then that blood feud would of course be neutralized. Is it one of the tragic ironies underlying this complex situation—another telling error of judgement which contributes to the tragic dénouement, for which no-one is really to blame, but for which everyone carries a certain responsibility—that Hippolyte should feel so inhibited about even mentioning what is in some respects an obvious way out? Even before Phèdre is discredited in his eyes, Hippolyte considers that he has 'de véritables droits' (l. 491) over her eldest son,[4] so if a real succession crisis had existed, the union of Hippolyte and Aricie would have been a genuine possibility. On the return of Thésée, is our frustration not increased by the awareness that there is no reason why Hippolyte should not look Thésée straight in the eye and explain that the feud is resolved? It is, under all the circumstances, amazing that Aricie should have responded to his amorous approach, but now that she has done so, they can ensure—whatever happens to Phèdre and her line—that there will be no further rivalry between the line of Egée and the line of Pallas. It is the sort of scene Arthur Miller might enjoy writing, yet neither Racine nor any of his characters envisages it.

When Hippolyte does seek out Thésée, indeed, he entertains no notion of persuading him of the desirability of the match on logical grounds: the best he thinks he can hope for is to 'émouvoir la tendresse' of his father by an 'heureuse adresse' (ll. 997–8). But of course any hope he might retain, at the end of Act III, of achieving this, is dashed—without his realising it—by the false accusation which ensures that the two men are at cross purposes for most of the interview which fills IV, 2. It is here that the innocence and the guilt of Hippolyte, his righteous indignation and his sense of shame, are most finely, exquisitely and excruciatingly balanced by Racine. Intent on making a clean breast of a shortcoming which he knows in his heart is not seriously sinful, but which continues to cause him considerable personal unease, he finds himself incomprehensibly accused of treachery, monstrous behaviour and impurity (ll. 1044–6)—charges which the self-righteous misogynist of Euripides would laugh out of court, but which strike Racine's Hippolyte dumb precisely because of the hint of truth which he can misguidedly read into them. Those who (still) claim that Hippolyte is somehow to blame here for making no adequate attempt to defend himself, need to read this critical scene again, and remember the ambivalent nature of the father–son relationship, defined in the opening lines of the play, which underpins it. Remember, too, that Hippolyte has no idea at the start of the scene that he has been accused of anything—his worst fear is that Phèdre may have blurted out the truth—nor, as he pieces together the facts behind Thésée's ranting, is he given any clue as to Œnone's role: line 1084, indeed, suggests quite explicitly that the sword which has convinced Thésée of his guilt was in Phèdre's own hands.

Where does this leave Racine's insistence that his disloyalty to Euripides was motivated by loyalty to Aristotle? The argument of the *Préface* is entirely logical. Euripides had portrayed Hippolytos as 'un philosophe exempt de toute imperfection', as a result of which unnamed critics in Antiquity had complained that he was not a proper tragic character according to Aristotle's theory of hamartia. In order to correct this aesthetic weakness, Racine feels obliged to inflict on Hippolyte a moral weakness—'quelque faiblesse'—so that he acquires a certain degree of guilt—becomes 'un peu coupable'. Only thus can Racine prevent the character from being an innocent victim, and ensure that the emotion he inspires in audiences finds the correct balance between pity and fear to generate catharsis. So Racine makes his hero fall in love with his father's sworn enemy, and even allows him treacherously to offer her part of his father's empire. As we have seen, however, if Racine is right at all, it is for quite the wrong reasons. We do feel sorry for Hippolyte, most of us do consider him an adequate tragic character, yet no-one considers him remotely guilty.

The consequences of this conclusion must be troubling to any but the most iconoclastic scholars. Did Racine, whose place in world literature depends in large measure on his illumination of human guilt and his analysis of human love, really misuse the word 'coupable', and misapply it to a human emotional experience, in such an important document as this defensive *Préface* to a controversial play which meant so much to him? Did this almost obsessive disciple of Aristotle actually misunderstand his master's argument over the nature of hamartia and its relationship with catharsis? Or was Aristotle himself, whose analysis of the specific nature of the tragic experience has formed the basis of almost all subsequent discussion of dramatic theory, too dogmatic in his insistence that the suffering of a virtuous person was incompatible with the special status which he wished to accord to the tragic genre?

If there is a misunderstanding, it may reside in Racine's instinctive association of hamartia with guilt. It is scarcely surprising that the Jansenist, working in a context where all theatrical activity is charged with immorality, but anxious at all costs to prove its moral value, should assume that hamartia carries the meaning familiar to English scholars, the tragic flaw. The Greek word, however—although like all Aristotelian metaphors its implications are cryptic—seems more likely to have meant a miscalculation or error of judgement. The term, as in the classic case of Oedipus, is applied to a decision which is made, or an action which is carried out, without full control or knowledge of the facts: an act which is not of itself depraved, but which in specific circumstances has catastrophic repercussions. Since the harm that results from such acts is not intended, we pardon and pity the perpetrator; but since they are done intentionally, they cannot be dismissed as accidents, but involve some degree of responsibility, *as is shown by the fact that the doer regrets them and blames himself.*[5]

It is certain that if Aristotle had wanted the word hamartia to relate primarily to a culpable moral flaw, other words at his disposal would have made this clearer: *mochtheria*, moral depravity, applied to someone who simply does not know how to behave (the word is in fact applied by Aristotle precisely to the sort of morally vicious man whom he wishes to exclude from tragedy), or *akrasia*, moral instability—deliberate and calculated wrong-doing. His choice of the word hamartia, therefore, suggests an interest in the morally ambiguous area. The logic of chapter 13 of the *Poetics* clearly implies that something more complicated than moral error must be involved. Tragedy may portray *either* a man without a real moral flaw, but who makes a mistake of fact or judgement, *or* a man who is not above moral reproach, but to whom an objective observer (as opposed to the man himself, his enemies or his friends) would not wish to apply the more pejorative terms (*mochtheros*, etc.).

Does this enable us to see afresh how Hippolytos and Hippolyte resemble each other, and how they differ? Neither of them is really guilty, but both are out of their depth, and both miscalculate. Almost all Hippolyte's decisions and actions in the course of the play, in fact are the result of miscalculations, about the motives and likely reactions of all the other characters, including his closest friends, allies and divine protectors. Aricie does not make him guilty, but she blurs his judgement: buoyed up by human love, he fails to see the blatant injustice of the universe, the rash temper of his father, the lack of moral control in his step-mother, and the blind inhumanity of the supernatural forces in which he misguidedly puts his faith. The parallel with Phèdre is again striking: just as we have sought to defend Hippolyte by blaming human agents, we may also defend him by accusing the gods. His own appeals to divine justice have a poignant irony: his assumption that the universe is fair persistently conflicts with the play's affirmation that it is not:

> ... Dieux, qui la connaissez,
> Est-ce donc sa vertu que vous récompensez? (ll. 727–8)

> Mais l'innocence enfin n'a rien à redouter. (l. 996)

> Sur l'équité des dieux osons nous confier:
> Ils ont trop d'intérêt à me justifier. (ll. 1351–2)

Such blind faith is clearly the antithesis of guilt, yet it is in this, as Naneix pointed out, that Hippolyte's tragic quality resides:

> Pour le tragique, n'y en a-t-il pas autant et du plus cruel dans la destinée d'Hippolyte que dans celle de Phèdre? Admettons que ce soit réellement Vénus qui possède et détraque Phèdre. Celle-ci serait bien à plaindre. Mais elle ne fait pas aux dieux l'honneur de les croire incapables d'iniquité, elle s'attend aux mauvais traitements qu'ils lui infligent. Hippolyte, comme tous les grands cœurs, plus prompt à la confiance qu'à la méfiance, s'obstine à prêter à la divinité une noblesse, une droiture qu'elle n'a pas; ... il acquiert vraiment par ses mérites le droit d'espérer sa grâce de Neptune, la grâce du ciel. Cet espoir est chez lui tragiquement déçu.[6]

Racine the artist did all the right things in converting Hippolytos into Hippolyte. Racine the analyst was simply too concerned to prove the moral value of what he had created to realize that it was in fact profoundly disturbing to anyone who wished to believe that the universe had a moral foundation. This is where the aesthetic and emotional appeal of tragedy must lie: it has the ability—is perhaps defined by the ability—to retain the interest of audiences from a wide variety of moral and ethical backgrounds in areas of moral and ethical ambiguity. When a human being feels overwhelmed by the universe, unable to control the result of his actions, aware that matters over which he has no control impinge much more vigorously on his experience and on his fate than those which he does control, then the spectacle of a tragic hero, drawn with apparent inexorability towards a disastrous course of action which he knows will cause him to lose self-esteem, to feel shame and inadequacy, but for which he will always insist on seeking extenuating circumstances, excuses, finding someone else to share the blame if not take it over entirely—that spectacle will fulfil the function of true art to enable the common man to set his own experience—guilty helplessness in the face of an overwhelming and often apparently absurd universe—in a more rational perspective. He will be given healthy encouragement to face up to and escape from unhealthy and destructive feelings.

Or of course, *passim*, she/her. But this applies as much to Hippolyte as to Phèdre, to a male spectator as to a female.

Notes:

1   J.-L. Barrault, *Phèdre*, Paris: Le Seuil, 1946; L.-L. Naneix, *Phèdre l'incomprise*, Paris: La Pensée universelle, 1977. See also R.C. Knight, 'Hippolyte and Hippolytos', in *The Modern Language Review*, XXXIX, 1944, pp. 225–35; E. Méron, 'De l'*Hippolyte* d'Euripide à la *Phèdre* de Racine: deux conceptions du tragique', in *XVIIe siècle*, 100, 1973; and 'Hippolyte requis d'amour et calomnié', in P. Bénichou, *L'Ecrivain et ses travaux*, Paris: Corti, 1967.
2   Y. Stalloni, 'Hippolyte ou la passion impossible', in *Analyses et réflexions sur Phèdre de Racine*, Paris: eds. Marketing, 1983, p. 75.
3   R. Barthes, *Sur Racine*, Paris: Le Seuil, 1963, p. 111.
4   R.C. Knight, p. 232, points out the vagueness of this appeal; and Hippolyte in making the claim reveals the fragility of his status in Athens, although Racine stresses neither his illegitimacy nor the problems he may face as a result of his non-Attic mother.
5   See J. Hutton, *Aristotle's Poetics*, New York: Norton, 1982, 95. The italics are mine. Hutton's summary relates the concept of hamartia to Aristotle's *Ethics*, particularly *E.N.*, 5.10, 1135b12; 3.2, 1110b31; 3.2, 1110b17.
6   Naneix, op. cit., p. 78.

CHAPTER TWENTY

L'influence de Louis XIV sur la vie littéraire: pour un bilan critique

JEAN ROHOU

L'histoire politique a perdu sa prééminence et, malgré une récente réévaluation du niveau événementiel, nul ne songe plus, dit-on, à majorer l'influence des grands hommes en tous domaines, ni, par exemple, à faire du dix-septième siècle l'apanage de Louis XIV. A y regarder de près, l'évolution de la vision des choses me semble moins nette.

Certes, l'auteur du *Siècle de Louis XIV* a souvent majoré l'influence du souverain: il a réformé seul le goût de sa cour en plus d'un genre … 'Non seulement il s'est fait de grandes choses sous son règne, mais c'est lui qui les faisait'.[1] Néanmoins, il savait que *siècle* désignait d'abord la durée d'une génération, et il a parfois relativisé les implications de son titre. 'Ce n'est point simplement la vie de ce prince que j'écris …, c'est plutôt l'histoire de l'esprit humain à cette époque'.[2] Au XIXe siècle, il y a une majorité de louanges,[3] mais aussi de vigoureuses critiques.[4] Les unes et les autres révèlent souvent les implications politiques du sujet à un point qui devrait inciter à la prudence. Or, on retrouve récemment des affirmations trop absolues, surtout quand elles attribuent l'effet de tout un système, voire une évolution générale, au goût ou à la volonté personnelle du roi.[5] Il me semble qu'un bilan critique s'imposerait: je n'en propose qu'une esquisse.

Il faudrait d'abord préciser la question: quelle influence de quel Louis XIV sur quelle littérature? Il y a deux Louis XIV, très liés l'un à l'autre: l'individu, avec ses désirs et son goût personnels, et le roi, avec ses projets et besoins institutionnels; tous deux évoluent: celui de 1662, avide de plaisirs, ne ressemble guère, sauf par la même ambition de gloire, à celui de 1690, replié à Versailles et dans la dévotion. Tentons de distinguer la personne du personnage. Louis XIV fut un très grand roi parce qu'il occupa le trône au moment où l'absolutisme venait de triompher définitivement des forces du passé et n'était pas encore ébranlé par celles de l'avenir. Mais aussi parce qu'il eut l'ambition et la capacité de remplir pleinement ce rôle que l'histoire lui offrait. Il ne semble pas que ce fût une intelligence exceptionnelle: rien d'un Gustave–Adolphe ni d'un Napoléon.[6] Mais il eut—d'autant plus facilement?—l'intelligence d'une fonction qu'il rêvait de porter à sa perfection, c'est-à-dire le sens de ce qui convenait à sa gloire. Le résultat fut très heureux tant que cette gloire eut à s'imposer et fut le catalyseur des aspirations d'une élite en mal de sublimation de son assujettissement, tant qu'elle fut branchée sur les désirs d'une collectivité, avant de tourner au narcissisme tyrannique et creux et à cette dévotion pharisienne que dénoncera l'archevêque de Cambrai. Et c'est aussi cette intelligence plus fonctionnelle ou institutionnelle que personnelle ou originale qui lui permit de suivre et même au besoin de rectifier les avis des remarquables conseillers qui avaient construit son régime, avant que son orgueil susceptible ne les remplaçât par des médiocres. C'est peut-être tout cela que voulait dire Spanheim: 'Sans avoir rien de brillant ni de vaste ni de fort éclairé dans l'esprit, ... il a du choix, du discernement et de la pénétration suffisante ... pour faire justice au mérite où il en trouve'.[7]

Je ne crois pas que la politique culturelle mise en place à partir de 1662 fût l'effet d'une sollicitude personnelle de Louis Capet pour la littérature, ni surtout pour sa dimension artistique. En revanche, le développement des lettres, comme médias et comme œuvres d'art, était un besoin de l'absolutisme, régime de monopole, d'assujettissement et de représentation, qui cultive par nature propagande et prestige. Les Valois l'avaient déjà compris et surtout Richelieu avait protégé et gratifié les gens de lettres, par goût—plus, probablement, que Louis XIV—par souci de gloire et aussi pour amadouer une opinion publique rétive face aux exigences de sa politique: sa réputation de Mécène, les éloges de ses obligés, les écrits de ses journalistes et pamphlétaires eurent de fait une grande influence.

A la mort du cardinal, Louis XIII supprima toutes ces gratifications. Mazarin se montra fort pingre et ce fut l'une des raisons de la vigoureuse hostilité de la majorité des gens de lettres pendant la Fronde, tandis que Condé ou Retz, qui en gratifiaient, ne manquèrent pas de pamphlétaires. Il comprit sans doute son erreur. C'est pour lui que Charpentier, Costar et Ménage établirent, en 1655, une liste 'des gens de lettres ... les plus célèbres' en France et à l'étranger. Son secrétaire Colbert ne put ignorer cette initiative: peut-être même en fut-il le promoteur? En 1658, Colbert annote une autre liste. Cela n'aboutit à rien. Mais, parallèlement, à partir de 1657, le surintendant des finances, Fouquet, avide de plaisirs, de gloire et de pouvoir et successeur présomptif de Mazarin, se constitue une cour d'écrivains et d'artistes.

Tout cela réduit à l'improbabilité l'hypothèse d'une initiative personnelle de Louis Capet, sans diminuer le mérite du roi qui a su rassembler et orchestrer les moyens disponibles pour son glorieux absolutisme. Richelieu fournissait le modèle, Mazarin en soulignait *a contrario* l'intérêt, Fouquet l'avait ranimé et permettait de voir qu'une telle politique ne devait appartenir qu'au roi.[8] Vibrant admirateur du premier, féroce rival du second—auquel Chapelain est aussi vigoureusement hostile[9]—Colbert est certainement à l'origine du nouveau mécénat. Si Louis XIV le souhaita de son côté, ce fut sans doute surtout en réaction au prestige qu'il valait à Fouquet, ce prince de Vaux qu'il se hâta d'éliminer. Dans la décennie suivante, le goût de la belle-sœur du roi—qu'il trouvait lui-même si charmante et spirituelle—de Mme de Montespan et de sa sœur Mme de Thianges[10] eut sans doute plus d'influence sur la littérature d'art que celui du souverain.

Deuxième partie de la question: sur quelle littérature cherchons-nous à mesurer l'influence de Louis XIV? Celle que la postérité a sélectionnée, alors qu'à l'époque, et surtout pour la cour, Thomas Corneille et Quinault n'avaient pas tellement moins d'importance que Molière ou Racine? Celle des écrivains courtisans de 1670 ou celle de La Fontaine ou Mme de Lafayette, plus critiques car plus indépendants, ou celle de Bayle et Fontenelle? Quand nous disons Louis XIV et Molière, pensons-nous à l'auteur de *La Pastorale comique* ou à celui de *Dom Juan*?

Enfin, il faudrait préciser ce qu'on entend par *influence*: terme commode pour désigner une action diffuse. Par quels canaux[11] s'est-elle exercée, dans quels buts, à quels niveaux : sur les conditions de vie des écrivains, sur leur reconnaissance sociale, sur leur vision et leur style? Une influence ne peut s'exercer également sur l'ensemble d'un champ traversé de contradictions, où elle cherche à imposer une orientation nouvelle. De plus le mécénat est sélectif, par ses limites budgétaires, par ses intentions et préférences et par sa nature même: il ne peut 'produire d'effet pour la gloire de l'auteur et du donateur qu'à la condition de rester hautement distinctif, donc fortement sélectif'.[12] Il faudrait préciser quels étaient, en mars 1661, la constitution du champ littéraire, le poids relatif de chaque groupe, le dynamisme de chaque tendance, isoler l'influence gouvernementale et personnelle du roi de toutes les autres et mesurer le résultat tous les deux ou trois ans pour le moins. Il faudrait des analyses précises et subtiles, comme celles d'Alain Viala sur l'évolution des divers types de patronage et de consécration et des stratégies d'écrivains, ou celle de Fanny Népote-

Desmarres sur le détournement, en faveur du rituel absolutiste et de l'ascension de la bourgeoisie, des thèmes nobiliaires de la pastorale.[13] Je me contenterai de proposer quelques hypothèses et d'esquisser une périodisation. Quelle fut l'importance de la politique littéraire de Louis XIV, au regard de l'ensemble de son action et de son budget? Quel en fut l'esprit: propagande idéologique ou politique culturelle? A quel niveau la littérature en fut-elle influencée: dans ses thèmes, ses genres, sa vision, son style?

Le montant total des gratifications pour 1663 est de 77,500 livres, dont le tiers (25,300 livres) pour seize hommes de lettres français. Il culmine à 110,000 environ en 1669, soit 0.085% du budget de l'Etat et 1.16% de celui de la Cour, pour descendre à 86,000 en 1672, stagner quelque temps autour de 45,000, décliner jusqu'à 11,000 livres en 1690, et disparaître. C'était, pendant la première décennie, plus du double de ce qu'accordait Richelieu (environ 40,000 livres par an), mais au total moins du vingtième de ce que Louis XIV donna, en deux fois moins de temps, à Mme de Montespan, sa brillante maîtresse. Autre comparaison possible: dans la lettre du 30 juin 1665[14] que Chapelain adresse à l'Italien Dati pour lui fournir le canevas d'un panégyrique de Louis XIV, il y a 30 lignes sur les exploits militaires, 79 sur l'administration économique et la diplomatie, 9 sur les gratifications (5 pour les lettres, 4 pour les arts). Mais, pour l'époque, c'était déjà exceptionnel, du moins pendant la première décennie.

Pourquoi le soutien à la littérature eut-il malgré tout une importance considérable? Il est peu vraisemblable d'en attribuer le mérite à Louis XIV personnellement. L'amour des lettres n'est pas primordial dans sa culture ni dans ses aspirations, nettement inférieures sur ce point à celles de François Ier, Richelieu ou Fouquet. Enfant et adolescent, il a vécu parmi les chefs-d'œuvres architecturaux, plastiques, chorégraphiques et musicaux. Son parrain Mazarin, surintendant de son éducation est un grand collectionneur, un amasseur de trésors et un amateur de spectacles. Louis est lui-même fort bon danseur et fier de l'être. En revanche sa formation intellectuelle et sa culture littéraire—qu'on avait pu juger moins importantes pour un futur souverain de majesté dont on ne pouvait prévoir qu'il serait aussi un roi bureaucrate—étaient médiocres. Et malgré des panégyriques qui ne valent pas témoignage, fussent-ils signés de Molière,[15] rien de précis ne vient garantir la qualité de son goût littéraire personnel, souvent vanté avec trop d'assurance.[16] Parmi les tragédies, celle 'qui lui plaît le plus',[17] c'est *Mithridate*, conçue en effet pour satisfaire le goût de l'élite sociale: synthèse mélodramatique d'héroïsme pompeux, de romanesque, de tendresse galante et pathétique. Malheureusement, c'est l'une des moins bonnes tragédies de Racine. Passons à Molière: ce que le roi attend de lui, ce sont des divertissements, si possible spectaculaires, comme les comédies-ballets en musique (deux sur sept pièces entre janvier 1664 et août 1666, onze sur quinze de décembre 1666 à 1673), et non pas des chefs-d'œuvres littéraires. Il n'a jamais vu *Dom Juan*, ni probablement *Le Misanthrope*. Et s'il a sans doute voulu *Tartuffe*[18] c'est qu'il lui était politiquement nécessaire de discréditer l'association secrète des dévots pour assurer son pouvoir absolu, sa liberté de mœurs et son orgueilleuse hauteur envers le Pape. Rien de littéraire dans sa motivation.

Les raisons de ce mécénat ne sont pas artistiques ou culturelles, mais politiques: bien plus que chez Fouquet et même un peu plus que chez Richelieu. Chaque gratifié sera 'un des instruments de la gloire du Roi par les ouvrages d'esprit'.[19] Qu'ils n'aillent pas croire 'que les faveurs du Roi ne sont que le paiement de leur mérite'.[20] Il s'agit de contribuer à la gloire du règne, en France, dans le monde et dans les siècles des siècles. Si Chapelain, dans sa réponse à Colbert, propose la poésie autant ou plus que les médailles et mouvements, c'est pour sa pérennité. 'Pour les vers, Monsieur, vous ne pouvez rien imaginer qui allât plus droit à votre but. De toutes les choses durables, c'est sans doute celle qui se défend le plus contre l'injure du temps, lorsqu'une bonne main s'en mêle. Tous les tombeaux, tous les portraits, toutes les statues les plus renommées ont fait naufrage contre cet écueil' (18 novembre 1662).

Il s'agit même de faire directement l'éloge du roi—ce qui ne peut guère donner que des œuvres fort plates. Non seulement cette politique veut propager l'image avantageuse d'un souverain qui veut s'imposer par la splendeur et régner par l'admiration, mais il y a des vues plus précises et plus 'politiciennes'. Si l'historien Mézeray vient en tête des écrivains gratifiés, avec 4,000 livres, contre 3,000 à Chapelain et 2,000 à Corneille, c'est parce que l'histoire doit célébrer le présent et le passé de la nation et de la dynastie, et montrer ses droits, à l'intérieur, face aux aspirations provinciales d'autonomie relative, comme à l'extérieur, pour justifier d'éventuelles annexions.[21] Si plusieurs orientalistes sont sur la liste, c'est parce que la France veut garder de bonnes relations là-bas, dans le dos de l'empire austro-hongrois. Les érudits étrangers[22]—parmi lesquels ne figure aucun sujet du roi d'Espagne, le grand rival du début du règne—ne sont pas gratifiés seulement comme tels, mais aussi pour leur importance politique: ambassadeur de Hollande en Suède, conseiller du roi de Danemark ou du duc de Brunswick, secrétaire du duc de Modène.

Les gratifiés sont donc priés de célébrer le roi et sa politique, pour mériter leur inscription ou son renouvellement. Chapelain a proposé

Heinsius; mais il lui demande un effort, lui fournissant thème et canevas:

> Si ... vous vouliez aider mon dessein par quelque ouvrage de prose latine que vous m'adresseriez en forme d'éloge du Roi, où vous parlassiez avec votre éloquence ordinaire de ses actions, de ses vertus, de sa valeur, de sa prudence, de la résolution qu'il a prise et qu'il exécute de conduire sa barque sans autre pilote que lui-même, chose inouïe en une jeunesse de vingt-quatre ans, de sa bonté, de son équité, de la connaissance qu'il a de ses droits et de sa vigueur à les maintenir, de la protection qu'il donne à ses alliés jusqu'à sacrifier à leurs intérêts les siens propres, de celle qu'il veut donner aux Muses, de l'ordre qu'il met à ses places, à ses troupes, à ses finances, de sa modération dans les divertissements, de sa royale gravité mêlée d'une douceur qui lui attire le respect aussi bien que l'amour des peuples, de ses richesses, de ses magnificences jointes à sa mine héroïque, à sa force infatigable et aux grâces qui n'abandonnent jamais la moindre de ses actions, si, dis-je, vous touchiez tout cela comme de vous-même sur le bruit que font jusqu'au fond du Nord toutes ces merveilles, je verrais bien plus d'apparence au succès.[23]

Dans sa réponse, Heinsius fait l'éloge du roi. Joie de Chapelain : cela 'me servira à faire voir à M. Colbert que vous étiez digne de l'honneur qu'il vous a procuré'. Mais il faudra aussi exalter le ministre. Car le renouvellement ne sera pas automatique: 'Selon que les gratifiés en useront, les gratifications pourront être continuées' (8 juin 1663). On mesure ici toute l'importance du terme. Les *gratifications* sont des versements ponctuels par opposition aux pensions, qui impliquent une pérennité, souvent garantie par brevet.

Chapelain, poussé par Colbert, incite les bénéficiaires: 'Ne manquez pas de remercier par écrit M. Colbert. La reconnaissance complète serait de faire comme tous les gratifiés quelque chose pour Sa Majesté'.[24] Le hasard fait bien les choses : début juin 1663, alors que se font les premiers versements, Louis XIV se remet d'une rougeole. Chapelain anime ses thuriféraires 'à célébrer sa convalescence'. Sept poètes s'y attellent, dont 'un jeune homme appelé Racine' (9 juin).

Chacun des gratifiés de 1663 poussera son remerciement, même si certains, gênés, se font tirer l'oreille par Chapelain, comme Huet. 'Si le Roi le désire et que M. Colbert s'en soit expliqué comme vous me l'apprenez et comme le P. Rapin me le confirme, ajoutant même que ceux qui y manquent seront remarqués, la honte et bassesse qui peut être en cela n'est-elle pas couverte et effacée par le commandement?' Quelques-uns font du zèle, notamment le jeune Racine. Et si les frères Boileau critiquent fort ce mécénat, c'est parce qu'ils n'en bénéficient pas. Motif: ils ont trop d'esprit critique, alors que Racine se montre fort courtisan et fait sa cour à Chapelain depuis 1660. Bien entendu, tous les textes écrits en sollicitation ou remerciement d'une gratification sont fort médiocres, fussent-ils de Corneille, Molière ou Racine.

Quand s'imposeront les restrictions budgétaires, après 1680, on ne gratifiera plus que des savants—utiles à l'économie, sinon à la guerre—des propagandistes de l'idéologie, des hauts-faits et des mondanités et les membres de la Petite Académie, chargés d'immortaliser en inscriptions et médailles les exploits du règne: 'Je vous confie la chose du monde qui m'est la plus précieuse, qui est ma gloire', avait dit le roi aux membres de cette institution.

Nous pouvons regretter les critères de sélection des gratifiés. Mais évitons les critiques anachroniques. La reconnaissance de ce que nous appelons littérature y est importante au regard de l'idée qu'on s'en fait alors et de ce qu'est, à toutes époques, une politique culturelle. Le XVIIe siècle n'avait guère l'idée de l'indépendance de l'écrivain ni de la littérature. Il ne pouvait l'avoir: elle suppose le développement de l'individualisme, de la démocratie, du public intellectuel, et une diversification des pratiques qui permette une nette distinction entre la littérature et l'idéologie, la religion, la morale ou la politique. Pour la grande majorité des intellectuels des années 1660—bien plus nettement que vers 1620 ou sous la Régence—la littérature est, à travers le plaisir, une éducation à l'ordre social, idéologique et moral. Ne prenons pas pour finesse critique ce qui serait inintelligence anachronique. Le mécénat louis-quatorzien fut largement positif pour la vie littéraire. Non seulement par ses gratifications qui représentaient, pour les bénéficiaires, le quart de ce qu'il leur fallait pour vivre à l'aise à Paris. Mais surtout par les motivations qu'il accroît et par la volonté dont il témoigne de promouvoir les arts et lettres dans une société où la plupart des nobles les dédaignaient au profit des armes. La réaction de Bussy-Rabutin et Mme de Sévigné au choix de Boileau et Racine, deux intellectuels bourgeois, comme historiographes d'un roi conquérant, seront à cet égard significatives.

Ne croyons pas non plus que Chapelain ou même Colbert fussent bornés au point de préférer une médiocrité encomiastique à un chef-d'œuvre artistique. Même s'il cherchait surtout le prestige du règne, le ministre savait que celui-ci en donnerait plus que celle-là. S'il apprécia *Britannicus* et *Bérénice*, comme en témoignent les dédicaces, ce n'est certes pas pour l'image du souverain que donnent Agrippine, Néron ou même Titus, accablé par sa charge. Non seulement la cérémonie absolutiste comportait un certain défoulement, mais elle admettait des critiques relatives, utiles soupapes de sécurité. Celles des prédicateurs bien sûr, mais aussi celles des écrivains, notamment contre les flatteurs (Racine), les petits marquis (Molière), mais même contre les souverains, à condition d'excepter Louis XIV des défauts de sa catégorie. Si La Fontaine fut tenu à l'écart—sans plus[25]—c'est sans doute moins pour ses critiques politiques, pourtant vives, que pour sa fidélité à Fouquet, son hostilité à Colbert, son allergie à une attitude courtisane et l'immoralité de ses *Contes*. Si, malgré le faible intérêt personnel du roi pour la littérature, elle a une importance relativement considérable dans la politique culturelle de 1662, c'est en partie grâce à l'exemple donné par Fouquet qui, lui-même, prenait modèle sur les salons. C'est aussi grâce à Chapelain, un humaniste de vieille école, aux antipodes de certaines vedettes médiatiques—notamment Lully— que va favoriser le système. Et c'est enfin parce que la littérature classique a commencé à se développer un peu avant 1662, parallèlement à l'absolutisme et non pas seulement grâce à lui. Ils ont été favorisés par la même adhésion à l'ordre retrouvé et par la réaction à la même aporie à laquelle ils offraient sublimation. Quand Louis XIV prend le pouvoir, en mars 1661, la plupart des grands auteurs des deux décennies suivantes—La Rochefoucauld, La Fontaine, Molière, Bossuet, Pierre et Thomas Corneille, Quinault, Furetière, voire Mme de Lafayette, Mme de Sévigné et Boileau[26]—sont déjà maîtres de leur talent et presque tous en ont donné des preuves. Parmi les grands auteurs de la première moitié du règne, seuls Racine et Guilleragues seront véritablement nouveaux. Dès l'été 1658, il est clair qu'une grande époque s'ouvre: la France va retrouver paix et prospérité; elle dominera l'Europe; Paris et la cour, les fêtes et les arts vont se développer et gagner en prestige. Au-delà de raisons particulières, c'est aussi pour cela que Molière (octobre 1658) et Bossuet (janvier 1659) s'installent à Paris et que Corneille revient au théâtre (*Œdipe*, 24 janvier 1659). Louis XIV n'y est personnellement pour rien, mais le mouvement qui le porte et auquel il saura donner toute son ampleur, anime déjà les lettres et les arts.

Il ne faut pas majorer les effets de la politique de gratifications décidée en novembre 1662. Parmi ceux que nous considérons comme de grands écrivains, seuls sont concernés Corneille, qui avait fait ses preuves depuis trente ans, Molière, reconnu et subventionné par le roi avant cette date,[27] et, bon dernier de la liste, un Racine qui est encore loin d'être le nôtre. Et surtout les premiers chefs-d'œuvre véritablement classiques sont antérieurs à cette décision. Bossuet se distingue depuis 1659 et sa plus remarquable série de sermons, celle du carême du Louvre, va du 26 février au 9 avril 1662. *La Princesse de Montpensier* est achevée d'imprimer le 20 août 1662, *L'Ecole des Femmes* est jouée le 26 décembre.

L'absolutisme louis-quatorzien eut une influence certaine sur l'équilibre des genres littéraires. Une politique de prestige aime particulièrement les arts du spectacle, cérémonies, où l'on rassemble la foule pour l'impressionner sinon la domestiquer. On peut y appliquer ce que Louis disait à son fils à propos de ses imposants travaux d'architecture:

> Un roi de France doit voir dans ces divertissements autre chose que de simples plaisirs. Les peuples se plaisent au spectacle ... Par là, nous tenons leurs esprits et leurs cœurs quelquefois plus fortement peut-être que par la récompense et les bienfaits, et, à l'égard des étrangers, ce qui se consume en ces dépenses, qui peuvent passer pour superflues, fait sur eux une impression très avantageuse de magnificence, de puissance, de richesse et de grandeur.

Je proposerai dans un autre article une périodisation de l'influence du système louis-quatorzien sur la vie littéraire. Jusque vers 1666, tout en poussant à la discipline et à la majesté, il suscite aussi la critique (Boileau, Bossuet) et peut même la promouvoir (*Tartuffe*). On peut espérer que sa politique sera celle du 'juste milieu, dans lequel seul se trouve la justice, la raison et la vérité' (*Lettre sur l'Imposteur*). De 1666 à 1673, c'est l'heureux équilibre d'une discipline sans contrainte. Puis se développent les inconvénients de ce régime de monopole et de narcissisme: il réquisitionne à son seul profit Bossuet (1670) et, plus nettement, Racine et Boileau (1677); il favorise le théâtre spectaculaire et superficiel au détriment du théâtre littéraire. Enfin, à partir de 1682, installé dans la dévotion, il censure les thèmes et les séductions de l'art (cet ersatz de religion qui n'est qu'un pernicieux *divertissement*), développe la censure, même contre ses fidèles (Boileau), voire contre ses propres créations (*Athalie*), mais suscite une remarquable littérature de réaction (Bayle, Fontenelle, *Télémaque*), par une influence aussi importante que celle de 1662. Du moins jusque vers 1695 ou, au plus tard, 1699. De 1700 à 1715, je ne vois plus de relation importante entre Louis XIV et la vie littéraire.

Notes:

1   Lettre à Milord Hervey, 1ᵉʳ juin 1740.
2   Lettre à l'abbé Dubos, 30 octobre 1738.
3   Cuvillier-Fleury, qui se félicite de faire partie des 'hommes de la réaction' (p. 17) à un moment où, comme Scylla après Charybde, 'le socialisme a pris la place du romantisme' (p. 19), exalte 'cette période de soumission morale' (p. 23), 'la plus grande dans l'histoire de l'esprit humain' (p. 28): de tous les grands auteurs du moment, 'il n'en est pas un seul qui ne soit, à quelques années près, contemporain du Roi, vivant sous son influence, animé et inspiré de son souffle' (article du 14 octobre 1849, repris dans *Etudes historiques et littéraires*, t. I, 1854, p. 28).

4   Le républicain Henri Martin, tout en admettant que 'l'influence personnelle de Louis XIV sur le développement de la civilisation française fut éclatante' (p.96), l'accuse d'avoir proscrit une seule science, mais la plus importante: 'la science *générale*, la science des idées' (p. 23). En 1667, il interdit les funérailles solennelles de Descartes, à cause de la 'répulsion de la royauté politique pour la royauté de l'intelligence', de 'cette crainte des idées naturelle à tout pouvoir absolu; le protecteur des lettres et des arts défend de prononcer publiquement l'éloge funèbre du plus grand génie qui ait illustré les lettres françaises' (*La Monarchie au XVIIᵉ siècle. Etude sur le système et l'influence personnelle de Louis XIV*, thèse de doctorat, 1848, p. 20). Au début du Second Empire, Eugène Despois estime que si 'le grand roi a été animé d'intentions excellentes à l'égard des gens de lettres ...', ces générosités si vantées n'étaient ni intelligentes, ni spontanées, ni surtout aussi abondantes qu'on le suppose à distance' ('Des influences royales en littérature. I. Louis XIV', *La Revue des deux mondes*, 15 juin 1853, p. 1231). N'en déplaise à Voltaire, Lesueur, Poussin, Descartes, Pascal, Corneille ne doivent rien à Louis XIV. Certes, il 'n'a pas étouffé le génie de Molière! C'est très bien, sans doute; mais prétendre faire du génie de Molière un des fruits du pouvoir absolu ..., c'est une dérision, quand ces bienfaits du pouvoir envers lui se réduisent à lui avoir laissé un peu de cette liberté qu'un gouvernement plus libéral lui eût accordée tout entière' (p. 1235). 'Chez les écrivains de la seconde génération', que Louis XIV a vraiment pu influencer, comme 'Racine et Fénelon', 'l'inspiration est devenue moins originale et moins puissante, [...] la langue, plus délicate et plus souple, a perdu ce caractère de mâle vigueur' (p. 1236). Enfin, 'il n'y a peut-être pas un seul exemple, dans notre littérature, d'une stérilité aussi déplorable que celle que présentent les vingt dernières années du grand roi' (p. 1239), sauf dans la mesure où, réagissant contre lui, 'Fontenelle et quelques autres préludent discrètement aux témérités philosophiques du siècle qui va suivre' (p. 1240). Conclusion: 'qu'on l'admire pour avoir recueilli cette moisson glorieuse qu'il n'avait pas semée, soit; mais qu'on daigne alors nous expliquer pourquoi à cette fécondité puissante succède une si surprenante stérilité' (p. 1239). Et pour finir cette pointe assassine: 'Auguste n'a pas fait Virgile, mais il a tué Cicéron. C'est, de toutes ses influences littéraires, la seule qu'il ne soit pas permis de contester' (p. 1246).

5   'Il réunissait en lui l'éclat et le goût' (Madeleine Bertaud, *Le XVIIᵉ siècle*, P.U. de Nancy, 1990, p. 101). 'Il ne faut pas oublier que, pour Molière ou pour Racine, Louis XIV est légitimement un arbitre du goût' (E. Bury, *Le Classicisme*, Nathan, 1993, p. 39). Dans un riche article pour 'une esquisse de la place de la littérature sous Louis XIV', Mᵐᵉ Népote-Desmarres écrit qu'il 'réordonne au profit du Bien Commun un projet culturel global, le Classicisme' et parle de 'l'harmonie classique d'inspiration royale' (dans *Le Mécénat capétien*, Carrefour universitaire méditerranéen, Nice, 1989, pp. 35 et 37).

6   De cette 'médiocrité' en mal de dorure, les arts bénéficient peut-être d'une certaine façon. 'Louis n'a point la stature du roi qu'il rêve d'être. Aussi, n'étant point le personnage, se voit contraint de le jouer. C'est en cela que Versailles devient un gigantesque théâtre, grandiose et dérisoire'. C'est une des raisons pour lesquelles, dans les divers secteurs de son activité, après de remarquables débuts, 'la forme a très rapidement pris le pas sur le fonds' (D. Dessert *Louis XIV prend le pouvoir. Naissance d'un mythe?* Editions Complexe, 1989, pp. 39 et 37).

7   *Relation de la cour de France en 1690*, éd. Bourgeois, 1900, pp. 67–68.

8   'Les Muses mêmes et toutes les sciences couraient risque de tomber dans cette nécessité de n'avoir à louer que la corruption', écrira Colbert, champion de la transformation d'un règlement de comptes politique en supériorité morale (Clément, *Lettres, mémoires et instructions de Colbert*, 1863, t. II, p. 17).

9   'Il n'y eut jamais de plus impudent voleur, de dissipateur plus aveugle, ni d'ambitieux plus insensé' que 'ce misérable'. Chapelain qualifie même de 'canaille intéressée' les écrivains qui acceptaient sa protection (lettres du 7 octobre et du 9 décembre 1661).

10   Pour la première on se reportera à la dédicace d'*Andromaque* et à *l'Histoire de Madame Henriette d'Angleterre* de Mᵐᵉ de Lafayette. En 1675, Mᵐᵉ de Thianges offre au fils de sa sœur, bâtard préféré du roi, une *Chambre Sublime*, sorte de Panthéon culturel où Boileau fait signe à La Fontaine (que Louis XIV n'apprécie guère) d'entrer, pour y rejoindre La Rochefoucauld, Mᵐᵉ de Lafayette, Bossuet et Racine.

11   Y compris les voies indirectes: l'arrestation de Fouquet, les galanteries, les guerres, le repli sur Versailles, la Révocation de l'Edit de Nantes, les avatars des relations avec Port-Royal, etc.

12   A. Viala, *Naissance de l'écrivain*, Ed. de Minuit, 1985, p. 78.

13   'Molière auteur pastoral? Aperçu sur quelques rapports avec la politique de Louis XIV', *Littératures classiques*, 11, 1989, pp. 245–257.

14 Publiée par F. Waquet, *Studi francesi*, 89, 1986, pp. 248–251.

15 Ce monarque, dont l'âme aux grandes qualités
Joint un goût délicat des savantes beautés,
Qui, séparant le bon d'avec son apparence,
Décide sans erreur, et loue avec prudence ...
(*La Gloire du Val-de-Grâce*, vv. 293–296)
Il était indispensable, dans un poème destiné à célébrer Mignard jusqu'à critiquer son rival Le Brun (vv. 340–352), que préféraient le roi et son ministre, de célébrer le goût du souverain et du 'grand Colbert'. Louis XIV avait loué la fresque de Mignard 'de deux précieux mots',
Et l'on sait qu'en deux mots ce roi judicieux
Fait des plus beaux travaux l'éloge glorieux (vv. 301–302).

16 'Une heureuse fortune a permis que Louis XIV eût le goût aussi bon que l'élite des 'honnêtes gens' ' (Lagarde et Michard, *XVIIᵉ siècle*, Bordas, 1952, p. 9).

17 Journal de Dangeau, 5 novembre 1684.

18 Il est inconcevable que cette pièce d'un auteur bien en cour, dont elle n'entachera pas la faveur, ait été représentée aux grandioses fêtes d'inauguration de Versailles malgré une démarche de la Compagnie du Saint-Sacrement auprès du roi, sans un soutien résolu de celui-ci ... qui se hâta de l'interdire une fois le coup porté.

19 Chapelain, Lettre à Colbert, 5 décembre 1665.

20 Id., 20 novembre 1665.

21 La reine, fille d'Espagne, n'avait renoncé à son patrimoine qu'au prix d'une dot qui ne fut pas versée. D'où, en 1667, un *Traité des droits de la Reine sur divers états de la monarchie d'Espagne*, aussitôt adressé pour diffusion aux gratifiés étrangers, et suivi de la guerre de Dévolution — c'est-à-dire de transmission d'héritage — et de l'annexion de Lille, Douai et dix autres places fortes.

22 Neuf en 1664 et 1665, quatorze en 1666 et 1667, treize en 1668, dix en 1669, mais plus aucun à partir de 1674. Parmi eux, aucun sujet du roi d'Espagne, le grand rival du début du règne; mais plusieurs hollandais: ce pays est encore de nos amis jusqu'en 1667.

23 Lettre du 12 avril 1663. Je suis ici Georges Couton, 'Effort publicitaire et organisation de la recherche; les gratifications aux gens de lettres sous Louis XIV', *Le XVIIᵉ siècle et la recherche*, éd. R. Duchêne, CMR17, Marseille, 1977, pp. 41–55.

24 Lettre à Perrot d'Ablancourt, 6 juin 1663.

25 Il peut dédier son premier recueil de *Fables* au Dauphin, le second à Mᵐᵉ de Montespan, le troisième à l'aîné des petits-fils du Roi. Celui-ci s'est contenté de retarder de cinq mois son admission à l'Académie Française, qui avait eu le tort de le préférer à Boileau, historiographe de Sa Majesté depuis six ans. Notons qu'il s'agissait de succéder à Colbert, sans doute la principale cible des *Fables*.

26 La première a tout juste vingt-sept ans, mais *La Princesse de Montpensier*, achevée d'imprimer le 20 août 1662, montre la plénitude de son talent et ne doit rien au nouveau souverain. Mᵐᵉ de Sévigné en a trente-cinq; son talent mondain est conforme à l'orientation de la décennie précédente; sa confirmation, à partir de 1671, dans une correspondance privée, est due au départ de sa chère fille, et nullement au nouveau gouvernement. Boileau a rédigé une première version de la *Satire I* en 1657 et jusqu'en 1665, il s'escrime contre le nouveau système — qui a notamment le tort de ne pas le reconnaître.

27 Sa troupe est invitée à jouer à la cour du 8 au 14 mai 1662.

Index